TRANSCENDENTAL HEIDEGGER

Transcendental Heidegger

Edited by
STEVEN CROWELL
and JEFF MALPAS

Stanford University Press
Stanford, California
2007

Stanford University Press
Stanford, California

Printed in the United States of America on acid-free, archival-quality paper

Library of Congress Cataloging-in-Publication Data

Transcendental Heidegger / edited by Steven Crowell and Jeff Malpas.
p. cm.
Includes bibliographical references and index.
ISBN 978-0-8047-5510-8 (cloth : alk. paper)—ISBN 978-0-8047-5511-5 (pbk. : alk. paper)
1. Heidegger, Martin, 1889-1976—Congresses. 2. Transcendentalism—Congresses. I. Crowell, Steven Galt. II. Malpas, J. E.

B3279.H49T635 2007
193—dc22 2006100035

Typeset by Classic Typography in 10.5/12 Bembo

Contents

Contributors

WILLIAM BLATTNER is Associate Professor of Philosophy at Georgetown University and the author of *Heidegger's Temporal Idealism* (1999), as well as articles on Heidegger, Kant, and Dewey. He is also a devoted fan of the Washington Nationals.

DAVID CARR is Charles Howard Candler Professor of Philosophy at Emory University. He is the translator of Husserl's *The Crisis of European Sciences and Transcendental Phenomenology: An Introduction to Phenomenological Philosophy* (1970); and the author of *Phenomenology and the Problem of History* (1974), *Time, Narrative, and History* (1986), *Interpreting Husserl* (1987), *The Paradox of Subjectivity* (1999), and of essays on phenomenology, Husserl, and the philosophy of history.

STEVEN CROWELL is Joseph and Joanna Nazro Mullen Professor of Philosophy, and Professor of German Studies, at Rice University. He is the author of *Husserl, Heidegger, and the Space of Meaning: Paths Toward Transcendental Phenomenology* (2001), and editor of *The Prism of the Self: Philosophical Essays in Honor of Maurice Natanson* (1995). With Burt Hopkins, he edits *The New Yearbook for Phenomenology and Phenomenological Philosophy*.

DANIEL O. DAHLSTROM, Professor of Philosophy, Boston University, is the author of *Heidegger's Concept of Truth* (2001), and the translator of Heidegger's first Marburg lectures, *Introduction to Phenomenological Research* (2005). His article, "Heidegger's Transcendentalism," can be found in *Research in Phenomenology* (2005).

KARSTEN HARRIES was born in Jena, Germany, and trained at Yale University, where he has taught since 1961, interrupted only by two years as an assistant professor at the University of Texas in Austin (1963–65) and several years spent in Germany. He is the author of more than 170 articles and reviews and five books: *The Meaning of Modern Art* (1968), *The Bavarian Rococo Church: Between Faith and Aestheticism* (1983), *The Broken Frame: Three Lectures*

(1990), *The Ethical Function of Architecture* (1997; winner of the American Institute of Architects Eighth Annual International Architecture Book Award for Criticism), and *Infinity and Perspective* (2001).

JOHN HAUGELAND is Professor of Philosophy at the University Chicago. His research focuses mainly on the early Heidegger, the metaphysics of truth, the philosophy of science, and the philosophy of mind. He is the author of *Artificial Intelligence: The Very Idea* (1985), and *Having Thought: Essays in the Metaphysics of Mind* (1998); the editor of *Mind Design* (1981) and *Mind Design II* (1997); and coeditor, with James Conant, of *The Road Since Structure* (2000).

CRISTINA LAFONT is Professor of Philosophy at Northwestern University. She is the author of *The Linguistic Turn in Hermeneutic Philosophy* (1999) and *Heidegger, Language, and World-Disclosure* (2000). Some of her recent articles include: "Heidegger's Hermeneutics," in *The Blackwell Companion to Heidegger* (2005); "Was Heidegger an Externalist?" *Inquiry* (2005); "Précis of *Heidegger, Language, and World-Disclosure*" and "Replies," *Inquiry* (2002); "The Role of Language in *Being and Time*," in *Heidegger Reexamined: Heidegger and Contemporary Philosophy* (2002).

JEFF MALPAS was born in Sydney, Australia, but grew up in New Zealand. He is a graduate of the University of Auckland and the Australian National University. Since 1999, he has been Professor of Philosophy at the University of Tasmania. He has been a Humboldt Research Fellow at the University of Heidelberg and Ludwig-Maximilian University, Munich. His work encompasses both the phenomenological-hermeneutic tradition, especially Heidegger and Gadamer, and Anglo-American thought, particularly as centered around Davidson and Rorty, and includes research in applied ethics, philosophical methodology, and the philosophy of place and space. He is the author of *Place and Experience* (1999) and of *Heidegger's Topology: Being, Place, World* (2006), and the editor of *Gadamer's Century* (2002), among many other works.

DERMOT MORAN was born in Dublin and is a graduate of University College Dublin and Yale University. He is, since 1989, Professor of Philosophy at University College Dublin and Founding Editor of the *International Journal of Philosophical Studies*. Professor Moran has been Visiting Professor at Yale University, Connecticut College, and Rice University, and has taught at Queen's University Belfast and Maynooth University. He is author of *The Philosophy of John Scottus Eriugena* (1989), *Introduction to Phenomenology* (2000), and *Edmund Husserl: Founder of Phenomenology* (2005). He has edited Husserl, *The Shorter Logical Investigations* (2001), and *The Logical Investigations*, 2 vols., trans. J. N. Findlay (2001); and coedited, with Tim Mooney, *The Phenome-*

nology Reader (2002), and, with Lester Embree, *Phenomenology: Critical Concepts*, 5 vols. (2004).

MARK OKRENT is Professor of Philosophy at Bates College. His recent publications include essays on Heidegger, Kant, and the relations among intentionality, normativity, and teleology. He is the author of *Heidegger's Pragmatism: Understanding, Being, and the Critique of Metaphysics* (1988).

HERMAN PHILIPSE studied law at the University of Leiden, the Netherlands, and philosophy in Leiden, Oxford, Paris, and Cologne. He was Full Professor of Philosophy at the University of Leiden from 1985 to 2003 and is now University Professor at the University of Utrecht. He has published widely on issues in epistemology, metaphysics, and the philosophy of religion, and on authors such as Descartes, Kant, Husserl, and Heidegger. His extensive historical and critical analysis of Heidegger's oeuvre, *Heidegger's Philosophy of Being: A Critical Interpretation*, was published by Princeton University Press in 1998.

ROBERT B. PIPPIN is the Evelyn Stefansson Nef Distinguished Service Professor in the Committee on Social Thought, the Department of Philosophy, and the College at the University of Chicago. He is the author of several books on German idealism and later German philosophy, including *Kant's Theory of Form* (1982), *Hegel's Idealism: The Satisfactions of Self-Consciousness* (1989), and *Modernism as a Philosophical Problem* (1997). He also wrote a book about literature: *Henry James and Modern Moral Life* (2000). A collection of his recent essays in German, *Die Verwirklichung der Freiheit*, appeared in 2005, as did his most recent book, *The Persistence of Subjectivity: On the Kantian Aftermath*. He is a former Humboldt Fellow, the winner of the Mellon Distinguished Achievement Award in the Humanities, and was recently a Fellow at the Wissenschaftskolleg zu Berlin.

RACHEL ZUCKERT is Assistant Professor of Philosophy at Northwestern University. Her publications include "A New Look at Kant's Theory of Pleasure," *Journal of Aesthetics and Art Criticism* (2002); "Awe or Envy: Herder Contra Kant on the Sublime," *Journal of Aesthetics and Art Criticism* (2003); "Boring Beauty and Universal Morality: Kant on the Ideal of Beauty," *Inquiry* (2005); and *Kant on Beauty and Biology: An Interpretation of the "Critique of Judgment,"* forthcoming from Cambridge University Press.

CHAPTER 1

Introduction

TRANSCENDENTAL HEIDEGGER

Steven Crowell and Jeff Malpas

THE TRANSCENDENTAL is a key notion in Heidegger's thought. Not only does Heidegger's early work stand within the framework of transcendental phenomenology as established by Husserl—even though it also contests and revises that framework—but that thinking also stands in a close relationship to the critical philosophy of Immanuel Kant, and specifically to the transcendental project, and modes of argument, of Kant's *Critique of Pure Reason*. Moreover, while the idea of the transcendental is explicitly disavowed in Heidegger's later thought, there still seems to be an important sense (though one that remains in need of clarification) in which that thinking retains a broadly "transcendental" character. It is perhaps surprising, then, that more attention has not been paid so far to what may be thought of as the "transcendental Heidegger"—to the role of the transcendental in Heidegger's thinking as well as Heidegger's stance toward the tradition of transcendental thought as such.[1] This collection aims to go some way toward remedying this apparent neglect, and to argue for the continuing significance of the transcendental for understanding Heidegger's thinking, both early and late. In so doing, it also makes a case for the continuing significance of the transcendental in philosophy more broadly.

Of course, what is meant by the term *transcendental* is an unavoidable and underlying issue here. As Heidegger himself uses it, the term is almost always understood in relation to Kant, and to the idea of "transcendence," which Heidegger—following Husserl in this regard rather more than Kant himself—takes to lie at the heart of the Kantian critical enterprise: the transcendental names that which makes possible the structure of transcendence.

In consequence, the shift away from the transcendental as a key term in Heidegger's thinking goes hand in hand with a shift away from the focus on transcendence, and, at the same time, from Kant, as well as from Husserl and the language of transcendental phenomenology. Basing oneself on Heidegger's overt—and often polemical—self-interpretation, then, one might be tempted to find a radical discontinuity between Heidegger's earlier and later thinking; indeed, the celebrated "turning" in Heidegger's thought has been seen chiefly as a turning away from the transcendental and all that is associated with it. Yet in spite of Heidegger's adoption of this specific reading of the notion, the transcendental is by no means an idea to which there attaches a simple or settled interpretation. Indeed, ever since Kant's appropriation of the term from the language of scholastic logic and metaphysics, the idea of the transcendental has given rise to discussion and debate—debate that has often, particularly in Anglo-Saxon philosophical circles, been rather negatively disposed.[2] So while it is obviously important to understand and acknowledge what Heidegger himself says about the transcendental, there is also a need to interrogate the term in a way that is sensitive to the possibility that it may harbor a significance exhausted neither by Heidegger's explicit usage nor by some of the other interpretations that have circulated around it. Could the transcendental refer us, for instance, to a distinctive mode of nonreductive analysis that aims to analyze phenomena in a way that draws only on elements already given in the phenomena as such?[3] Although such a characterization is extremely general, it would seem to conform, in its general outline, to certain key aspects of the analytic of Dasein in *Being and Time* as well as the account of the structure of the Fourfold in a late essay such as "The Thing."

How we should understand the idea of the transcendental is a topic that informs many of the discussions that appear in this collection, even if it is not always addressed explicitly. But such a topic can hardly be raised without confronting an extraordinary range of general philosophical issues. We may introduce some of the many topics of investigation on offer in the present volume by reflecting on three areas in which the transcendental tradition from Kant to Husserl gave rise to intense debate: the *scope* of the transcendental question itself; the *character* of transcendental inquiry; and the appeal to *subjectivity*, with its concomitant question of *idealism*.

1. The Scope of the Transcendental Question

Kant can reasonably be understood as having raised the question of the conditions that make a certain kind of knowledge possible—namely, rational knowledge that claims to "transcend" what can be given in sense experience. Perhaps the most well-known feature of Heidegger's Kant interpretation is his rejection of this "epistemological" reading of Kant; instead he favors the claim that Kant's enterprise was really an "ontological" one. As David Carr's contribution to this volume shows, this widening of the scope of the transcendental question stemmed from Heidegger's appreciation of what Husserl's transcendental phenomenology had already accomplished, namely, a "break with the way of ideas," that is, a break with an understanding of intentionality as something that is mediated by mental "representations." To understand transcendental philosophy essentially as an answer to a certain kind of skepticism (that is, as primarily an epistemological enterprise) is to remain within the Cartesian framework in which alone such a problem can arise. Heidegger's reading of Kant makes explicit the tension within Kant himself between a residual Cartesianism and a new paradigm, in which mind is always in the world and subject and object cannot be thought as separate.

For Heidegger, then, the scope of the transcendental question is not restricted to the conditions of cognitive experience, but to all intentionality—all consciousness of something *as* something—as such. Contributions by Mark Okrent and Steven Crowell explore some consequences of this widened scope. For Okrent, one of Heidegger's most important insights is that the intentionality of judgment rests upon a more basic, "practical" intentionality of the sort found in our dealings with tools. Crowell, in turn, argues that Heidegger's analysis of conscience, in *Being and Time*, should be understood as an account of how the norms inherent in such practical intentionality arise in experience. As with all such fundamental issues, there are disagreements: for Okrent, Heidegger's argument fails to make clear why only entities that have "world" in his sense can intend entities; whereas for Crowell, analysis of conscience—and the practice of reason-giving that emerges from it—are precisely what clarify this matter.

These treatments of intentionality show that for Heidegger the real scope of the transcendental question is not limited even to intentionality in the broadest sense, but rather to the "understanding of being" upon which all directedness toward objects "as" something depends. Indeed, as Robert B. Pippin maintains, if Heidegger's "question of being" is not to be construed as a MacGuffin, we should understand it precisely as a question into the very possibility of any intelligibility or meaning at all. In his reading of Heidegger's reflections on *Angst* and *das Nichts*, Pippin argues that what is most interesting about Heidegger's account is his claim that meaning can *fail*, that things can present themselves as wholly lacking in significance. This is in contrast to the Hegelian view that a collapse of meaning—a collapse of a way of looking at the world—can only be part of a dialectical emergence of new meaning. But it also, according to Pippin, shows that Heidegger's inquiry cannot be truly transcendental in Kant's sense, since Kantian conditions of possibility *cannot* fail.

This widening of the scope of the transcendental question is carried forth into Heidegger's later work, as Jeff Malpas shows in his reconstruction of the traces of "topographical" thinking that are present already in Heidegger's early work but come to full expression in his late reflections on the topology of being. If the transcendental question concerns the conditions that allow entities to come to presence, then *Being and Time*—in which this possibility is traced back to the presence of one of those entities, Dasein—might seem to suffer from disabling circularity. But Malpas shows how the later Heidegger provides a solution by recasting thought as a kind of topographical process, which maps conditions of possibility from within the field they govern, rather than by appealing to some single ultimate ground. The notion of the Fourfold, and the emphasis on the way places constellate around particular things, are thus seen to belong to a kind of transformed transcendental project.

2. The Character of Transcendental Inquiry

All this gives rise to more questions: What *are* "conditions of possibility"? How do we discover them? For Kant, the answer is that such conditions include a set of concepts whose a priori application to objects is established through transcendental arguments—in particular through a transcendental deduction.[4] Heidegger clearly follows Kant in his idea that what distinguishes philosophical inquiry from empirical science is its concern with "a priori" conditions of experience, that is, conditions that do not themselves derive from experience. Equally clearly, however, he rejects Kant's idea that these conditions stem from a faculty of "pure reason." Rather, their origin lies in the temporality of Dasein, toward which Kant is understood to have been groping in his treatment of imagination in the first *Critique*. Further, taking his cue from Husserl's phenomenological approach, Heidegger famously argued that there is no need for the centerpiece of Kant's thought, the *quaestio juris*, the question that a transcendental deduction is supposed to answer. Rachel Zuckert's contribution to this volume subjects this chapter in Heidegger's reading of Kant to close examination. She recognizes that in his "temporalized" interpretation of the a priori Heidegger is trying to come to terms with a question that even today continues to trouble Kant scholarship—namely, is synthesis a real psychological activity or a purely logical condition?—but she criticizes him for sidestepping the problem of explaining the application of the categories. Heidegger's claim that categories do nothing but make explicit the preconceptual synthesis of imagination, while not as outrageous as some commentators have held, leaves important questions unexplored. Zuckert then argues that Kant himself seems to have moved closer to Heidegger's position with late concept of "reflective judgment," whose principle—"purposiveness"—has a temporal structure that closely resembles Heidegger's idea of projection. In the end, however, Zuckert finds that Heidegger too easily abandoned the strong claims for necessity, which, for Kant, distinguished the categories as something in need of transcendental inquiry in the first place.

This point is echoed in Cristina Lafont's treatment of the a priori in Heidegger. For her, Heidegger's thought exhibits the "hermeneutic" transformation of Kant's Copernican revolution that is characteristic of an important strand of German thought since Wilhelm von Humboldt. Under such a hermeneutic transformation a priori conditions are no longer traced back to a pure transcendental subject but to a merely *factic* one; they are embedded in the particular, historical languages that inform Dasein's "understanding of being." Heidegger follows Kant in claiming that no access to entities is possible outside of such an a priori context (a particular understanding of being), but because his synthetic a priori is merely factic he cannot employ Kant's argument for this claim, namely, that a particular understanding is necessary for *all possible* experience. Rather than drop the strong notion of the a priori, however, Heidegger embraces an unstable linguistic idealism. Lafont contrasts such idealism with the "contextual a priori" in Hilary Putnam's internal realism—a position that, in Heideggerian terms, is purchased at the cost of abandoning the ontological difference, the absolute distinction between ontic (a posteriori) and ontological (a priori) knowledge.

A similar tension is uncovered by William Blattner, who finds Heidegger's notion of a priori conditions to be caught between two important currents in his understanding of philosophical inquiry: the pragmatic strand, and the aspirations for a transcendental ontology. The pragmatic strand uncovers conditions on meaning—such as skills and capacities—that cannot be captured in concepts and propositions. The transcendental strand seeks an ultimate ground for this sort of "understanding of being" in a theory of original temporality. But the transcendental aspiration involves an objectifying conceptual thematization of a priori conditions, which contradicts the very character—preconceptual, resistant to propositional formulation—of these conditions (skills, practices) themselves. Blattner suggests that Heidegger chose to drop the transcendental idea of a scientific ontology in his later work. But he leaves us with the crucial question regarding the character of philosophical inquiry: To what extent can philosophical expression be other than conceptual or theoretical? Is propositionality an obstacle to our access to being?

Several chapters—for instance, those of Pippin, Carr, and Dermot Moran—take note of the fact that Heidegger's transcendentalism is a placeholder for the idea that there is something distinctive about philosophical inquiry vis-à-vis other intellectual pursuits. In a wide-ranging chapter on this topic, Karsten Harries explores how Heidegger's approach to the transcendental draws upon far more than Kant and Husserl. The notion first emerges from Heidegger's early theological concern with "eternal truths" and their relation to human beings, a concern evident in Heidegger's commitment in his earliest publications to the strong program of transcendental logic. But even in *Being and Time*—which, as Lafont argued, submits Kant's Copernican revolution to a "hermeneutic" finitization—he still struggles to preserve something of the a priori. Harries presses the issue: is not thinking always in some sense a transcendence of the finite? In his 1929 Davos dispute with the neo-Kantian philosopher Ernst Cassirer,[5] Heidegger emphasizes the limits of transcendental reflection: can it really dictate conditions for all possible experience, or is it not limited to experience as it has actually arisen under specific historical, and therefore contingent, conditions? Where Cassirer reads the self-transcendence of the human being as a "homecoming" (a term that itself has important connotations in Heidegger's own thought), Heidegger sees it as a kind of *anxiety*. Following Nietzsche, Heidegger begins to see that a more positive characterization of self-transcendence, and of thinking, is blocked by the scientific pursuit of truth itself, which has no room for many forms of experience—of the beautiful, for instance, or the good—that, consequently, seem to disappear from the science-dominated world. Heidegger's late thought, then, can be seen as a continuation of the pursuit of transcendence that attempts to do justice to these excluded experiences in an age that puts roadblocks in the way of such reflection.

3. The Role of Subjectivity and the Question of Idealism

Heidegger is rightly understood as an implacable foe of the Cartesian picture of an isolated subject cut off from the world; being-in-the-world is nothing if not a challenge to such a picture. One might expect, then, that Kant's appeal to the "I think" as the cornerstone of his transcendental philosophy would find little resonance in Heidegger's thought. But this is by no means the case. Instead, Dasein comes to occupy the position of the transcendental subject, with corresponding fractures introduced into the project. As we learn in Dermot Moran's contribution—which traces in detail the interconnections between Heidegger's "question of being" and Husserl's idea of transcendental phenomenology as "first philosophy"—the fundamental question that troubled Husserl was the "paradox of subjectivity." For Husserl, the transcendental subject is not, as it was for Kant, a formal principle or logical postulate; it is the concrete locus of the intentional "constitution" of entities in the world. At the same time, as human subjectivity it is itself one such entity in the world. Moran shows how Husserl attempted to solve this problem by means of the phenomenological reduction, through which a distinction is made between a world-involved "natural attitude" and a world-bracketing "transcendental" attitude. If Heidegger rejects the reduction—and so this sort of solution to the paradox of subjectivity—does he not fall back into the problem that one entity, Dasein, is both "in" the world and also the condition of the world's very appearing?

However it stands with this ultimate question—and the chapters by Dahlstrom, Malpas, Philipse, Lafont, and Harries, among others, all register its effects on Heidegger's thought—Heidegger's approach can also be seen to illuminate the apparent necessity by which philosophy continually has recourse to some form of subjectivity. Mark Okrent, for instance, shows how Heidegger's notion of the *Worumwillen*—the sort of self-understanding that I have when I am engaged in practical, goal-directed activities—avoids problems that arise when one starts with the Kantian "I think," that is, with the subject of cognition or judgment as representation. Such a subject can only become aware of *itself* by means of a representation, which leads to an infinite regress. Heidegger, in contrast, conceives the subject first of all as *practical*, and in practical activity my self-understanding is a function of the holistic and typical structure of such activity: in acting, I act "as" something—gardener, teacher, husband, and so on. Such self-understanding is not a second-order reflection, but it makes possible the kind of explicit cognizing and representing that finally gets formulated in the practice of judging.

This pragmatic transformation of the transcendental subject has implications for the vexed question of idealism. As Carr's chapter points out, Kant himself did not fully break with the Cartesian picture that gives rise to something like a "problem of the external world." His "Refutation of Idealism"—the focal point of many earlier discussions of the nature and scope of transcendental arguments[6]—has thus been variously understood. Heidegger claimed that the problem of the external world was a pseudoproblem, but his own stance toward the realism/idealism debate, and toward transcendental idealism in particular, has been widely disputed. In his contribution to the volume, Herman Philipse compares Heidegger's strategy of "debunking" skepticism about the external world with similar strategies in Husserl, G. E. Moore, and Rudolf Carnap, and asks whether the resulting concept of "world" can avoid the problem of the *Ding an sich*. This chapter, which proceeds by unpacking the various possible senses of "idealism" and "realism" in several famous puzzle passages in *Being and Time*, poses a question similar to the one that occupied Lafont, namely, whether there is, on Heidegger's view, the possibility of encountering entities outside the global transcendental framework, "world." Where Lafont answers in the negative—thereby attributing to Heidegger a kind of linguistic idealism where meaning determines reference—Philipse explores the idea that the access to entities in the phenomenon of *Angst* might provide an alternative to such idealism.

Philipse argues that one can accept Heidegger's "realism" only if one gives up scientific realism—the idea that science is our best access to things in the world. What, then, is one to say about scientific practices within the framework of Heidegger's transcendental philosophy? This is equivalent to asking how it is that Dasein's understanding supplies the "enabling conditions" for the "being of entities." In place of Kant's view that such conditions "synthesize" the manifold of space and time, Heidegger holds that they "let beings be." John Haugeland carefully unpacks this central Heideggerian thought, moving from simpler cases—the idea that in order for something to be a baseball or a hammer there must be certain social practices and skillful abilities (which Heidegger associates with Dasein's "understanding of being") that let such things show themselves as such—to the harder case of how we are to understand the idea that Dasein's understanding also lets mere natural entities "be." Through a series of careful phenomenological distinctions, Haugeland shows how the scientific practices of theory construction and experimentation, together with the existential commitments that are bound up with them—provide necessary conditions for bringing natural things out of their "obscurity." Because this obscurity is deep, the project of science is difficult. In Kantian terms, we certainly end up with an empirical realism here. Is this also a scientific realism? Haugeland's account of the relation between Newton's laws and Einstein's laws emphasizes the role of commitment in scientific practice, and he argues that the urge to say which one is "really" true is a holdover of the desire for a God's-eye view that Heidegger's thought should help us resist.

Of course, the problem of truth—so closely related to questions of transcendental idealism and the transcendental subject—has long been a disputed topic in the Heidegger literature. Ernst Tugendhat's argument that Heidegger's identification of truth with "disclosedness" abandons the critical concept of truth in favor of a concept with no normative force is often seen as having been so persuasive that, on its basis, Heidegger himself came to reject the idea that the openness of beings can rightly be called "truth." Daniel O. Dahlstrom revisits this issue, arguing that Heidegger's earlier notion of transcendental truth as the condition for the possibility of propositional truth did undergo a major transformation. This transformation was not the result of Tugendhat's arguments, however, but of Heidegger's own gradual move away from posing the question of transcendence in terms of the ontological difference between being and beings. As Dahlstrom argues on the basis of passages from Heidegger's *Contributions to Philosophy (From Enown-*

ing) (*Beiträge zur Philosophie [Vom Ereignis]*), to pose the question that way merely reproduces the problem of treating being in the manner of an "idea." Heidegger's later approach to being as the event of the presencing-absencing of beings terms it the "truth that prevails [*west*]," and Dahlstrom argues that this new approach retains a kind of transcendental structure, since such prevailing, or valence, is the condition of the *bi*valence on which Tugendhat insisted in any concept of truth. In his final writings Heidegger does reject the idea that this prevailing is properly called "truth," but he continues to maintain that such prevailing—including its necessary relation to human beings or "mortals"—makes bivalence possible. Here we recognize the same move that Crowell's chapter attributes to the analysis of conscience in *Being and Time*: Heidegger wants to exhibit the source of our responsiveness to the normative as such, which provides the ultimate conditions for intentionality, meaning, and ontic truth. In Heidegger's later thought, as in the earlier, there thus remains an important relation to the transcendental tradition.

This collection does not claim to provide a definitive account of the "transcendental Heidegger," nor does it resolve the question concerning Heidegger's status as a transcendental thinker or the many issues concerning his relation to Kant or Husserl. But it does allow the controversies surrounding the transcendental in Heidegger's thought to take center stage, with the hope that the richness of these themes will spur further philosophical investigation.

*

Earlier versions of the chapters in this volume were delivered at the conference Heidegger and Transcendental Philosophy, held at Rice University, Houston, in April 2003. The editors would like to thank Rice University's Humanities Research Center for significant financial support of this conference. Further funding, for which we are also grateful, came through the office of the President and the office of the Provost of Rice University. Professor Werner Kelber, Director of the Humanities Research Center, and Sandra Gilbert, Associate Director, together with graduate students Matthew Burch, Irene McMullin, and Matthew Schunke made crucial contributions to the organization and facilitation of the conference itself. We are very pleased to have the chance here to acknowledge these contributions with gratitude. Finally, James Phillips was responsible for preparing the manuscript of this volume for submission. Special thanks are due him for his careful and timely work.

CHAPTER 2

Ontology, the A Priori, and the Primacy of Practice

AN APORIA IN HEIDEGGER'S EARLY PHILOSOPHY

William Blattner

IN THE PAST, I have argued simultaneously for two theses about Martin Heidegger's early philosophy that one might well fear are inconsistent with one another.[1] I have maintained that Heidegger's early philosophy embraces a thesis that I call "the primacy of practice," namely, that the intelligence and intelligibility of human life is explained primarily by practice and that the contribution made by cognition is derivative. I have also contended, however, that Heidegger's ontological project, inspired by Kant, constitutes an attempt to acquire a priori knowledge of being. In short, I have been arguing that Heidegger is both a transcendentalist and something of a pragmatist. It is not at all clear that one philosopher can be both.

In this chapter I explore whether the primacy of practice, as I have developed it on Heidegger's behalf, is in fact inconsistent with his aspirations to develop a transcendental ontology. To do so, I will draw upon some of my readings of Heidegger, to spell out both the primacy of practice and the nature of Heidegger's vision of an a priori ontology.[2] I shall argue that the primacy of practice and a priori ontology are not directly inconsistent, but only indirectly inconsistent, if we add a further and rather natural assumption into the mix, namely, that the a priori ontology for which we aim is meant to be, in Heidegger's words, "theoretic-conceptual" (*theoretisch-begrifflich*).[3] These three assertions together are inconsistent, and they force Heidegger into a difficult choice. Finally, I shall show how the argument I develop here both supplements and supports the narrative of Heidegger's early methodological agonies, as developed by Theodore Kisiel in his study of the genesis of *Being and Time* (*Sein und Zeit*).[4]

1. The Primacy of Practice

In section 13 of *Being and Time*, Heidegger announces that cognition (*Erkenntnis*) is a founded mode of being-in-the-world, thus that cognition is derivative of some more basic aspect of human existence.[5] He does not devote a lot of space in this section to explaining just how he means to argue for this thesis, but if we put section 13 into the context of Heidegger's discussion of understanding and interpretation, we can see that Heidegger's reasoning runs roughly as follows:

1. Cognition is a form of taking-as, that is, all intending is intending-as.
2. The as-structure constitutes interpretation.
3. Interpretation is derivative of understanding.[6]
4. Therefore, cognition is derivative of understanding.

No single sentence of *Being and Time* announces (1), but it is hard to know what the argument structure of the crucial paragraph from *Being and Time* (88–89/61–62) would be, unless Heidegger had (1) in mind. He begins the paragraph by asking what we may learn by examining cognition phenomenologically, and then narrows his focus down to a relatively "pure" case of cognition, "observational determination" (*betrachtendes Bestimmen*). He characterizes such observation as "looking at" (*Hinsehen*) and says that it is a consummate form of "taking a thing in" (*Vernehmen*). All taking-in, moreover, is interpretive, in other words, taking-as: "Taking-in [*Das Vernehmen*] has the same mode of accomplishment as *addressing* and *discussing* something as something. On the basis of this *interpreting* in the broadest sense taking-in becomes *determining*."[7] This reading of the passage is supported by Heidegger's claim in *Being and Time* that "all prepredicative, simple seeing of something available is in itself already understanding and interpretive" (189/149). In other words, the argument of the paragraph in question seems to run like this: not even the best candidate for an interpretation-free form of cognition, not even "rigidly staring" (*starres Begaffen*) at something, escapes the function of interpretation. All cognition, all intending, is a taking-in or taking-as. All cognition is interpretation.

Whereas we have to do a little work to tease (1) out, Heidegger does assert (2) directly,[8] as we shall explore below. The third point is the burden for sections 31 and 32 of *Being and Time*. Now, if Heidegger does endorse (1)–(3), then (4) follows. To work out, therefore, Heidegger's celebrated section 13 claim that cognition is a founded mode of being-in-the-world, we must get a handle on the distinction between understanding and interpretation.

By *understanding* Heidegger means "neither a *sort of cognition*, distinguished in some way from explaining and conceiving, nor even cognition in general in the sense of thematically grasping [something]."[9] What does Heidegger have in mind with a sort of understanding that is not thematic, not cognitive? In ontic (i.e., everyday) discourse we often use the expression *to understand something* to mean "to be able to manage a thing," "to be equal to it," "to be capable of something." In understanding, as an existentiale, "that of which one is capable is not a What, but rather being as existing."[10] Understanding is, thus, a capacity or ability by means of which I manage or know how to do something, but which is not "thematic." *Interpretation*, by way of contrast, emerges, when we are not equal to a task, when we cannot manage what we are doing.

> Circumspection uncovers, and that means that the world that is already understood gets interpreted. The available comes *explicitly* into the sight that understands. All preparing, setting aright, repairing, bettering, filling out are accomplished by laying apart [*auseinandergelegt*] the circumspectively available entity and concerning oneself with what has become visible in accordance with this laying-apart. That which has been circumspectively laid apart with respect to its in-order-to, that which has been *explicitly* understood, has the structure of *something as something*.[11]

Interpretation emerges when it is necessary to "set things aright," to "repair" them, "better" them, "fill them out," that is, when felt difficulty arises, or as Heidegger puts it in *Basic Problems*, when Dasein's dealings are "disturbed."[12] Such interpretation involves both the "explicitness" of its object and the "as-structure."

What does Heidegger mean to emphasize, when he contrasts the inexplicit, nonthematic nature of understanding with the thematic, explicit constitution of interpretation? What does he mean by "thematic" and "explicit"? Hubert Dreyfus has offered, in fact, two different ways of understanding the distinction, neither of which is quite right, however.[13] First, we may note that in understanding, Dasein is "absorbed" (*aufgenommen*) in its activities; the paraphernalia with which Dasein deals, when it genuinely understands it, "withdraws into its availability."[14] This can suggest that by "thematic" and "explicit" Heidegger means conscious, so that understanding is an un- or preconscious form of dealing with the world, whereas interpretation is a conscious form of doing so. If this is how Heidegger means to distinguish understanding from interpretation, what becomes of the argument of section 13 of *Being and Time*? The thesis that cognition is founded in a more basic form of being-in-the-world is then specified into the claim that conscious experience is founded in un- or preconscious "absorbed coping."

This may well be true—and Dreyfus offers powerful phenomenological evidence to this effect—but it cuts philosophical ice only against Descartes or any other philosopher of cognition who regards all cognition as conscious. Clearly, this is far too narrow a construal of Heidegger's target in section 13.

If the Cartesian notion that all cognition is conscious is not Heidegger's target in section 13, then what is? A more plausible target is the Kantian-Husserlian conception that cognition is a self-sufficient, subjective activity, one that can be consummated without the assistance of any noncognitive skills or capacities. Heidegger suggests this target in section 13, when he writes,

> In directing-itself to . . . and grasping Dasein does not somehow first come out of an inner sphere in which it is primarily enclosed [*verkapselt*], but rather, in accordance with its primary sort of being it is always already "out there" amid the encountering entities of the world that has in each case already been discovered. When Dasein visits with [*das bestimmende Sichaufhalten bei*] the entity to be cognized and determines what it is, it does not somehow abandon the inner sphere, but rather, insofar it "is out there" amid the object, Dasein is also "inside" in the properly understood sense; that is, it itself is as cognizing being-in-the-world. And conversely, taking [*Vernehmen*] the cognized [object] in is not returning into the "box" of consciousness with the booty Dasein has won, in which it has recorded the object, but rather, also in taking, preserving, and retaining the object Dasein *remains* cognizing Dasein *as Dasein out there.*[15]

Dreyfus indicates this approach as well, when he describes the target of Heidegger's criticism as "a relation between a *self-contained* subject with mental content (the inner) and an independent object (the outer)."[16] What sort of conception of cognition does such an approach invite or imply? Cognition would be self-contained if it were governed by rules. In this case, the mind could apply its rules to the data of experience and thereby not rely on anything beyond its own intelligence in understanding.[17] Construing cognition as rule-governed or algorithmic data processing would then be a second approach we might consider.

There is a certain historical plausibility to this way of looking at things, since Kant and Husserl both understood concepts (or noemata) as rules for experience. Not only would Kant and Husserl move into Heidegger's crosshairs here, but so would the modern "cognitivist" project of artificial intelligence on which Dreyfus has focused much of his attention. The drawback of approaching Heidegger this way is twofold, however. First, there are very few references in *Being and Time* to rules and their limits,[18] which makes textually implausible the suggestion that this is the key to reconstructing the distinction between understanding and cognition. Second, if this were the right way to read Heidegger, it would limit Heidegger's contemporary applicability to the field of artificial intelligence. Although this second consideration is hardly decisive, it would certainly be a welcome development if Heidegger's analysis of cognition could cast a wider net, including such recent examples of cognition-centered thinking as John Searle and Donald Davidson.

With this in mind, thirdly and finally, I have suggested that we take the distinction between understanding and interpretation in *Being and Time* as focused on the line between those forms of intelligence that can be captured in propositions and those that cannot. If we approach Heidegger this way, then his claim is that the most fundamental ways in which we understand the world cannot be expressed in propositional content. This puts Heidegger at odds not only with Kant but also with both the "linguistic turn" in Anglo-American philosophy, which has generally been tantamount to a "propositional turn," as well as the logicist tradition represented by the neo-Kantians and logical empiricists.

Beyond these broad historical advantages, I think we can also connect this construal of the understanding-interpretation distinction with the text. Heidegger's official account of interpretation lays emphasis upon two features of interpretation: its *explicitness* and the *as-structure*. Interpretation is a "development" (*Ausbildung*) of understanding, specifically a development in which understanding has become explicit and characterized by the as-structure. Indeed, Heidegger essentially identifies these two features when he writes, "The 'as' makes up the structure of the explicitness of what is understood; it constitutes interpretation."[19] To be explicit, therefore, is to be characterized by an "as." But what is it to be characterized by an "as"?

There is a fairly clear connection in the text of *Being and Time* between the as-structure, aspectuality, conceptuality, propositionality, and the fore-structure of interpretation. Let me now summarize these connections. In section 32 Heidegger spells out the internal "forestructure" (*Vorstruktur*) of interpretation as a trio of phenomena that together constitute interpretation: "forehaving" (*Vorhabe*), "foresight" (*Vorsicht*), and "foreconception" (*Vorgriff*). Heidegger writes:

> An available entity is always already understood in terms of the totality of involvements. This totality does not have to be grasped explicitly by a thematic interpretation. Even when it is passed through such an interpretation, it recedes back into the understanding that has not been raised up. And precisely in this mode it is an essential foundation of everyday, circumspective interpretation. This interpretation is grounded in a *forehaving*. It moves, as an appropriation of understanding, in the understanding being toward such an understood totality of involvements.[20]

The appropriation of an entity in explicit interpretation rests on the "foundation" of our prior understanding of a totality of involvements. Our forehaving, what we have in advance of interpretation, is our understanding, the inexplicit grasp that we have of the entire framework and environment in which we are operating.

Such understanding bridges to interpretation by way of foresight.

> The appropriation of what is understood, but still veiled, carries out its unveiling always under the guidance of an aspect, which fixes that in terms of which the entity that is understood is supposed to be interpreted. Interpretation is always grounded in a *foresight*, which "cuts" what has been taken in forehaving "down" to a determinate interpretability.[21]

Interpretation appropriates something "understood, but still veiled." That is to say, interpretation is directed to something that falls within the ambit of our understanding but which is opaque, resistant, or problematic in some way. This fits the general contours of the distinction I indicated above: interpretation emerges when Dasein's dealings are disturbed, when Dasein confronts something it has not mastered already. The foresight focuses the interpretation upon some specific way in which the entity can be interpreted, that is, it selects an aspect in terms of which the entity is grasped. Such an aspect in terms of which the entity is grasped is something as which we take the object. The as-structure, therefore, emerges with the foresight of interpretation. Foresight in interpretation correlates with the *as* on the side of the object.

Further, this as-structure requires a certain kind of conceptuality, a fore- or protoconceptuality:

> The item understood . . . becomes conceivable through interpretation. Interpretation can create the conceptuality that belongs to the entity to be interpreted in terms of this entity itself, or it can force the entity into concepts that it resists in accordance with its sort of being. As always, interpretation has in each case already, either with finality or with reservations, decided itself in favor of a determinate conceptuality; it is grounded in a *foreconception*.[22]

To take an entity as something, to grasp it under an aspect, is to subject it to, or let it be seen by way of, a certain conceptuality. Heidegger's language here is a bit ambivalent between conception and conceivability, between conceptuality and foreconception or protoconceptuality. Why? In discussing perception, Heidegger comments that perception is an act of interpretation.[23] This is to say that all seeing, for Heidegger, is seeing-as. Still, Heidegger admonishes us not to infer from the absence of "the explicitness of an assertion" in simple seeing that all interpretation is absent: "All predicative, simple seeing of something available is in itself already understanding and interpretive [*verstehend-auslegend*]. . . . That in simple seeing the explicitness of an assertion can be missing does not justify denying all articulating interpretation, and therewith the as-structure, to this simple seeing."[24] Why would one be inclined to make the mistake Heidegger is concerned to avoid? Noticing that the full determinateness of propositional content on display in an overt assertion or covert judgment is missing, one might be inclined to conclude that perception does not have any sort of propositional content. But this would be a mistake. Perception, indeed, interpretation at large, does have a sort of propositional content. That content is, however, "modally vague."

In *The Critique of Pure Reason* Kant distinguishes between an appearance in general, which is the object of a perception, and the content of a judgment, by arguing that an appearance is "indeterminate." That is, for example, whereas the judgment that my cat is white is definite with respect to modality (possibility, necessity, actuality), the mere perceptual experience of my white cat is not so definite. When a perception is expressed in the form of a judgment, the modal indefiniteness of the perception has to be resolved. This contrast between indeterminate perception and determinate judgment, however, does not prevent Kant from concluding that "the same function which gives unity to the various representations *in a judgment* also gives unity to the mere synthesis of various representations in *an intuition*."[25]

In essence, a perception has modally or grammatically vague propositional content, whereas a judgment or assertion has modally or grammatically definite content. What is the "function of unity" shared by an indeterminate perception and a determinate judgment or assertion? It is the unity of a concept. In the assertion "my cat is white" and the perception of my white cat, the concept *cat* unifies the content of the experience and judgment. This is to say, then, that all perception and judgment, all interpretation in Heidegger's accounting, is conceptually articulated. And this explains why all interpretation is "grounded in a foreconception."

Understanding, on the other hand, is *not* grounded in a foreconception, which is to say that it does not have even the determinacy of conceptual articulation. Understanding is preconceptual, rather than merely preconscious. Not only is it not rule-governed, it is not concept-governed at all. Understanding lacks the structure of the *as*.[26] Furthermore, this way of reading Heidegger suggests that when he characterizes interpretation as *explicit* (*ausdrücklich*), he does not mean *conscious*, but rather *articulate*, specifically, *conceptually articulate*. Indeed, the German word here, *ausdrücklich*, is built on the term *Ausdruck*, expression, which certainly suggests linguistic expressibility. In short, I am recommending that we read the fault line between understanding and interpretation as the distinction between those forms of dealing with the world that are conceptually articulated and those that are not. If my line of interpretation is correct here, then Heidegger would be committed to the conclusion that interpretation can be captured in propositional form. Indeed, he draws just this inference: "What has been taken-in and determined can be expressed in propositions [*Sätze*]; it can be retained and kept as something asserted [*als solches Ausgesagtes*]."[27]

By implication, what has not been taken-as and determined, that is, understanding, cannot be expressed in propositions, cannot be asserted. Finally, this also makes sense retrospectively of Heidegger's mysterious comment about understanding, that "in understanding . . . that of which one is capable is not a What, but rather being as existing."[28] The content of understanding is not a What, a propositional content; it is, rather, an activity.

So, the primacy of practice, the thesis that the intelligence and intelligibility of human life resides primarily in precognitive practice, and that cognition is derivative of such practice, takes form in *Being and Time* by way of the distinction between understanding and interpretation. Cognition is taking-as, grasping things under a conceptually articulated aspect, in such a way that the content of one's taking-as can be expressed in propositional form, asserted. Understanding is what Dreyfus calls "absorbed coping," an inexplicit mastery of one's world and oneself. Such mastery is inexplicit, however, not in the sense that it is un- or preconscious (though it may well mostly be), nor in the sense that it is not rule-governed (though it surely is not), but rather in the sense that it is preconceptual, prepropositional. Precognitive understanding cannot "be expressed in propositions," it cannot "be retained and kept as something asserted." This moves Heidegger's thought into the neighborhood of John Dewey's pragmatism, even if it does not exactly make Heidegger a pragmatist.[29]

2. *Heidegger's Transcendentalism*

Heidegger does not only have deep affinities with the pragmatism of John Dewey, but also with the transcendentalism of Immanuel Kant. Heidegger appears to want to deploy some form of transcendental method in order to establish his ontology on an a priori basis. How does he try to do this? In *Being and Time*, Heidegger contrasts the status of what he is pleased to call the "productive logic" that lays the ground for the sciences and the "'logic' that limps along afterward," and merely catalogs and organizes the results of scientific inquiry. Productive logic, Heidegger argues, lays the ground for the sciences in the specific sense that it generates an "a priori material logic" of the regions of being studied by the sciences:

> Such laying the ground for the sciences is fundamentally unlike the "logic" that limps along afterward, which investigates the contingent condition of a science with respect to its "method." It [namely, Heidegger's ontological reflection] is productive logic in the sense that it leaps ahead into a determinate region of being, discloses it for the first time in its ontological constitution, and makes the structures that are disclosed in it available to the sciences as transparent directives for inquiry. So, for example, what is philosophically primary is not a theory of historical concept formation, nor a theory of historical knowledge, nor even a theory of history as the

object of the discipline of history, but rather the interpretation of authentically historical entities in terms of their historicality. Thus, the positive results of Kant's *Critique of Pure Reason* rest upon an approach to working out what belongs to a nature in general, and not upon a "theory" of knowledge. His transcendental logic is an a priori material logic of the region of being of nature.[30]

For this reason, ontological reflection is immune to refutation by empirical inquiry. As he puts it in his lectures on Kant's first *Critique*: "The basic concepts of philology cannot be clarified with the help of philological methods; and the basic concepts of history cannot be determined by researching the sources, let alone be grasped by such research. . . . Latent in every science of a realm of entities there always lies a regional ontology which belongs to this science, but which can never in principle be developed by this science."[31] Thus, ontology is a priori in the specific sense that it does not depend upon, and is not open to, refutation and revision by empirical scientific inquiry.

In developing an interpretation of this aspect of Heidegger's thought,[32] I have contended that Heidegger's argument for this position in his Kant lectures does not warrant the general conclusion he draws. Heidegger does not offer sufficient justification for the conclusion that the regional ontologies specific to individual sciences are a priori disclosable, therefore, properly philosophical. Rather, his argument can only reach so far as to conclude that the very broad ontologies of the large-scale regions of being analyzed in *Being and Time*—namely, the occurrent or present-at-hand, the available or ready-to-hand, and the existent or human—are a priori, hence philosophical. In order to defend the heart of Heidegger's apriorism in *Being and Time* and his early lectures, we must abandon the most aggressively anti-empirical aspects of his attitude toward the sciences. To see this, we must understand a little more about Heidegger's actual argument in his Kant lectures.

Heidegger argues that any act of conceptual understanding depends on forms of unity that run deeper than any concept.[33] In an astonishing act of exegetical bravura, Heidegger argues that the temporal form of intuition in Kant's Aesthetic is to be identified with the temporal structure of the threefold synthesis of experience in the A-Deduction, and both of these are in turn to be assimilated to transcendental apperception and the pure productive imagination, the common root of the two stems of cognition, intuition, and understanding. This is all to say that, according to Heidegger, the temporal structure of experience is a fundamental form of unity that lies at the foundation of all more explicit, conceptually articulated activities. The specific argument in the Kant lectures, as I have reconstructed it,[34] runs like this.

The temporal form of intuition is not conceptually articulate, because it is a condition of the possibility of any act of concept formation. According to Heidegger, conceptualization and intuition both require an "antecedent zone," "a dimension within which I can move while" either intuiting or forming concepts:

> This "grasping in *one*" cannot at all be identical with seeing pregiven representations together in terms of the "unity of the concept." This "grasping in one" is by no means the logical act of concept-forming reflection, but rather is the act of the same synthesis on the basis of which a many is pregiven as *a* many for a thinking seeing. I see a pine tree *and* a willow tree *and* a lime tree. I do not see them successively by losing sight of the one seen before. Rather this many must be given to me *in one* so that I have a dimension within which I can move while comparing. What encounters [me] must in a certain way belong *to me*, must lie before me in a surveyable *zone* [*Umkreis*]. The unity of this zone, which, so to speak, antecedently holds the manifold together in advance, is what is ultimately meant by "grasping in one."[35]

Concept formation requires that representations of a sample of objects be able to come before the mind, so that their differences can be excluded in light of what they have in common. There is much to say about how such a process works—and neither Kant nor Heidegger in his Kant lectures says much that is very illuminating about it, since they both rely upon an abstractionist account of concept formation—but this much, at least, Heidegger thinks is presupposed: the representations that are compared and processed must all, as Heidegger says, belong *to me* and be available *to me*. Thus, the "surveyable zone" to which Heidegger refers is the zone of my self-consciousness, what Kant calls "transcendental apperception."

Heidegger argues that this "zone" of availability is the pure form of time. In order to learn to see unity in a sample of experiential data, I must be able to hold the data together through time.[36] This requires the abilities to "apprehend" the data in sequence, to "reproduce" or retain the data through the flow of time, and "recognize" or identify their unity. These abilities in turn require that the temporal flow of my experience itself possess unity. Unless the past remains available to me, not as an explicit object of recollection but as a retained repository of information, I could not "reach back" to the data once present to me in order to identify the specific regularity or commonness I am learning to see. This unitary temporal flow of experience is a necessary condition of my capacity to learn concepts. In a nutshell: *however it is that we learn or come to identify conceptual patterns in experience*, such identification presupposes the temporal unity of the flow of experience, what Heidegger calls "temporality" (*die Zeitlichkeit*).

The temporal unity of experience, temporality, is not merely necessary for concept formation, but Heidegger suggests, sufficient for ontology. The fundamental unity of the antecedent zone of temporality gives rise to an understanding of being. In the peculiar, hybrid language of Heidegger's *Kantdeutung*, he writes, "*But if the synthesis of understanding*, as synthesis of recognition in the concept, *is related to time and if categories emerge from just* this *synthesis as activity of understanding*, that is, if the three syntheses are interrelated on the basis of time, *then the origin of the categories is time itself*."[37]

The categories together make up "the concept of the object in general." Note that the "concept of the object in general" is not a single, simple concept. It is, rather, a complex construction assembled from the Kantian categories. Instead of "concept of the object in general," it is probably clearer to say "conception of objectivity in general." This conception of objectivity in general is the correlate in Kant of ontology in Heidegger. Kant's Analytic of Principles in the *Critique of Pure Reason* is an analysis of the temporal structure of any object simply insofar as it is an object, just as the promised (but never completed) third division of Part I of *Being and Time* was intended to be a temporal analysis of any entity just in so far as it is. So, when Heidegger interprets Kant he writes (above) that "the origin of the categories is time itself," that is, the origin of the conception of objectivity is time itself, Heidegger implies that for him the origin of ontology is time itself. In other words, the unity of temporality is rich enough to *generate on its own* the understanding of being.

To sketch briefly how this would go, consider the following picture. What is it to be occurrent (present-at-hand)? In Division One of *Being and Time*, the concept of the occurrent is focused on independence: to be occurrent is to be independent, both of other objects and of the subject, the understanding. The occurrent contrasts, therefore, with the available (ready-to-hand), which is dependent both on other objects (its "co-equipment," so to speak) and on the human practices in which it is involved. In the final quarter of *Being and Time*, however, Heidegger restates his analysis, and perhaps deepens it, in terms of temporal structure. The occurrent is what shows up in the temporal structure of "ordinary time," that is, shows up for Dasein insofar as Dasein exhibits the temporality of detached cognition. Occurrent objects, that is, subsist in a temporal form in which the manifold of past-present-future is a series of contentless and mutually indifferent moments or stretches of time. Available objects, on the other hand, subsist in a temporal form in which the past-present-future is a contentful manifold defined by its relation to the project of use in which the available entity is caught up. Paradigmatically, the future that defines equipment is specified by the task or goal that Dasein aims to accomplish insofar as it relates to the equipment. Finally, human beings, Dasein, are defined by a temporal manifold that does not make up a sequence or series at all, in which the unattainable future that I can-be is not later than the past that I have-already-been.

The details of this comparative analysis of sorts of being are less important than the general structure of Heidegger's ontological project.[38] Heidegger attempts to extract an ontology of each of the three large-scale regions of being from the temporal structure of the region. And this temporal structure correlates with the temporal structure of Dasein's mode of relating to the region. The occurrent is disclosed in detached cognition and exhibits the temporal structure revealed in such detachment. The available is disclosed in practical manipulation and use and exhibits the temporal structure of such use. And the human is disclosed in self-understanding and exhibits the temporal structure of such self-constitution.

Ontology, therefore, is a priori, because it is the expression of the forms of temporality that underlie and make possible all attempts to articulate in conceptual form the nature of the objects we confront. Whatever we might want to say about philology's relationship to language, we can say, if Heidegger's argument is sound, that the large-scale ontology contemplated in the preceding paragraphs is immune to refutation by empirical investigation, since it makes up a condition of the possibility of all empirical concept formation.

Finally, to draw some of this together and bring it into contact with the theme of transcendentalism, Heidegger's ontology is transcendental, in the specific Kantian sense, in that it is "occupied not so much with objects as with the mode of our knowledge of objects in so far as this mode of knowledge is to be possible *a priori*."[39] Heidegger's ontology presents to us what we may know about objects a priori, namely, their temporal structure.

3. Are Heidegger's Transcendentalism and Pragmatism Inconsistent?

I have thus far maintained in two parallel arguments that Heidegger's philosophy has deep affinities both with Deweyan pragmatism and with Kantian transcendentalism. Heidegger embraces both the primacy of practice and the apriority of ontology. One is likely to suspect, however, that pragmatism and transcendentalism, as philosophical attitudes, if not movements, are incompatible. The transcendental and the a priori are two of the prime targets of much pragmatist anti-epistemology. Despite the confident feeling that pragmatism and transcendentalism are incompatible, the upshot of Heidegger's *Kantdeutung* appears to be that Kant's transcendentalism actually presupposes the primacy of practice. We have seen that for Heidegger, whereas interpretation can be captured in propositions and thus brings in the entire apparatus of aspectuality, conceptuality, and cognition, understanding is precognitive, engaged coping. Ontology expresses the a priori form of temporality, the temporal structure of experience more fundamental than any conceptual articulation of it. Ontology is a priori precisely *because* it gives expression to what underlies and makes possible all concept formation. Ontology is immune to empirical refutation, because no conceptually articulate, empirical activity can violate, and hence call into question, the results of ontological inquiry. Ontology is a priori, then, because it expresses our preconceptual pre-ontological understanding of being. Put in the exegetical context of Heidegger's *Kantdeutung*, we may say that Heidegger's reconstruction of Kant's first *Critique* shows how in order to defend the a priori status of ontology, Kant must ultimately turn to Heidegger's antirepresentationalist quasi-pragmatism.

The primacy of practice and transcendental ontology are, therefore, not inconsistent, at least not simply as such. If we take into consideration, however, a further aspect of Heidegger's conception of philosophical method, we do confront an inconsistency, one that I believe is irresolvable. According to the Heidegger of the mid-1920s, ontology must be articulated conceptually and expressed propositionally. Ontology is, after all, a science. It is theoretical in nature. It is expressed in *Being and Time* in a web of propositions. Heidegger could not put it more clearly than he does in *Basic Problems*, when he writes, "Philosophy is the theoretic-conceptual interpretation of being, its structure, and its possibilities."[40] It is for this reason, if no other, that Heidegger is not by his own lights an existentialist, that he is no Kierkegaard or Jaspers. In the hands of Kierkegaard and Jaspers philosophy is merely edifying; in Heidegger's hands it is scientific.

Heidegger's writings from the mid- to late 1920s are filled with this rhetoric of scientificity: the opening sections of *Basic Problems* lay great stress on the scientificity of philosophy, which is to say ontology, and contrast scientific ontology with mere "worldview philosophy." In the process of developing this theme of scientificity, moreover, Heidegger emphasizes the mere "positivity" of worldview philosophy.

> Every world- and life-view is positing [*setzend*], that is, is related existingly [*seiend*] to entities. It posits entities, it is positive. . . . To worldview belongs this multifaceted positivity, such that it is in each case rooted in a thus and so existing Dasein, is related to the existing world, and interprets the factically existing Dasein. Because this positivity, that is, the relatedness to entities, the existing world, and existing Dasein, belongs to the essence of worldview and thereby to the construction of worldviews in general, the construction of worldviews precisely cannot be the task of philosophy.[41]

Philosophy does not concern itself with the positive, with what is merely given, the way human life happens to be constituted here and now. Philosophy focuses, instead, on what is necessary, what underlies all positivity. As Kant argued in the first *Critique*, necessity is the hallmark of the a priori. What is necessary must be known a priori. Scientific philosophy, in contrast with pseudo-philosophical worldview thinking, must be an a priori science.

Heidegger's point here, moreover, is not just a negative rhetorical jab at worldview philosophy. It informs his detailed conception of phenomenological method.

Being should be apprehended and made into a theme. Being is in every case the being of an entity, and for this reason it is accessible primarily only in reference to an entity [*im Ausgang von einem Seienden*]. Therefore, phenomenology's apprehending vision must be directed to an entity, but in such a way that the being of the entity thereby becomes salient and available for thematizing [*zur Abhebung und zur möglichen Thematasierung kommt*].[42]

Phenomenology *thematizes* being. According to *Being and Time*, "thematizing objectifies."[43] From Kant forward there is an intimate connection between objectivity and conceptuality. In section 19 of the B-Deduction, Kant links objective validity with judgment, which is propositional or conceptual. For this reason, according Kant, the understanding—Kant's understanding, not Heidegger's—is the faculty of both concepts and objects. There can be no objectivity without conceptuality. Thematizing in *Being and Time* is therefore a matter of interpretation, putting understanding into conceptual form. This explains why interpretation, but not understanding, is *thematic*.

If phenomenological ontology is conceptually articulated and propositionally expressed, what does this tell us about the understanding of being to which it gives voice? It entails that the understanding of being can be captured in propositions. (At least, unless ontology is a hopeless distortion of the understanding of being.) However, if the understanding of being can be captured in propositions, then it is, by the analysis above, not understanding at all, but rather interpretation. Put the other way around, whatever it is that ontology puts into words, it cannot be an *understanding* of anything, including being. And if it is not an understanding of being, that is, does not line up with the pure productive imagination of Heidegger's Kant, then it cannot enjoy a priori status. It does not capture something more fundamental than the conceptual, something that would thereby prove to be immune to empirical refutation.

Therefore, there is nothing inconsistent in Heidegger's transcendentalist quasi-pragmatism until we add into the brew the notion that ontology is "theoretic-conceptual." Heidegger does face an aporia in his early conception of philosophy, but it is not a simple inconsistency between transcendentalism and the primacy of practice. The aporia is a triadic inconsistency between the primacy of practice, the transcendental conception of ontology as a priori, and the further expectation that ontology is scientific, that is, theoretic-conceptual.

One might object: "But surely Heidegger saw these difficulties and offered a method for overcoming them, namely, hermeneutics!" In the words of *Being and Time*,

From the investigation itself it will emerge that the methodological sense of phenomenological description is *interpretation*. The *logos* of the phenomenology of Dasein has the character of *hermeneuein*, through which the authentic sense of being and the basic structures of its own being are *made known* to the ontological understanding that belongs to Dasein itself. The phenomenology of Dasein is *hermeneutics* in the original meaning of the word, according to which it designates the business of interpretation.[44]

Hermeneutics is the practice of putting understanding into words, of giving voice to what lies below the level of articulate expression. Putting the understanding of being into words, then, is a hermeneutic act. Scientific ontology, if it is to be possible at all, must be hermeneutic. This argument, unfortunately, does not so much resolve our worries as give them a name. Certainly, if the understanding of being could be expressed in propositional form, then the business of doing so would deserve the name of *hermeneutics*. Giving the method of ontology a name does not clarify its inner possibility, and it is precisely this possibility that we have called into question. It is noteworthy, then, that *Being and Time* does so little to clarify the nature of hermeneutics, so little to explain to the puzzled reader how ontology could be a matter of hermeneutic interpretation.[45]

If hermeneutics is not the answer to our worries,[46] then we will have to abandon one of the three jointly inconsistent elements of Heidegger's method. Which should it be? To those who are attracted to the transcendental-phenomenological Heidegger, the answer is obvious: we should abandon the primacy of practice. We saw above, however, that Heidegger's justification of the transcendental status of ontology relies upon the primacy of practice. Thus, we cannot resolve the aporia by abandoning the primacy of practice. We are forced to choose between transcendentalism and scientific ontology. This is to say, Heidegger cannot have it both ways, he cannot simultaneously insist that ontology is immune to empirical refutation and that it is a scientific theoretic-conceptual enterprise.

We find historical confirmation of the stubbornness of this aporia in the vicissitudes of Heidegger's methodological reflections prior to *Being and Time*. Theodore Kisiel has described in great detail Heidegger's inconsistent attitude toward the theoretic-conceptual nature of philosophy.[47] In his early Freiburg lecture course *The Idea of Philosophy and the Problem of World-Views* (*Die Idee der Philosophie und das Weltanschauungsproblem*),[48] Heidegger toys with the idea of abandoning the theoretic-conceptual nature of philosophy. He suggests that Husserl's "principle of principles" "does not have a theoretical character."[49] Phenomenology is meant to be "the primordial bearing of life-experience and life as such," and this bearing "becomes absolute when we live in it—and that is not achieved by any constructed system of concepts, regardless of how extensive it may be, but only through phenomenological life in its ever-growing self-intensification."[50] He follows these remarks up in the next subsection of the lecture (section 20a) with the *sug-*

gestion—and this is all it is here—that phenomenological language might not be theoretical, conceptual, and generalizing.

The problem of method presented itself in the form of the question of the possible description of experiences. The crudest but already sufficiently threatening objection pertained to *language*. All description is a "grasping-in-words"—"verbal expression" is generalizing. This objection rests on the opinion that all language is itself already objectifying, that is, that living in meaning implies a theoretical grasping of what is meant, that the fulfillment of meaning is *only* object-giving.[51]

In the next paragraph he labels the assumption that "grasping-in-words" is always theoretical an "undemonstrated prejudice." If this were so, he concludes, then it would be false that "all verbal meaning consists in nothing but" theoretical universality.[52] So, in these passages Heidegger aims to undercut the assumption that all hermeneutic expression is theoretic-conceptual. In defending hermeneutic interpretation as the method of phenomenology, Heidegger does not try to explain how the precognitive understanding of being can be put into "theoretic-conceptual" propositional form. Rather, he suggests that the verbal expression of phenomenology is nonconceptual: nontheoretical, nonpropositional, nonscientific. Ontology is not scientific, but rather aims for "self-intensification."[53] In another of his early Freiburg lecture courses, published as *Ontology: The Hermeneutics of Facticity* (*Ontologie: Hermeneutik der Faktizität*), he describes the aim of philosophy to be "wakefulness."

Steven Crowell has (in a gentle and friendly fashion) criticized Kisiel's narrative of the genesis of *Being and Time* by arguing that Kisiel arbitrarily deemphasizes Heidegger's affinity with Husserl's phenomenology.[54] Husserl's phenomenology provides Heidegger with a model of a formal science of being. Phenomenology gives us access to the formal structure of objectivity, rather than merely to the general content of objects. Phenomenology thus allows philosophy to escape from the prospect of merely integrating the results of empirical research, the prospect of remaining a logic that merely "limps along afterward." Phenomenology delineates the special topic of philosophy, namely, being, the formal structure of what is, and gives us nonempirical access to it, that is, access independent of empirical science, so that philosophy can become a "productive logic" of being. Crowell makes a convincing case that this model of phenomenological science had a grip on Heidegger. That the *aspiration* to an a priori formal ontology plays a significant role in Heidegger's development does not show us, however, how that aspiration can be realized. When Heidegger does actually turn to the foundations of a priori ontology in his Kant lectures, we see that the way in which he defends the apriority of ontology is incompatible with its scientificity. Because the Kant lectures postdate *Being and Time*, Kisiel does not explore them and the light they shed on Heidegger's proposed methodology. Had he done so, he could have supplemented the *narrative* of Heidegger's early Freiburg years with an *argument* drawn from the Marburg years, an argument that shows how Heidegger is forced to choose between apriority and scientificity.

Not long after *Being and Time* and the Kant lectures Heidegger seems once again to give up on scientific ontology.[55] After returning to Freiburg, Heidegger begins to move back toward a nonscientific conception of philosophy. Indeed, Heidegger seems to be struggling to define how we can talk about being nonscientifically. In his 1929 inaugural lecture at Freiburg, "What Is Metaphysics?" he is driven to the conclusion that ontology is about the Nothing.[56] It may well be that metaphysics is about nothing, not only because we are invited into it by anxiety, but also because we cannot say anything disciplined, *wissenschaftlich*, theoretic-conceptual about being from within anxiety. Looked at in this way, the position of "What Is Metaphysics?" is a desperate halfway house between the scientific ontology of *Being and Time* and the later, poetic vision of the discourse of being that emerges in the 1930s. "What Is Metaphysics?" may then represent an all-or-nothing response to the collapse of transcendental phenomenology: science or nothing, the Nothing.

In the 1930s Heidegger turns away from the failed models of philosophy of the 1920s and gropes around for something new. Through all the details of Heidegger's path from *Being and Time* to "Time and Being," the one constant remains that Heidegger seeks to develop and perhaps stabilize a discourse of being. He holds on to the idea that this discourse of being is more fundamental than empirical scientific research and immune to revision by the impress of such research. His *name* for the discourse of being changes through the years: phenomenological ontology, metaphysics, thinking. Whatever it is called, it maintains its apriority, its priority to empirical science. That the discourse of being retains its apriority, even when it escapes scientificity, is an indirect confirmation of my account above: the apriority of the discourse of being is not a consequence of its scientificity, but rather of the primacy of practice. The attempt to put this discourse into theoretic-conceptual form as a *science* of being fails, and when it does, Heidegger gives up on the science, not on being.

In an especially clear statement of this in "Time and Being," Heidegger states that even trying to relate thinking in the form of a lecture is dubious, because lectures speak "merely in propositional statements."[57] Propositionality—that is, conceptuality, interpretation, cognition—is an obstacle to our access to being. This explains Heidegger's attraction to poetry as a form of thinking, for poetry eschews propositional-conceptual representation in favor of a more direct and evocative encounter with being. Heidegger's turn away from philosophical science is, therefore, not merely a spasmodic display of some crypto-religious mysticism of the sort identified by Herman Philipse in his book on Heidegger's philosophy of being.[58] It is, quite surprisingly, a disciplined response to a philosophical aporia that besets his early conception of ontology.[59]

CHAPTER 3

Heidegger on Kant on Transcendence

David Carr

THE CENTERPIECE of Kant's *Critique of Pure Reason* is called the "transcendental deduction of the pure concepts of the understanding." Kant explains that he has chosen the term *deduction* by analogy to juridical procedure. Jurists distinguish between questions of fact (*quid facti*) and questions of law or right (*quid juris*), he says,[1] and the answer to the latter sort of question is called a deduction. Kant has drawn up a list or table of the pure concepts of the understanding, or categories, and the "deduction" is meant to answer the question: *by what right* are these categories applied a priori to objects? It is a question, he says, of "how *subjective conditions of thought* can have *objective validity*."[2]

In his reading of this part of Kant's *Critique*, Heidegger takes Kant to task for his choice and explanation of the term *deduction*. "The transcendental deduction, conceived as *quaestio iuris*, is the most fatal part of Kant's philosophy to which one can appeal. The transcendental deduction is untenable almost throughout [*fast durchgängig unhaltbar*]."[3] "The *questio juris* should not be taken as the guiding thread for the interpretation of this central chapter of Kant's."[4] The problem of the section called "transcendental deduction," he says, is "*ganz und gar keine juristische Geltungsfrage*"—not at all a juridical question of validity.[5] In fact, "*eine juristische Fragestellung [hat] keinen Sinn*," a juridical inquiry makes no sense here,[6] and by introducing the *quid juris* Kant is guilty of nothing less than a "misunderstanding of the problem of transcendence [*Verkennung des Transzendenzproblems*]."[7] Heidegger is critical of Kant on many points in his interpretation of the *Critique*, but these are certainly the harshest and most emphatic expressions he uses; Heidegger seems irritated, if not angry, an indication that something important is at stake. This is remarkable, since on the whole, of course, Heidegger views

Kant very positively and wants to enlist him as a forerunner of his own project. How can we reconcile this with Heidegger's view that Kant has gone wrong at the very heart of his major work? This is the question I want to explore in the following pages.

A few words on the background and context of the passages I just quoted. The years before and immediately after the publication of *Being and Time* (*Sein und Zeit*; 1927) were the years of Heidegger's most intense preoccupation with Kant. That work itself contains many discussions of Kant. The same is true of the lecture course *The Basic Problems of Phenomenology* (*Grundprobleme der Phänomenologie*; 1927), which was followed in the winter semester of 1927–28 by the course *Phenomenological Interpretation of Kant's "Critique of Pure Reason"* (*Phänomenologische Interpretation von Kants "Kritik der reinen Vernunft"*), from which the above passages were taken. Heidegger's celebrated debate with Cassirer at Davos, primarily on Kant, took place in early 1929, and it was followed in the same year by the publication of *Kant and the Problem of Metaphysics* (*Kant und das Problem der Metaphysik*). One thing that strikes readers of Heidegger on Kant in these writings is that his analysis is very detailed and close to the text, but it is focused entirely on the first *Critique*, and indeed goes no farther than the first third of that work. He has almost nothing to say about the "transcendental dialectic" and its critique of traditional metaphysics, in which the first *Critique* culminates, much less about Kant's moral philosophy, for which the first *Critique* is preparing the way. Heidegger returns to Kant in texts of the 1940s, 1950s, and 1960s, notably in the Nietzsche lectures, in "Kants These über das Sein" ("Kant's Thesis About Being") and in *Die Frage nach dem Ding?* (*What Is a Thing?*). But these later reflections derive, I believe, from a very different perspective not only on Kant but on the history of modern philosophy generally. I will not be concerned with them here.

Heidegger is admirably open about what he admits is the "violence" of his interpretation of Kant. In his 1950 foreword to the second edition of *Kant and the Problem*, he is sympathetic to the misgivings of historians of philosophy whose methods are those of "philosophical philology," and admits that he is operating according to different rules. He even admits, in retrospect, that his procedure has led to "omissions and shortcomings" in his book, though he does not say what they are.[8] In the preface to the *Phenomenological Interpretation*, Heidegger predictably cites Kant's well-known comment, with reference to Plato, that it is not unusual that we can understand an author better than he understood himself, and a lesser-known complaint Kant makes against historians of philosophy, who in their concern with what philosophers said, overlook what they wanted to say—comments Kant probably wishes posthumously he had never made, since they are so easily turned against him.[9] The declared focus of Heidegger's interpretation is "das, was Kant hat sagen wollen [what Kant wanted to say]," or, "die Fundamente dessen, was er meint [the basis of that which he intended]."[10]

In the 1950 foreword mentioned above, Heidegger says, as the translator puts it, that "readers have taken constant offense at the violence of my interpretation." I have to confess that, more often than not, I have been among those readers. To be sure, when one reads Heidegger on Kant, or Heidegger on any other philosopher for that matter, one expects to learn more about Heidegger than about the philosopher in question. But surely there are limits to this principle of charity. Heidegger goes too far, it has always seemed to me, when he says that Kant is engaged in a "Grundlegung der Metaphysik [laying the ground for metaphysics]" rather than a *critique* of metaphysics, and that his project has "nothing to do" (*nichts zu schaffen*) with epistemology or philosophy of science.[11] And when he says of Kant that "the I, the ego, is for him as for Descartes the *res cogitans, res, something* [*etwas*] that thinks,"[12] and that it occupies the role of the *hypokeimenon* in traditional metaphysics,[13] I have to wonder, in all seriousness, if Heidegger ever got as far as the Paralogisms in his reading of the *Critique*.

When I first came across Heidegger's assertion that the transcendental deduction is not a deduction, then, my reaction was similar. Granted, there is little agreement on how to interpret it. But to say that it is not a deduction, as Kant himself defines that term? That seemed to me to go too far. Some reflection has convinced me, however, that in this case Heidegger has got it exactly right. Whether or not he has discovered what Kant wanted to say, he has at least correctly articulated what Kant should, and perhaps should not, have said in this context, and I want to explain why I think this is so.

1. *The Problem of Transcendence*

Let's explore first what Heidegger means by his criticisms of Kant's idea of "deduction." In saying that Kant misunderstands "the problem of transcendence" Heidegger is suggesting that the problem of transcendence is what Kant should be understanding, and indeed his whole reading of Kant is centered around the notion of transcendence as the central problem for Kant. Indeed, it is from this problem that, according to Heidegger, "transcendental philosophy" gets its name.[14] Since this is certainly not Kant's way of characterizing his central preoccupation, or of explaining what transcendental philosophy is, we must ask what Heidegger means when he imputes this problem to Kant.

In *Kant and the Problem of Metaphysics*, Heidegger defines "Transzendenz" as "das Überschreiten der reinen Vernunft zum Seienden, so dass sich diesem allererst als möglichem Gegenstand Erfahrung anmessen kann."[15] Roughly: pure reason steps beyond itself to what is, so that the latter can function as an object for experience. In *Phenomenological Interpretation* he speaks of the phenomenon of transcendence as "das Gegenstehen des anschaulich Begegnenden [the standing over against of what is intuitively encountered],"[16] "das Gegenstehen von etwas als Gegen-stand [the standing over against of something as ob-ject]."[17] Objects can be known empirically only if they are already objects, not just intuitions. The Copernican turn is rephrased: "Only when objects qua objects conform to objectivity can empirical knowledge conform to objects." In Heidegger's language this means: "Ontic truth presupposes ontological truth."[18] Transcendence can be named, in much more Kantian language, "die apriorische Konstituierung der Gegenständlichkeit."[19] Thus the problem of transcendence is to show how "Gegenstandsbeziehung [the a priori constitution of objectivity]" is possible a priori, that is, how it is possible that what is encountered in intuition stands over against us as an object before, or so that, it can be known empirically.[20]

Everything Kant says in the transcendental deduction, according to Heidegger, circles as it were around the phenomenon of transcendence, coming at it from different sides, and "at times it looks as if Kant in fact had a real grasp of the phenomenon."[21] But then he misunderstands it in the way he sets up the problem. Heidegger's objection to the *quid juris* conception of the deduction lies in his view of how Kant thinks of transcendence as a problem and how he envisions the solution to this problem. The key to the problem lies in turn in how Kant thinks of the a priori. "A priori is what belongs to the subject, what is in the mind [*Gemüt*]."[22] The categories are then conceived of as a priori in this sense. But how can something in the mind have validity for what is outside the mind? "By what right can the subjective be taken for something objective as well, which essentially it is not?"[23] In short, transcendence can be a problem, in the way Kant envisages it, only on the basis of a "transcendence-free conception of the a priori" and a conception of the mind as "isolated subject."[24] Thus subject and object are conceived, in Heidegger's language, as "zwei vorhandene Seiende [two occurrent entities]" and the problem is that of how representations in the subject can meet up—"zusammentreffen"—with their objects outside.[25]

What has happened here, according to Heidegger, is that Kant's approach to this problem, indicated by his choice of the word *deduction*, is "polemical," that is, it has been dictated by the way his opponents posed the questions. But this means that "Kant is seeking the solution of the problem while being guided by a kind of question which is already in itself finally impossible."[26] I take this to mean that in using this terminology, Kant has, according to Heidegger, reverted to the framework that set the terms of the debate about knowledge carried out by Kant's predecessors, beginning with Descartes. If we begin with the Cartesian isolated subject, and conceive of the world to be known as a transcendent realm of objects, then any claim that the subject's representations correspond to this outside world must be proved or justified. We would then be in the business of comparing our representations with their objects, a task that is futile, as Hume saw. Since Hume still accepts the traditional terms of the debate, the only outcome for him can be skepticism. And if Kant also accepts these terms and sees the problem in the same way, Heidegger seems to be saying, then Kant is no better off.

The point Heidegger is making is that if Kant's contribution is to have any value, then it cannot consist in just another attempt to solve the old problem of skepticism; it must be seen as overthrowing the old problem and raising a new question. This actually happens in the section called "The Deduction of the Pure Concepts of Understanding," as we can understand if we are able to see beyond the polemical framework suggested by its title and Kant's explanation of it. When Kant describes the transcendental deduction, in a formulation Heidegger seems to prefer, as "the explanation of the manner [*Art*] in which concepts relate themselves a priori to objects,"[27] then we must read the word "explanation" (*Erklärung*) to mean not justification or proof that they do so relate themselves, but as answering the question: "what is the nature [*Art*] of these concepts . . . that they have objective reality a priori?"[28] In other words, it is a question of the essential nature of these concepts. It is senseless to first list the categories and then ask after their possible application to objects, for "this application 'to objects,' this object-relation [*Gegenstandsbeziehung*] as such, is constituted precisely by them."[29] As Kant says in a passage Heidegger is fond of quoting, "the a priori conditions of a possible experience in general are at the same time conditions of the possibility of objects of experience."[30]

But this search for conditions leads to the even more fundamental question of the essential nature of the subject to whom these concepts belong. The question of the possibility of experience is the question of the "transcendental character [*transzendentale Beschaffenheit*] of the subject."[31] Translating this unabashedly into his own terminology, Heidegger says it is a question of the "Seinsverfassung des Daseins [the ontological constitution of Dasein]"[32] The latter is not an isolated subject; it is "ein Seiendes, das wesenhaft außer sich ist [a being which is fundamentally outside itself]"[33] And because it is essentially outside itself, it can also come back to itself and remain with and in itself. Thus, "Die Transzendenz ist die Voraussetzung fur die Möglichkeit des Selbstseins [Transcendence is the presupposition for the possibility of being a self]."[34] The "explanation" of "Gegenstandsbeziehung," then, lies in the "Transzendenz-Struktur des Daseins."

This structure is revealed, Heidegger thinks, in the theory of the threefold synthesis and the concept of transcendental apperception which are exposed in the first part of the A-Deduction. He quotes Kant's distinction, at

Axvif, between the subjective and the objective "sides" of the transcendental deduction, in which Kant declares the former "not essential" to his main purpose, which lies in the objective side. But Heidegger thinks he has got it precisely backward. It is the objective deduction that Kant casts as a juridical procedure, and in so doing he misunderstands the internal connection between the two sides. "More than that: he fails to see that precisely the *radical execution [radikale Durchführung] of the subjective side of the task of the deduction also accomplishes [mit erledigt] the objective task*."[35]

In the second-edition version of the transcendental deduction Kant largely suppresses the subjective side of the deduction, and this is why Heidegger takes the first edition as his focus. Kant thus departed from his original insight, limited as he was by what he saw as the options open to him. Having introduced the distinction between the "faculties" of sensibility and understanding, Kant knew that his investigations of them could not be empirical or psychological in the manner of the empiricists (he mentions Locke). But the only alternative he knew was the rational or logical. So he wavers [*schwankt*] between psychology and logic, and his uncertainty at the level of content is the result of his uncertainty of method. "In place of an unclear mixture of psychology and logic, what was needed was the clear insight that it was a matter of a purely phenomenological interpretation of human existence [Dasein] as knowing—a phenomenology that supports [*trägt*] [both] psychology and logic."[36]

The essential task of the transcendental deduction is this: before Kant can reveal the categories in particular in their relation to objects, he must show how "überhaupt" anything like a relation to an object, "oder das Gegenstehen eines Gegenstandes," is constituted.[37] This is accomplished in the description of the threefold synthesis—or would be, if Kant had correctly understood its implications. For Heidegger it reveals the role of the imagination as productive and transcendental, and is ultimately grounded in temporality. For Kant this analysis culminates in the idea of transcendental apperception, which functions as a sort of "Urkategorie" (primordial category) or "vehicle" for all categories and all concepts.[38] But Heidegger sees this section as deeply ambiguous. He thinks that Kant has produced two conflicting maps of the mind. In one, which emerges as his official doctrine, he divides the mind into *two* "Grundquellen" (basic sources) or "Stämme" (roots) of knowledge, sensibility and understanding, and then gives the "I think," as the principle of the understanding, the role of unifying the two. In the other, he lists *three* "Erkenntnisquellen" (sources of cognition), namely sense, imagination, and apperception,[39] and even suggests in one passage that synthetic unity of apperception presupposes a pure synthesis of imagination.[40] Kant's twofold division wins out in the end, because Kant is too much of a rationalist to give such a central role to imagination. But Kant is not entirely happy with this version either, according to Heidegger, because in the introduction, where he first introduces the twofold division, he suggests darkly that the two faculties "perhaps spring from a common, but to us unknown root."[41] Heidegger believes that Kant actually discovered that root in the transcendental imagination but "shrank back" from what he had seen.[42] In the end, for Heidegger, the imagination is not merely on an equal footing with sense and understanding, but is prior to both.

For Heidegger apperception, as the unifying principle of the understanding, must be reinterpreted in light of its relation to the threefold synthesis and the unifying role of the imagination. Rather than standing outside of and opposed to time, as Kant seems to suggest, the "I think" must be conceived as temporal synthesis. Only when it is understood in this way can it be "that which at the deepest level makes the relation to an object possible [*das, was im innersten Grunde die Gegenstandsbeziehung möglich macht*]."[43] This is the very subjectivity of the subject, its character of being essentially outside itself. For Heidegger, Kant's thesis is that "the representing of something—or the representedness of something—is not possible unless the representer, the subject, *is in itself transcendent*, unless *Sich-verhalten-zu* [comportment toward], *Offenheit-für* [openness for], *Hinausstand* [standing out], *Exstasis*, belong to its *Existenz*."[44] This is what Heidegger calls the "ekstatische Grundverfassung des Subjekts."[45]

2. *Kant and Intentionality*

It is Heidegger's interpretation of the threefold synthesis and his treatment of the productive or transcendental imagination as the "unknown root" of sense and understanding that is rightly regarded as the centerpiece of his reading of Kant. It is also that part of his analysis that tells us more about Heidegger, I think, than it does about Kant. For this reason I will not go into it further here. In the foregoing I put the emphasis on Heidegger's denunciation of the *quid juris* derivation of the term *deduction* because, as I said, I think this part of Heidegger's reading can really tell us something about Kant, especially about his place in the *historical* context and his relation to his predecessors. In other words, it actually helps us understand Kant and his role and place in modern philosophy. In this section I will try to show how this is so.

Heidegger's attack on the *quid juris* question is much more prominent in the *Phenomenological Interpretation* than it is in the Kant book, though it is there as well. There is no doubt that it plays an important part in Heidegger's *Auseinandersetzung* with the neo-Kantians, especially those of the Southwest school, who place the notion of the *Geltung* (holding) or *Gültigkeit* (validity) of judgments at the heart of their own interpretation. This is also an aspect of Heidegger's interpretation that I choose not to explore, interesting as it is, since again this is more about Heidegger and his contemporaries than about Kant. With reference to Heidegger's own situation, however, I will say that I think the Kant interpretation reveals the deep and pervasive, though here unacknowledged, influence of *Husserl* on Heidegger, at a time when he is trying to divest himself of that influence. We should note the central role of the concept of *Gegenstandsbeziehung* in his treatment of transcendence as Kant's central concern in the *Critique*. Heidegger is, after all, talking about intentionality, though he steadfastly refuses to pronounce the word. It might be suggested that he avoids the word because it is anachronistic and does not belong to Kant's vocabulary. But that is also true of *Gegenstandsbeziehung*, and for that matter, *Transzendenz*. In any case, the influence of Husserl on Heidegger's treatment lies not in his choice of this theme, or even in his preference for the A-Deduction, which he also shares with Husserl. It lies much deeper, as we shall see later.

Whatever name we choose, it is obvious that intentionality or *Gegenstandsbeziehung* is the heart of Kant's concern. But that should not be surprising, since in a way it has been the major concern of all modern philosophers since Descartes. Husserl preferred the term *intentionality*, but he did not invent the thing to which it refers. Everyone had always recognized that the whole point, we might say, of consciousness or mind is that it supposedly reaches out beyond itself and puts us in contact with a world of independent reality. The question for Kant's predecessors was how or indeed whether it actually does what it purports to do.

What I want to argue is that Kant's originality lies in seeing beyond this question and then transforming the traditional approach to it, something he does with some hesitation, confusion, and backsliding. This, I think, is what Heidegger has correctly seen and to some extent shown in his analysis.

In the transcendental deduction, when Kant introduces the transcendental unity of apperception or self-consciousness, and distinguishes it from empirical self-consciousness, he is already introducing intentionality into his analysis, if only grammatically, just as Descartes had done with the cogito: the cogito requires its cogitatum; thinking is thinking of or about something or that something is the case. Here, of course, Kant is interested in a particular kind of thinking, namely that which is involved in our knowledge of the sensible world. The question here is: how is experience, that is, empirical knowledge, possible? Such knowledge requires that our thinking be linked with intuitions as sense-representations. But what is the nature of that link? One might expect that, since thought requires an object, it is these sense-representations that serve as its objects.

Kant's rejection of this idea is the very heart of his approach to the problem of knowledge. It might be said that Kant here rejects the so-called way of ideas which had dominated the treatment of knowledge since Descartes, and which was notoriously explained by Locke when he wrote that the term *idea* "serves best to stand for whatsoever is the *object* of the understanding when a man thinks."[46] Kant indeed sometimes uses the term *Vorstellung* in a way that corresponds roughly to the term *idea* and its cognates in other languages, as used by Locke and other modern philosophers. And he talks about sense-representations, even giving them at one point the Humean designation *impressions* [*Eindrücke*],[47] and asserts that they are necessarily involved in our knowledge of the sensible world. But these representations are "a mere determination of the mind [*Bestimmung des Gemüts*]."[48] Knowledge of the sensible world is not about our mind or its contents, but precisely about the sensible world, or rather about objects in the sensible world. This knowledge requires that we have sense-representations, but it also requires that, by their means, *objects* be thought. Sense-representations must be united not in the subject that has them, but in an object. Another way of putting this is to say that, in order to have knowledge of the sensible world, it is not enough that we *have* sense-representations; we must also take them to *be* representations, that is, to present or stand for something beyond themselves. This act of taking them to be so, is just what is expressed in the apperceptive "I think," which must mean in this context: "I am representing an object."

This is clearly expressed in the doctrine of the transcendental object, the "*etwas überhaupt* = *x*," as the object that corresponds to but stands over against (*gegenübersteht*) the knowledge we have of it.[49] The condition for this is a transcendental, not merely empirical, apperception. In the B-Deduction he speaks of the *objective* unity of apperception. This apperception represents the "I" not merely as unity of its own representations, but as an ability to think objects through those representations.

Having articulated the object-relation in this way, it seems clear that Kant is not asking *whether* the mind is so related, but *how*. To ask *whether* would be to attempt to refute skepticism regarding our knowledge of nature. To be sure, a long tradition of commentators has taken Kant to be doing just that. But it is hard to square this view of Kant's project with the fact that he unequivocally affirms, at the starting point of his inquiry, and so as one of its assumptions, that "we are in possession" of a priori knowledge of nature, that "even common sense is never without it."[50] He also affirms emphatically that, with regard to mathematics and natural science, it is not a question of asking whether such knowledge is possible, since it so clearly is actual. The question for Kant is *how* such knowledge is possible. Thus Kant here seems to depart completely from the concerns of his predecessors, from Descartes on, who thought that science must look to philosophy for a warrant it is incapable of providing for itself. Indeed, he notes that in his own day, "the study of nature has entered on the secure path of a science,"[51] presumably without the help of philosophers, since he takes a dim view of what his predecessors had accomplished.

But if Kant is not out to defeat skepticism, what then is he doing? Skepticism arose out of the traditional conception of what it means to have knowledge. According to this conception, knowledge of the real world meant knowledge of things in themselves. As Kant says, if we begin with this idea of knowledge (he calls it "transcendental realism"), we will surely end in skepticism. "After wrongly supposing that objects of the senses, if they are to be external, must have an existence by themselves, and independently of the senses, [the realist] finds that, judged from this point of view, all our sensuous representations are inadequate to establish their reality."[52] To argue against skepticism on these terms would be to argue that our representations *are* somehow adequate to establish the reality of objects. Instead, Kant wants to revise the idea of knowledge and the whole conceptual framework which allows the problem of skepticism to arise. When he rejects the *whether* question about empirical knowledge in favor of the *how* question, he is really raising the *what* question, that of the essence of knowledge. This is the sense in which he is interested in the possibility, or conditions of possibility, of empirical knowledge, even though its actuality is for him never in doubt.

Kant's revised conception of *what* knowledge is attacks both the subjective and the objective sides of the transcendental realist position. The objective side is addressed, of course, by Kant's distinction between things in themselves and appearances, but that distinction is possible only in connection with a revised conception of the knowing process itself. This brings with it a radically revised theory of mind and subjectivity.

The so-called way of ideas, which Kant is seeking to supplant, is a characterization not only of the knowing process but also of the knowing subject. It is the view that the mind is a thing that has certain properties, and these properties are thoughts, ideas, or representations. But Kant affirms, as we have seen, that the mind must not merely have representations, it must also take them to be representations, and thus refer beyond themselves. But the tradition has no place in its theory of mind for this act of taking. This act is nothing other than the "I think" whereby I relate my representations to objects by means of concepts. If we start with the traditional conception, its relation to the world has to be explained after the fact. Kant is saying that we must begin with a mind that is characterized by intentionality, a mind whose essence is to refer beyond itself. Kant calls the unity of apperception the "supreme principle of all employment of the understanding."[53] Thus he places it even above the categories. His transcendental argument for the unity of apperception is similar to that for the categories, but it must take precedence over them. His argument for causality is that it cannot be derived from experience, and without it experience would not be possible. Hence it must be considered a priori and transcendental, a condition of the possibility of experience. But causal relations are relations among objects, not representations. Hence the a priori object-related (i.e., intentional) character of experience establishes in general the domain to which the categories apply.

In other words, agreeing with Hume that neither reason alone nor sense experience (in the empiricist sense) could ever guarantee the connection between ideas and things, Kant concluded that the connection must be a priori. It is not to be derived from experience, but is a condition of the possibility of experience, that the "I think" accompany all my representations and in doing so relate them to objects. This, it seems to me, is the only way to understand Kant's use of the terms *a priori* and *transcendental* when he applied them to the "I think," the unity of apperception, and the relation of representations to an object. He is saying that these constitute the very essence of experience, and that philosophically we cannot expect to derive them from anything simpler or more basic. Kant's starting point is that "we are in possession" of certain cognitions, which means that we *have* experience, in his own full-fledged sense of that term. This is Kant's response to Descartes' starting point and the Humean skepticism to which it ultimately leads. Rather than accepting that starting point and then somehow defeating the skepticism it implies, Kant revises the starting point itself. Rather than starting with the encapsulated mind and then asking how we can get out of it to the world, we must begin with a notion of mind that is already (i.e., a priori) outside of itself and in the world.

3. Kant, Heidegger, and Husserl

This is the view of Kant's accomplishment that Heidegger's interpretation permits us to see. It is not so much a matter of what Kant wanted to say as of what Kant needed to think if his work was to constitute a new contribution to the development of modern philosophy, a genuine turn in its course rather than just another "move" in its game. To play the game means accepting its rules; it is altogether a different thing to change the game and thus overthrow the rules. If Kant was doing the former, he was not only a less important philosopher, he was also, I think, not very successful at it. Only if he was doing the latter does he deserve the position he has been accorded. Which was he doing? The problem—and this Heidegger has also seen—is that he was doing both.

Heidegger's attack on the *quid juris* derivation of the term *deduction* suggests that Kant is accepting that aspect of the modern project which is focused on the refutation of skepticism with regard to empirical knowledge. This is not the only place in which Kant's project can be read that way; the Refutation of Idealism, introduced in the second edition, contributes to the sense that the whole Analytic of Principles can be read as a series of arguments against skepticism. Many commentators have read Kant in this way, and of those many conclude that Kant does not succeed. But to argue against skepticism is to accept the presuppositions according to which skepticism needs a refutation. These presuppositions include a view of what objects are, what the subject is, and in what knowledge consists or would or should consist. As we have noted, Kant denounces these presuppositions under the heading of Transcendental Realism; but his explanation of the deduction, Heidegger rightly points out, suggests that concepts essentially belong to the subject and that their application to objects needs a justification. It thus runs counter to what is genuinely innovative in Kant's theory of concepts and even to his basic idea of the Copernican turn. But more important, the idea of "deduction" suggests a theory of the mind more in keeping with that of Kant's predecessors and with transcendental realism: a mind which appears essentially self-enclosed whose relation to objects and to the world has to be established. In other words, it would be to accept the "way of ideas."

Heidegger's insight is that if Kant's theory of the a priori is to have any significance, it must be more than a designation of what belongs to the mind, to the exclusion of object and world. It must consist in the claim that the *Gegenstandsbeziehung*—intentionality—is essential to the mind itself, not some external fact about it that has to be proved. But this insistence is merely a repetition of the strategy adapted by Husserl in this regard, a strategy which constitutes a primary feature of Husserl's philosophy, although it is not often recognized as such.

What is important about Husserl in this regard is not that he asserts the central importance of intentionality, and takes it as his theme, but rather how he places it in the order of philosophical priorities. The rejection of the "way of ideas" can be seen as the primary impetus of Husserl's philosophy, from the *Logical Investigations* (*Logische Untersuchungen*) on. There, his attack on the empiricist theory of the mental image or representation is of a piece with his attack on psychologism in logic. Though they deal with different domains of objects, both are attempts to collapse the object of consciousness into consciousness or to confuse the two. Attacking representationalism, Husserl does not first assume that we have mental representations and then ask what we need in addition that will somehow secure the object-relation, but rather shows that the idea of such representation cannot be backed up by phenomenological description. In *Ideas I* (*Ideen I*) he devotes a section (section 42) to what he calls the "fundamental error" of believing that perception presents us not with a thing but only a picture of it, or perhaps a sign or symbol for it. This error draws on the common experience we have of representations or images, as when we see pictures or photographs of objects. But it overlooks that here the idea of representation presupposes the idea of direct seeing, in the double sense that (1) the image depicts something that could be directly seen, and (2) the image is itself directly seen and not depicted. In spite of being "transcendent," in the sense of belonging to the world and not to consciousness, the object of perception is present, directly given to the perceiver "in the flesh" (*leibhaftig gegeben*).

For Husserl it is not just the object of perception but reality as a whole, the *world*, that transcends consciousness in this sense. But consciousness is not something that could be cut off from this transcendence; on the contrary, it is as transcendent that object and world are given, indeed directly given to consciousness. This is because, for Husserl, consciousness, as intentional, is nothing that could be cut off: it consists entirely in its *Gegenstandsbeziehung*, or *Weltbezug*. World and object, in turn, make no sense if we assume that they are cut off from the mind.

This is the view, then, that Heidegger takes over from Husserl, urging it as the proper understanding of Kant. Its primary feature is that it puts intentionality or *Gegenstandsbeziehung* first, rather than trying to establish or justify it. In the historical sense it might be viewed as a *faute de mieux* or a cop-out: since the pre-Kantians failed to establish the object-relation, we simply assume it, glossing over the problem instead of actually solving it. But that would be to recognize the legitimacy of the problem. What Husserl and Heidegger, and to some extent Kant, have done is to unearth the assumptions on which this supposed problem depends, assumptions about the nature of mind, object, and world that amount to deep ontological commitments. The attempt to derive intentionality from something more basic, and thus to reduce it to a confused amalgam of resemblance, causality, and logic, is characteristic not only of the pre-Kantian moderns but also of contemporary materialists. They all share the unargued commitment to an ontology in which intentionality has no place and is thus an anomaly that has to be explained or justified. Husserl and Heidegger turn the tables on this assumption, and Heidegger claims to see this happening already in Kant, even though Kant only fitfully recognized it.

Another aspect of Heidegger's Kant interpretation that is indebted to, or at least strongly reminiscent of, Husserl, is his claim that Kant is kept from recognizing the significance of what he is doing because of methodological limitations. Kant wavers (*schwankt*) between psychology and logic, Heidegger says, because he fails to see any third alternative. He decides to downplay the subjective deduction and finally to jettison it altogether because he thinks it too psychological and perhaps even empirical, opting instead for a logical version of transcendental apperception as the source of unity between sense and understanding. He should have envisaged the possibility of a "phenomenological interpretation" as intermediary between psychology and logic. Here we are reminded of Heidegger's efforts in *Being and Time* to distinguish sharply between his own *Daseinsanalyse* and anything psychological, anthropological, or otherwise "regional" in character.

Husserl's phenomenology, of course, emerges in the intersection between psychology and logic. His efforts to articulate the distinctiveness of his method can be traced to his efforts to defend his *Logical Investigations* against the charge that they represented a relapse into the very psychologism he had rejected in the first volume of the same work (this is part of his own *Auseinandersetzung* with the neo-Kantians). He puts forward the idea of a metaphysically neutral description of mental activity that does not subscribe to the ontological assumptions of the psychological and the empirical. In the course of this development, from 1900 to 1913, he first emphasizes the "eidetic" character of phenomenology, and then begins to characterize it less as a science of essences and more as a critique of reason and as a transcendental philosophy. But this explicit adoption of Kantian themes goes hand in hand with a critique of Kant that anticipates Heidegger's. He thinks that Kant misunderstood the A-Deduction as psychological,[54] replacing it by a theory of mind based on a series of arguments, even as it failed to free itself from the dubious legacy of mental-faculty psychology. In the end he characterizes Kant's theory of mind as "mythical constructions,"[55] and portrays Kant as a philosopher who was seeking but failed to find transcendental phenomenology.

Husserl's designation of his phenomenology as transcendental philosophy emerges when he begins employing the terminology of the immanent and the transcendent in the years leading up to *Ideas I*. His use of the term *transcendence* and his own understanding of the meaning and derivation of the term *transcendental philosophy* are evident in an early section of *Cartesian Meditations* (*Cartesianische Meditationen*) (section 11), under the heading "The Transcendence of the World":

> Neither the world nor any worldly object is a piece of my ego, to be found in my conscious life as a really inherent part of it, as a complex of data of sensation or a complex of acts. . . . If this "transcendence" . . . is part of the intrinsic sense of the world, then, by way of contrast, the ego himself, who bears within him the world as an accepted sense and who, in turn, is necessarily presupposed by this sense, is legitimately called *transcendental*, in the phenomenological sense. Accordingly, the philosophical problems arising from this correlation are called transcendental-philosophical.[56]

Thus both Heidegger's terminology of transcendence and important aspects of his Kant interpretation have their unacknowledged origins in Husserl.

But behind both of these influences lies the much more important issue of how to treat transcendence (or intentionality) as a philosophical issue, an issue Heidegger articulates in his rejection of the "deduction" as a juridical procedure. Kant's great insight was, or should have been, that we don't have to ask permission, as it were, to apply the categories to objects or to relate the mind to the world. Asking "by what right" we do this is to take on a burden of proof that has dubious assumptions and that should not be accepted in the first place.

It should be pointed out that the question of "right" makes a good deal more sense as part of Kant's *critique* of traditional metaphysics, a topic which Heidegger neglects, as we pointed out. The question here is to determine whether we have the right to employ concepts of the understanding, like causality and substance, beyond the limits of all possible experience. But the answer to this question, in the Dialectic, is to deny us the right to so employ our concepts, and so to undercut the pretensions of traditional metaphysics, rational psychology, and natural theology. Here the issue of skepticism is also appropriate, but Kant's purpose is not to defeat skepticism about traditional metaphysical knowledge; if anything he plays the role of the skeptic himself. Thus the idea of a "deduction" of certain concepts, conceived as a question of their legitimacy, would seem appropriate in that context. But it seems oddly placed in the early sections of the Analytic, which is designed to display the entirely legitimate employment of pure concepts within the empirical realm. And here Heidegger's point, and the key to his well-founded critical reading of Kant, is that the question of their legitimacy should not arise.

CHAPTER 4

Conscience and Reason

HEIDEGGER AND THE GROUNDS OF INTENTIONALITY

Steven Crowell

1. Transcendental Philosophy and Intentionality

According to Kant, transcendental philosophy embodies the kind of knowledge "by which we know that—and how—certain representations . . . can be employed or are possible purely a priori"; that is, "such knowledge as concerns the a priori possibility of knowledge, or its a priori employment."[1] In Kant's language, to say that a representation is "possible" is equivalent to saying that it can be "employed," and that, in turn, is equivalent to saying that it has "content," that is, "relation to [an] object."[2] All representations, as such, *purport* to have content, but not all of them *do*. In showing "that and how" representations can have content, transcendental philosophy is concerned with the issue of *intentionality*, with showing that entities in the world are there for us, how our mental life discloses what there is. At first, however, its approach to this issue seems restricted to showing "that and how" certain representations can have a relation to objects "purely a priori"—that is, without reference to any experience in which objects can be given. In this sense, transcendental philosophy specifically concerns the intentionality of *reason*, where reason is the power of producing representations whose purported content does not derive from experience. How can representations that have their seat purely in thinking be shown to have a relation to an object? Kant answers that this is possible only if the content of such representations can be shown to be the condition for the possibility of intentionality as such, that is, only if it makes "objects"—entities that are there for us—possible. In fact, then, the *Critique of Pure Reason*'s approach to the question of intentionality is not at all restricted. By showing that and how certain representations are employable a priori it shows how *any* representation could have relation to an object at all.

I have opened this chapter with some well-known features of Kant's enterprise in order to specify a context for what looks, on the face of it, to be a somewhat quixotic task—namely, to argue that Heidegger's fundamental ontology is concerned precisely with the question that concerned Kant: how does *reason* make intentionality possible? It is clear that Heidegger aims to give an account of intentionality (he says so in many places),[3] but it seems equally clear that the account turns not on reason but on the understanding of being (*Seinsverständnis*). More concretely, Heidegger traces the possibility of encountering entities as entities not, as does Kant, to the self-determining spontaneity of transcendental apperception, the "I think," but to the thrown-projective "care" structure of Dasein as being-in-the-world. For Heidegger, what Kant mistakenly attributes to reason has deeper roots, and though Kant may succeed in uncovering conditions for a certain kind of intentionality (the regional ontology of nature as the occurrent), this is accomplished only by concealing those deeper roots through an aporetic approach to the "subject" as something equally occurrent. It is not reason, then—the power of combining representations into judgments, the power of subsuming representations under rules, or drawing inferences—that explains how entities show up for us, but rather Dasein's "transcendence," its "projection of possibilities for being its self" in light of which things can show themselves as what they are.

I do not wish to contradict the claim that Heidegger advances the tradition of transcendental philosophy beyond Kant precisely by recognizing that care is ontologically prior to reason, that Dasein's transcendence is the ground of self-consciousness. But I shall argue that just this priority of care over reason and self-consciousness provides a *better* explanation of reason's contribution to the account of intentionality. Unlike the transcendental unity of apperception, the care structure involves an inner articulation, and my aim is to show reason's place within it.

Here, however, lies a second objection. For though the care structure is internally articulated, reason is apparently not one of its elements. Whether one takes care to involve "existentiality, facticity, and falling" or "understanding, disposition, and discourse," reason is conspicuously absent.[4] Indeed, it has long been assumed that Heidegger's ontology occludes reason. For some—those who applaud Heidegger's frequent remarks dismissing *ratio*, *Vernunft*, as "the most stiff-necked adversary of thought"[5]—this occlusion is a welcome departure in the dreary history of Western rationalism. For others—those who associate the putative absence of reason with dangers best emblematized by Heidegger's involvement with National Socialism—the occlusion is symptomatic of the general failure of Heidegger's position. For these critics, Heidegger's attempt to subordinate reason to care ends with his failure to do justice to the normative aspects of our experience.

The classic formulation of this objection is found in *Der Wahrheitsbegriff bei Husserl und Heidegger* (*The Concept of Truth in Husserl and Heidegger*), where Ernst Tugendhat claims that in Heidegger's attempt to ground propositional truth in the "more primordial" truth of Dasein's disclosedness "the specific sense of 'truth' is lost."[6] The predicate *true* properly applies to propositions because they can be assessed in terms of a distinction between correct and incorrect, measured against the entity as it is in itself. Heidegger argues that for an entity to serve as such a measure it must show up in a holistic context of significance ("world") that has been disclosed in advance, a disclosedness he terms "ontological truth." Such truth does not stand in normative relation to falsity but to "closed-off-ness." However, Tugendhat argues that because Heidegger provides no explanation of what governs this distinction in the way that appeals to the entity as it is in itself governs the distinction between correctness and incorrectness, it is pseudonormative: rather than being something assessable in terms of success or failure, disclosedness is something that merely *occurs*. As a condition for any encounter with entities, disclosedness provides a "*conditio sine qua non*," but the "specific sense of the truth relation"—its distinctive normativity—"is not clarified."[7]

Tugendhat deems a failure Heidegger's attempt to define the normative content of disclosedness by means of the concept of authenticity, a judgment that is followed by many. In the following reading of Heidegger's remarks on conscience—which is where the ontology of reason is to be found—I will argue that Tugendhat and others miss the point. First, however, I will consider in somewhat more detail a few objections to Heidegger's approach.

2. *Robert Pippin's Criticisms*

Let us begin by considering what any explanation of intentionality must provide. Intentionality is philosophically perplexing because by means of it we are not simply in causal interaction with entities but have to do with them *as* something. One way to get at this distinction is to say that to be involved with something "as" something is to be governed by the conditions that the thing must satisfy in order to *be* what it is *taken* to be. This means that intentionality is a normative notion, governed by conditions of success or failure. For instance, for me to experience something as a pen (for it to be the "intentional content" of my "state"), I must be responsive to the rules which constitute something as a pen.[8] Stating what these rules are can be difficult—indeed, *whether* they can be stated at all is a matter of some dispute—but only if it is true that in the face of the thing's failure to live up to (some of) its satisfaction conditions I would admit that my experience "had not been" *of* a pen, I could not have been involved with it *as* a pen at all.

Now Heidegger appears to have an account of this sort of normativity. In keeping with his rejection of a Cartesian subject whose mental states determine the content of its experience, Heidegger locates the norms governing intentionality not in the individual subject's representations but in social practices. Before being an individual subject, Dasein is a socialized One (*das Man*), constituted by what is "average" (the normal) and *thereby* caught up in what is normative.[9] It is because I conform to the way "one" does things that entities can become available to me as *appropriate* and so "as" pens, shoes, eating utensils, and the like. Such normativity simply arises in the course of practices; it is not the result of (and hence not explicable in terms of) reason. Intentionality rests not upon a transcendental *logic* but upon the de facto normativity of practices.

Robert Pippin, however, has questioned the adequacy of this account, arguing that it explains only how we act in accord with norms, when what really needs explaining is how we can act in *light* of them. By emphasizing "mindless" conformism over any "quasi-intentional features of *taking up* or *sustaining* a practice,"[10] this interpretation conceals a moment of self-conscious agency that has not been given its due: even to say that I am conforming to a norm is to say more than that my behavior just happens. When Heidegger suggests that in practices I "let" things "be involved," this implies more than simply using things appropriately; it implies that I use them "in light of such appropriateness." Social practices are such that one can be doing them only if one *takes* oneself to be doing them.[11] The Kantian rationalist will explain the distinction between acting merely in accord with norms (conformism) and acting in light of them by appealing to self-legislation or pure practical reason, and Pippin acknowledges that Heidegger's rejection of such rationalism has some plausibility: "We do of course inherit and pass on much unreflectively, or at least in a way that makes the language of self-imposition and justification look highly idealized."[12] Nevertheless he requires that Heidegger provide some account of "the internal structure of . . . sustaining and reflecting" social practices, without which we cannot distinguish acting in accord with norms from acting in light of them. Because Heidegger does not provide such an account, his appeal to sociality is ultimately aporetic.[13]

Pippin recognizes that such an account should be given in Division Two of *Being and Time*, but he believes that "the themes of anxiety, guilt, the call of conscience, authenticity, and resoluteness do not shed much light" on the problem. Because they represent a "total" breakdown of the seamless conformity to the norms grounded in *das Man*, they provide merely an "indeterminate negation" of the conformist self, one that reveals no positive resources for a normatively oriented "sustaining and reflecting" of inherited norms.[14] In short, Heidegger lacks an adequate concept of self-consciousness in Hegel's sense: because these chapters present Dasein's authentic disclosedness not as something it works toward by "reasoning, reflecting, contestation with others" but as an "original event," Dasein's authenticity, its "'acting for the sake of its own possibility,' cannot be rightly understood as acting *on*, or 'having' reasons, as if it came to its ends, or could come to them as its own, only by virtue of such reasons. This would be a secondary manifestation for Heidegger and would suggest an unacceptably subjectivist understanding of such activity (as if the subject were the 'origin')."[15] Thus, on Pippin's reading, Heidegger's position offers nothing but the mindless social conformism of the One, the "arch, defensive neo-positivism" of a disclosive event that simply reifies "mentalités, epistemes, 'discourses,' 'fields of power,' and so on."[16]

But is it true that Division Two of *Being and Time* sheds no light on this problem? Can the existential analyses of anxiety, conscience, and resoluteness really be relegated to the scrap heap of "indeterminate negation"? Pippin challenges us to look again at these chapters to see whether they might yield something like a notion of normative self-consciousness—something that would illuminate what it means to act in light of norms, or to act on reasons, without implying (as Pippin, following Hegel, does) that authentic disclosedness must be a *consequence* of deliberation, or "reasoning, reflecting, contestation with others." Perhaps critics have been putting the wrong question to these chapters, one that conceals the place that reason already occupies there.

3. Ernst Tugendhat's Criticisms

It is in fact possible to identify precisely where the wrong question gets asked if we return to Tugendhat. Elaborating the critical insight underlying his *Wahrheitsbegriff*, Tugendhat has argued that "the moral, and indeed the normative in general, does not appear" in *Being and Time*. Of course, *das Man* involves a kind of normativity, but this is entirely "conventional," and so, he argues, compatible with Dasein's being "hardwired" for it. True normativity is distinguished from the conventional precisely in that it involves "a claim to grounding," and so includes a "specific depth dimension" of deliberation and reason-giving.[17] Corresponding to this is the existential condition of *Eigenständigkeit* (literally, "independence"), a kind of freedom constituted by a concern for this depth dimension of reasons. Just this, Tugendhat argues, is absent from *Being and Time*: "it emerges that of the three crucial concepts that were mentioned—deliberation, reasons, norms—not a single one is found in *Sein und Zeit*; they neither occur there, nor is there anything remotely resembling them."[18] The individuality and freedom required for deliberation do appear in connection with authenticity, but it is precisely there that no trace of deliberation and reasoning is to be found; indeed "resoluteness *excludes* deliberation."[19] Hence *Being and Time* provides no account of the depth dimension of reasons.

But just where should we expect reason and deliberation to show up in an account of resoluteness? Deliberation concerns the reasons for what I do, considers which possibilities are "better grounded."[20] Tugendhat distinguishes between two levels at which the call for deliberation might arise. At the first level—that of moral and prudential deliberation—I consider the relative weight that a given desire should have in the order of my willing. Though I deliberate as an individual, my appeal to reason here ensures that my answer will remain general—an expression of how *one* should live. At the second level, however—that of authenticity as Tugendhat interprets it—it is my set of desires as a whole that is at stake, and I am faced with the question of how *I* should live: in the face of death I ponder whether I have really lived my life or whether life has passed me by. Heidegger's account of resoluteness is said to address this issue. In what sense, then, does it exclude deliberation?

First, there is the trivial sense in which Heidegger's text offers no account of prudential and moral deliberation, but since Tugendhat correctly sees that authenticity is "not equivalent to the question of what is morally right,"[21] one cannot infer that *Being and Time*'s ontology excludes such an account. Instead, Tugendhat argues that the *question* to which resolute choice is the answer excludes deliberation, noting that the question of what my life means (who I should be) is not the sort of thing on which deliberation can get a grip. The very singularity of the question seems to exclude the publicity and universality of reason-giving. Because there is no "depth dimension of reasons" to appeal to here, Tugendhat suggests that "ultimate enlightenment lies in realizing the senselessness of the question."[22] He therefore heaps scorn on what he takes to be Heidegger's appeal to guilt and conscience as ersatz norms that would substitute for the impossibility of deliberation.[23] But what if these notions are not intended to supply nonrational standards for a choice where reason can no longer be invoked—that is, in relation to the *ontic* question of who I should be? What if they serve the *ontological* function of clarifying how any answer to that ontic question brings with it an orientation toward reasons, thus making deliberation possible? In that case, Heidegger's identification of resoluteness with existential truth would not, as Tugendhat believes, amount to "an attempt to banish reason from human existence, particularly from the relation of oneself to oneself,"[24] but would rather be the account of why reason belongs to that relation.

Tugendhat claims that though Heidegger's concept of resolute choice appears to be an irrational decisionism, it must nevertheless, if it is to be a choice, remain tacitly supported by an orientation toward reasons. A genuine choice "must be able to rest upon justification, that is, it is grounded in the question of truth, even though it cannot be fully resolved in this question."[25] Heidegger's clinging to the notion of existential *truth* is said to be grudging acknowledgment of this. But what sort of grounding is it that orients choice toward truth and justification even though it cannot be "fully resolved in this question"? How do I *come to be* so oriented; how do I *enter into* the depth dimension of reasons? Just this—and not the question of how I should live my life—is at stake in Heidegger's ontological discussion of conscience. Consider the issue from another angle: Tugendhat argues that one who deliberates morally seeks those reasons for acting that are reasons for everyone, that is, to do that which everyone would be justified in doing. This means that the deliberator is one for whom this "universal justifiability has become a motive," and, as Tugendhat notes, how such a thing can become a motive "is not self-evident."[26] Before the ontologist delves into the practice of moral deliberation, then, he might well wish to understand how the actor comes to be *concerned* with reasons at all. If Tugendhat is right that Heidegger has little to say about the first, he misses the fact that Heidegger has much to say about the second. The chapter on conscience does not supply ersatz criteria for an otherwise irrational choice: it articulates our capacity for entering into the space of reasons.

4. *Locating Reason in Being and Time*

Can such an assertion—which certainly does not sound very Heideggerian—be supported by the text of *Being and Time*? It can, but the evidence will require a good deal of unpacking. In explicating his "formalized" concept of guilt, Heidegger writes: "The self, which as such has to lay the ground [*Grund*] for itself, can *never* get that ground into its power; and yet it has to take over being the ground existingly [*existierend*]." In case this is not crystal clear, Heidegger goes on to explain: Dasein is "*not through* itself, but [is] *released to* itself from the ground, in order to be *as this* [ground]. Dasein is not itself the ground of its being, insofar as this [ground] first springs from its own projection; but as being-a-self [*Selbstsein*] it is indeed the *being* of the ground. This ground is always only ground of an entity whose being has to take over being-a-ground."[27]

The burden of my argument is to show that "taking over being-a-ground" must be understood as including a reference to ground as *reason*. First, however, two preliminary comments are in order, one concerning transcendental philosophy, the other what is to be understood by "reason."

As Carl-Friedrich Gethmann has shown, this passage represents the crux of Heidegger's transformation of the transcendental philosophy of Kant, Fichte, and Husserl; here the transcendental subject, as care, is conceived not as "the constituting entity but as the entity that *facilitates* [*vollziehend*] constitution." In contrast to the transcendental subject in Fichte (and Husserl), Dasein's "primal act" is "not the positing of itself as positing, but rather the positing of itself as posited."[28] As our passage indicates, Dasein, as thrown, must acknowledge a ground from which it is "released to itself," and which is, in Gethmann's term, "out of reach" (*unverfügbar*). Thus, as Gethmann explains, Dasein "presents [*stellt dar*] the ground for all entities (positing) and is itself grounded [*begründet*] by means of the ground."[29]

At first glance this threatens to annul the transcendental point of departure altogether. If the so-called transcendental subject is itself grounded in something out of reach—whether reified epistemes, power structures, or capital-*B* Being—won't the ground that it presents for intentionality simply have the character of a fact? What will keep dogmatism and skepticism from resuming their eternal dialectic? Haven't we simply generated another version of Tugendhat's criticism, namely, that Heidegger's ontology allows no room for the normativity of reason?[30] To respond to this worry it is necessary to recognize that the passage in question entails two distinct notions of ground: ground as *facticity* and ground as *reason*.[31] Taking over being-a-ground—where "being" must be understood existentially as ability-to-be—names the point at which Dasein becomes accountable: the factic ground that remains out of reach is reflected in a normative project of grounding (accountability) that first makes *possible* something like reasons.

What, then, is to be understood by "reason"? The link between the idea of conscience as taking over being-a-ground and the concept of ground as reason is to be found in the character of conscience as a call, that is, in its character as discourse. For reason has a double connection to discourse. First, reasoning is a *discursive practice* in which something is offered or given—support for one's judgment, justification for one's behavior. Second, that which is given, the reason, is itself something that, in Tugendhat's translation of T. M. Scanlon's phrase, *speaks for* something else—not in the sense of speaking in place of something but in the sense of telling in favor of it.[32] Corresponding to this double connection is a double normativity: first, as a practice, reason-giving, like all practices, depends on constitutive rules that determine what counts as success or failure; and second, what is given in this practice itself stands in a normative relation to something, namely, that for which it supplies a reason.[33]

The attempt to link conscience to reason by means of its character as a call—that is, as a mode of discourse—may seem unpromising if we recall certain passages about discourse in *Being and Time*. Everywhere Heidegger seems keen to disassociate language from reason—to "liberate grammar from logic," as he puts it (209/165). Far from seeing an intimate connection between discourse and reason, such as one might find in contemporary attempts to link linguistic meaning to truth conditions or to spell out the semantics of language with the help of logic, Heidegger argues that the logical forms of language—*apophansis*, predicative assertion—are parasitical on a more primordial sense of *logos* as "letting be seen." Further, "assertion is not a free-floating kind of behavior which, in its own right, might be capable of disclosing entities . . . in a primary way" (157/199). Primordial disclosure is, rather, a function of Dasein's pre-predicative involvements.[34] However, the thesis being advanced here is not that the call of conscience is itself a mode of discourse that speaks for something else, a practice of reason-giving that employs predicative assertion. The claim is, rather, that the discourse of conscience is the ontological condition of that practice that explains its double normativity: the rule of accountability inherent in the practice of giving and the rule of legitimation that underlies speaking for something. To flesh out this claim—and so to read our initial passage with more insight—we must locate conscience within the structure of Dasein's being, care, as a whole.

5. *Conscience and the Structure of Care*

Discourse (*Rede*) is one of the three existential structures that go to make up Dasein's disclosedness, that is, that account ontologically for the fact that I am "in" a "world," a context of significance within which things can be encountered in all the ways they are so encountered. The other two structures are disposition (*Befindlichkeit*) and understanding (*Verstehen*). Together, these three make up the framework of Heidegger's account of intentionality. The broad outlines of Heidegger's position are well known, so I will only mention them. First, disposition is that aspect of my being thanks to which things *matter* to me. I do not inhabit a world in which things are merely arranged around me in neutral fashion; rather, they have a particular salience, they are alluring or repelling or irritating. This is because I am present to myself not first of all through a theoretical reflection but always through the "feeling" of my own having-to-be. I can be disposed in various ways but I am never without some mood. Second, understanding is not a mental operation but a *sein-können*, an "ability-to-be," a skill or know-how, which Heidegger terms the "projection of possibilities for being." It is because I possess such skills and abilities that I can encounter things in *their* possibilities—that is, that things can prove useful or appropriate for the tasks in which I am engaged. Understanding in this sense yields a teleologically structured "relevance totality"—things are there "in order to" accomplish some specific end, which in turn appears as something in order to accomplish some further end—a totality that is anchored in an "end in itself," referred back to the being who acts "for the sake of" what it is (practical identity). Discourse, thirdly, is what Heidegger calls the "articulation of intelligibility"—namely, the articulation of that intelligibility that has its roots in disposition and understanding. Though disposition and understanding are necessary conditions for intentionality, they are not sufficient. For things to be significant they must not merely be useful for something but also *tellable*: what I am doing must be able to be named. Only so is it possible that things can show up *as* what they are, and without this "as"—one that encodes the normative sense of the "proper" in any given world—we do not have intentionality.

Heidegger initially describes care in its "everyday" modality and argues that the self of everyday being-in-the-world is the One (*das Man*). That is, what makes up the significance of the world into which I am geared is not some content that belongs to my consciousness, in terms of which I represent the world; rather, it belongs to the "public," the always historically and culturally particular social practices of those among whom I find myself. I conduct myself as "one" does in the roles I adopt, and in telling myself and others what I am up to, I speak as one does: "the 'One' itself articulates the referential context of significance" (167/129). The conformism that this picture of everyday Dasein evokes correlates to another aspect of everydayness, namely, that my way of gearing into the world is not a function of deliberation but rather a "mindless" coping in which my abilities take the lead. To say that everydayness is mindless is not, however, to say that it is *opaque*. On the contrary, it is precisely "cleared" (*gelichtet*): a necessary condition for the possibility of encountering things as meaningful is the habitual conformity to public norms, to the normal and average, and to the name.

Although my everyday gearing into the world is not a function of deliberation, deliberation, as a kind of practice, must find *its* ontological clarification at the level of the One. Heidegger analyzes the way that disturbances in the smooth flow of my activities can occasion a transition in my dealings with things: from their being "available" things become merely "occurrent"; accordingly, I no longer simply deal with them but rather—at the extreme—merely stare at them. Such disturbances provide the occasion for deliberation—that is, for technical, strategic, and prudential consideration of what is to be done. It must be possible, therefore, to give an ontological account of deliberation as a specific modification of the care structure.[35] Appreciation of this point allows us to see why the everyday one-self is a necessary, but not a sufficient, condition for intentionality.

First, when I deliberate about how to go on I do so in terms of some disposition. Things (including my own beliefs and desires) will present themselves as salient, as "weighty" or not, according to how I am disposed. Upon deliberation I may be less likely simply to act on the faces that things show me according to my mood than I would be when absorbed in worldly affairs, but this is simply because the project of deliberation is to deliberate *about* my action. If I am finally moved to act "in spite of" the way I feel about things, "because" it is called for or reasonable, this will only be because I am so disposed that I can feel the weight of the reasons brought forward. Second, deliberation involves making explicit what belongs to understanding—the particular in-order-to relations grounded in the specific for-the-sake-of that informs my smoothly functioning practice. I make these elements explicit to the extent that I am able, and I consider them as indications of how to go on. Such explication is, finally, discursive: I articulate courses of action, weighing evidence and considering reasons for going on in one way or another. The significant thing to note is that deliberation takes place (as did the action from which it arose) within the constitutive rules of the "world" in which I remain engaged. That is, I deliberate as that which I was understanding myself to be, in terms of my "practical identity" as husband, as teacher, as American citizen. Thus, while only an individual can deliberate, I do not deliberate as my ownmost self. Rather, the reasons I adduce and the evidence that I find salient will normally be those typical of the current cultural, historical composition of the One. I deliberate in order to restore equilibrium in a context that otherwise remains fixed; I consider things in light of how *one* ought to go on. This does not mean that my reasoning is nothing but the rationalization of specific cultural conditions, but it does mean that the practice of deliberation, like all practices, is grounded ontologically in what is public, typical, and normative in a given community. That deliberation is explicitly oriented toward "reasons for" does not, ontologically, get us any further than the analysis of everyday coping. For in spite of its being a product of a disturbance in the smooth flow of my comportment in the world, adjusting to the world, deliberation does not disclose any aspect of myself that would not already be governed by the public, anonymous One.[36]

Heidegger does, however, consider a more extreme possibility—not the disturbance of everyday coping but its complete breakdown—in which the self is explicitly called into question *as* a self. Here deliberation is impossible because the everyday world on which it depends "has the character of completely lacking significance" (231/186). Yet it is only in light of this liminal mode of being that the sufficient condition of intentionality—the possibility of a genuinely first-person stance—is made evident. As I shall argue, the account of conscience that finds its place here articulates what it means to say "I," such that I—and not only some "one"—have, and can have, reasons about which I deliberate; it explains how *one's* reasons can be *my* reasons. For Heidegger, conscience is not itself a kind of private reason but an ontological condition for distinguishing between external and internal reasons, between a quasi-mechanical conformism and a commitment responsive to the normativity of norms.

The liminal condition of breakdown is a modification of the care structure and thus involves the three elements of disposition, understanding, and discourse. As the sort of discourse that belongs to this modification, conscience will articulate the intelligibility of the self as disclosed through the other two elements: the disposition of *Angst* and its corresponding mode of understanding, *death*. For our purposes what matters most about these controversial analyses is the way "everyday familiarity collapses," so that Dasein is "brought face to face with itself as being-in-the-world" (233/188).

Anxiety is a distinctive disposition because it neutralizes the claims things normally exert on me and so also the reasons they provide for what I do. Anxiety "tells us that entities are not 'relevant' at all" (231/186). This does not mean that significance and reasons disappear; I still register their demands, but they no longer grip me. As Heidegger puts it elsewhere, anxiety reveals the "strangeness" of the fact "*that* they are beings—and not nothing"; beings are simply there, inert.[37] This is because, second, anxiety does not "concern a *definite* kind of being for Dasein or a *definite* possibility for it" but rather "discloses Dasein as *being-possible* as such" (232/187–88). Things become insignificant, reasons lose their grip, just because I am no longer drawn into the world in terms of some definite possibility, some specific practical identity. "We ourselves . . . slip away from ourselves,"[38] and with that go the constitutive rules that, belonging to our roles and practices, provide the terms in which I understand how to go on. Without these, I am able neither to act nor to deliberate. Conceived as a mode of understanding (ability-to-be), this being individuated down to my sheer "being-possible" is, as William Blattner has shown, an "*in*-ability-to-be"—that is, "death" as the "possibility of no-longer-being-able-to-be-there" (294/250).[39] Death is not a matter of bodily demise but an existential condition in which I am no longer able to gear into the world in terms of roles and practices, with the result that things have properties but no affordances, and the motives and reasons the latter once supplied now take on the character of something closer to simple facts, items in the world of which I can take note but which do not move me. The question that arises here is not how they could ever have *been* valid for me (as the one-self I am defined by such validity), but how they could be valid for me now—that is, for the one who genuinely says "I." How can any reason be *my* reason?

This question, I claim, is answered by the mode of discourse that articulates the intelligibility of breakdown, namely, the call of conscience. What is "given to understand" in the call? Heidegger answers: "guilty" (*schuldig*)—but such guilt cannot be explained with reference to any law, whether conventional, rational/moral, or divine. Because conscience articulates a condition in which such laws have ceased to make any claim on me and persist merely as facts, inert items that lack normative force, what I am given to understand about myself in conscience cannot be explained through transgression of them. Heidegger expresses this by saying that the term *guilt* must be "formalized" so that "all reference to law, ought, and social relations drops out" (328/283). But can the notion of guilt make sense without reference to any law or ought? Owing something to someone is more than simply possessing what he once possessed; rather, a law or norm governing exchanges must be in place. But Heidegger's formalization is meant to bring out a further ontological point, namely, that my relation to such a law or norm must be of a certain character. If I am incapable of placing myself under the law—as may occur through various mental or physical incapacities—then I cannot be said to owe something. *Angst* in Heidegger's sense reveals something like a *global* incapacity vis-à-vis the normativity of all laws and oughts: existing norms present themselves as mere facts; they have no more normative force than does the code of Hammurabi. It may be true that a valid law obligates me whether or not I recognize it, but the point of Heidegger's formalization is to highlight the way law and ought can come to have standing from the first-person point of view.

Thus the role the analysis of guilt is to play is relatively clear. To say that "this 'Guilty!' turns up as a predicate for the 'I am'" (326/281) means that it belongs to my radically individualized mode of being, independent of any grasp of myself as this or that (including as rational being or as believer). Further, what conscience gives to understand thereby is "the ontological condition for Dasein's ability to come to owe anything in factically existing" (332/288). Heidegger thus examines conscience in order to explain how I can come to be *obligated*. Since there is no question about how *one* comes to be obligated (the one-self simply conforms to constitutive rules), Heidegger's concern here is to show how, given the fact that the one-self can break down, something like a responsiveness to norms as norms is possible. If that is so, we have the context necessary for understanding our initial text, since Heidegger offers it to unpack his formalized definition of guilt as "being the ground of a nullity" (329/283). That context, as John Haugeland correctly sees, is Heidegger's account of responsibility, for which reason Haugeland translates *schuldig* not as "guilty" but as "responsible"—in the sense both of "at fault/culpable and obliged/indebted/liable."[40] Yet "being the ground of a nullity" signifies responsibility in a further sense not noted by Haugeland: that of being *answerable* (*verantwortlich*) (334/288). To see how this discursive sense is already at stake in our passage is to understand how conscience provides an ontological condition for reason.

To make that case I will argue, first, that conscience accounts for how grounds become reasons, in the sense of "my" reasons—that is, that conscience explains my ability to act not just in accord with, but also in light of, norms; and second, that the notion of resoluteness, as the authentic response to the call of conscience, entails the project of *giving* reasons (to oneself and to the other).

6. Being-Guilty and the Space of Reasons

As a "predicate for the 'I am,'" being-guilty as "being the ground of a nullity" is not the simple state of an occurrent entity but a way of existing, a modification of the care structure. The complexity of Heidegger's attempt to explain such being-a-ground arises from the fact that the notion of ground itself is twofold, thanks to the two equiprimordial aspects of Dasein's being, thrownness and projection.

Heidegger first introduces the notion of ground in terms of Dasein's thrownness: Dasein has "*not* laid that ground *itself*," and yet "it reposes in the weight of it, which is made manifest to it as a burden" in its mood (330/284). What does "ground" mean here? Formally, as Gethmann observed, it is simply what is out of reach (*unverfügbar*), that which the transcendental subject must posit itself as being posited *by*. Less formally, however, several attempts to specify such a ground have been made. Heidegger sometimes suggests that it be conceived as "nature" (or "cosmos"), as *das Übermächtige*—which leads, perhaps, to some form of theological conception.[41] Gadamer suggests that this dimension of Dasein's ground is language and tradition, which is always "mehr Sein als Bewußtsein."[42] Dreyfus glosses the notion by appeal to background practices belonging to one's sociocultural milieu.[43] We need not decide the merits of any of these suggestions, since our concern is with what it might mean to be grounded in any of these ways, and my claim is that such grounds, *to the extent that they remain out of reach*, cannot be conceived as *reasons*. This is clear if the factic ground is conceived as nature, for to say that I am grounded in nature is to say that I find myself within a causal nexus over which I have no control: the forces of nature that cooperate in ensuring that I do what I do cannot be confused with the reasons why *I* do it. Nature in this sense lies outside the space of reasons because its constraint on me is not normatively assessable; it simply is or is not.

Something similar holds if the ground is conceived either as history, tradition, or social practices—so long as we insist, with Heidegger, that it functions as factic ground precisely to the extent that it is out of reach. For though we can see that social practices, for instance, must be understood normatively—that is, that they involve reasons in the sense of an in-order-to and a for-the-sake-of and so are assessable in terms of success or failure—it is not from the point of view of one's everyday coping that we make this judgment. The agent functions within the nexus of such practices in much the way that she functions within the constraints of nature: she acts in accord with norms but not in light of them; hence such behavior is largely predictable from a third-person point of view. This is the picture of the functioning of norms within social practices we get from Division One of *Being and Time*, where it is difficult to distinguish human from animal teleological action.[44] Though we might be willing to describe animal behavior as being based on reasons, such reasons would be external: there are reasons for what Larry Bird does on the court, just as there are reasons for what the wasp does, but neither does them *for* those reasons, in light of them. In *Angst*—which is possible for Bird but not for the wasp—this difference comes to awareness: that in whose grip I was when geared into the world now confronts me as an inert fact, something without normative force.

Robert Pippin is surely right to object that this strikes a false note as a picture of human meaningful activity, but this is not an objection to Heidegger. For the latter, we are never simply grounded by the sort of thrown ground disclosed in mood; instead, though Dasein "can *never* get that ground into its power," it "has to take over being the ground existingly" (330/284). In the structure of my being as care, my facticity is always ramified by my existentiality—that is, my "projection of possibilities for being a self." What does "ground" mean when it is ramified by existentiality? The answer must be given at an appropriately formalized level. Recall that in *Angst* the concern is not for a "*definite* kind of being for Dasein or a *definite* possibility for it," but rather for "being-possible as such" (232/187). Thus, taking over the ground existingly may be described formally as a "possibilizing" of the factic ground: what the call of conscience gives to understand is that that which I can never get into my power—what grounds me beyond my reach—is nevertheless *my* possibility. This, I suggest, can only mean that factic grounds become subject to a choice for which I am accountable; they are thereby taken up into the normative space of reasons.

The argument for this remains largely implicit in *Being and Time*. However, in the 1929 essay "Vom Wesen des Grundes" ("On the Essence of Ground"), Heidegger provides a crucial clarification of how factic grounds enter the space of reasons when Dasein takes over being-a-ground.[45] The essay follows *Being and Time* in arguing that the in-order-to relations informing Dasein's practical dealings with things are anchored in Dasein's self-awareness as that "for-the-sake-of-which" (*Umwillen*) it is so engaged. This possibility for being (or ability-to-be) discloses a totality of significance ("world") in terms of which entities can "gain entry into world"—show themselves in *their* possibilities—and thereby "come to be 'more in being'" (EG, 123). We should understand this "more" as entities' being held up to constitutive standards, and the essay makes clear what *Being and Time* did not, namely, that the worldhood that makes such standards possible is grounded in the *normative* orientation of Dasein's first-person self-awareness. Heidegger here calls this orientation "sovereignty."

In 1929 Heidegger glossed the care structure—transcendence of beings toward their being—with the Platonic notion of an *epekeina tes ousias*: a "beyond beings." This suggests that transcendence is connected with the Good, so Heidegger asks: "May we interpret the *agathon* as the transcendence of Dasein" (EG, 124)? According to Heidegger, Plato's *agathon* is "that *hexis* (sovereign power) that is sovereign with respect to the possibility (in the sense of the enabling) of truth, understanding, and even being." Such "sovereignty," however, also describes the *Umwillen* of resolute, individuated Dasein. Thus the "essence of the *agathon* lies in [Dasein's] sovereignty over itself as *hou heneka*—as the 'for the sake of . . . ', it is the source of possibility as such" (EG, 124). By thus equating authentic *Umwillen* with the ancient *hou heneka* and its orientation toward the good or what is "best," Heidegger lets us see that to "possibilize" factic grounds by taking over being-a-ground is to act in light of a *normative* distinction between better and worse. By grasping my situation in the normative light of what is best, the factic grounds into which I am thrown become reasons for which I am responsible.[46]

To take over being-a-ground, then—that is, to possibilize what grounds me—is to transform the claims of nature or society (what "one" simply *does*) into first-person terms, into my reasons for doing what I do. Conscience discloses that I am a being for whom thrown grounds can never function simply as causes: because Dasein has been "*released* from the ground, *not through* itself but *to* itself, so as to be *as this* [ground]" (330/285), grounds take on the character of reasons for which I am accountable. My natural impulses are not within my power, but it is I who make them normative for me, make them reasons for what I do. My gearing into the world must take place in terms of social practices whose rules are not within my power and so function essentially as grounds in the sense of causes. However, it is I who transform such functional effectuation into reasons for being—namely, by answering for them as possibilities. If conscience articulates the intelligibility of the first-person stance that emerges in the collapse of the one-self, Heidegger's gloss of the call in terms of *schuldig-sein* identifies the ontological condition whereby one's (factic) grounds become my (normative) reasons and thus explains how Dasein can act not only in accord with norms but also in light of them.

7. *Being-Guilty and Giving Reasons*

There is a further aspect to the project whereby Dasein enters into the space of reasons through the possibilizing of factic grounds. Heidegger terms such a project "resoluteness" (*Entschlossenheit*), defined as "the self-projection upon one's ownmost being-guilty" (343/297). To "hear" the call of conscience "correctly is . . . tantamount to having an understanding of oneself in one's ownmost potentiality for being" (333/287)—that is, to *be* guilty, to *take over* being-a-ground. With the help of "On the Essence of Ground" we have understood resoluteness as sovereignty, as Dasein's awareness of itself as being-possible, acting for the sake of what is best (*agathon*). But what belongs to such an ability-to-be? On the one hand, I cannot improve on the answer that John Haugeland has provided in terms of his notion of "existential commitment." To be resolved is to take responsibility for the standards inherent in the practices in which I am engaged; only so is it possible for there to *be* practices rather than mere occurrences. For instance, if something can be a rook only because there is a practice, chess, in which it *counts* as such a thing, the idea of "counting" itself depends on my commitment to the game, without which the standards that determine success or failure might have normative authority but would lack normative force. This is not to say that, lacking *my* commitment, there could be no rooks—institutions and practices are social, after all—but neither do these things exist apart from all first-person commitment.[47]

On the other hand, this notion of commitment does not tell the whole story, for it does not reflect the specifically discursive aspect that, for Heidegger, belongs to taking over being-a-ground. To be responsible is to be *answerable* (*verantwortlich*) (334/288), and to be answerable for something is to be accountable for it, that is, to be prepared to *give* an *account* of oneself. Adumbrated here is a necessary connection between resoluteness—as the possibilizing of factic grounds into normative reasons—and the practice of giving reasons. To say that something becomes a reason for me is to say that it speaks for something else, justifies it; and such a thing makes sense only within the constitutive rules of a *practice of giving reasons*. Thus, whatever be the particular project on which I resolve—whatever it is to which I commit ontically—I always at the same time commit myself to accountability as giving an account (*ratio reddende*). The practice of giving reasons has its origin in the call of conscience; it is the "discourse" of an authentic response to the call.

However, this claim appears to run afoul of the fact that Heidegger defines authentic discourse as "reticence," not "giving reasons" (343/298). On the received view, authentic Dasein does not try to justify itself by giving an account of what it is doing; rather, it goes silently about the world-historical business upon which it has resolved in its decisionistic way. Now it would be possible to undermine the received view drawing solely upon *Being and Time*—reticence is compatible with the discursive project of giving an account *to oneself* and, thereby, being prepared to account for oneself to others—but that would still leave a central question unanswered: if Heidegger meant us to understand that resoluteness entails the practice of giving reasons, why didn't he say so? The answer is that he *did* say so, only not in *Being and Time*. To establish a specific textual connection between authentic discourse and the project of reason-giving we must return to the essay "On the Essence of Ground."

"To what extent does there lie in transcendence the intrinsic possibility of something like ground [*Grund*; reason] in general" (EG, 125)? Though "On the Essence of Ground" does not discuss conscience explicitly, in answering this question it suggests how resoluteness entails the practice of giving reasons. Identifying transcendence with a notion of freedom that is ontologically more original than that drawn from the concept of causality, Heidegger notes that prior to all comportment freedom is the condition for being gripped by the normative. Transcendence means that human beings "can be obligated to themselves, i.e., be free selves." And this, in turn, makes possible "something binding, indeed obligation in general" (EG, 126). Hence freedom—what *Being and Time* calls "taking over being-a-ground"—is the "origin of ground in general. Freedom is freedom for ground" (EG, 127). In unpacking what this latter claim means, Heidegger shows us where the project of reason-giving arises.

There are three ways that "in grounding, freedom *gives* and *takes* ground" (EG, 127), and each of these ways corresponds to one aspect of the care structure. First, there is grounding as "taking up a basis" (*Bodennehmen*) within beings, a kind of "belonging to beings" whereby Dasein is "thoroughly attuned by them" (EG, 128). This factic grounding corresponds to care as *disposition*. Second, there is grounding as "establishing" (*Stiften*), which "is nothing other than the projection of the 'for-the-sake-of,'" that is, Dasein's *understanding*. Formally conceived as taking over being-a-ground, understanding opens up the space of reasons through orientation toward the normative, the *agathon*, seeing in light of what is "best." Neither form of grounding is itself "a comportment toward beings," but together they "make intentionality possible transcendentally in such a way that . . . they co-temporalize a *third* manner of grounding: grounding as the grounding of something [*Begründen*]." It is this form of grounding, Heidegger insists, that "makes possible the manifestation of beings in themselves, the possibility of ontic truth" (EG, 129).

Now as we would expect, this third form of grounding belongs to *discourse* as the remaining moment of the care structure. First, Heidegger tells us that the "originary" sense of *Begründen* means "making possible the why-question in general" (EG, 129). Thanks to the "excess of possibility" that is given in the "projection of world" (i.e., the excess, grounded in the for-the-sake-of as *agathon*, that constitutes world as a normative totality of significance and brings entities "more in being" by holding them to constitutive standards), "the 'why' question springs forth" in relation to those beings "that press around us as we find ourselves" (EG, 130). If, in *Being and Time*, Heidegger defined authentic discourse as reticence—the silencing of the everyday way things are talked about so that the call of conscience can be *heard*—he now makes plain that *answering* the call involves discourse as *Begründen*, answering for oneself and for things. In the face of the collapse of the one-self, Dasein confronts the question "Why *this* way and not otherwise?" (EG, 130), and thereby becomes accountable.

As Heidegger explains, the "ontological ground of beings" lies in our "understanding of being," which provides "the most antecedent *answer*" to the why-question (EG, 130). But an answer to the why-question is a *reason*. "*Because* such *Begründen* prevails transcendentally from the outset throughout all becoming-manifest of beings (ontic truth), *all* ontic discovery and disclosing *must* account [*ausweisen*] for itself" (EG, 130; my emphasis). To account, in this sense, is to give reasons: "What occurs is the referral [*Anführung*] to a being that then makes itself known, for example, as 'cause' or as the 'motivational grounds' (motive) for an already manifest nexus of beings"—a referral that is "*demanded*" by the "what-being and how-being of the relevant beings" (EG, 130).[48] And only because there is such a demand can Dasein "in its factical accounting and justifications, cast 'reasons' aside, suppress any demand for them, pervert them, cover them over" (EG, 131). Lest there be any doubt about the matter, Heidegger terms the transcendental answering, which makes this ontic reason-giving possible, "legitimation" (*Rechtgebung*) (EG, 132). Conscience, then, calls one to take over being-a-ground, to answer for oneself, to legitimate by *giving* grounds, that is, reasons. Hence Heidegger concludes his essay by bringing these two elements of conscience (hearing and answering) together in relation to the regrettably undeveloped, but essential, reference to the one *to whom* reasons are finally given and without whom the whole thing makes no sense: "And only being able to listen into the distance"—that is, *vernehmen* as registering the call—"awakens Dasein as a self to the answer of the other Dasein, with whom it can surrender its I-ness"—that is, to whom it must account for itself—"so as to attain an authentic self" (EG, 135).

Needless to say, all this calls for more scrutiny. Even if the textual evidence of a connection between conscience and reason is sufficiently persuasive, it would still be necessary to examine more closely the connection between understanding (the for-the-sake-of as *agathon*, normativity) and conscience both as hearing the call and as giving reasons. And it would be necessary to show how these two moments of conscience remain decisive in Heidegger's later writings, when he inquires into the two aspects of reason—reason as *Vernehmen*, hearing, taking to heart, *heißen*, and *nous*, on the one hand; and reason as *ratio reddende*, account-giving, legitimation, and *logos* on the other. But it is already something to have shown that *Being and Time* retains an important place for reason, that conscience underlies both our responsiveness to reasons and our practice of giving them.[49]

CHAPTER 5

Transcendental Truth and the Truth That Prevails

Daniel O. Dahlstrom

ACCORDING TO Heidegger in *Being and Time* (*Sein und Zeit*), the primary locus of truth is not an assertion or judgment and its essence does not consist in the correctness of an assertion or judgment, that is, its correspondence with an object. Heidegger argues that truth in the most original sense of the word is, instead, the disclosedness of being-here and, as such, the "ontological condition of the possibility" of the truth and falsity of assertions.[1] The locution "condition of the possibility of . . . ," recurring throughout *Being and Time*,[2] suggests that this "original phenomenon of the truth" has a structural role akin to that of transcendental truth in Kant's theoretical philosophy. This kinship is not surprising, since, as we now know from Heidegger's lectures and other writings shortly before and after the composition of the final draft of *Being and Time*, his thinking at this time takes a decidedly Kantian turn, lamented by some, applauded by others.[3]

Yet one good turn deserves another, and in *Contributions to Philosophy (From Enowning)* (*Beiträge zur Philosophie [Vom Ereignis]*) Heidegger tells us that fundamental ontology was merely "transitional," its transcendental path "provisional," and its account of truth "insufficient."[4] Beginning in 1930, Heidegger turns from transcendental truth and the truth of being-here to "the truth of being" and "the truth that prevails," a change in focus that persists for the better part of the next three decades. This change in focus, moreover, dominates Heidegger's work during this period. In 1938 he himself alerts his readers to nine different addresses and writings composed since 1930 on the question of truth. Nor does this emphasis on the question of truth fade from his writings and addresses in the years just before, during, and after the war.[5] In the discussions of truth after 1930, being-here or Da-sein continues, to be sure, to play a crucial role. However, it is no longer the center of gravity of the analysis. One important clue to this difference is the emphasis in *Contributions to Philosophy* that Da-sein, far from being something that we can assume as the starting point of analysis and far from meaning something like "human existence," is something whose existence depends very much on the future and, indeed, is the ground of a humanity yet to come (*Beiträge*, 300ff.).

There is a great deal more that would need to be said about these differences, but the brief précis given here suffices to pose the first question that I would like to address: why does transcendental truth, the truth of Da-sein, the enabling disclosedness of what it means to be, as unpacked in *Being and Time*, come to seem insufficient, if not inadequate, to Heidegger? In order to give even a semblance of an answer to this question, it will be necessary to elaborate a bit more on the account of transcendental truth in *Being and Time* and, above all, to indicate why Heidegger takes his subsequent treatment of truth to be an advance over that account.

Though essentially posed as historical, this first question is connected to matters of considerable consequence and controversy in regard to Heidegger's thinking. These issues can be put into relief by considering two famous criticisms of Heidegger's account of truth after 1930, the first by Ernst Tugendhat, the second by Heidegger himself. According to Tugendhat, the answer to our first question lies in the glaring absence of any measure or criterion within the account of truth as disclosedness in *Being and Time*.[6] Not that Tugendhat thinks that Heidegger's subsequent attempt to identify the openness of things as the measure fares any better. In a justly celebrated critical review, Tugendhat insists, as is well known, that Heidegger's mature philosophy merely exacerbates matters since there is nothing against which to measure the openness of being, once the latter has been construed as the measure or source of the measure itself.

In 1964, merely two months after Tugendhat first voiced his criticism publicly (though others, e.g., Karl Jaspers and Karl Löwith, had been saying much the same thing for years), Heidegger makes two substantial retractions in connection with his account of truth.[7] He calls "untenable" the claim that truth underwent some essential transformation from unhiddenness to correctness among the Greeks, thereby recanting a thesis that he had advanced repeatedly since 1930. Even more significant is his observation in this same context that it was "inappropriate and misleading" to designate the clearing (*aletheia*, in the sense of unhiddenness) the "truth."[8] This second retraction is staggering, when one considers how intensely Heidegger had belabored variations on this very theme since 1930.

Not surprisingly, some, such as Karl-Otto Apel, have interpreted Heidegger's remarks in 1964 as an admission of the trenchancy of Tugendhat's criticism. On Apel's interpretation, Heidegger was effectively repudiating the theme of the predisclosedness of being that had obsessed him throughout his career. Apel goes so far as to claim that Heidegger is acknowledging that his talk of truth in an original sense was not so much a clearing as it was a clearinghouse of meanings, only some of which prove to be true. As Apel reads it, Heidegger had long been guilty of a fundamental confusion of meaning with truth and, in the twilight of his career, with Tugendhat's exposure of his folly looming on the horizon, finally confesses to that confusion.[9]

One of my aims here is to suggest why such readings of Heidegger's 1964 remarks overreach. But while I think that Apel's interpretation is wrong, I think that it is usefully wrong because it helps us become clearer about what Heidegger is up to and to reconsider critically its strengths and weaknesses. Indeed, even if we give Heidegger's self-critical remarks in 1964 a generous reading, we are still left with the question of the sort of revisions they require.[10] In other words, what are the implications of Heidegger's severing the sort of connection between truth and being he had been insisting on for over thirty years? And, given the admission of mistake in this regard, why did he make this mistake? What motivated him to make what must be considered an egregious error, even if one interprets his 1964 remarks generously? I do not hope to answer all these questions in this setting but the second question that I would like to address in the following remarks is posed with a view to answering them: what is the significance of Heidegger's 1964 concessions to critics of his account of truth after 1930? This second question is obviously related to the first since the account of truth after 1930 is motivated, as Heidegger himself iterates, precisely by a sense of the shortcomings of the theory in *Being and Time*. Even if Tugendhat is wrong (as I think he is) about some of the details, he is right that Heidegger's turn is largely motivated by dissatisfaction with the account of transcendental truth in *Being and Time*.

My chapter is divided into two parts, corresponding to the two questions posed in my opening remarks. The first part outlines Heidegger's criticisms of the transcendental account of truth in *Being and Time* and his elaboration, on the basis of those criticisms, of a different way of speaking of truth, namely, as a "truth that prevails." Following this review of the development of Heidegger's mature conception of truth, I turn in the second part to the question of the import of the retractions mentioned above for this conception.

1. The Turn in Heidegger's Conception of Truth

Heidegger instructively criticizes the project of *Being and Time* by situating it within a taxonomy of kinds of transcendence. The birthplace of all the different notions of transcendence is, he contends, Plato's construal of entities in terms of the constant look that they present over many different and changing circumstances. From this vantage point, the beingness of a being is the *idea* or *eidos* that is common (*koinon*) or generic (*gene*). With the positing of this idea common to and yet beyond any particular beings, its separateness from beings is also instituted and this, Heidegger insists, is "the origin of 'transcendence' in all its forms."[11] Against this Platonic backdrop, Heidegger proceeds to identify four subsequent senses of "transcendence": ontic, ontological, epistemological, and fundamental-ontological.[12]

Ontic transcendence is, paradigmatically, that of the supreme being, the creator who reigns above and over all other entities (though he adds that God is also confusedly deemed "the transcendence" himself—like "the magnificence"!—and even "being").

Ontological transcendence refers to the sort of ascendancy over entities that lies in beingness as the generality "over" and "prior to" all entities (and, hence, a priori with respect to them). Since Heidegger has some philosophical tradition after Plato in mind, he is probably thinking of the scholastic doctrine of transcendentals, those predicates that, because they range over all the categories, cannot be defined in terms of them. Scotus's definition of metaphysics as the *scientia transcendentalium* comes to mind. At the outset of *Being and Time* Heidegger himself hearkens back to this second sense of transcendence when he places "*veritas transcendentalis*" in apposition to "phenomenological truth" (*Being and Time*, 62/38).

Epistemological transcendence is the sort of transcendence that takes its bearings from Descartes' notion of the subject. The question of epistemological transcendence is the question of whether that subject gets beyond or "transcends" itself and manages in some sense to reach an object (*Beiträge*, 217ff., 355). This notion of transcendence, Heidegger adds, is overturned as soon as Da-sein forms the point of departure (*Beiträge*, 176, 217ff., 252). But the fact that epistemological transcendence is "from the outset surpassed" by the standpoint of Da-sein indicates by no means that the standpoint of *Being and Time* is not itself a transcendental one.

A fourth sense of "transcendence" is, as Heidegger himself puts it, the *fundamental-ontological* transcendence elaborated in *Being and Time*. Here, he notes, the term in its original sense as a climbing over or exceeding (*Übersteigerung*) is construed as a mark of being-here (Da-sein), in order to indicate that it always already stands in the open amid entities. But, Heidegger contends, strictly speaking the term *transcendence* is inapplicable, since being-here as such is that opening (the opening of the concealment). Besides, he adds, transcendence presupposes levels and is in danger of being misconstrued as an action of an ego and subject. Accordingly, Heidegger concludes that, in this context, "the notion of 'transcendence' in *every* sense must *disappear*" (*Beiträge*, 216ff., 322, 337).

Heidegger thus places *Being and Time* within the tradition of philosophies of transcendence with the aim of elaborating what, in his eyes, is problematic about his early work. That problem is perhaps most visible in light of the work's proximity to Kant's transcendental philosophy, a proximity that Heidegger takes pains to determine at several junctures in *Contributions to Philosophy*. To be sure, Heidegger protests with some annoyance against construals of his transcendental project in *Being and Time* as an "existentiell" or "modernized" Kantianism (*Beiträge*, 253). Whereas the notion of Da-sein supposedly overturns any sort of subjectivity, it is precisely subjectivity that Kant grasps as "transcendental"; whereas the being, disclosed in and by Da-sein is not to be identified with an object (only entities can be objects) or with a concept of an object, Kant's transcendental subjectivity relates singularly to the objecthood of objects as the condition of their possibility (*Beiträge*, 250). Yet despite these considerable differences and others, Heidegger saw an opportunity, as he puts it, to give his contemporaries a closer glimpse of the relation of being-here and being, by looking back to Kant's project, especially since he viewed Kant as the only one since the Greeks to interpret beingness in terms of time.[13]

Nevertheless, even though Heidegger's retrospective on Kant took the form of a violent reading that broached a conception of the transcendental project allegedly more basic than anything in the critical philosophy, Heidegger came to recognize that the effort to invoke a kinship with Kant was doomed. (As we now know, Heidegger burned the rest of the manuscript of *Being and Time*, though, of course, this fact in itself says nothing about the finished or unfinished state of those writings.) What doomed the effort was precisely what motivated it: the attempt to maintain the ontological difference between being and beings. The aim of insisting on the ontological difference was to pose the question of the truth of being in a way that sets it off from all questions about this or that particular being. Yet as soon as the distinction was made, it fell back onto the path from which it derives, where beingness is constrasted with beings, precisely as an idea, a universal (*ens transcendens*), or as the objecthood of objects of experience, the condition of their possibility. As a result, Heidegger continues, he tried to overturn his first approach to the question of being, undertaken in *Being and Time* and the Kant book, by attempting in various ways to get some control over the ontological difference. As he puts it: "Thus, it became necessary to endeavor to free oneself from the 'condition of the possibility' as a merely 'mathematical' regression and to grasp the truth of being in the basis of its *own* prevailing (the event)" (*Beiträge*, 250). Herein, too, Heidegger adds, lies the tortuous and ambiguous character of the ontological difference. For, as necessary as the distinction is to procure an initial perspective on the question of being, it is also fatal since it stems from the question of the entity as such, that is, its beingness, a path, Heidegger is quick to point out, that never leads to the question of being as such. "Hence, it is a matter," he concludes, "not of passing beyond the entity ([not of] transcendence) but instead of moving beyond this difference and with it, moving beyond transcendence, and questioning from the outset from the standpoint of being and truth" (*Beiträge*, 250ff.).[14]

Being, as Heidegger understands it in *Contributions to Philosophy*, is accordingly not supposed to be transcendent in any of the senses of the word glossed earlier; that is, it is neither transcendent nor transcendental in Kant's sense. Being is not something that is universally accessible or common; it is not some cause or all-encompassing factor behind things; it is not the most general, albeit yet-to-be-conceived determination of entities with which we are otherwise quite familiar (*Beiträge*, 258ff.). Nor is it some universal principle projected by a transcendental subject by virtue of which objects might be known. Being is also not a projection by/of Dasein in terms of which entities are uncovered and their manners of being disclosed (*Beiträge*, 251, 256, 258). Far from being separate from entities, being is the historical event of their presencing and absencing, an event that Heidegger also describes in the 1930s as the conflict of world and earth, a conflict that prevails as the timely spacing and spacious timing of entities (*Beiträge*, 260ff.). Its prevailing in just this way is what Heidegger deems "the truth of being" and "the truth that prevails."

A great deal more, of course, needs to be said and many more questions raised about this account. But we now perhaps have enough clues to begin to indicate why Heidegger finds his account of transcendental truth in *Being and Time* inadequate. True to its name, the transcendental truth in *Being and Time* passes beyond the entities to the respective conceptions of their being, what Heidegger calls their respective beingness (*Seiendheit*), for example, their readiness-to-hand, present-at-handness, temporality, and so on, a move reflected in the distinctions between ontic and ontological and between existentiell and existential that run throughout fundamental ontology. (Interestingly enough, this is precisely the aspect of fundamental ontology criticized by Derrida much later.) In addition, construing the disclosive projection of and by Da-sein as the condition of possibility renders its truth an action of Da-sein, initiated by Da-sein, regardless of the extent of its thrownness, and thereby reinscribes the transcendental-phenomenological subject.[15] In spite of Heidegger's best efforts, the question of being, as it is posed in *Being and Time*, falls into the traps that, in his view, victimized Plato and Kant, namely, the confusion of being with an idea or concept of beings in general, that is, in the final analysis, nothing else but Da-sein's projection (understanding).

Nevertheless, being, as Heidegger construes it in *Contributions to Philosophy*, does echo one aspect of the traditional notion of transcendental truth. Being needs human beings and, indeed, needs them precisely in connection with its truth. To be sure, Heidegger is quick to advise that talk of a relation between being and being-here is misleading in this connection to the extent that it suggests that being obtains of itself and that being-here happens to assume a stance toward it, like a subject to an object. Nevertheless, being, Heidegger insists repeatedly, only prevails by appropriating being-here. "Being needs the human being so that it might prevail and it is only by belonging to being that a human being achieves his consummate vocation as Da-sein."[16] The interplay of this needing and belonging constitutes what Heidegger means when he speaks of the event (*Ereignis*) of being, and he adds that this event is the very first thing that we have to consider (*Beiträge*, 251). The truth of being, as opposed to transcendental truth, even the transcendental truth of *Dasein*'s disclosedness, is the event in which being prevails precisely by making being-here its own.

The difficulty of speaking about a "relation" in this connection between being and being-here has already been noted. While being-here is always a way of being, it may or may not own up to this truth. Herein lies yet another connotation of the *Er-eignen*—the process of coming into its own and making being-here its own—by means of which Heidegger characterizes the event (*Er-eignis*) of being, already signaled by the talk of authenticity and inauthenticity in *Being and Time*. Whereas in 1927 Heidegger puts the emphasis on the authenticity (*Eigentlichkeit*) of resoluteness as the "most original, because *authentic* truth of being-here," in 1936 he is concerned to demonstrate that being-here is grounded in the truth of being as the event in which being appropriates being-here as a clearing for its (being's) self-concealment (*Being and Time*, 343–48/297–301; *Beiträge*, 298ff., 303). Not coincidentally, talk of authenticity and inauthenticity gives way to talk of simply being-here or being-away (*Beiträge*, 301ff., 323ff.).

In keeping with this shift in focus from the truth of being-here to the truth of being, Heidegger reconfigures the notion of a clearing. In *Being and Time* "clearing" was a synonym for the "disclosedness" of/by Dasein, and Heidegger did not shy away from linking it to its etymology and to traditional metaphors of light, even hearkening back to Descartes' *lumen naturale*. The metaphor suggests that the truth of Dasein is that medium in and by virtue of which things present themselves and thus are said to be. But this image, with its Platonic roots, suggests that being is the presence of things or even the paradigmatic, constant presence by virtue of which things are present. Hence, when Heidegger turns to his account of the clearing as the truth, not primarily of Dasein, but of being, he drops the association with light in favor of the normal use of the term for a fortuitous opening in a forest. A clearing in the latter sense is a limited setting that shades off into the darkness of the forest, but in the process makes it possible for things to show themselves without showing itself in any comparable way. So, too, the truth of being is the presencing and absencing of things, the event in which and out of which and by which they make themselves present and ultimately absent themselves. But this event, encompassing the presencing no less than the absencing, is as such hidden. In Husserlian terms, it is unavailable to any sensory intuition and only accessible by way of a categorial intuition, though it should be obvious that Heidegger himself must eschew any talk of intuition in this connection, given the implication that the presence of something is required in order for it to be intuited.

Part of what Heidegger means by the truth of being can be appreciated by considering the fact that entities do not wear their being (i.e., their eventfulness in his special sense of the term) on their sleeves like their color or size or relation to other things. This observation corresponds to Kant's claim that being is not a property or a "real" predicate.[17] In analogous fashion, we know the difference between an open and a closed sentence, between a free and a bounded variable; it makes all the difference in the world to say "Fx" and "(∃x)Fx" but that difference cannot be expressed by saying that "Existence exists," which makes about as much sense as quantifying over the quantifier itself. To say that there exists an *x* which is *F* is not simply to entertain the logically possible state of affairs "*x* is *F*" but to affirm the presence of an entity with the property *F*. Stipulation of the distinction between open and closed sentences is a recognition of this difference, even if that presence as such is, according to the story that Heidegger wants to tell, typically passed over in favor of consideration of the entity itself and its properties and relations to other entities. Perhaps the most notable symptom of this Western forgottenness of being is the reduction of the significance of the statement that something exists to a matter of belief (Hume), positing (Kant), or judgment (Frege).[18] (Here we see the vestiges of the phenomenological reduction even in Heidegger's mature work).

But if the way in which the existential quantifier must be distinguished from what is quantified, as well as from any property indicated by a predicate, corresponds in some sense to Heidegger's distinction between an entity and its being, it only tells part of the story. For exclusive consideration of the being of an entity in these terms might still amount to identifying being with the presence of this or that or even all entities. But being conceals itself not only as the presence, but also as the absence of an entity in all the senses of its time-space horizon, that is, the different senses of its absence before, during, and after its presence. In other words, the hiddenness of being is the hiddenness of not only the entity's presence (shades of the scholastic distinction between essence and existence) but also its absence.

The truth of being is thus the clearing for its self-concealing in both senses of the term. Being conceals itself both as the presence of what is present and as its absence. But this clearing is not static; it is an event in which being as such prevails. As Heidegger puts it: "Truth for us is not something that is already in principle settled, that suspicious descendant of things valid in themselves. But it is also not the mere opposite, the raucous flux and fleetingness of all opinions" (*Beiträge*, 331). He accordingly speaks equivalently of "the truth of being" and "the truth that prevails." Those familiar with Heidegger's later works, particularly *Contributions to Philosophy*, have probably guessed by now what German word I am translating from when I speak of the truth that prevails. The term is Heidegger's verbal use of *wesen* (sometimes translated aptly as "unfolding"). Heidegger reserves this verbal use for being and, ostensibly because it belongs so essentially to being, for truth. In other words, whereas beings or entities can be said to be but not to prevail, only being and truth can properly be said to prevail—"das Seiende ist, das Seyn ist nicht, sondern west" (*Beiträge*, 254, 255, 260, 286, 289, 342). Since Heidegger reserves this term *wesen* or "prevailing" for being and truth, it provides an important clue to his understanding of the truth of being.

This choice of terminology is also cause for confusion, since Heidegger at times invokes the term *Wesen* in its traditional significance as "essence," in contrast to *Wesung*, where he is unambiguously signaling the sense of "prevailing." More to the point, one might object that translating *west* as "prevails" is out of line in this connection, given Heidegger's repudiation of axiology in any traditional sense and his antipathy to talk of values, let alone truth values. But Heidegger's rejection of value theory should not be confused with a disavowal of valuation. For he repeatedly alludes to the way in which being, in its appropriation of being-here, is the source of measures and constraints. Or, as it might be put in more contemporary parlance, the event of being is precisely what yields constraints in general, including normative constraints. Herein, I submit, lies the basic reason why he speaks of the clearing as the truth of being and why I suggest that *wesen* might be translated as "prevailing." The historical event of being *prevails* precisely in the sense that its valence underlies all bivalence, whereby its prevailing is not to be confused with the constancy of something ever on hand somehow or somewhere, but the historical pre-valence of what is always already coming to us. Heidegger is, if not stubbornly taciturn or reticent, then at least distressingly indirect, when it comes to elaborating what the pre-valence of being means for beings and being-here. But he seems to have remained confident to the end that the human dilemma in the present, that is, nihilism, rests upon an obliviousness to being's prevalence (the infamous *Seinsvergessenheit*).

2. Heidegger's Retractions

These remarks bring us to the second question raised at the outset, namely, the question about the significance of Heidegger's concessions, in 1964, that he should not have used the term *truth* to characterize the clearing of being. Here, too, Heidegger is perfectly unambiguous about the way in which the clearing gives rise to constraints. As he puts it: "Without the foregoing experience of *aletheia* as the clearing, all talk of constraints and lack of constraints [*Verbindlichkeit und Unverbindlichkeit*] remains groundless."[19] But, while echoing this constant refrain of his account of truth after 1930, Heidegger now acknowledges that it was "inappropriate" and "misleading" to apply the label "truth" to it. But why exactly does he now find it "inappropriate" and "misleading"? After all, more than once, beginning already in 1927, he had inferred that what makes truth in the sense of discovery or correctness possible "must" be called "true" in an even more original, more essential sense.[20] The inference hardly seems valid, at least not without much further ado, and Heidegger's retractions in 1964 may well be an admission of its invalidity, especially in light of his acknowledgment that "truth" had always stood for a kind of agreement or correspondence (for example, already in Homer, he concedes, *aletheia* signified *homoiesis*). In other words, Heidegger is acknowledging that correspondence and bivalence are necessary elements of the original and rightly enduring conception of truth. In light of this canonical understanding of truth, it is inappropriate and misleading to speak of two truths and, indeed, of a truth more original than truth as correctness or correspondence.

But these concessions, it should be obvious, do not amount to a retraction by Heidegger of his account of the clearing, that is, that event in which being appropriates being-here to itself and constitutes the presencing and absencing of beings. Nor does he budge on the basic insight that led him to infer—erroneously, it would seem—that the clearing is the truth in a more original sense. For, as noted earlier, Heidegger continues to insist that the way in which being prevails in the clearing, appropriating being-here to itself, grounds measures, constraints, and the lack of them, and thus historically affords the possibility of truth in the sense of correspondence.[21] After affirming that the clearing, while not yet truth, grounds the truth, Heidegger asks rhetorically whether it is, therefore, something more or less than the truth. Thus, while refraining from calling it truth in some more original sense than truth as correctness or correspondence, he repeats the same basic move that he has been making since *Being and Time*. Not truth as correctness or correspondence as such, but what underlies and secures it: that for Heidegger is what stands in question—what needs to be thought (*die Sache des Denkens*)—at the end of philosophy, that is, the end of metaphysics.

A final word in this connection. In his 1964 remarks, Heidegger often omits the word *possibility* and simply observes that the clearing "affords" or "grants" (*gewährt*) truth as *adaequatio* or *certitudo*. This omission is probably quite deliberate since Heidegger clearly does not understand the clearing as merely one necessary condition among others. Whatever the merits of Apel's reading on other grounds, it simply does not stand up as an accurate interpretation of what Heidegger understood to be the import of his self-critical remarks in 1964. In other words, his retractions cannot be construed legitimately as an acknowledgment that the clearing is merely a condition of the possibility of truth, a clearinghouse, if you will, for meanings that may or may not prove true. Indeed, if it were not inappropriate to employ the metaphysical framework of necessary and sufficient conditions, one would be tempted to construe the clearing as a sufficient condition, since Heidegger challenges thinking at the end of philosophy to take up the task of asking why it is that the clearing appears *only* as correctness and reliability. Here again it is telling that Heidegger trots out a familiar argument. The clearing appears only as correctness, Heidegger submits, because we think of what the clearing affords and secures rather than what it is itself; and the fact that we do so is no accident since self-concealing, a sheltering self-concealing, lies at the heart of the clearing. In sum, while Heidegger is plainly admitting mistakes in his account of the scope of what "truth" designates, he is by no means prepared to jettison his account of being revealing and concealing itself as the historical event, the clearing that grounds truth as correctness or correspondence.

CHAPTER 6

The Descent of the 'Logos'

LIMITS OF TRANSCENDENTAL REFLECTION

Karsten Harries

1. The Death of God and the Claim to Truth

Are there eternal truths? Heidegger raises this question in *Being and Time* only to dismiss it. For what would it mean to claim such truths? Traditionally truth is located in our judgments or assertions. As Thomas's much-cited definition has it, "Truth is the adequation of the thing and the understanding."[1] This is to say that there is no truth where there is no understanding. As Heidegger puts it in *Being and Time*: "Because the kind of Being that is essential to truth is of the character of Dasein, all truth is relative to Dasein's being."[2] And is there Dasein other than human Dasein? Despite the efforts of those who search for intelligence somewhere "out there" in space, so far all such efforts have been disappointed. For all intents and purposes we human beings appear to find ourselves alone here on this earth. To show that there are eternal truths, would we not have to show that the understanding, too, is eternal? As Heidegger might put it: would we not have to show that there always has been and will be Dasein? But can this be shown? The fable with which Nietzsche, borrowing from Schopenhauer, begins "On Truth and Lies in a Nonmoral Sense" comes to mind, quite representative of gloomy post-Copernican meditations on the immensity of the cosmos that would seem to make human existence no more than an insignificant cosmic accident: "Once upon a time, in some out of the way corner of that universe which is dispersed into numberless twinkling solar systems, there was a star upon which clever beasts invented knowing. That was the most arrogant and mendacious minute of 'world history' but nevertheless, it was only a minute. After nature had drawn a few breaths, the star cooled and congealed, and the clever beasts had to die."[3] Nietzsche here calls attention to the disproportion between the human claim to truth and our peripheral location in the cosmos, to the ephemeral nature of our being. Will the time not come, when there will no longer be human beings, when there will be no understanding and hence no truth? Thomas Aquinas, to be sure, would have had no difficulty answering Nietzsche. His understanding of God left no room for thoughts of a cosmos from which understanding would be absent. But the author of *Being and Time* was too convinced that, for the philosopher at least, God had died, to give such an answer. Absolute truth and the absolute subject are declared residues of Christian theology philosophy ought to leave behind:

> The ideas of a "pure 'I'" and of a "consciousness in general" are so far from including the a priori character of "actual" subjectivity that the ontological characters of Dasein's facticity and its state of being are either passed over or not seen. Rejection of a "consciousness in general" does not signify that the a priori is negated, any more than the positing of an idealized subject guarantees that Dasein has an a priori character grounded upon fact. Both the contention that there are "eternal truths" and the jumbling together of Dasein's phenomenally grounded "ideality" with an idealized absolute subject, belong to those residues of Christian theology within philosophical problematics which have not as yet been radically extruded.[4]

This suggests that any appeal to an idealized subject in an attempt to ground truth borrows illegitimately from the Christian understanding of God. Kant's transcendental subject invites such a charge: is its constitutive power more than an illicit projection of God's creative power unto man? Because of Kant's failure to subject his understanding of the transcendental subject and, with it, of objectivity and truth to sufficiently critical attention, his Copernican revolution remained incomplete. The charge is indeed obvious, and Herder already protested both Kant's elision of the person and his elision of language. Challenging Kant, Herder insists that we can think only in our own natural language. If those metaphysicians Kant criticizes have lost themselves in airless realms, Kant himself, Herder suggests, tries to rise even higher, losing himself in an empty, merely formal transcendence. Instead of a critique of pure reason, Herder therefore demands a physiology of man's faculties and a study of language as it is.

In *Being and Time* Heidegger offers a succinct argument in support of what is essentially the same position: "Discourse (*Rede*) is existentially language (*Sprache*), because that entity whose disclosedness it Articulates according to significations, has, as its kind of Being, Being-in-the-world—a being which has been thrown and submitted to the 'world.'"[5] This denies the traditional distinction between a timeless *Rede* or *logos* and concrete language. Because human being is always bound into the world and that means also into a particular historical situation, language can never be pure or innocent.

Essentially the same argument challenges the distinction between the transcendental subject and the person.

All this suggests that if we are more radically critical than Kant and free his crucial insight from remnants of the Christian understanding of truth, which would ground truth in the creative and aperspectival vision of God, we will be forced to submerge both subject and *logos* in the world and subject both to time. In different ways both Heidegger's *Being and Time* and Wittgenstein's *Philosophical Investigations* bear witness to such a submersion.

When Heidegger speaks in *Being and Time* of residues of Christian theology that have to be radically extruded from philosophy, he is also criticizing himself. He had begun, as we know, as a Catholic theologian, and he never succeeded altogether in leaving his theological origins behind. This inability need not be seen as a philosophical failure, but can be understood as bound up with a recognition of what philosophy can and cannot do. I would thus resist those interpretations that, invoking Heidegger's supposed *Kehre* ("turn"), draw a sharp distinction between the later mystical and post-metaphysical Heidegger to the earlier still transcendental and still metaphysical Heidegger.[6] I would claim rather that from beginning to end we meet in Heidegger the admittedly shifting and evolving tension between what I want to call a theological and a philosophical strand. Thus we meet again and again, paging through the many volumes of his collected works, reflections that make one think of words by "the great Görres," as Heidegger called him in a review of Friedrich Wilhelm Forster's *Autorität und Freiheit*: "Dig more deeply and you will hit Catholic ground."[7] "Ground" should not be understood here as meaning a firm foundation. Even as a theology student Heidegger did not find himself truly sheltered inside what he called "the tent of Catholic philosophy."[8] From the very beginning we sense tension between Heidegger's faith, his theological studies, and an emphasis on self and self-realization. To be sure, the sentence that in the review precedes the cited Görres quote would seem to include the young Heidegger: "He, who never stepped on false paths and did not allow himself to be blinded by the deceitful light of the modern spirit, who in true, deep, and well-grounded self-denial dares walk through life in the shining light of truth, will find in this book a message of great joy; he will become conscious once again of the great good fortune of being in possession of the truth."[9] But did Heidegger at the time think himself in possession of the truth? The fact that in this review he does not simply condemn "the much praised personality cult" raises questions. He is, we should note, quick to add that this cult can flourish only when one's "own spiritual freedom" remains in "the inmost contact with the richest and deepest well-spring of religious-moral authority. This can, by its very nature, not dispense with a venerable, outer form."[10] Freedom, in other words, must be bound by authority. Here already we meet with a critique of that "negative freedom" that in the "Rectorial Address" was to turn into an attack on "academic freedom." This critique is a presupposition of Heidegger's receptivity to National Socialism and of his attacks on democracy and liberalism, reaffirmed in the Spiegel interview.[11]

Kant knew too that freedom requires authority. But if autonomy is to be preserved, such authority must be sought within one's own self, where Kant was thinking of practical reason. The young Heidegger, on the other hand, was thinking first of all of a personal faith. But although personal and private, this source of all moral-religious authority yet required an "external form" to become communicable. Without such a form it would remain voiceless, a pealing of silence, as Heidegger was later to say. But every form that seeks to fix this wellspring threatens to turn what was authentic into something inauthentic and external. Does it help to insist that the form must be venerable or *ehrwürdig*? That it is part of our inheritance? Heidegger will repeat this suggestion in *Being and Time*. But our inheritance includes all too much that we cannot honor. Does responsible self-development not demand that we critically confront our inheritance? Where is such a confrontation to find its measure? In *Being and Time* Heidegger was to say: "Resoluteness constitutes the loyalty of existence to its own Self. As resoluteness which is ready for anxiety, this loyalty is at the same time a possible way of revering the sole authority which a free existing can have—of revering the repeatable possibilities of existence."[12] "Repeatable possibilities of existence" here takes the place of "religious-moral authority," which cannot dispense with "a venerable, outer form." But there are far too many such possibilities to offer an orientation. Faced with often competing possibilities, what justification can there be for elevating one above the others? Dasein loses its way, where the experience of thus having lost one's way is also an experience of our freedom.

Of special interest among Heidegger's early writings is the essay "Remarks on the Philosophical Orientation for Academics" ("Zur philosophischen Orientierung für Akademiker"), which looks ahead to his later ideas concerning how the university should be reformed, ideas that are hinted at in "What Is Metaphysics?" and developed in the "Rectorial Address." "Philosophy," we read in the early essay, "in truth a mirror of the eternal, today often reflects no more than subjective opinions, personal moods and wishes."[13] Such a turn to subject and person is said to lead to a disoriented "fluttering about," to have made philosophical questioning a matter of taste. But such a degradation of philosophy into a kind of intellectual game, enjoyed by philosophical gourmets, is said to be unable to do justice to a "desire for final and definitive answers to the final questions of being," questions that may suddenly seize us, seemingly arriving from nowhere, questions that weigh on our "tortured soul, which know neither goal nor way."[14] Here it is precisely the turn to a subject that refuses to accept an eternal measure that is said to threaten a loss of our true self. *Being and Time* will turn this claim around.

Reason, the young Heidegger is convinced, will show us the right path. Strict logical thinking will put us on firm ground. To be sure "a strict, icy-cold logic" will be resisted by the "delicately feeling modern soul," which refuses to be bound by "the unmovable eternal barriers of the logical laws." That requires a certain self-transcendence. "A certain amount of ethical power, the art of self-appropriation and self-surrender, is indispensable to strict logical thinking, which has to hermetically seal itself off from every affective influence of the mind."[15] For the sake of what is eternally valid the self has to surrender itself in one sense in order to truly gain itself. Thinking of the authority of pure practical reason, Kant could have said something similar.

In these remarks Heidegger's thinking already circles around the self. The theology student thus wants the philosophical training of theologians to place greater emphasis on what he calls a "justified egoism." All other projects and endeavors are to be subordinated to "the fundamental demand for the intellectual and ethical strengthening of one's own personality and its continued development."[16] Such development "cannot be allowed to take a back seat to an ever more intensive involvement with what is alien to the self."[17] Here already the opposition between *Eigenentwicklung*, development of one's ownmost self, and *Fremdverwicklung*, being caught up in what is alien, threatens to call into question the authority of the inherited faith, for first of all that faith presents itself as something we cannot possess, relying on our reason, but as a gift that must possess us.[18] The path of self-development has to call into question this faith and "the treasures of truth" it mediated. The young Heidegger knows how questionable his striving for these treasures is. "To be sure, this fundamental demand (*Grundforderung*) with its high inner value includes also all the difficulty of its adequate fulfillment."[19]

In this connection the young theologian acknowledges the importance of lectures that would strengthen students in their faith.

> About the pressing need for amore thorough apologetic education there is no doubt. A timely thought is being realized in these religious-scientific lectures. Sketched in broad strokes, delivered in finely wrought language, the basic truths of Christianity in their eternal greatness present themselves to the soul of the Catholic student, arouse enthusiasm, remind him "what we have," more precisely put, what the single individual has potentially. The actual possession of these treasures of truth demands, however, a ceaseless self-engagement beyond merely listening to lectures.[20]

This "justified egoism" remains central to Heidegger's thinking and is presupposed by what he later has to say about "authenticity" (*Eigentlichkeit*). And already in these first publications "justified egoism" is opposed to false subjectivism—what Heidegger elsewhere calls "individualism,"[21] or "unfettered autonomism."[22] Heidegger never lets go of this opposition. What changes most fundamentally is his understanding of the binding *logos*. Here already we meet with the conviction that genuine self-possession presupposes the continued strengthening of the self.

How is such a strengthening to be thought?[23] How are we to distinguish between justified and unjustified egoism? The juxtaposition of "strict, icy-cold logic" and the delicately feeling modern soul, fluttering about without a clear sense of direction, gives us a pointer: the twenty-one-year-old Heidegger seeks support in the eternal barriers of the fundamental laws of logic. In his long essay "New Research on Logic" ("Neuere Forschungen über Logik"), he enthusiastically endorses the progressive liberation of logic from psychologism, inaugurated by Kant, and to which the neo-Kantians, Husserl, and Frege had made such important contributions. The basic question of logic is said to be: what are the conditions that make any knowledge whatsoever possible?[24] Logic is transcendental. That is as true for the young Heidegger as it is for the author of the *Tractatus*. And Heidegger's focus, too, is here on mathematics and the sciences. Crucial is the distinction between temporal reality, with which the empirical sciences are concerned, and the realm of ideal, atemporal meaning, presupposed by all merely ontic inquiry. As the *zoon logon echon*, the *animal rationale*, the human being is able to raise himself beyond that inevitably care- and perspective-bound individual we all are first of all and most of the time, thereby recognizing our kinship to a realm of timeless meaning. In logic Heidegger thus discovers, as Dieter Thomä notes, "a kind of theological stand-in."[25] "The universal validity of the laws of thought" grants us something like a foundation.[26] Egoism is justified only when it limits itself, binds itself to the eternal, generally accessible, universally valid *logos*. Mental health and logic, logic and ethics belong together, as already Plato thought. Logic helps to make us more receptive to the timeless treasures opened up by faith.

Fifteen years later Heidegger decisively divorces philosophy from theology—still in the name of self-affirmation and autonomy. Theology, he points out, has its foundation in faith. To be sure, it understands itself as a science. In the Marburg lecture "Phenomenology and Theology" (1927), Heidegger even calls theology a "positive science," the latter defined as "the justifying disclosure of some present being that has in some manner disclosed itself."[27] What in this case is present is being Christian, *die Christlichkeit*, the essence of the relation, determined by Christ, of faith to the cross:

But faith also understands itself always only by faith. The believer does not know, and never knows, say on the basis of a theoretical experience, about his specific existence; rather, he can only "believe" this possibility of existence as one that the Dasein in question never has in its power, in which it has rather become servant, brought before God, and thus reborn. The authentic existential sense of faith is accordingly: faith = rebirth. And rebirth not in the sense of a momentary endowment with some quality, but rebirth as mode of the historical existing of the factically believing Dasein in that history, which begins with the event of the Revelation; in the history that, according to the spirit of Revelation, has already been provided with a definite, final end. The happening of Revelation, which comes down to faith, and which accordingly happens in faith itself, discloses itself only to faith. Luther says: "Faith is making oneself a prisoner in the things we do not see."[28]

The will to believe is a will to allow oneself to be taken prisoner. Faith is bondage. But understood in this way, faith has to be, as Heidegger puts it, "the mortal enemy" of philosophy, at least if we understand with Heidegger "the free self-possession of the entire Dasein" as the "factically highly variable form of existence that belongs essentially to philosophy."[29] Philosophy and faith are opposed now as autonomy is opposed to heteronomy. The philosopher has to insist on what the young Heidegger called *Eigenentwicklung*, has to refuse to let himself become a prisoner. But faith demands such imprisonment. Does it not follow from this that every theological philosophy is, as Heidegger says of a Christian philosophy, a "wooden iron"?[30]

In *Being and Time*, as we saw, Heidegger's commitment to *Eigenentwicklung* turns against the high hopes he once had for transcendental inquiry. He had come to see the transcendental subject and the associated thought of eternal truths that had once helped support his own embrace of logic as just such a wooden iron.

2. *Truth and Self-Transcendence*

But is this judgment justified? The transcendental subject is not dismissed quite that easily. What is at issue shows itself in Heidegger's Davos disputation with Ernst Cassirer. Cassirer seizes on the central point when he points out that having made truth relative to Dasein, Heidegger has to face the question: how then does such a finite being arrive at knowledge, reason, truth?[31] "Does Heidegger," Cassirer asks, "want to renounce all objectivity, this form of absoluteness that Kant insisted on in the realm of ethics, theory, and in the *Critique of Judgment*? Does he want to retreat entirely into the finite being, or, if not, where does he see the opening to this sphere? I ask this because I really do not know."[32]

This, it seems to me, remains the most fundamental question we can ask Heidegger and his followers. Both, Heidegger and Cassirer, recognize what we can call the self-transcendence of human being, which is just another way of saying that both recognize the importance of freedom. Freedom presupposes that human beings, even as they find themselves inescapably in some particular time and place, are not imprisoned by a particular point of view, a particular perspective. Whatever limitation such placement may entail, it does not mean that imagination and thought do not allow us to transcend whatever would imprison us. "Thoughts are free," as an old folk song has it. Such freedom is constitutive of thinking and of truth.

Both agree that we do not comprehend freedom. Heidegger finds the question "How is freedom possible?" meaningless, meaningless because presupposed by all possibility.[33] "From this," he adds, "it does not follow that we are left, so to speak, with a problem of the irrational. However, because freedom is not an object of theoretical comprehension, but an object of philosophizing, this can only mean that freedom is and can only be in liberation. The only adequate relation to freedom is the self-liberation of freedom in the human being."[34]

Cassirer agrees with this formulation, and he also agrees that such self-liberation has its basis in our finitude. But this basis is not enough. The human being must also possess what Cassirer calls "the metabasis that leads him from the immediacy of his existence into the region of pure form. And only in this form does he possess his infinity."[35] That metabasis that demands the possession of infinity in form, Cassirer suggests, is inscribed into freedom. That is to say, freedom has its measure in the fusion of infinity and form. To be sure, Kant already pointed out that the question "How is freedom possible?" cannot be answered. We comprehend only that freedom cannot be comprehended. But, as Cassirer reminds us, Kant's ethics allows us to say rather more. Insofar as we are ethical beings, we transcend ourselves as merely finite beings of nature: "The categorical imperative must be such that it is valid not only for human beings but for all rational beings whatsoever. Here there is this strange transition. Our being limited to a definite sphere suddenly falls away. The moral leads beyond the world of appearances. And is not this what is decisively metaphysical, that in this place there is a breakthrough? What is at issue is a gate to the *mundus intelligibilis*."[36] And does such a gate not also open up whenever we claim truth for an assertion? Do we not lose the very meaning of truth when we make it relative to a knower bound by a particular place and perspective? Is truth not in its very essence transperspectival? Do we not measure ourselves, in this case too, by what holds for all rational beings?

Heidegger no doubt would have insisted that when we speak that way we misinterpret the self-transcendence of Dasein that he, too, recognizes—misinterpret it in a way that cannot hide its debt to the Christian tradition. In *Being and Time* that alleged debt is made explicit when Heidegger first introduces his understanding of the essential transcendence of Dasein. Briefly he touches here on the traditional understanding of man as *zoon logon echon* and as *animal rationale*. But more space is given to the transformation of this understanding by "the anthropology of Christian theology." To be sure, "in modern times the Christian definition has been deprived of its theological character. But the idea of 'transcendence'—that man is he who reaches beyond himself—is rooted in Christian dogmatics, which can hardly be said to have made an ontological problem of man's Being."[37] For illustrations Heidegger turns to Calvin, who says that man has been given "reason, intelligence, prudence, judgment" not only so that he might govern his earthly life, "but that by them he might ascend beyond, even unto God and to eternal felicity."[38] And Heidegger also refers to Zwingli, who understands man as the being who, created in the image of God, "looks up to God and his Word" and "is drawn to God."[39] Cassirer's understanding of man as the being in whom the finite opens up to the infinite and absolute recognizes the same verticality. In the Davos disputation Heidegger recognizes the need to acknowledge and to account for such self-transcendence. He points out that his claim that truth is relative to Dasein should not be misunderstood ontically, as if he were claiming that each individual had his or her own truth. Heidegger grants the possibility of revealing what is as it is for everyone. He, too, attempts to show how the commitment to objectivity that characterizes science is possible. But, he insists, while the "trans-subjectivity of truth" does mean that, so understood, truth calls on the inquirer to rise above his concrete being-in-the-world, he yet remains caught up in what is, confronts what is, facing the possibility of shaping it.

What can be abstracted here as objective knowledge does indeed have a truth content—this content does indeed say something about what is—but it also accords with the existing individual who thus seeks truth. Yet the distinctive validity that is ascribed to this truth content is ill-interpreted when one says: in opposition to the stream of experience there is something enduring, the eternal meaning and concept. I counter by asking: what does "eternal" here really mean? Is not this eternity only enduringness in the sense of the *aei* of time? Is it not only possible on the ground of an inner transcendence of time itself?[40]

In the "Rectorial Address" Heidegger will locate the origin of science in this power of self-transcendence, which always remains bound to human beings who can only exist at a particular time and place:

But if there should be science and it should be for us and through us, under what conditions can it truly exist? Only if we place ourselves under the power of the beginning of our spiritual-historical existence. This beginning is the departure, the setting out, of Greek philosophy. Here, for the first time, Western man rises up, from a base in a popular culture [*Volkstum*] and by means of his language, against the totality of what is and questions and comprehends it as the being that it is. All science is philosophy, whether it knows and wills it—or not. All science remains bound to that beginning of philosophy.[41]

With much of this Cassirer could have agreed. But he would not have agreed with the way Heidegger here substitutes a horizontal for the traditional vertical interpretation of the self-transcendence of Dasein. Time itself is now said to be the condition that alone makes transcendence possible. Only the horizon of present, future, and past constitutes our understanding of what endures or is eternal.

Time is also the condition of transcendental arguments. Even as such arguments seek to inquire into what is presupposed by, say, all possible experience, they can never make sure that the space of possibility has been adequately surveyed. For that space has no boundaries. It is thus always possible that in the light of changed experiences the space of what is thought possible will have to be expanded. In this sense transcendental arguments cannot lay an unshakable foundation. In principle they are always revisable, but this is not to say that they are therefore useless. Transcendental arguments help us to clarify our presuppositions. What they cannot do is provide us with anything resembling an ought. They cannot tell us what to do or think. For to the extent that they succeed, they have to be based on an understanding of what we now consider all possible experience, or all possible thinking, or all possible speaking. But this means that we cannot help but experience, think, or speak in a way that accords with what such arguments establish. Arguments that look transcendental but appear to have a normative conclusion—consider, for example, Wittgenstein's *Tractatus*—operate with a restricted understanding of what constitutes experience, thought, or language, which can then be opposed to the way we often experience, think, or speak.

Just this question of the normative significance of transcendental reflection is at issue in the Davos debate. The infinite, Cassirer insists, must be understood not only negatively, in opposition to the finite, but as constituted precisely as the fulfillment of the finite as totality, where Cassirer reminds his listeners of the end of Hegel's *Phenomenology of Spirit* and cites Goethe: "If you want to progress into the infinite, just explore the finite in all its many aspects."[42] Heidegger might have replied that Hegel's absolute owes too much to the old God, and that Cassirer's finding it appropriate to cite him here shows that Cassirer's attempt to bend together infinity and totality still betrays a borrowing from the theological tradition that transcendental reflection cannot legitimate.

What separates the two philosophers is put into sharp focus by Heidegger's questions: "To what extent does philosophy have the task to liberate us from anxiety? Does it not rather have the task to expose man to anxiety?"[43] Cassirer answers with what he calls "a kind of confession."[44] He, too, takes the task of philosophy to be the ever-progressing liberation of human beings. But such liberation Cassirer understands also as a liberation from the anxiety that is part of our earthly being. Such liberation is to compensate us for a reality in which we can never quite feel at home, not, to be sure, by offering us a metaphysical spirit realm but by turning to a realm that our spirit has created. This is how Cassirer would have us understand the slightly transformed Schiller quotation with which Hegel concludes his *Phenomenology*: "aus dem Kelche dieses Geisterreiches/schäumt ihm seine Unendlichkeit." Anxiety is left behind as human beings raise themselves beyond the everyday in which the spirit never can feel at home, and raises above it a *Geisterreich*, a spirit realm, which beckons us as our true home.

Cassirer here might have cited a passage from Kant's discussion of the sublime in the *Critique of Judgment*: "But the mind listens to the voice of reason within itself, which demands totality for all given magnitudes. . . . Reason makes us unavoidably think of the infinite (in common reason's judgment) as given in its entirety (in its totality)."[45] And it is just this ability to think an infinite whole which opens a window in the realm of nature to the supersensible: "If the human mind is nonetheless to be *able to even think* the given infinite without contradiction, it must have within itself a power that is supersensible, whose idea of a noumenon cannot be intuited but can yet be regarded as the substrate underlying what is mere appearance, namely our intuition of the world."[46] The experience of the sublime opens a window to the noumenal as our true home.

Key here is the fusion of infinity and totality, which is also the fusion of freedom and reason. Heidegger calls just this fusion into question. To be sure, he too gives entirety, totality, unity a normative significance. We understand Dasein primordially only when we grasp it as a whole; and similarly, in the call of conscience Dasein is called to seize itself as a whole. But can Dasein even be understood as a whole? Is such completeness not denied by Heidegger's understanding of Dasein as essentially care? As long as it is, Dasein is not at its end and in this sense is incomplete. Dasein comes to its end only with death. But Heidegger would not have us understand the call of the whole as the call of death. "The 'ending' which we have in view when we speak of death, does not signify Dasein's being-at-an-end, but a *Being-towards-the-end* of this entity. Death is a way to be, which Dasein takes over as soon as it is."[47] In our very essence we are mortals, and only as such can we truly affirm ourselves. Such affirmation presupposes an appropriation of what Heidegger calls Dasein's essential guilt, of the fact that, even while we are called to freedom, that is to say to take possession of ourselves, we have to recognize that we have not chosen to be cast as mortals into a world that all too often seems indifferent to our wishes and desires. "To project oneself upon this Being-guilty, which Dasein is as *long as it is*, belongs to the very meaning of resoluteness. The existentiell way of taking over this 'guilt' in resoluteness, in its disclosure of Dasein, has become so transparent that Being-guilty is understood *as something constant*."[48] To think this constancy I have to think the self as constant.[49] But what allows me to speak of myself, as I have been and will be, as my and thus as one and the same self? How is the unity of the self to be thought? Heidegger rejects appeals to a soul substance. And Kant, too, despite his rejection of all attempts to interpret the self as particular substance, is criticized for clinging to the ontological concept of the subject, which "*characterizes not the Selfhood of the 'I' qua Self, but the selfsameness and steadiness of something that is always present-at-hand.*"[50] To give unity and constancy to our being-in-the-world, Heidegger appeals instead to death as the possibility that allows us to possess our life as a whole. As Heidegger himself reminds us, in *Being and Time* the appeal to death plays a part that invites comparison with that allotted by Kant to the transcendental subject. But more important to me here than this similarity is what distinguishes the two. The unity provided by the transcendental subject is said by Kant to be constitutive of all possible experience, that is to say of all experience I am able to conceive, not just of all experience I might possibly have. I can thus think of a great many experiences that I could not possibly have, for example, experiences someone had long before I was born or experiences my grandchildren will have when I am no longer. In thinking the transcendental subject the mortal self transcends its mortality, if only in thought, transcends indeed all facticity toward a boundless logical realm. It was precisely in such self-transcendence that Cassirer found something like a spiritual home and an answer to Heideggerian anxiety. But Heidegger might ask what account Cassirer, or for that matter Kant, is able to give of the fusion of totality and infinity that would alone justify talk of a homecoming? Does the very anxiety that is awakened when, thinking, I transcend the limits of my Dasein, awaken anxiety and open up an abyss that swallows all thoughts of homecoming? Does the invocation of totality not require transcendental justification? To appeal to the human power of self-transcendence to justify the possibility of the scientific pursuit of objective knowledge is one thing; to extend such justification to ethics and aesthetics in an attempt to make sense of a spiritual homecoming quite another.

3. Power and Poverty of Transcendental Reflection

To dramatize Heidegger's question "Are there eternal truths?" I turned in the very beginning of this chapter to Nietzsche's "On Truth and Lies," which has of course become a favorite text with postmodernists—one reason why I chose it. It contains the following passage, which has become almost a sacred text:

What then is truth? A movable host of metaphors, metonymies, and anthropomorphisms, a sum of human relations which have been poetically and rhetorically intensified, transferred and embellished, and which, after long usage, seem to a people to be fixed, canonical, and binding. Truths are illusions which we have forgotten are illusions; they are metaphors that have become worn out and have been drained of sensuous force, coins which have lost their embossing and are now considered as metal and no longer as coins.[51]

The passage is representative of what I have called a third Copernican revolution, which challenges Kant's attempt to justify our claim to knowledge by appealing to the human power of self-transcendence, pointing out how inextricably we remain mired in our natural and cultural situation. What separates Kant, who would have us dwell contentedly on the island of truth, from Nietzsche, who again and again beckons us to venture into uncharted seas? Here Kant:

> We have now not merely explored the territory of pure understanding, and carefully surveyed every part of it, but have also measured its extent and assigned to everything in it its rightful place. This domain is an island, enclosed by nature itself with unalterable limits. It is the land of truth—enchanting name!—surrounded by a wide and stormy ocean, the native home of illusion, where many a fog bank and many a swiftly melting iceberg give the deceptive appearance of farther shores, deluding the adventurous seafarer ever anew with empty hopes, and engaging him in enterprises which he can never abandon and yet is unable to carry to completion.[52]

Just what is the nature of Nietzsche's disagreement? What does he mean by truth? Accepting the traditional understanding of truth as *adaequatio intellectus et rei*, Nietzsche, too, points out that full adequacy would mean the disappearance of what distinguishes the two. In God's creative understanding intellect and thing were thus thought to coincide. Following Kant and Schopenhauer rather than Thomas Aquinas, Nietzsche understands "truth" as the correspondence of our thoughts to the things themselves. But "'the thing in itself' (which is precisely what the pure truth apart from any of its consequences would be) is likewise something quite incomprehensible to the creator of language and not in the least worth striving for."[53] Kant, no more than Nietzsche, would claim that we can know truth in that sense. His understanding of truth is quite different. He understands truth in terms of the adequacy of the intellect, not to the things in themselves but to the objects. These objects should not be confused with the things of everyday experience. What we experience are only the subjective appearances of the objects, constituted by our embodied understanding, inescapably situated in a particular here and now, bound by both nature and culture, as Nietzsche emphasized. But while the objects as such are never given in experience, they haunt all appearance and provide science with a regulative ideal. To understand that something presents itself to us as it does only because of our particular situation and point of view is to have already begun a journey that aims at an ever more adequate understanding of the objects. Such understanding let the Ionian philosophers ask long ago: what are things really made of? Here we have the key to that beginning of philosophy to which, according to Heidegger, all science remains bound.

Would Nietzsche have disagreed with any of this? He himself points out how difficult it is to take seriously what is urged by the third Copernican revolution:

> Every person who is familiar with such considerations has no doubt felt a deep mistrust of all idealism of this sort: just as often as he has quite clearly convinced himself of the eternal consistency, omnipresence, and infallibility of the laws of nature. He concludes that so far as we can penetrate here—from the telescopic heights to the microscopic depths—everything is secure, complete, infinite, regular, and without any gaps. Science will be able to dig successfully in this shaft forever, and all the things that are discovered will harmonize and not contradict each other.[54]

To be sure, Nietzsche does go on to remind us of the many ways in which the manifest image of the world is limited by all sorts of perspectives, shaped by all sorts of metaphors. But he concludes the first part of the essay by pointing out

> that the artistic process of metaphor formation with which every sensation begins in us already presupposes these forms [the Kantian forms of pure intuition] and thus occurs within them. The only way in which the possibility of subsequently constructing a new conceptual edifice from metaphors can be explained is by the firm persistence of these original forms. That is to say, this conceptual edifice is an imitation of temporal, spatial, and numerical relationships in the domain of metaphors.[55]

This explains why the extent to which science trades metaphorical for mathematical forms of description is a measure of its progress.

Borrowing from Schopenhauer, who in turn relies on Kant, Nietzsche here sketches with a few strokes his version of a transcendental justification of the scientific pursuit of objective knowledge. The problem with the pursuit of truth so understood, for Nietzsche, is not that it rests on shaky foundations but that it is all too successful, even as it threatens to render our life-world ever more uninhabitable. The pursuit of objective truth has to lead to nihilism. Essentially the same claim is made by Heidegger when he understands our age as the age of the world picture; and by Wittgenstein when in the *Tractatus* he lays out the conditions that make meaningful speech possible, where meaning is understood in its relation to objective truth. Wittgenstein's logical space is essentially the same space in which we must look for Kant's island of truth. But, as Wittgenstein makes clear, logical space has no room for anything resembling values or persons. That is why human beings will refuse to dwell contentedly on Kant's enchanting island, why they will be lured ever again to explore the stormy ocean that surrounds that island. Nietzsche and Heidegger were such sailors. And must not the same be said, finally, of Kant? Did he too not recognize that his island knew neither persons nor values. The understanding of experience presupposed by the first *Critique* binds it to objective truth in a way that has to lose sight of moral and aesthetic experience. But, as Kant of course knew, we do experience persons and we do experience beauty. An adequate understanding of experience has to do justice to both. It is his wrestling with such questions that presides over the progress of Heidegger's thought and helps to explain the transformation of the transcendental into the oracular, mystical Heidegger. Our task is to understand the necessity of thought that governs that transformation.

4. *Of Gods and Angels*

At issue here is the meaning of experience. What is experience? Do we do justice to it when we use the relation between subject and object as a guiding thread? Heidegger recasts this question as follows: What is a thing? Is it to be understood as something present-at-hand? *Being and Time* calls this answer into question. The being "in itself" (*an sich*) of things is there determined as readiness-to-hand, inviting a pragmatic reading of Heidegger's fundamental ontology. By putting the "in itself" into quotation marks, he lets us think of the Kantian thing-in-itself even as he invites us to question his appropriation of Kant's terminology. It is indeed to suggest that readiness-to-hand is not to be understood subjectively, as merely a way of taking them, *als bloßer Auffassungscharakter.*[56] First of all and most of the time we encounter things as ready-to-hand. But in a later marginal comment Heidegger expresses a reservation: "aber doch nur Begegnischarakter [but nevertheless only a way of encountering them]."[57] And already in *Being and Time* he points out that "only by reason of something present-at-hand 'is there' anything ready to hand?"—only to follow this with the question: "Does it follow, however, granting this thesis for the nonce, that readiness-to-hand is ontologically founded upon presence-at-hand?"[58] This rhetorical question demands a negative answer, but this does not mean that the being of the thing is adequately understood as readiness-to-hand. In "The Origin of the Work of Art" ("Der Ursprung des Kunstwerkes"), Heidegger turns to the work of art to gain a deeper understanding of the being of the thing, a turn that invites the question: how does this turn compare with Kant's turn to the aesthetic in the *Critique of Judgment*? That turn also would seem to represent a deepening of Kant's concept of experience, and invites the question: how is experience, thus expanded, possible? What is new in "The Origin of the Work of Art" is Heidegger's insistence that the being of equipment is understood properly only when we understand it as a belonging to the earth, where the earth is understood by Heidegger as that which shows itself only when it remains undisclosed and unexplained. "Earth thus shatters every attempt to penetrate into it. It causes every merely calculating importunity upon it to turn into a destruction. This destruction may herald itself under the appearance of mastery and of progress in the form of technical-scientific objectification of nature, but this mastery remains an impotence of will. The earth appears openly cleared as itself only when it is perceived and preserved as that which is by nature undisclosable, that which shrinks from every disclosure and constantly keeps itself closed up."[59]

"Earth" here names what can be called "material transcendence." What is transcended is every linguistic or conceptual space. Transcended also is what Heidegger calls the "world," which names a space of intelligibility in which things must take their place if they are to be disclosed and explained. But even if they are constituted by our language or concepts and as such are appearances, the things that thus appear are not created by us but given. Inseparable from our experience of the thingliness of things is a sense of this gift, a recognition of the fact that the rift between thing and word, between earth and world, cannot be closed or eliminated.

Continued reflection of what is presupposed by our experience of what makes a thing a thing pushes Heidegger still further, to a point where transcendental reflection invites a turn to what we may want to call the mystical. In this connection Heidegger introduces the fourfold, the *Geviert*, that is said to be copresent in the presencing of things. If the *Geviert* is indeed constitutive of things, it would seem that transcendental reflection should open up an easy path to it. What makes this path not so easy is the fact that our own time, Heidegger insists, blocks adequate access to things. Heidegger is aware of the untimeliness of his speaking of the "united four," of earth and sky or heaven (*Himmel* can mean either), of the divine ones, *die Göttlichen*, and mortals. Such talk may be understood as the nostalgic accompaniment of his understanding of the modern age, shaped as it is by science and technology and thus by metaphysics, as the age of the world picture or the *Gestell*, both terms meant to characterize the *Verwahrlosung* in question. That our age will stumble over Heidegger's understanding of the *Geviert* and the associated understanding of the thing is only to be expected.

Three of the terms are easy to understand.

1. *Earth* names first of all the ground that supports us. But it also names what I have called "material transcendence," the thingliness of things that will always elude our conceptual nets.
2. Heidegger's *Himmel* too is familiar. It means first of all the ever-changing sky above. But we should not forget that looking up to the sky we experience ourselves as not bound by the here and now. The word *spirit* points to the possibility of such self-transcendence.

The word thus means not only the sky above, but the spiritual, ecstatic dimension of our being, the space presupposed by every logical or linguistic space.

3. The least problematic term is the fourth, *die Sterblichen*. As *Being and Time* had shown, our being is, in its very essence, that of mortals.
4. But what does Heidegger mean by *die Göttlichen*, the divine ones? How are we to think these? Heidegger here is thinking of Hölderlin, who speaks of gods, angels, the divine ones, and the Godhead. Especially important to Heidegger is his line "it is the Godhead with which man measures himself."[60] To exist authentically, Heidegger now seems to be saying, human beings must measure themselves by something divine. But how does such a repetition of the familiar understanding of the human being as *imago Dei*, to which Heidegger himself referred in *Being and Time*, agree with the concept of authenticity that he there developed? His argument would seem to leave no room for something divine that provides human being with a measure.

Once again following Hölderlin, Heidegger speaks not only of the Godhead, but of gods. Thus we read in "Hölderlin and the Essence of Poetry": "Human Dasein is brought in a firm relation and placed on a ground when the gods are named primordially and the essence of things is allowed to speak so that only now things shine forth."[61] This claims that language is a necessary condition of the presencing of things. But further it claims that language presupposes a primordial naming of the gods. How are we to understand this?

A successful naming of the essence of things presupposes that these must already have touched human beings in some fashion. To find the right word, to take the proper measure, we have to experience how things belong together. Think of perceiving a family resemblance. We can perceive such a resemblance without being in possession of the concept that would explain it. To name a god is to find a word for the ground of such a belonging-together of things. Hölderlin's and Heidegger's gods thus recall Plato's ideas. According to Plato we remember these ideas. Baumgarten might have spoken of a clear but confused perception of perfection; Kant of an aesthetic judgment. Heidegger speaks a different language: the gods themselves have to let us speak.[62] That is to say, our *logos* has to respond to a transcendent *logos*. As Heidegger says of the call of conscience in *Being and Time*, the call of this *logos* has to be a wordless call. Heidegger therefore calls "the divine ones" the beckoning messengers of the godhead.[63] Once again, following Hölderlin, Heidegger will also speak of angels. The poet hears and responds to their message and make it public. Such ability to hear binds poetic imagination. But every attempt to thus name the gods and to make public what remains incomprehensible, in order to give human beings the measures they need to come together as a community, does violence to what surpasses comprehension. Again and again we will replace gods with golden calves.

What is such talk of gods and angels to us today? Would we philosophers not have been better served had Heidegger listened more to Kant than to Hölderlin? Are we not talking here about the productive imagination as the ground of all our concepts, where the German *Einbildungskraft* points to the gathering together of some manifold that Heidegger connects with the word *logos*? As Kant recognized, we cannot look for the ground of such gathering in either the subject or the object. It surpasses our understanding and it is therefore not surprising that we should grope for it with inadequate symbols.[64] But what can be understood is that without this ground there can be no authentic Dasein.

As Heidegger makes clear in *Being and Time*, his talk of authenticity presupposes an ideal of human existing that can hardly be realized in our world. At bottom it is still the same ideal that the young Heidegger understood as "the free self-possession of the entire Dasein." There was a time that this ideal let him understand philosophy as the mortal enemy of the faith in which all theology has its ground. But the more resolute the attempt at such "free self-possession," the more inescapable the recognition that such self-possession demands that freedom be bound by something like faith. In his "Dialogue with a Japanese," Heidegger calls the relation between the word of scripture and theological-speculative thinking that occupied the young theology student the same relation that, then still concealed, was later to occupy him as the relation between language and being.[65] The statement is a bit surprising. Did Heidegger not say in the *Introduction to Metaphysics* that a world separated the Christian conception, which understood *logos* as a being, from the understanding that we meet with in a thinker such as Heraclitus, who understood being as *logos* and *logos* again as "primordial gathering?"[66] In the Old Testament *logos* means the word in the sense of commandment; the Ten Commandments were *hoi deka logoi*. "*Logos thus means*: the *keryx*, *angelos*, the herald, the messenger who transmits orders and commandments."[67] In his conversation with the Japanese Heidegger thus bridges this onto-theological difference. And when he there says of his theological origin that origin also awaits us as a task, he invites philosophy to return to onto-theology. Our task is to make a transition from being understood as *logos*, as gathering, to some concrete being that we experience and that gathers us.

Still concealed, the relationship between the word of scripture and theological-speculative thinking is said by Heidegger to be the same relationship as that between language and being.[68] In a different and yet similar way it also conceals the relationship between divine and human *logos*. Both being and language Heidegger thinks again and again as *logos*, understood as "the constant gathering" of beings.[69] And when we read in *Being and Time*, "Discourse is existentially language," that is, beings, "because that entity whose disclosedness it articulates according to significations, has, as its kind of Being, Being-in-the-world—a Being which has been thrown and submitted to the 'world,'"[70] the same argument can be used to support the following: the divine Heraclitean *logos* must descend into the realm of beings; it has to become concrete and visible. The *logos* has to become flesh. Philosophy cannot comprehend such incarnation, nor can it force such a descent. But it can show that such a descent is demanded by Heidegger's concept of authenticity. Authenticity demands windows in the house that objectifying reason has built, windows to transcendence. How is such transcendence experienced? One such experience is the experience of the beautiful. Another is the experience of a person.

CHAPTER 7

Letting Be

John Haugeland

1. *The Problem*

The official aim of *Being and Time* is to reawaken the question of the sense of being—the project Heidegger calls "fundamental ontology." In that work, and others from the same period, he employs, as a new technical term, the expression *sein lassen*, "to let be." This is a compound transitive verb, the subject of which (if made explicit at all) is generally Dasein or Dasein's world, and the direct object of which is entities, or some species thereof. So, simple uses of the term might be claims like "Dasein lets entities be" or "The everyday world lets equipment be." Moreover, there are also a number of broadly related verbs, used in similar ways, such as: *begegnen lassen*, "to let show up"; *bewenden lassen*, "to let have-a-role"; *entlassen*, "to release"; and even *freigeben*, "to set-free." Again, in all these cases, the active subject (if mentioned at all) is typically Dasein or its world, and the passive objects are entities of some sort.

Various of these points are illustrated by a well-known paragraph from section 18 (worldishness) of *Being and Time* and a shorter one from section 26 (others and *Mitsein*):

> Ontically, to let-have-a-role means this: within some factical carefulness, to let something available *be* thus and so, *as* it thenceforth is, and *in order that* it be so. We take this ontical sense of "letting be" as fundamentally ontological. And that's how we interpret the sense of the antecedent setting-free of what is intraworldly available from the outset. To let "be" antecedently does not mean to bring something first into its being and produce it, but rather to discover "entities" already in their availability and, so, to let entities with this being show up.[1]

And:

> Dasein's world sets free entities that are not only quite different from equipment and things, but which, in accord with their sort-of-being as Dasein themselves, are "in" the world by way of being-in-the-world—the world in which they at the same time show up as intraworldly. These entities are neither occurrent nor available, but rather are *just like* the very Dasein that sets them free—*they are there too, co-there.*[2]

The latter passage not only explicitly mentions Dasein's world as the subject of the verb, but also makes clear that its objects are not limited to available equipment—since other people and occurrent things are likewise explicitly mentioned.

Now, the first substantitive point I want to make is that this is very *weird*. What could it *mean* to say that Dasein's world "lets entities be" and "sets them free"? Free from what? And what would happen if it *stopped* doing that? Would all entities cease to be—or cease to be free? But Dasein's world is only insofar as Dasein is. Does that mean that if there were no Dasein there would be no entities at all? To be sure, some of these questions may be misguided; but, unless we confront them, we'll never find out how or why. If we don't acknowledge at the outset how odd and alien Heidegger's claims are, we have no hope of figuring out whatever it was he was trying to say.

So I propose to take it very slowly, and see what sense we can make, step by step—starting with a brief survey of how the verb phrase "let be" is used *in English*. It seems to me that, very roughly, we can distinguish four basic senses—which might be called the *acquiescing*, *allowing*, *enabling*, and *effecting* senses—as follows:

> *Acquiescing*: This is what we mean by "let it be," when we advise someone not to struggle with something—for instance, not to respond (to an insult), not to intervene (in a fight), or just not to keep trying (with some hopeless effort). (The title of the Beatles' song has this acquiescing sense.)
>
> *Allowing*: To let be can mean to permit—in the sense of not preventing—as when the Robinsons let their children be a little rowdier on Saturday nights.
>
> *Enabling*: Or it can mean to permit in another way, as making possible—as when a new highway lets a city be approached from the south, or a dam lets the spring floodwaters be held for the summer crops.
>
> *Effecting*: Finally, to let something be can be to bring it about or make it so—as when God said, "Let there be light" (and there was light). But it's the same sense, I think, when a geometer says, "Let *C* be the

midpoint of line *AB*," or the ball players say, "Let this sidewalk be the goal line."

Now, though Heidegger's word—*lassen*—is cognate and mostly synonymous with the English *let*, they are of course not fully equivalent in all contexts. Even so, I suggest that distinguishing these four senses will be all the "dictionary work" we need. For fundamental ontology makes us push and twist our vocabulary in any case; and English words are as malleable as any.

2. *Letting Equipment Be*

We can begin with the same special case that Heidegger himself does: everyday intraworldly equipment. It is in this context that he introduces the other two *lassen*-verbs mentioned above: *bewenden lassen* and *begegnen lassen*. But it's not so hard to see how these work, so long as we're careful about the rest of the terminology too. In sections 15 and 18, respectively, *Zuhandenheit* and *Bewandtnis* are both defined as the *being* of equipment. But they're not the same. The difference between them is what Heidegger calls the *articulation* of being into *that*-being and *what*-being (compare the actuality/essence distinction—of which more below). The *that*-being of an item of equipment (what's at stake in whether it is at all or not) is its *Zuhandenheit* (what I call *availability*). Its *what*-being (what's at stake in what "kind" of thing it is) is its *Bewandtnis*—which I therefore translate as its (equipmental) *role*. So: availability is the equipmental analog of actuality; and roles are the analog of essences.

Now, these various roles, to which equipmental entities are "assigned," only make the sense they make *in relation to* one another (hammer/nail/wood, pen/ink/paper, and so on). Heidegger calls the relational character of those assignments "signifying," and the totality of such signifyings "significance." And that significance, in turn, is what makes up the structure of the world—the world of everyday Dasein. But, with these points and terms in place, it's not so weird after all to say that Dasein's world *lets* intraworldly entities "have their roles" (*bewenden lassen*), or even that it *lets* them "show up" as anything whatsoever (*begegnen lassen*). For the world is *defined*, in effect, as the totality of all those roles in their essential interrelations. Hence, without it, nothing could show up as—or, therefore, be—anything equipmental at all. Or, to make the same point by means of a special case, who could deny that the "world" of baseball *lets* certain discernible configurations *be* strikes, home runs, and the like?

The problem with this kind of case is not that it's unpersuasive (as far as it goes) but that it's too easy. It's not big news that, without Dasein, nothing would be a hammer or a home run. But what about entities that have been around since long before there was Dasein, and still will be long after—entities that are (as we want to say) *independent* of Dasein? This question, however, cannot even be addressed without some grasp of the relevant sense of "independence"; and that turns out to presuppose the concept of that-being.

3. That-Being and Production

The articulation of being into that-being and what-being is one of the four basic problems identified in *The Basic Problems of Phenomenology* (*Die Grundprobleme der Phänomenologie*). In the chapter of that work addressed to this problem—or, rather, the chapter devoted to the historical background prerequisite to addressing the problem—Heidegger begins with the scholastic distinction between *essentia* and *existentia*, and the problem of how they could come together in an entity. In the case of finite entities (creatures), they are officially brought together in the causal *act* of divine creation: entities are at all in that they are *enacted* or *actualized* by God. So, *existentia* = createdness = enactedness = actuality.

The trouble is: if you just say that this "bringing together" is an "actualizing act" (of "causal creation"), you haven't really said anything about what that amounts to, or therefore thrown any light on what "being actual" in fact *means*. It is better, Heidegger suggests, to keep track of the original sense of *existentia* itself, and then trace that sense back to its roots in *Greek* ontology. Thus, the verb *existere* came to mean "to exist" from the more original meaning of *ex-sistere*: to cause to stand out, stand forth, or stand still. With that in mind, we can then ask the obvious question: why would a verb with *that* original sense come to mean anything like "is actual" or "has that-being"? Prima facie, for instance, its inner semantic motives are quite different from those of the Kantian definition of existence as "absolute position."

And here is where returning to the formative Greek sensibilities can shed some real light. Briefly, the Kantian definition makes sense within what Heidegger calls the horizon of *perceptual* comportment; that is, Kant's understanding of "empirical" entities as such takes its guidance from the perspective of their being knowable, going back ultimately to intuition. By contrast, Heidegger suggests, the *Greek* understanding of that-being—in which the scholastic concept *existentia* is still rooted—makes sense within the horizon of *productive* comportment.

Though we care more about what Heidegger's going to make of it than how he gets there, what he says is roughly the following. Greek *ontology* understands *morphe* (the shape or form of a thing) as grounded on *eidos* (the "look" of the thing)—even though, *conceptually* (not to mention, *perceptually*), the form is prior to the look.[3] And this surprising *ontological* ordering can only be explained if we see that the Greeks understood *being* not within the horizon of perception, but rather that of *production*. Thus, if we consider *seeing* a pot, then the pot itself must already have its form before the look of it can be taken in by the viewer; so *morphe* is prior to *eidos*. But if we consider, instead, *making* a pot, then the potter must *already* have the look in mind, to guide him in giving the requisite form to the clay; hence, the resulting *morphe* itself is grounded in that prior *eidos*.

Morphe and *eidos* are both associated with *what*-being (ancestors of *essentia*). But what interests us is how this "reversing" of their respective priorities might affect the understanding of *that*-being (*existentia*). Within the horizon of perception, the "object" is understood as *already* existing (actual); and so such existence itself can (only) be grasped as standing-over-againstness (*Gegenständlichkeit*, objectivity), with no further insight into what that amounts to. Within the horizon of production, on the other hand, the entity to be produced is precisely not understood as already existent—but rather merely what *can* be—and, more specifically, can, via this very production, *come into* being (*become* an entity) for the first time. Thus, existence—that-being—is somehow to be "conferred upon" or "accorded to" something (determined by the *eidos*) that does not yet "have" it. And the idea is that this "*according* of existence to"—"*letting* be"—can in turn be a clue to that which is accorded by it (= that-being).

Return to the potter. What exactly does he *do*, that *lets* the pot *be*? Well, of course, he shapes it, dries it, colors it, fires it, and so on. But any or all of those could conclude with an angry smash and a pile of rubble—which is to say, neither produce a pot nor let it be at all. Genuine, successful *production* of a pot—that is, *finishing* it, and, in fact, *letting* it be—is something more like *letting go of* or *releasing* it: that is, handing it over to the customer, or putting it in the cupboard, available to be used. And here the connotations of allowing and acquiescing, mentioned earlier, begin to get a grip—as, indeed, does "setting-free."

Yet, even in the special context of craftwork, letting-go-of cannot alone suffice as an account of what the producer does in "according" that-being to the product. For if, as soon as the producer let go, the intended product had crumbled or vanished, it still would not have been *produced*. So productive letting-be has to have the further character of setting the product out on its own, to stand up and be (persist as) what it is—*establishing* it, so to speak. But, if what is involved in coming-to-be is being set out on its own and established in this way, then we can see how the phrase *ex-sistere*—to cause to stand out or stand forth—could be taken to express it. What's more, we get at least a glimmer of how independence (out-on-its-own-ness) could be not merely compatible but conceptually connected with letting be.

But, finally, in order to establish and set the product up in that way, the producer has to give it (arrange for it to have) the capacities and capabilities that it will need in order to *be* on its own. A pot, for instance, may need a certain strength, stability, and waterproofness; and so the potter must ensure that it has them. In other words, in producing, the producer must *enable* the product to be whatever it is to be, and, in so doing, *enable* it to stand on its own—which is to say, to *be* or *ek-sist* at all. And precisely within that *enabling* lies the intelligibility of creation as actualization—the possible union of essence and existence.

Therefore, at least within the horizon of production, the enabling sense of letting-be is ultimately the deepest.

4. Scientific Discovering

It is one thing to say that Dasein "lets" its own equipment "be," that it "sets" the products of its own labor "free"; but it's quite another to say any such thing about protons, planets, or prehistoric lizards. Yet it's perfectly clear that Heidegger wants to make that claim too: "[Scientific projection = *thematizing*] aims at a setting free of entities that show up intraworldly, in such a way that they can 'throw themselves against' a pure discovering—that is, can become objects. Thematizing objectifies. It does not first 'posit' entities, but rather sets them free in such a way that they become 'objectively' questionable and determinable."[4] But—we have to ask again—what could it *mean* to say that Dasein's thematizing sets protons and planets *free*? What prison are they in? How do we "let" them out? How can we enable them to "throw themselves against" a pure discovering?

Now, what is perhaps the biggest surprise in this context is that these questions do have answers. If you will pardon my tweaking the metaphors a moment longer, we can answer this way: until Dasein releases them, entities remain in the darkest of all prisons, the prison of utter obscurity; we let them out by bringing them to light (into the clearing); and we enable them to throw themselves against a pure discovery by erecting a pure discovery in their path and accepting what happens as the result of their coming up against it. Or, less metaphorically, we introduce measuring instruments and accept their "readings" as evidence.

The crucial insight is this: letting entities throw themselves against a pure discovery is not easy, nor even easily recognized when achieved. Thus, when Galileo's peripatetic opponents argued that the specks of light visible in his telescope were not moons of Jupiter but rather mere artifacts of the instrument itself, they were being neither entirely obstreperous nor obtuse—and Galileo knew it. As a point of comparison, suppose a colleague claimed that four invisible "Martians" accompany your every lecture—and produced the videos to prove it (made with a special new camera, of course). Wouldn't you suspect that those "Martians" have more to do with that "special" camera than with your lectures? Likewise, Galileo's contemporaries had all kinds of good reasons to doubt the ostensible "evidence" he was offering them. And therefore, most of the work he had to do was to *show*, step by step, question by question, that what appeared in the telescope really was something "out there."

And, what did it take to do *that*? Well, he made multiple telescopes and showed that what you saw was the same, no matter which one you used. He showed and explained how they were constructed and why they would let distant objects seem closer and larger. He invited people to look at distant *terrestrial* objects—objects the existence and appearance of which they could independently confirm. He showed that, not only did those specks stay with Jupiter as it moved against the fixed stars, but also that they themselves visibly moved relative to Jupiter in just the way they would if they were separate bodies orbiting around it. Only after all of this, and more besides, could people so much as *see* what was in some sense "right before their eyes."

It is this sort of work—often *hard* work—that Heidegger means by "letting entities show up" (*begegnen lassen*) and, more specifically, letting them "throw themselves against" (*entgegnenwerfen*) a pure discovery. Such "letting" is clearly more than mere allowing or acquiescing-in, but also and especially *enabling*. In fact, in the sense in which discovery (observation) is *essentially* an acquiescing-in—accepting of—whatever is discovered, acquiescing itself is part of what is *enabled*.

Now, in German, the words themselves lubricate the transition from *begegnen lassen* and *entgegnenwerfen* to *Gegenstand* and *gegenständlich*; but, philosophically, those moves still have to be paid for—in other words, explained and justified. It's one thing to say that Dasein enables entities to show up; but it's quite another to say that it enables them to be—or, be objects—at all. Yet the latter, I'm convinced, is the claim he is really trying to make—or, more cautiously, was setting himself up to make in Division Three.

5. *Scientific Laws*

It might seem that Heidegger explicitly repudiates the thesis I just attributed to him. For he says, in section 43: "If Dasein does not exist, then 'independence' 'is' not either, nor 'is' the 'in-itself.' . . . It can be said *then*, neither that entities are nor that they are not. But *now*, so long as the understanding of being is, and with it the understanding of occurrentness, it can perfectly well be said that entities will still continue to be *then*."[5] And he adds in the next section: "*'There is' truth only so far and so long as Dasein is*. Only *then* are entities discovered; and they are disclosed only *so long as* Dasein *is* at all."[6] And finally, on the following page: "That, prior to Newton, his laws were neither true nor false, cannot mean that the entities those laws discoveringly point out were not [there] prior to him. Through Newton, the laws became true; with them, the entities in themselves became accessible to Dasein; with the discoveredness of these entities, they show themselves as precisely the entities that already were previously."[7] This all sounds straightforward enough: there are (past, present, and future) whatever *entities* there are, whether *Dasein* is then—to "let" them be—or not. What depends on Dasein, when it exists, is not what there is at that time, but only what can be said, pointed out, or accessed then—hence, what can be true or false. So, for instance, the force of gravity didn't come into existence the day Newton discovered his law about it; rather, it just *showed itself* for the first time, but showed itself *as* an entity that had been there all along and would also continue to be. What could be more obvious?

All the same, it is a little odd to say that the law of gravity wasn't *true* before Newton discovered it, especially since one of the things he did with it was retrodict various eclipses, comet sightings, and the like, back to antiquity. And, in the meantime, there remains the question of what to say about *Einstein*'s discovery that there is (was and will be) no force of gravity after all—just curved space-time. Does this mean that, through Newton, his laws *became* true, but *only for a while*? But that seems crazy: if Newton's laws were ever true, then they always were and always will be; that's the kind of laws they are—and the same goes for Einstein's.

(It may be worth noting that this line of questioning about *physical Being and Time* is not disconnected from the text *Being and Time*. In section 3, Heidegger motivates the entire project of fundamental ontology in terms of its relevance to foundational crises in the sciences; and, though briefly, he explicitly mentions physics and the theory of relativity as one example. So it's hard to believe he didn't have that issue in the back of his mind when making the claims we're now considering about Newton.)

So, how *does* physics (Newtonian physics, say) *let* physical objects *be*—"stand on their own, over against us"? Well, everything said above about Galileo still applies; Newton had to do that kind of hard, justificatory work too. But, with Newton, a further and even more fundamental element comes clearly into view: those very laws about which Heidegger makes such an odd claim. These laws, I will argue, are one version of a more general sort of factor that is essential in every understanding of being and every way of letting entities be. The advantage of proceeding via scientific laws is that the form of their contribution is especially clear.

In order to let entities be, Dasein must somehow discover them—which, in science, generally means to observe or measure them. But observation and measurement only make sense if there is, in principle, some way to distinguish between *correct* and *incorrect* results. Now, some invalid results may be detected by flagging technical errors or equipmental failure. But the only fundamental way to establish that something must be wrong is to show that some plurality of results are not mutually compatible. And that, finally, presupposes antecedent constraints on what combinations would and would not be possible—which is to say, *laws*.

Thus, Newton and his colleagues could have far better astronomical *data* than could Galileo, not simply because of technical advances but rather and mainly because they had much better laws. Knowing, as they did, with far greater accuracy, what *had to* be the case, they could calibrate and fine-tune their instruments and techniques in ways their predecessors could scarcely dream of.

Superficially, there might seem to be a problem here, with the credibility of the theory depending on the empirical evidence for it, while the accuracy of that evidence, in turn, is made possible by the theory. But—without even appealing to Heidegger's fondness for circles—we can see that the worry is misplaced. For, no matter how the methods are fine-tuned in general, they do still have to produce particular results in practice, independent of any particular predictions; and that still leaves room for empirical failure.

The point can be put more generally this way. It is in some sense "easy" to concoct a rich and powerful descriptive vocabulary. It is in some sense "easy" to concoct precise, general methods for investigating the entities putatively so describable. And it is in some sense "easy" to concoct strict laws constraining the results of those investigations. What is not at all easy is to do all three at once in such a way that, when those investigations are assiduously carried out, the actual results are consistently in accord with the laws.

Now, according to me, succeeding at that difficult but not impossible threefold task is the general form of discovering entities and *letting* them be—at least in the special case of scientific investigations. The crucial role of laws is to *restrict* what there *can* be by ruling out various conceivable combinations. Only by virtue of that restrictive function can subsumption of particulars under laws render the actual *intelligible*—that is, *explain why* one thing happened rather than another. And I take this to be the scientific version of what Heidegger means more generally when he allows that *understanding* entities is projecting them onto their *possibilities*.

6. Scientific Change

If the preceding is the general form of scientific letting-be, and if the that-being of scientifically discovered entities is *Gegenständlichkeit*—being-an-object or objectivity—then the relevant sense of letting be is again the *enabling* sense. For the upshot of subsumption under laws is to *enable* entities to *stand up against* observations and measurements—that is, to defy and repudiate them.

And the crucial prerequisite for this defiant repudiation is, as we have seen, the law-mandated impossibility of certain combinations of observed characteristics or measured magnitudes.

More particularly, we now see how, through Newton and his laws, the entities of Newtonian physics became accessible as the entities they already were and would continue to be. What remains utterly opaque, however, is what could be meant by saying that, through Newton, his laws *became* true—not to mention the inevitable follow-up question of whether they became neither-true-nor-false again through Einstein. What's worse, with this opacity, the force of the seemingly clear "as they already were and would continue to be" becomes pretty murky after all. What could Heidegger have been thinking?

I think *Being and Time* will support an extrapolation in terms of which this question might be answerable. (Whether the answer could ever be acceptable is another issue.)

Remember first that there are different sorts of time in *Being and Time*, including originary time, world time, and vulgar time. Originary time is not sequential at all. Simplifying ruthlessly, I understand it as the temporal character of a commitment to an understanding of being. When Heidegger says that, through Newton, his laws became true, he is referring to the undertaking of such a commitment. Thus, it is ultimately that undertaking which lets the Newtonian entities be. These entities are, of course, in time—and also in space. But this time does not at all have the character of a commitment (nor even the significance and datability of Dasein's everyday world). Rather, it has only the mathematical character of so-called Newtonian space-time. And it is in *this* time that those entities show themselves as precisely the entities that already were previously, and, moreover, will continue to be.

Now, when Einstein comes along, he has a different commitment to a different understanding of physical being, which, in turn, likewise lets entities be. These entities also show up as ones that already were previously and will continue to be—though, of course, in *relativistic* space-time. It is a difficult and vexing problem to say just what the relationship is between the respective sets of entities, but simple identity seems ruled out.

The easiest (and therefore most tempting) line is to say that, *really*, only one set of laws has ever been true, and only one set of entities—the entities that *those* laws let be—is actual, in some timeless sense of "is actual." Thus, what Einstein showed us is that, contrary to what we thought, Newton's laws were *never* true and the Newtonian universe of entities was *never* actual. Rather, it has always only ever been Einsteinian.

One problem with this interpretation is that it's incompatible with what Heidegger explicitly says. Another problem is that it's unlikely to be a stable position. For, by the same reasoning, we would have to say, *even now*, that it's *really* always only ever been an *X*-ian universe, where *X* is Einstein's successor—or, rather, the ultimate end of the line in that successorship, assuming there "is" such an end and science lasts long enough to get there.

Why would that idea ever strike anyone as the easiest and most tempting thing to say? I suspect that it is more of the legacy of scholasticism. The original and final science—the only one that's ever *really* been right—is *God's* science: the *scientia* of omniscience. This *scientia* is supposed to be absolutely and eternally correct, literally *by* fiat—the *effecting* sense of "letting be." No one who has ever tried to think about it could imagine that "getting over" this legacy is or will be easy. It will require at least a profound reconception of reality as such—which is to say a new and deeper understanding of being.

What I have tried to show is that the idea of *letting be*, taken not as effective and divine but as enabling and human, is an integral part of that larger endeavor.

CHAPTER 8

Heidegger and the Synthetic A Priori

Cristina Lafont

IN HIS BOOK *The Genesis of Being and Time*, Theodor Kisiel introduces his analysis of what he calls "the Kantian draft of *Being and Time*" with the following remark: "When was Heidegger not a Kantian? It is almost like asking, 'When was Heidegger not a German?'"[1] There are many senses in which Kisiel's observation is indisputably correct and which ensure the fruitfulness of an in-depth investigation of the relationship between Heidegger and transcendental philosophy. From a historical point of view, perhaps the fact that best supports Kisiel's remark is the one he points to immediately thereafter, namely, the neo-Kantianism that pervaded the air of the German university in Heidegger's formative years and, in particular, Heidegger's allegiance to the "Southwest German school of neo-Kantianism" as a student of Rickert. However, in what follows I would like to focus on the relationship between Heidegger and transcendental philosophy more from a systematic than from a historical-genealogical point of view.

Needless to say, any attempt to explain the sense in which Heidegger was a Kantian necessarily involves explaining the sense in which he was not. For it is surely beyond question that he was not an orthodox Kantian. Heidegger makes explicit his own view of the tension between his thought and Kant's in his lectures of the winter semester of 1927–28, entitled *Phenomenological Interpretations of Kant's Critique of Pure Reason* (*Phänomenologische Interpretation von Kants Kritik der reinen Vernunft*). There he characterizes the importance of Kant's philosophy for the very enterprise of *Being and Time* in the following terms: "If we radicalize the Kantian problem of ontological knowledge in the sense that we do not *limit* this problem to the ontological foundation of the positive *sciences* and if we do not take this problem as a problem of *judgment* but as the radical and fundamental question concerning the possibility of *understanding being in general*, then we shall arrive at the philosophically fundamental problematic of *Being and Time*."[2] Thus, *Being and Time*'s radicalization of transcendental philosophy has as its target the *scope* of the problem of ontological knowledge rather than the *Kantian model* for understanding it. As I will try to show in what follows, Heidegger sees indeed his own project as Kantian to the extent that it incorporates the core of Kant's Copernican revolution into the most important categorical distinction of his philosophy, namely, the *ontological difference*. On the other hand, though, as a consequence of his interpretation of the ontological difference Kant's transcendental idealism is transformed into a hermeneutic idealism. Accordingly, Heidegger's radicalization of transcendental philosophy aims to show, among other things, that what Kant erroneously thought were the invariant features of any human experience whatsoever (i.e., the pure forms of intuition and the categories) are just a special case of what is in fact a much broader phenomenon, namely, the necessarily circular (i.e., temporal) structure of all human understanding.[3] In this sense, Heidegger welcomes Kant's discovery of the synthetic a priori that is at the core of his Copernican revolution, but he thinks that the special function and status of the synthetic a priori is not an issue that concerns some specific judgments (at the basis of the positive sciences) but one that concerns understanding being in general. Seen in this light, an analysis of Heidegger's hermeneutic transformation of the synthetic a priori seems crucial to determining the precise nature of Heidegger's Kantianism.[4]

Earlier in the above-mentioned lectures Heidegger explains the connection between Kant's discovery of the synthetic a priori and the so-called Copernican revolution. His explanation is very helpful in this context, for it shows the exact way in which Kant's transcendental idealism gets transformed into Heidegger's hermeneutic idealism via the ontological difference. Commenting on the problem of the synthetic a priori Heidegger remarks:

> Briefly the problem is the following: How can understanding open up real principles about the possibility of things, i.e., how can the subject have in advance an understanding of the ontological constitution of the being of a being? Kant sees this correlation, one which we formulate in a more basic and radical manner by saying: *Beings are in no way accessible without an antecedent understanding of being*. This is to say that beings, which encounter us, must already be understood in advance in their ontological constitution. This understanding of the being of beings, this synthetic knowledge *a priori*, is crucial for every experience of beings. This is the only possible meaning of Kant's thesis, which is frequently misunderstood and which is called his Copernican revolution.[5]

Heidegger's claim that there can be no access to entities without a prior understanding of their being is thus the core of his hermeneutic transformation of Kant's transcendental idealism. Paraphrasing Kant's highest principle of synthetic judgments,[6] Heidegger's claim would read as follows: the conditions of possibility of understanding the being of entities are at the same time the conditions of possibility of the being of those entities. Heidegger makes this idealist view explicit right at the beginning of *Being and Time*, when he equates what we could call the "hermeneutic" with the "realist" meanings of "being." According to his explanation of the meaning of "being," "that which determines entities as entities" is "that on the basis of which entities are always already understood."[7] Whereas from a realist perspective it is assumed that what determines entities as entities is something that belongs to those entities themselves, that is, some ontic structure or properties that those entities have and others do not, the idealist perspective that Heidegger favors assumes that "there is being only in an understanding of being," and thus that "being can never be explained by entities but is already that which is 'transcendental' for every entity."[8] In Heidegger's view this idealism follows from recognizing the ontological difference itself, that is, the fact that "the being of entities 'is' not itself an entity."[9]

As Heidegger explains in his discussion of realism and idealism in section 43 of *Being and Time*, recognition of the ontological difference involves at least two separate claims. On the one hand, realizing that *being cannot be reduced to entities* implies realizing (against any naïve realism) that what determines entities as entities is our understanding of being, and not something ontically present in those entities and thus independent of our understanding of them. This is the idealist content of Heidegger's interpretation of the ontological difference that he expresses with the claim that the *being of entities must be projected* in order for these entities to be accessible to us. On the other hand, realizing that *entities cannot be reduced to being* implies realizing (against any absolute idealism) that entities cannot be reduced to our understanding of them. Parallel with Kant's attempt to reconcile a transcendental idealism with an empirical realism, one could say that Heidegger aims to be an ontic realist and an ontological idealist. On the one hand, this view is opposed to what Kant called "transcendental realism" and these days is usually called "metaphysical realism": the world is not made out of self-identifying entities; we are the ones who divide the world into different entities according to our interpretation of their being. On the other hand, this view is not supposed to lead to anything like what Kant called "empirical idealism" à la Berkeley, that is, it does not question the existence of entities independent of us. As Heidegger would put it, *that* there are entities has nothing to do with us, but *what* they are depends on our prior projection of their being.[10] Regardless of whether Heidegger's attempt to combine realism and idealism is in the end defensible or not,[11] what matters in our context are the implications of his hermeneutic idealism for an understanding of our experience (that is, of the conditions of possibility of our access to entities).[12]

According to this view, our understanding of the being of entities is synthetic a priori in the specifically Kantian sense that it is, as Heidegger puts it, "*prior* to all ontic experience, but precisely *for* it."[13] That is, our understanding of the being of entities is not taken from experience (1), but at the same time it determines all experience (of those entities) (2). However, this cannot be so for Kantian reasons. According to Kant, the apriority of this special kind of knowledge is due to the (alleged) fact that no human experience would be possible without said knowledge and thus is due to its universal validity. But according to Heidegger a factual Dasein's understanding of being is itself "essentially factical" and changes historically by virtue of our contingent projections. Thus, we need to know what other sorts of reasons Heidegger has to offer to justify the a priori status of our understanding of the being of entities.

The answer to this question lies at the core of Heidegger's transformation of the Kantian notion of apriority into the hermeneutic notion of the *perfect tense a priori* (i.e., the "always already"). This notion is supposed to both preserve and transform the Kantian notion of apriority in the following way. On the one hand, as Heidegger is keen to insist, the priority implicit in this notion does not merely have the *temporal* sense of indicating something ontically past but, as its name suggests, it also has the *normative* sense of conferring to that which is in each case prior the status of an *absolute authority over us* that a priori knowledge is supposed to have.[14] On the other hand, though, the fact that it includes the temporal sense expressed by the "in each case" is what is specifically incompatible with the traditional, Kantian notion of apriority, for it eliminates the implication of universal validity from the absolute authority of the a priori. In light of its historical alterability, that something is "a priori" no longer means that it is "universally valid," but at most that it is "unquestionable from within" (i.e., by those who share it). From this point of view, the crucial challenge to transcendental philosophy in *Being and Time* is to be found in Heidegger's claim that Dasein's "disclosedness is essentially factical."[15]

In light of this claim, though, one may well wonder whether Heidegger's aim is really to transform the notion of apriority or rather to simply reject it altogether. For the claim that our disclosedness is essentially factical seems to imply precisely that nothing in it has the kind of normative status that a priori knowledge is supposed to have. However, that this is not the intended interpretation becomes entirely clear when Heidegger claims that Dasein's disclosedness is "*truth* in the most primordial sense."[16] Thus, the crucial issue behind Heidegger's hermeneutic notion of apriority seems to lie in whether it can succeed in making these two characterizations of our disclosedness (as "essentially factical, but true") compatible. This brings us back to our former question. Given that our disclosedness is merely the result of a historical, contingent process of cultural interpretation, we need to know what reasons Heidegger can offer to ascribe to our understanding of the being of entities the Kantian features of synthetic a priori knowledge.

The first part of the claim—namely, that the understanding of being *is not taken from experience*—is just the expression of Heidegger's idealism, as already discussed. Being must be projected in advance in order for entities to be accessible as such entities.[17] This is such a basic presupposition within Heidegger's philosophy that he seems never to have felt the need to offer an elaborated justification for it. There is indeed a hermeneutic reason that Heidegger alludes to repeatedly, although he never discusses it in detail. Perhaps the best way to express it would be with the help of Quine's maxim "no entity without identity."[18] In our context, the idea behind it could be made explicit through the following argumentative lines: given that entities are not self-identifying, one has to identify which entities one is talking about in order to be able to distinguish them from others. And one cannot do so unless one has an understanding of what distinguishes these entities from others, that is, an understanding that provides the resources to identify entities as *what* they are, that is, in their *being*. Heidegger suggests such a line of argument in multiple places. For example, at the beginning of his lectures of the winter semester of 1931–32, entitled *The Essence of Truth* (*Vom Wesen der Wahrheit*), he explains:

> We wish to consider the essence of truth. "Truth": what is that? The answer to the question "what is that?" brings us to the "essence" of a thing. "Table": what is that? "Mountain," "ocean," "plant"; in each case the question "what is that?" asks about the "essence" of these things. We ask—and yet we already *know* them! Indeed, *must* we not already know them, in order afterward to ask, and even to give an answer, about *what* they are? . . . Clearly, we must *necessarily* already know the essence. For how otherwise could we know what we should provide when we are requested to name truths? . . . We must already know what and how the thing is about which we speak.[19]

Thus, that an understanding of the being of entities must be prior to any experience of those entities is just a consequence of a hermeneutic constraint, namely, that the way in which entities are understood must determine in advance which entities we are referring to or, in general terms, that *meaning must determine reference*. This hermeneutic constraint explains why understanding is necessarily projective. It also provides a more or less trivial justification for the second part of the claim, namely, that the understanding of the being of entities *determines all experience* of those entities. Given that the prior understanding of the being of entities is what makes our experience an experience of some specific entities (rather than others), it determines what these entities are (for us),[20] that is, it determines *what* they are accessible to us *as*.[21] Thus, that our experience is determined by a priori structures is not a consequence of its being constituted by some invariant set of conditions to be discovered once and for all, as Kant thought. It is actually a consequence of the circle of understanding, that is, of the fact that "every interpretation . . . must *already* have understood what is to be interpreted."[22] It is for this hermeneutic reason that entities can only be discovered by the prior projection of their being.[23] As Heidegger explains in *Basic Problems of Phenomenology*: "An entity can be uncovered, whether by way of perception or some other mode of access, only if the being of this entity is already disclosed—only if I already understand it. Only then can I ask whether it is real or not and embark on some procedure to establish the reality of the entity."[24]

Although the priority of an understanding of being over and above any experience of entities is, according to Heidegger, a general feature of all human understanding, the paradigm example that Heidegger favors in order to show the plausibility of this hermeneutic idealism is scientific knowledge. For scientific theories, as opposed to most ordinary understanding, are explicit and highly articulated kinds of interpretation, which for this reason allow for closer scrutiny as to their origin, structure, relationship to experience, and so on. Still, as a kind of interpretation they are subject to the same circular (and thus projective) conditions of understanding. In his lectures of the winter semester of 1928–29, entitled *Introduction to Philosophy* (*Einleitung in die Philosophie*) Heidegger explains:

> A determinate scientific investigation moves within a determinate problem, a determinate question posed to that which is its theme. Thematization presupposes the givenness of an object. But an object can only be given to me in the act of objectivation. I can only objectify something if this something is already manifest to me in advance. A manifest entity as entity can only be manifest, if this entity in its being is already understood in advance with regard to its being, that is, if it is projected. Thus, we see a completely determinate sequence within the structure of science. The central phenomenon is this projection of the constitution of being.[25]

In *What Is a Thing?* (*Die Frage nach den Ding?*) Heidegger offers a very detailed explanation of the structure and characteristics of such a projection with the help of an analysis of the transformation of science from the ancient conception of nature into modern natural science. He interprets this transformation as a change of "metaphysical projection" or, as it is called these days, a paradigm shift. Heidegger makes clear that the core of this paradigm shift does not consist in the emphasis on observation or experimentation, but on the projection of an entirely different understanding of the being of entities, a new world-disclosure brought about through the establishment and definition of new basic concepts by modern scientists such as Galileo and Newton.[26] According to Heidegger, to the extent that these new concepts organize all possible experience in advance, the grounding postulates or axioms of these modern theories through which these concepts are defined have the status of synthetic a priori knowledge.[27] For only on the basis of such postulates and axioms is something like empirical knowledge possible at all. In *Kant and the Problem of Metaphysics* (*Kant und das Problem der Metaphysik*) Heidegger explains this view as the correct insight behind Kant's Copernican revolution. Commenting on Kant's claim that "reason has insight only into that which it produces according to its own projections," he adds:

> The "previously projected plan" of a nature in general determines in advance the constitution of the being of entities, to which all questions that are investigated should be capable of being related. This *prior* plan of the being of entities is inscribed within the basic concepts and principles of the science of nature to which we already referred. Hence, what makes the comportment toward entities (ontic knowledge) possible is the *prior* understanding of the constitution of being, ontological knowledge. . . . This known quiddity of the entity is brought forward *a priori* in ontological knowledge prior to all ontic experience, although precisely for it. Knowledge that brings forth the quiddity [*Wasgehalt*] of the entity, i.e. knowledge which unveils the entity itself, Kant calls "synthetic." Thus the question concerning the possibility of ontological knowledge becomes the problem of the essence of a priori synthetic judgments. The instance capable of establishing the legitimacy of these material judgments concerning the being of the entity cannot be found in experience, for experience of the entity is itself always already guided by the ontological understanding of the entity, which in some specific respect must become accessible through experience.[28]

In spite of Heidegger's brilliant effort to have Kant speak in the language of *Being and Time*, the de-transcendentalization of synthetic a priori knowledge implicit in Heidegger's interpretation of the Copernican revolution becomes clear just by comparing the way in which the term *projection* is employed by both authors. For when Kant speaks of projections in his discussion of the structure of the empirical sciences, this term refers expressly to those projections to which *pure reason itself* gives rise, whereas for Heidegger these projections are merely a working-out of the basic concepts of the guiding understanding of being,[29] that is, they are just (historically alterable) *cultural productions*. But in this way, the properties of these projections in the two conceptions are radically different. For Kant, the appeal to the property of apriority implies ascribing to such projections (as products of pure reason) a strict *transcendental status* to which they would owe their necessity and universal validity, whereas the *prior* character of Heidegger's projections stems merely from the fore-structure of understanding.

However, once the transcendental status of the a priori is questioned, it is no longer clear that the features associated with this status can be preserved in the new conception. In particular, the claim that synthetic a priori knowledge determines all experience implies that this knowledge cannot be revised through experience, for no experience can contradict it.[30] But it is not at all clear that the hermeneutic reasons that we have considered so far are sufficient to support this implication. The mere fact that experimentation is guided by prior theoretical assumptions does not by itself imply their immunity from revision. Moreover, as Heidegger's own explanation of the evolution of modern science shows, these assumptions have in fact been revised. Thus, additional reasons seem necessary to justify the ascription of this important feature of the traditional notion of the a priori to Heidegger's hermeneutic a priori.

In *What Is a Thing?* Heidegger indeed offers such an additional hermeneutic reason. Drawing on what these days is called the underdetermination of theory choice by evidence, he tries to make plausible the immunity from revision based on experience that he ascribes to the basic principles and axioms of scientific theories. Heidegger appeals to the example of different explanations for "one and the same fact" within both the Aristotelian and Galilean paradigms, the fact that under normal conditions in the earth's field of gravitation, heavy bodies pass through a determinate distance faster than lighter bodies do. (This was described in Aristotelian physics by various inert properties lying in the nature of bodies, but was explained by Galileo as the consequence of the air resistance of bodies made of the same material but also of greater weight.) He comments: "Both Galileo and his opponents saw the same 'fact.' But they made the same fact or the same happening visible to themselves in different ways, interpreted it in different ways. Indeed, what appeared to them in each case as the authentic *fact and truth* was something *different.*"[31] It is thus the incommensurability among different projections that makes it impossible to interpret their historical change as a process of rational revision based on experience. As Heidegger claims in *Basic Questions of Philosophy* (*Grundfragen der Philosophie*): "It is simply pointless to *measure* the Aristotelian doctrine of motion against that of *Galileo* with respect to results, *judging* the former as backward and the latter as advanced. For *in each case, nature means something completely different.*"[32]

Given that, according to Heidegger, entities are only accessible through a prior projection of their being, it is clear that entities made accessible by genuinely different projections are, by definition, not the same entities. But only if they were, would it make sense to think of one as a correction of the other. Thus, an old projection cannot be *disproved* by a new one; at most, it can be put "out of force" by a different stipulation of what and how things are. Conversely, from the point of view of an old projection, the new one cannot be seen as better or worse but simply as meaningless; Heidegger remarks in *What Is a Thing?*: "[Newton's first law of motion] was up until the 17th century not at all self-evident. During the preceding fifteen hundred years it was not only unknown; rather, nature and *entities in general* were *experienced* in a way with respect to which this law *would have been meaningless*."[33] It is for this reason that Heidegger claims in *Being and Time* that "before Newton his laws were neither true nor false."[34]

This claim is based on Heidegger's distinction between two different senses of truth that correspond to the different senses of knowledge implicit here (namely, synthetic a priori and a posteriori). Whereas ontic knowledge of entities can be revised through experience and thus can turn out to be true or false in the standard sense, namely, in the sense of truth as correctness, ontological knowledge of the being of entities cannot be so revised and thus cannot turn out to be (empirically) false. Consequently, it must be true, although in an entirely different sense, namely, in the sense of unconcealment. Accordingly, the instituting of a new projection or world-disclosure as an unconcealing of the being of entities is a "happening of truth." On the one hand, it is a *happening* in the precise sense that it is a contingent, historical event; on the other hand, it is a happening of *truth*, to the extent that it cannot be questioned or revised through the experience that it makes possible and thus exercises an absolute normative authority over those who share it. The idea behind Heidegger's appeal to a more originary sense of truth could be expressed in the following terms. To the same extent that meaning determines reference, truth depends on meaning. After all, only meaningful statements can be true or false. Thus, what allows us to distinguish between meaningful and meaningless statements (i.e., our understanding of the being of entities), determines in advance what the possible truths are for those who share it, determining *which* ontic truths are accessible to them. In this sense, truth is relative to a prior understanding of being, which cannot itself be questioned in its validity. Thus, the attempt to conceive the historical changes in our understanding of being as a learning process is based on an illusion. There is no absolute truth across incommensurable understandings of being.[35] They are unrevisable from within and inaccessible (meaningless) from without.

In view of these consequences, though, Heidegger's attempt to retain the basic features of Kant's conception of apriority while transforming them hermeneutically becomes problematic. Precisely to the extent that Heidegger's transformation of the a priori makes us realize that our disclosedness is merely factical, and thus that no given world-disclosure is universally valid or absolute, we must realize that, unfortunately, it is not a happening of *truth*. Such a happening cannot borrow the normative feature of absolute authority from the notion of truth, for nothing "essentially factical" should have an absolute authority over us. We are back to our initial suspicion that Heidegger's characterization of our disclosedness as "essentially factical but true" is paradoxical, to say the least. However, the way from a mere suspicion to an argument may be harder than it seems. For the only alternative that Heidegger's arguments seem to leave open does not look much more appealing than his own proposal. His arguments show that questioning whether historical world-disclosures have absolute authority over those who share them requires accepting that the projection of the being of entities that they contain can turn out to be (empirically) false. However, this seems to be tantamount not only to a rejection of the synthetic a priori status as such; it seems to require defending the implausible claim that all knowledge is synthetic a posteriori, that is, directly revisable through experience. Thus, it seems that without a Kantian conception of apriority, however hermeneutically transformed, we would be condemned to go back to the old problems of either the empiricist or the rationalist conceptions.

In this context, though, I would like to point briefly to what I see as an interesting way out of the Heideggerian puzzle, namely, Putnam's conception of the "contextually a priori."[36] This conception, on the one hand, coincides with Heidegger's in recognizing the hermeneutic roots of the notion of apriority and thus in relativizing it against the Kantian and rationalist views. On the other hand, though, it shows how this can be done without either relativizing the notion of truth, as Heidegger does, or renouncing the notion of apriority entirely, as empiricists do.

Starting with the similarities between Heidegger's and Putnam's conceptions of apriority, both authors would agree that the distinction between synthetic a priori and a posteriori statements is sound and has methodological significance, as Putnam puts it.[37] In particular, both authors identify the same feature of the traditional conception of apriority as significant and worthy of reinterpretation, namely, the idea that there are statements that cannot be directly revised by experience or observation.[38] As Putnam explains in "'Two Dogmas' Revisited": "There are statements in science which can only be overthrown by a new theory . . . and not by observation alone. Such statements *have* a sort of 'apriority' prior to the invention of the new theory which challenges or replaces them: they are *contextually* a priori."[39] Finally, in contradistinction to Kant, both authors assume that what is behind the distinction is not, as Putnam expresses it, "the constitution of human reason" but, to put it in Heideggerian terms, a hermeneutic condition of understanding and interpretation.[40] Accordingly, both approaches temporalize (or detranscendentalize) the synthetic a priori status by understanding it as internal or relative to a specific body of theory and thus as something that changes historically.

In his article "Rethinking Mathematical Necessity," Putnam offers a short overview of the main features of the conception of the "contextually a priori" that he had put forward thirty years earlier in his article "It Ain't Necessarily So." He explains:

The way in which I proposed to draw that distinction is as follows: call a statement empirical relative to a body of knowledge B if possible observations . . . would be known to disconfirm the statement (without drawing on anything outside of that body of knowledge). It seemed to me that this captures pretty well the traditional notion of an empirical statement. Statements which belong to a body of knowledge but which are not empirical relative to that body of knowledge I called "necessary relative to the body of knowledge." The putative truths of Euclidean geometry were, prior to their overthrow, simultaneously synthetic and necessary (in this relativized sense). The point of this new distinction was, as I explained, to emphasize that there are at any given time some accepted statements which cannot be overthrown merely by observations, but can only be overthrown by thinking of a whole body of alternative theory as well. And I insisted (and still insist) that this is a distinction of methodological significance.[41]

So far, it may seem as if Putnam's transformation of the traditional notion of a priori coincides entirely with Heidegger's, at least to the extent that both transformations consist in a relativization of the a priori to specific theories or projections. However, if one looks at Putnam's explanation of the expression "necessary relative to a body of knowledge," the differences become clear. In "It Ain't Necessarily So" Putnam explains: "This notion of necessity relative to a body of knowledge is a technical notion being introduced here for special purposes and to which we give special properties. In particular, when we say that a statement is necessary relative to a body of knowledge, we imply that it is included in that body of knowledge and that it enjoys a special role in that body of knowledge. For example, one is not expected to give much of a reason for that kind of statement. But we do not imply that the statement is necessarily *true*, although, of course, it is thought to be true by someone whose knowledge that body of knowledge is."[42]

This is, of course, the crucial difference with Heidegger's approach. However, the question that this explanation immediately raises is whether this is not also the crucial difference with *any* conception of apriority. At least if one sticks to the traditional conception of apriority, according to which the special status or necessity of a priori statements consist in their being "true in all possible worlds," it seems clear that Putnam's expression "contextually a priori" is not meant to designate *a kind of a priori* knowledge.[43] But then what is the justification or the rationale for using the term *a priori*? According to Putnam's use of the expression, statements that are contextually a priori can indeed be overthrown by later theories and that means precisely that they turn out to be (empirically) false. But in his opinion it would be wrong to conclude from this fact that they were synthetic a posteriori all along. For, relative to the former body of theory, these statements were a priori in the specific sense that *they could not have been revised through the experience* available to that body of theory. This sense of the traditional conception of apriority is what Putnam wants to preserve in his notion of the "contextually a priori." In contradistinction to Heidegger, though, he questions the traditional assumption that the a priori or a posteriori status of a statement is fixed once and for all by virtue of its being the kind of statement that it is.[44]

The rationale behind Putnam's view could be explained in the following way. The need for a relativized notion of apriority is due to a repeated historical experience, namely, that what was once thought to be a priori true according to a body of theory turned out to be false according to the next theory. Now, if one does not question the assumption that "a priori" and "a posteriori" are permanent statuses of statements, this historical fact can only be interpreted in one of the following two ways. One option is to question that the statement at issue was a priori after all, precisely in view of our later judgment. Given that this can happen to any statement (for present evidence is in principle irrelevant according to this view), this option seems to lend support to the empiricist view that all statements are empirical statements.[45] The other possibility is to question that the statement really turned out to be (empirically) false:[46] as Putnam summarizes the argument, "if a statement which appears to be necessary relative to a body of knowledge at one time is not necessary relative to the body of knowledge of a later time, then it is not really the same statement that is involved, words have changed their meaning, and the old statement would still be a necessary truth if the meanings of the words had been kept unchanged."[47] His argument against this alternative is interesting in our context, for it targets precisely the kind of assumptions that are at the core of Heidegger's approach.

As we saw before, Heidegger's argument against the possibility of claiming that the Aristotelian doctrine of motion was proven false by Newton's doctrine was precisely that "in each case, nature means something completely different." This is, of course, only the outline of the argument. A displacement of meaning becomes an argument against the legitimacy of the comparison only under Heidegger's further assumption that meaning determines reference (and thus that a difference in meaning implies ipso facto a difference in reference). Given Heidegger's assumption that what "nature" in each case means determines that to which the respective theories refer, it follows that theories with entirely different conceptions of natural entities cannot be about the same entities. It is for this reason that Heidegger offers a very detailed analysis of Newton's first law of motion in order to show how it changes the Aristotelian understanding of the being of entities to such an extent that it projects an entirely new ontology; in this sense the Aristotelian and Newtonian projections are not about the same entities.[48] If this is the case, though, Heidegger is surely right in claiming that a comparison is meaningless, that according to the way in which nature and entities in general were experienced in the Aristotelian paradigm, Newton's law of motion "would have been meaningless." Thus, by the same token, after Newton's revolution the Aristotelian doctrine of motion became "meaningless" rather than empirically false.[49]

Putnam argues against this kind of view with the help of a different historical example, namely, the changes brought about by the development of non-Euclidean geometries, but this difference does not affect the argument.[50] In "It Ain't Necessarily So" he focuses on two statements of Euclidean geometry, namely, "that one cannot return to one's starting point by traveling on a straight line unless one reverses the sense of one's motion at some point, and that one can visit an arbitrary number of distinct and disjoint 'places' by continuing far enough on a suitable path."[51] He explains:

> If Euclidean geometry is only apparently false owing to a change in the meaning of words, then if we keep the meanings of the words *unchanged*, if we use the words in the old way, Euclidean geometry must *still* be true. . . . The statement that *there are only finitely many disjoint "places" to get to, travel as you may*, expresses a downright "conceptual impossibility" within the framework of Euclidean geometry. And one cannot say that all that has happened is that we have changed the meaning of the word "path," because in that case one would be committed to the metaphysical hypothesis that, in addition to the "paths" that are still so called, there exist others which are somehow physically inaccessible and additional "places" which are somehow physically inaccessible and which, together with what the physicists presently recognize as places and paths, fill out a Euclidean space.[52]

But, as Putnam argues:

> Where are these places? Where are these other paths? In fact they do not exist. If someone believes that they exist, then he must invent special physical laws to explain why, try as we may, we never succeed in seeing one of these other places or in sticking to one of these other paths. . . . Insofar as the terms "place," "path," and "straight line" have any application at all in physical space, they still have the application that they always had; something that was literally inconceivable has turned out to be true.[53]

Here Putnam's argument shows the untenable consequences of a conception of meaning and reference along Heideggerian lines.[54] As we saw before, Heidegger was able to incorporate most of the features of the Kantian conception of apriority into his own hermeneutic conception by incorporating Kant's transcendental idealism into his approach, although it had been transformed into a hermeneutic idealism. The key to this transformation was Heidegger's assumption that meaning determines reference or, to put it in his own terms, that our understanding of the being of entities is what determines entities as entities. Accordingly, a metaphysical projection is a priori in a very strong sense. As a projection of meaning it is at the same time responsible for the constitution of objects.[55] Thus, an alternative projection is (by definition) a projection of *different objects* and thus incommensurable with it. This view seemed to be confirmed by the fact that the experience made possible by the development of the new theory was indeed inaccessible within the framework of the prior body of theory. For what this fact indicates is that, from the point of view of the prior body of theory, objects under the descriptions of the later theory were indeed inaccessible, that is, "literally inconceivable." However, as Putnam argues, the same cannot be claimed of the objects of the prior theory. Given that they were already accessible, unless the mere existence of the new theory made them literally disappear, this view owes us an explanation of why these "different objects" are no longer there. In view of this difficulty, it seems a much better option to question the assumption that meaning determines reference, that is, to recognize that a projection of meaning is simply the best available account of objects, one that may turn out to be incorrectly described. Of course, this recognition is nothing other than a rejection of transcendental idealism in its hermeneutic variety.[56] As a consequence, a projection can be considered a priori only in a much weaker sense. For it is only the lack of an alternative way of accessing objects that makes a given understanding of their being contextually a priori within a given theory. Statements that express such understanding (definitions, axioms, etc.) do indeed have the special status that Heidegger ascribes to them, namely, they express the ontology of the theory. But, contrary to Heidegger's view, this only means that they cannot be meaningfully revised *until a better account of the same objects is available*. However, once such an account becomes available, the status of the prior statements changes in a very important way. Precisely as a consequence of having more than one way to access the same objects, these statements no longer have the status of *defining* which objects are being referred to; they just become one way among others of describing them and thus may turn out to be (empirically) false.[57] Thus, to put it in Heideggerian terms, what had the status of ontological knowledge in the previous theory turns out to be just ontic knowledge for the following one.

Seen in this light, Putnam's conception of the "contextually apriori" questions the core assumption of Heidegger's interpretation of the ontological difference, namely, that there is an absolute and permanent dichotomy between two different kinds of knowledge (ontic and ontological) and their respective kinds of truths. According to Putnam, a statement is contextually a priori relative to a given body of theory, if it is not possible within such a body of theory to specify a way in which it could be actually false.[58] As long as this is the case, Putnam would agree with Heidegger in claiming that this statement is "indispensable" for this body of theory in the specific sense that it cannot be questioned from within. But this by no means excludes the possibility that in the future some rival theory may be developed that will in fact show a specific way in which such a statement may actually be false and thus in need of revision. In this sense, Heidegger's relativization of the Kantian conception of apriority seems plausible in tracing its roots back to a hermeneutic origin, namely, the lack of interpretative alternatives in a given historical situation. But in the wake of Heidegger's hermeneutic idealism the lack of interpretative alternatives turns out to be an intrinsic (and thus permanent) condition of any understanding of being as such, for any alternative to it must be necessarily meaningless. However, without any independent reasons to accept this idealist assumption it does not seem plausible to interpret the lack of alternatives in a given hermeneutic situation as being anything more than what it seems, namely, an entirely contingent fact. To the extent that this situation cannot be overcome at will, it seems indeed justified to confer a special status to our understanding of being as contextually a priori. But, to the extent that it could in principle be overcome, there seems to be no reason to interpret this status in the normative terms of an absolute authority over us that knowledge a priori was supposed to have before its hermeneutic transformation.

CHAPTER 9

Heidegger's Topology of Being

Jeff Malpas

> The more I study nature around home, the more I am moved by it. The thunderstorm, perceived not only in its more extreme manifestations, but precisely as a power and feature among the various other forms of the sky, the light, active as a principle and resembling fate, working to impart national shape so that we might possess something sacred, the urgency of its comings and goings, the particular character of its forests, and the way in which the diversities of nature all converge in one area, so that all the holy places of the earth come together in a single place, and the philosophical light around my window—all this is now my joy. Let me not forget that I have come this far.
> —Friedrich Hölderlin[1]

HANS-GEORG GADAMER, perhaps Heidegger's best-known student, described his own work as an attempt to adhere to, and to make accessible in a new way, the line of thinking developed by Heidegger in his essay, first given as a series of lectures three times between 1935 and 1936, "The Origin of the Work of Art" ("Der Ursprung des Kunstwerkes").[2] In this essay Heidegger argues that the work of art is not to be construed in representational terms but rather in its character, as a work, in opening and establishing a world. Heidegger takes as his central example a Greek temple (in fact, he seems to have in mind a very specific temple, the temple of Hera at Paestum), of which he writes:

A building, a Greek temple, portrays nothing. It simply stands there in the middle of the rock-cleft valley. The building encloses the figure of the god, and in this concealment lets it stand out into the holy precinct through the open portico, By means of the temple, the god is present in the temple. . . . [The temple] first fits together and at the same time gathers around itself the unity of those paths and relations in which birth and death, disaster and blessing, victory and disgrace, endurance and decline acquire the shape of destiny for human being. The all-governing expanse of this open relational context is the world of this historical people. . . . The temple-work, standing there, opens up a world . . . the temple, in its standing there, first gives to things their look and to men their outlook on themselves.[3]

Crucial to this account is the role of the artwork in the establishing of a world, where such "establishing" is seen as identical with the "happening" of truth, understood, not uncontroversially, as that which first allows things to be seen and so enables the possibility of particular truths. Heidegger thus focuses on the way in which a particular thing opens up a realm of understanding and illumination that goes beyond the particular thing itself. The particular thing, most characteristically the artwork, stands at the center of a larger horizon in which other things, an entire world, are brought to light within an essentially relational context (for they are shown in their relation to the thing that stands at the center of the horizon). For Gadamer, this account provides the basis for the development of a hermeneutic theory as well as an aesthetics; for me, what is of interest is its broader significance for philosophy and ontology—as well as for the idea of the transcendental.

In "The Origin of the Work of Art," we see Heidegger trying to articulate what he later comes to call the "topology of being," that is, an account of the "place" in which things come to presence, in which they come to be. In "The Origin of the Work of Art," he refers to this "place" using the German *Stätte*, but elsewhere he talks of it in terms of *Topos*, *Ort*, or *Ortschaft* (all of which can be translated as "place," although *Ortschaft* is sometimes given as "settlement" or "locality"). Talk of "place" here carries a certain ambiguity, for the "place of being" names both a generalized structure that is variously described by Heidegger at different stages in his thinking (in "The Origin of the Work of Art" it is described in terms of the "strife" between the concealment of Earth and the openness of World that is the twofold established in and through the work that is the temple), but since that structure is always a structure given particular instantiation in *this* place, so it also names *each and every* place in and around which things are brought to presence and the "worlding" of world occurs.

The idea of the inquiry into being as an inquiry into the place of being is apparent very early in Heidegger's career, in his lecture notes from the course he gave in the summer semester of 1923 in Freiburg. There we find him preoccupied with what he calls "facticity," which he characterizes in terms of the way in which Dasein is "in each case 'this' Dasein in its being-there for a while at a particular time."[4] Facticity is that aspect of our own being according to which we find ourselves already given over to things, according to which our being is indeed always a being *there*—according to which it is always already "in" the world. If the analysis of facticity is a central concern here, then, so too is Heidegger concerned to investigate the nature of the world and of the "wherein" that characterizes our own being in relation to the world. The world, claims Heidegger, is that which environs or surrounds us and also that toward which we are oriented, about which we are concerned and to which we attend. But how do we encounter the world? And if our encounter with the world is always an encounter with respect to particular things and situations, how are these encountered?

Heidegger proposes to answer these questions by looking to our everyday, precritical encounter with things. The example on which he focuses is an ordinary thing of the home or the workplace, a table. How is the table first encountered? We might be inclined to say, as a material thing, as something "with such and such a weight, such and such a color, such and such a shape,"[5] as a thing that also offers an infinity of possible perceptual appearances. The thing as material, natural thing can be distinguished from the thing as it might be evaluated or used—as it might be significant or meaningful. Heidegger denies, however, that the thing grasped as mere object, either as natural object or as meaningful object, is what is first encountered. Instead what is prior is the "in the world" as such, as that is articulated in and around specific things such as the table, but not any table, this table, the table before us now. Thus Heidegger tells us, "This schema must be avoided: What exists are subjects and objects, consciousness and being."[6] We cannot first posit things aside from our dealings with those things nor the selves involved in those dealings aside from things. Instead Heidegger turns to an analysis of an example taken from his own being-there, a description of the table in his family home:

What is there in *the* room there at home is *the* table (not "a" table among many other tables in other rooms and other houses) at which one sits *in order to* write, have a meal, sew, play. Everyone sees this right away, e.g. during a visit: it is a writing table, a dining table, a sewing table—such is the primary way it is a being encountered in itself. This characteristic of "in order to do something" is not merely imposed on the table by relating and assimilating it to something else which it is not. Its standing-there in the room means: Playing this role in such and such characteristic use. This and that about it is "impractical," unsuitable. That part is damaged. It now stands in a better spot in the room than before—there's better lighting, for example. . . . Here and there it shows lines—the boys like to busy themselves at the table. Those lines are not just interruptions in the paint, but rather: it was the boys and it still is. This side is not the east side, and this side so many cm. shorter than the other, but rather the one at which my wife sits in the evening when she wants to stay up and read, there at the table we had such and such a discussion that time, there that decision was made with a *friend* at that time, there that *work* was written at that time, there that holiday celebrated at that time. That is *the* table as such it is there in the temporality of everydayness.[7]

There are a number of points that are worth noting in this passage. The first is the way in which Heidegger takes the encounter with the world to have its origin and focus in our prior involvement with a particular thing that is itself implicated in a larger system of relationships. The world is thus understood as relational but also as brought to focus around particular nodal points within the web of the relations that constitute the world. Moreover, in the encounter with the thing, we also encounter ourselves and others. What is primary, then, is not the bare encounter with some "de-worlded," disconnected "object," nor do we first find ourselves as that which stands in opposition to that object, but instead we find self and thing presented together as part of one system of interrelation. With more recent philosophical developments in mind we may say that the account Heidegger offers here is a form of "externalist" theory of the self; the account also bears comparison with Davidson's externalist position as articulated in papers such as "Three Varieties of Knowledge" (although there are notable differences).[8] But it may be better to say that what Heidegger does here is to reject both externalist and internalist accounts, presenting instead a view according to which what comes first is the world in which both self and thing are bound together and in which each is articulated in relation to the other.

The account that is adumbrated in the 1923 lectures on facticity is, of course, further developed in *Being and Time* (*Sein und Zeit*) published in 1927. The question of being posed in the latter work is answered by looking to an analysis of the structure of the mode of being of a particular being—the being for whom being is itself in question and to which Heidegger gives the name (at least in this work) *Dasein*. From the outset it is important to note, however, that Heidegger's question of being—not only in this work but throughout his thinking—is not a question that asks for some underlying principle or definition of being, nor is it a question that asks for some sort of analysis of the internal ontological structure of independently existing entities. The question of being is not a question about how things, already understood as present to us, are constituted as the beings that they are, but, prior to this, it asks how it is that any being can even come to be present.

In terms of the existing philosophical tradition, Heidegger's question of being must be understood as more closely related to the Kantian transcendental question concerning the conditions for the possibility of synthetic a priori judgment than it is to contemporary inquiries concerning identity, causality, and so forth as these relate to the structure of "reality" or the universe. Indeed, while this way of understanding the question of being is important for Heidegger's work as a whole, it is especially important for *Being and Time*, and the work of the late 1920s and early 1930s, precisely because of the way in which Heidegger's own thought during this period takes the form of a concentrated engagement with Kant, particularly with the *Critique of Pure Reason*. Thus the projected second Part of *Being and Time* was to have included a "de-struction" of the history of ontology, in which Kant was a major focus, while the second major work Heidegger published after *Being and Time* was entirely devoted to the *Critique of Pure Reason*—Heidegger's so-called *Kantbuch, Kant and the Problem of Metaphysics* (*Kant und das Problem der Metaphysik*) (1929).

Since *Being and Time* takes the question of being as a question to be pursued through an analysis of the structure of Dasein—literally there/here-being—and since Dasein is understood as being-in-the-world, so the analysis of Dasein is also an analysis of the structure of world or worldhood. As in the earlier work, this analysis gives priority to the relational structure of active engagement in which both we and the things around us are brought together and mutually articulated. Thus Heidegger focuses the early part of his analysis in *Being and Time* on Dasein as being-in-the-world, and so on the structure of "being-in" and worldhood. As in the earlier work, Heidegger sees the world as established through the interrelations that obtain between Dasein and the things around it, as well as through the interrelations between those things as such. Indeed, Heidegger analyzes the structure of world in terms of the structure of "equipment" (*das Zeug*), that together constitutes a system of relationships or "assignments" (one system of such assignments, or part of one, is seen in the workshop), and he famously talks of the way in which the world is itself brought to light through the breakdown in the system of relationships between equipment—through the broken tool:

> The structure of the Being of what is ready-to-hand as equipment is determined by references or assignments . . . When an assignment has been disturbed—when something is unusable for some purpose—then the assignment becomes explicit. Even now, of course, it has not become explicit as an ontological structure; but it has become explicit ontically for the circumspection which comes up against the damaging of the tool. When an assignment to some particular "towards-this" has been thus circumspectively aroused, we catch sight of the "towards-this" itself, and along with it everything concerned with the work—the whole "workshop"—as that wherein concern already dwells. The context of equipment is lit up, not as something never seen before, but as a totality constantly sighted beforehand in circumspection. With this totality, however, the world announces itself.[9]

The argument of *Being and Time* also makes clear, however, that the character of equipmental engagement is derivative of the structure of temporality—an idea present too in *The Hermeneutics of Facticity* (*Hermeneutik der Faktizität*). The ordering of self and thing within the larger horizon of the world is itself determined by the ordering of past, present, and future (something already indicated in the earlier work) and captured in terms of the notions of care (*Sorge*) and being-toward-death, both of which can be taken as tied essentially to facticity. It is through the being in question of Dasein's being, which is evident in care and in the recognition of death, that beings are themselves brought to presence. We might also say that it is through Dasein's "being-there," and so through the *Da* that is integral to Dasein's own being, and that is worked out in and through Dasein's concrete involvement with things, that any other being can be brought to light. The structure that is evident here is essentially the same as the structure that we saw earlier in "The Origin of the Work of Art": the coming to presence of things, the establishing of world, the happening of truth, occurs in and through a particular place or site, in and through the temple, in and through the *Da*, the here/there, the place, of *Sein*. What distinguishes *Being and Time* from the later discussions, however, is that the framework of *Being and Time* includes no specific reference to topology but is instead pursued from within a "transcendental" framework (one that is also hermeneutically and phenomenologically nuanced) that is in accord with the Kantian orientation of the earlier work.

It is significant, particularly in light both of *Being and Time*'s transcendental orientation and of Heidegger's own later critique of the earlier work, that in *Being and Time* it is the projective activity of Dasein that seems to establish the ordering of equipment and the ordering of the world that comes from this. Indeed, the projective activity of Dasein is itself based in Dasein's own being as that is determined by care, being-toward-death, and temporality. In this respect, temporality can be seen as opening up space—the space within which the structure of equipmentality is itself articulated—and thereby establishing a world. Rather like Bergson, Heidegger appears here to be temporalizing space, in reaction, perhaps, to the dominant spatialization of time. But insofar as the opening up of world is indeed based in Dasein's projecting character, and insofar as this is already presupposed in the idea of Dasein as the being for whom being is in question, so the structure of being, and the structure of world, is given just in the questioning, and questionable, character of Dasein's own being. World is founded in the projection of Dasein, which is not itself something that is determined by Dasein but is simply Dasein's own mode of being as such. The same is true in "The Origin of the Work of Art," although there the character of Dasein as "projecting" has been taken over by the role of the poet, or perhaps the statesman, as founding a world in the founding of a people and a destiny.

It might seem, however, that in its general form the account I have so far outlined is problematic, if for no other reason than that it appears to be circular. If what is at issue is the coming to presence or appearing of things that is identical with the establishing of world, and if this occurs only in relation to that kind of being which is being-in-the-world but which is itself worked out in relation to things and to world as such, then isn't this a strategy that looks to explain world, and the appearing of things within it, on the basis of that same world? Put more charitably, one might argue that Heidegger provides no real explanation, only a description. There is something right about this point—but it is correct only inasmuch as it reflects a core point in Heidegger's own approach. As Heidegger understands it, the question of being is not a question that is answered by looking to some explanatory or causal foundation, although to do so is precisely what metaphysics has traditionally attempted. But Heidegger claims that the metaphysical tradition has consistently misunderstood or forgotten being. Being is not some being apart from or in addition to beings. And that means there is nothing to which one can appeal in answer to the question of being other than being itself. It is this circularity that Heidegger himself brings to attention at a number of points in *Being and Time*.[10] So what then is being? Nothing other than the appearing or presencing of beings as such, and that means that being and world, or at least what Heidegger calls the "worlding of world," are closely tied together. Neither being nor world, however, can be explicated other than through an articulation of the structural elements that are integral to them. Thus the only possible strategy for Heidegger to adopt is indeed a certain "descriptive" strategy—a strategy that tries to explicate being through uncovering the structure within which certain elements are interrelated and unified. In this respect, Heidegger takes the Kantian idea of "analytic," as set out in the *Critique of Pure Reason*, as the basis for his own methodology. Thus Heidegger writes: "In the ontological sense, 'the analytic' is not a reduction into elements, but the articulation of the [a priori] unity of a composite structure [*Strukturgefüge*]. This is also essential in my concept of the 'analytic of Da-sein.'"[11] Elsewhere he talks of the "methodological tendency" "to derive everything and anything from some simple primal ground"—a tendency he rejects in favor of a structure of what he terms "equiprimordial elements."[12]

Gadamer himself addresses the aspect of Heidegger's approach that is at issue here, discussing its origins in the phenomenological method but also emphasizing its "descriptive" and "visionary" character—Heidegger was, he says, "a thinker who sees":

> And this "seeing" occurs not only in momentary evocations in which a striking word is found and an intuition flashes for a fleeting moment. The entire conceptual analysis is not presented as an argued progression from one concept to another; rather the analysis is made by approaching the same "thing" from the most diverse perspectives, thus giving the conceptual description the character of the plastic arts, that is, the three-dimensionality of tangible reality.[13]

Heidegger looks always, in his analyses of being, to the elaboration of a single structure. In doing so, he does not seek to explain by looking to some principle outside or beyond what is to be explained. Here his strategy is usefully illustrated by appeal to the idea, if not quite of topology, then of topography. The method of topographical surveying is one that looks to build up a map of a certain landscape, not by looking to some single vantage point from which all can be seen or by deducing that landscape from some underlying and determining structure, but rather by looking to the way that landscape is constituted through the inter-relations between the landmarks that make it up—a set of interrelations worked out through repeated triangulation and traverse.[14] This "topographical" method is what essentially underlies Heidegger's later development of the idea of topology—of what he terms a *Topologie des Seyns*—although in his earlier work it is also associated with an explicitly transcendental mode of proceeding. Indeed, the transcendental can perhaps itself be understood as attempting something like such a topology inasmuch as it too depends on the articulation of the unity of a set of interconnected elements within a single field.[15]

Heidegger comes only gradually to articulate the ideas that are crucial here. And the way he sets those ideas out in *Being and Time* presents some problems that are quite distinct from any simple "begging of the question." Those problems can be seen to underlie the shift in Heidegger's thinking that occurs around the time of "The Origin of the Work of Art" and in the period immediately before and after—the famous "Turning" or "Reversal" in his thinking (*die Kehre*) which he presented not as a break with his earlier work so much as a continuation and radicalization of it. The Turning is, however, an equivocal notion.[16] It already appears in the plan of *Being and Time*, inasmuch as Division Three of Part 1 of that work was supposed to have involved a "turning" from the temporality of Dasein to the temporality of being. Indeed, a common reading of the Turning in Heidegger's thought is that it is also to be construed as a turning from Dasein, from human being, to being as such. The Turning is thus often held to have its origin in Heidegger's inability to complete the project set out in *Being and Time*. There is no doubt that the Turning is associated with Heidegger's shift away from the framework of *Being and Time* (although that framework is still present in Heidegger's thinking until at least 1933, when it remains clearly present in the background of the infamous *Rektoratsrede*), but it is not to be simply assimilated to the same turning that was to have been accomplished in *Being and Time*. In fact, the Turning refers to a movement in thinking itself, a movement that involves a turning back to being from the usual forgetfulness of being that characterizes metaphysics. In this respect, and inasmuch as it does indeed represent a modification (but not rejection) of the project partially carried out in *Being and Time*, the Turning can be seen to involve a turning *away* from the transcendental, and, one might also say, metaphysical character of that project. Thus Heidegger himself criticizes *Being and Time*, particularly in the "Letter on 'Humanism'" ("Brief über den 'Humanismus'") of 1949, for remaining still too much within the framework of traditional metaphysics.[17] Indeed, what Heidegger says of *Being and Time* in this regard is especially illuminating. Repeating a crucial sentence from the introduction to *Being and Time*: "Being is the *transcendens* pure and simple,"[18] Heidegger comments that "whether the definition of being as the *transcendens* pure and simple really does name the simple essence of the truth of being—this and this alone is the primary question for a thinking that attempts to think the truth of being."[19]

The notion of transcendence that is at issue here is a notion central to much of Heidegger's thinking at least from the period 1926–29, but the content of the notion requires some clarification. In *The Metaphysical Foundations of Logic* (*Metaphysische Anfangsgründe der Logik*) from 1928, Heidegger writes that:

> *Transcendence* means the surpassing, the going beyond. . . . Transcendence is . . . the primordial constitution of the *subjectivity* of a subject. . . . To be a subject means to transcend. . . . Transcendence does not mean crossing a barrier that has fenced off the subject in an inner space. But what gets crossed over is the being itself that can become manifest to the subject on the very basis of the subject's transcendence. . . . Therefore, what Dasein surpasses in its transcendence is not a gap or barrier "between" itself and objects. But beings, among which Dasein factically is, get surpassed by Dasein . . . beings get surpassed and can subsequently become objects. . . . That "toward which" the subject, as subject, transcends is not an object, not at all this or that being. . . . That toward which the subject transcends is what we call world . . . because this primordial being of Dasein, as surpassing, crosses over to a world, we characterize the basic phenomenon of Dasein's transcendence with the expression being-in-the-world.[20]

This focus on the problem of transcendence, on being as transcendence, and on transcendence as naming the structure of human Dasein, of subjectivity, is characteristic of the framework that Heidegger develops in *Being and Time*.[21] It also indicates the indebtedness of that work to Husserl and Kant, and so the extent to which that work operates within a transcendental and phenomenological framework.

As Heidegger uses the term *transcendental*, however, it refers us to two senses of transcendence. The first is the sense outlined above—the way in which Dasein transcends beings in the direction of world (or, as Heidegger puts it elsewhere, transcends objects in the direction of their objectness). The second is the sense involved in the idea of the transcendent as that which goes beyond world and from which Kant himself clearly distinguishes the idea of the transcendental.[22] The transcendental can be said to be that which underlies the structure of transcendence in both of these senses—as it refers us to the structure that makes possible transcendence in the first sense and also marks off as unfounded transcendence in the second sense[23]—although it is to the first of these two senses that it relates more directly, and so, for Heidegger, the transcendental is most often understood as that which makes possible the transcendence of things in the direction of world. As it underlies such transcendence, so the analysis of the transcendental structure is always directed at the analysis of the structure of Dasein on the basis of which such transcendence is possible. In this respect, the transcendental as it appears in Heidegger is always associated with a particular set of philosophical, one might almost say metaphysical, commitments, and it is this on which Heidegger himself seems to focus in his discussions of the transcendental. The transcendental is always, for Heidegger, tied to the attempt to articulate the possibility of transcendence as it is grounded in the structure of human Dasein and understood in terms of Dasein's surpassing of beings in the direction of world and of being. It is perhaps no surprise, then, that Heidegger comes to view *Being and Time* itself as indeed still enmeshed in metaphysics inasmuch as it remains preoccupied with the problem of transcendence. Moreover, since the focus on transcendence, and on the transcendental, is also part of Heidegger's engagement with Kant, so Heidegger's working through the problem of the transcendental is also a working through Kant—a working through from which he eventually emerges in the mid-1930s. As Heidegger later wrote in the preface to the republished edition of the Kant book: "With *Being and Time* alone—: soon/ clear that we did not enter into/the real question. . . . A refuge—underway and/not new discoveries in Kant Philology."[24]

The "Turning" in Heidegger's thinking is thus itself a turn back to being away from the oblivion of being that is characteristic of metaphysics, away from forgetfulness of the proper relation between being and human being, away from the transcendental and the focus on transcendence, away from the preoccupation with the objectness of the object. So, in *Contributions to Philosophy (from Enowning)* (*Beiträge zur Philosophie [Vom Ereignis]*), Heidegger writes:

Even when "transcendence" is grasped differently than up to now, namely as *surpassing* and not as the *super-sensible* as a being, even then this determination all too easily dissembles what is ownmost to Dasein. For, even in this way, transcendence still presupposes an *under and this-side* [*Unten und Diesseits*] and is in danger of still being misinterpreted after all as the action of an "I" and a subject.[25]

Moreover, just as the idea of transcendence drops away, so too is the notion of Dasein reconfigured. Thus, while Heidegger often insists that *Being and Time* had already clearly rejected any simply subjectivism or idealism, nevertheless he also tells us that "in *Being and Time*, Da-sein still stands in the shadow of the 'anthropological,' the 'subjectivistic,' and the 'individualist,' etc."[26] In fact, the term *Dasein* appears less frequently in Heidegger's work after the mid-1930s. And if we look to the *Beiträge*, some ten or so years later than *Being and Time*, we find that Da-sein is regularly hyphenated and also seems no longer to refer to the essence of human being in the way it had in 1927.[27] If Da-sein does continue to refer to the essence of human, that is, mortal, being, then it does so by naming that in the sway of which mortal being always stands but which also encompasses the other elements of world as their origin and ground. In the *Beiträge*, Da-sein names something much closer to a *topos*, a place, and instead of the structure of being-in-the-world that was the focus of *Being and Time*, Heidegger now elaborates a structure that is the structure of the *Da* of *Sein*, the *topos* of being. Da-sein is the opened, cleared realm, the "between" that unites as well as differentiates the elements of world, thereby allowing the world itself to open (indeed, the world is this disclosive opening), revealing the things that stand within that world, giving to humans the possibility of a history and a future. As Heidegger comments, "Da-sein is to be taken as time-space, not in the sense of the usual concepts of time and space but as the site for the moment of the grounding of the truth of being,"[28] and again: "Da-sein is the turning point in the turning of Ereignis. . . . Da-sein is the *between* [*das Zwischen*] between man (as history-grounding) and gods (in their history). The between [*Zwischen*] [is] not one that first ensues from the relation of gods to humans, but rather that between [*Zwischen*] which above all grounds the time-space for the relation."[29] Moreover, while Da-sein is to be understood as this "between," it is nevertheless not to be understood in terms of transcendence: "This 'between' is, however, not a 'transcendence' with reference to man. Rather it is the opposite: that open to which man belongs as the founder and preserver wherein as Da-sein he is en-owned [*er-eignet*] by be-ing itself—be-ing that holds sway as nothing other than en-owning [*Ereignis*]."[30] Transcendence itself can only be understood on the basis of this owning and opening. The Turning is thus the Turning of the *Ereignis* itself, in which mortals are brought into the sway of being and in which a world is established through the opening of the *Da*, the there, the place.

The shift away from transcendence, away from human Dasein as identical with transcendence, is inevitably, of course, a shift away from the framework of *Being and Time*. Gadamer directs attention to a marginal note in *Being and Time* in which Heidegger talks of "the place of the understanding of Being" (*Stätte des Seinsverständnisses*), an expression with which, says Gadamer, "Heidegger wants to mediate between the older point of departure from Dasein (in which its being is at stake) and the new movement of thought of the 'there' [*Da*] in which *das Sein* or Being forms a clearing. In the word place [*Stätte*] this latter emphasis comes to the fore: it is the scene of an event and not primarily the site of an activity by Dasein."[31] The core concepts are now the concepts of truth, understood as *aletheia*, uncovering, and openness, as the opening of the place of being. Thus, at the end of the 1964 essay "The End of Philosophy and the Task of Thinking" ("Das Ende der Philosophie und die Aufgabe des Denkens"), Heidegger writes: "Does the name for the task of thinking then read instead of Being and Time: Opening and Presence?"[32] In this way we can characterize the Heideggerian shift away from the transcendental precisely in terms of a shift in how Heidegger understands the *Da*. Yet in characterizing the shift in this way, what remains constant is the essentially topological orientation of Heidegger's thought—an orientation that is constant from the period of *Being and Time* and earlier, through to the *Beiträge*, and after. Heidegger's abandonment of the transcendental is thus an abandonment of the preoccupation with transcendence, not an abandonment of the topology that is itself a crucial element in the idea of the transcendental and that is even present, I would suggest, in Kant.[33]

The structure that we see set out in the *Beiträge* is developed further in Heidegger's later thinking. In particular, the *Ereignis* structure we find in the *Beiträge*, expressed in terms of the Fourfold (*Das Geviert*) of earth, sky, gods, and mortals—itself understood as the gathering and establishing of world—is the explicit focus of essays such as "The Thing" ("Das Ding") and "Building Dwelling Thinking" ("Bauen Wohnen Denken"), from 1950 and 1951. But as in his earlier work, this *Ereignis*, this gathering of world and of the elements of world to one another, while it is a gathering that can be described in ways that are not dependent on any particular place or thing, nevertheless occurs always in relation to specific things and places. In "Building Dwelling Thinking," Heidegger uses the example of a bridge, and one of the bridges he has in mind is clearly the Alte Brücke in the city of Heidelberg:

> The bridge swings over the stream "with ease and power." It does not just connect banks that are already there. The banks emerge as banks only as the bridge crosses the stream. . . . With the banks, the bridge brings to the stream the one and the other expanse of the landscape lying behind them. It brings stream and bank and land into each other's neighborhood. The bridge *gathers* the earth as landscape around the stream. . . . The bridge lets the stream run its course and at the same time grants their way to mortals so that they may come and go from shore to shore. . . . Always and ever differently the bridge escorts the lingering and hastening ways of men to and fro. . . . The bridge *gathers*, as a passage that crosses, before the gods—whether we explicitly think of, and visibly give thanks for, their presence. . . . The bridge *gathers* to itself *in its own* way earth and sky, divinities and mortals. The bridge is a place. As such it allows a space into which earth and sky, gods and mortals are admitted.[34]

Significantly, while the bridge only appears within a cleared realm, a world, that itself necessarily involves mortals, as it also involves the gods, earth, and sky, still the bridge is not something that is brought into salience merely through the projective activity of mortals. The building of the bridge is something mortals do, but the appearing of the bridge as a bridge is brought about through the worlding of the world, that is, through the world's coming to be as world, through the gathering of the elements of world within the differentiating unity of the Fourfold. In this latter respect, the ordering and establishing of world that enables the bridge to appear as a bridge also enables the mortals themselves to come to light. This means, of course, that the mortals come to light precisely as mortal—as beings that die—but here it is not so much death as our "ownmost possibility" that is given primary emphasis—death as a mark of radical finitude, of essential uncanniness, which was the focus of *Being and Time*—but rather death as nothingness, as the ultimate ungroundedness of things, death as the marker of our belonging to the constant "sway" of being.

Recognizing our being as mortals, then, is not a matter simply of facing up to the fact that we die, but more significantly, it means recognizing the way in which we are already given over to the world, to the Fourfold that also encompasses the gods, earth, and sky—it is a matter of recognizing our own belonging within the sway of being, of our own already being gathered into the opening and presencing of what Heidegger calls *Ereignis*. To say that we dwell is to say that we already belong, as mortals, to the Fourfold, but it is also to call upon us to grasp the fact of that dwelling. And while Heidegger is not clear on this point, dwelling would seem to refer to both our prior belonging in this fashion (to our being always already given over to dwelling and so to gathering of *Ereignis*) and to the possibility of that prior belonging itself becoming a determining element in the manner of that dwelling. Dwelling is a matter of our prior belonging, and it is also a matter of our being recalled to that belonging—a matter of remembrance and of return.[35]

The happening of world that occurs in and through the gathering of the Fourfold is also, in the language of the *Beiträge*, the happening of Da-sein—it is, we might say, the "place-ing of being." Similarly, *Ereignis* is a matter of topoi-esis—a gathering/opening of/into place. As the manner of mortal being is dwelling, so dwelling is always a being-in-place (and not merely "being-in-the-world"). Yet although the place at issue here is not the idea of some abstract generality—we are always brought to place here/there, in this very spot—still there is no one place that can be given primacy here, no one place that is privileged in respect of being, no one place that alone allows us properly to dwell. The happening of place, as a gathering of world, and so as an opening and presencing, does not distinguish between the Black Forest or a Greek island, between Times Square or the Australian outback. There may well be differences in the exact manner of the gathering and happening of place in these cases, but in each there is a placing, a gathering, an *Ereignis*. Aside from attentiveness to the different character of each such placing, the difficulty is to keep sight of the way in which the happening of being is always such a coming to place, and so is always concretely placed in this way and yet is not exclusive to any one such place. Yet inevitably, of course, one will find oneself calling upon one's own place, one's vocabulary of place, in the attempt to talk about the happening, the place-ing, that is at issue here, and Heidegger is certainly no exception in this regard.

Nevertheless, inasmuch as Heidegger is indeed centrally concerned to understand place as the *Da* of Being, so the place he seeks to understand is not any particular place but rather the place that makes every such place possible. In the "Conversation on a Country Path" ("Feldweg-Gespräch"), we find Heidegger struggling to find a language in which to express this idea.

> The region gathers, just as if nothing were happening, each to each and each to all into an abiding, while resting in itself. Regioning is a gathering and re-sheltering, for an expanded resting in an abiding. So the region itself is at once an expanse and an abiding. It abides into the expanse of resting. It expands into the abiding of what has been freely turned toward itself.[36]

This regioning is just the idea of the coming to be of a place that is the place of the Fourfold, but that is not a place that looks inward so much as expanding outward—a place that opens into world. Indeed, the Heideggerian idea that the fundamental concern of thinking is to uncover and to articulate this "place of being," which is that which opens out to a world while it also enables mortals to see themselves in their relation to the elements of the world—earth, sky, and gods—can be seen as telling us something about both world and place. On this account, place is indeed an opening or clearing, while the world is that which can only come to pass inasmuch as it is opened up through such a clearing. Yet no one clearing achieves this: the clearing occurs everywhere that gods and mortals, earth and sky are brought together. Only in and through such a clearing is world possible, because only in and through such a clearing can the interconnectedness of world be brought into its proper, if differentiated, unity. Moreover only in and through such a clearing can world be constituted as an opening into possibility, into infinity:

> Infinite means that the ends and the sides, the regions of the relation do not stand by themselves cut-off and one-sidedly; rather, freed of one-sidedness and finitude, they belong infinitely to one another in the relation which "thoroughly" holds them together from its centre. The centre, so-called because it centres, that is, mediates, is neither earth nor heaven, God nor man. The in-finity that is to be thought here is abysmally different from that which is merely without end, which, because of its uniformity, allows no growth. On the other hand the "more tender relation" of earth and heaven, God and man, can become more in-finite. For what is not one-sided can come more purely to light from the intimacy in which the named four are bound to each other.[37]

The world is thus not, contra Wittgenstein, "all that is the case"—it is not a mere sum or totality—but a complex, differentiated, and infinite unity.

The emphasis on the complex unity of the world, and on place as the focal point for such unity, is particularly significant, for it is already evident in the idea of the transcendental as concerned with explicating the structure of transcendence in terms of the integral connection of what Heidegger terms "equiprimordial" elements. The problem with the transcendental is that it sees the structure at issue here as having to be grounded in the structure of a Dasein that is itself tied, in one way or another, to human subjectivity. Moreover, inasmuch as it is already based on the idea of an explication of the structure of transcendence as a "surpassing" by Dasein in the direction of world, so it already presents a bifurcation between Dasein as that which is the ground of transcendence and world as that toward which transcendence must move. Transcendence thus arises as a problem out of the distinction between Dasein and its world that the transcendental aims to overcome—this is itself evident in the bifurcation in the idea of transcendence that enables it to refer both to the idea of Dasein's reaching out beyond objects to their objectness, beyond beings to world, and to that which goes beyond Dasein and world. The problem with the transcendental, then, is that in spite of its already topological orientation, it is nevertheless predicated on a way of understanding being that is already disjunctive, already threatens the unity of being's occurrence. Indeed, one might go so far as to say that this disjunction remains present to some extent in that central Heideggerian idea of the ontological difference and its emphasis on the distinction between being and beings. It is precisely for this reason that the ontological difference must be understood not in terms of the disjunction between being and beings (this is how the metaphysical tradition has understood, and thereby misunderstood and obliterated, the difference), but rather in terms of their essential belonging together. The ontological difference thus properly names the same belonging together that is referred to in terms of the "between" that holds open the structure of world.[38] It is this same "difference" that is referred to by Heidegger in his poem on Cézanne:

> In the late work of the painter the twofoldness
> of what is present and of presence has become
> one, "realised" and overcome at the same time
> transformed into a mystery-filled identity.[39]

The attempt to articulate the place of being is itself an attempt to articulate what Cézanne paints: the differentiated unity that is the happening of world in and through place.

The explicit focus on place—on *topos, Da, Ort, Ortschaft*—in Heidegger's late thinking is thus not tied up with some romantic longing or nostalgia for a "heimisch" origin. Instead, it follows from the topological character of

Heidegger's thinking as a whole and is a direct consequence of the attempt to address the question of being in a way that remains to true to being as such, but which is also true to the belonging together of being and beings, of presence and what is present. All of Heidegger's thought, as he himself said, can be construed as an attempt to articulate the place of being.[40] And in doing this, what Heidegger attempts is something that is difficult and even obscure, largely because it is so fundamental, so simple and so close: "The one thing thinking would like to attain and for the first time tries to articulate in *Being and Time* is something simple. As such, being remains mysterious, the simple nearness of an unobtrusive prevailing."[41] And elsewhere he writes: "To think being does not require a solemn approach and the pretension of arcane erudition, nor the display of rare and exceptional states as in mystical raptures, reveries and swoonings. All that is needed is simple wakefulness in the presence of any random unobtrusive being, an awakening that all of a sudden sees that the being 'is.'"[42] The homecoming that Heidegger finds spoken of in Hölderlin is thus a homecoming that indeed consists in a remembrance of and a return to a place that properly we can never leave.[43] Heidegger's task of thinking is to achieve such a homecoming, a homecoming that must always be carried out in each and every place and time. We may choose to say that, for Heidegger, philosophy itself is such a homecoming, but we may also wonder, as Heidegger did himself, whether it is proper to speak of this still as philosophy at all. Heidegger talks of thinking, a kind of meditative thinking, that looks to preserve the place of being, to speak it, and in so doing provide us with a reminder of who and what we are, of our own being as mortal creatures, born and destined to die, and yet nevertheless given over to a world that itself shines, as Heidegger puts it, as a world, as a world that shines in the truth and beauty of gathered place.

CHAPTER 10

Heidegger's Transcendental Phenomenology in the Light of Husserl's Project of First Philosophy

Dermot Moran

IN THIS CHAPTER I want to interrogate Heidegger's commitment to a transcendental phenomenology during his so-called "phenomenological decade" (roughly 1919–29) in relation to Husserl's parallel project of transcendental "first philosophy" in those same years. Husserl initially conceived of phenomenology in the *Logical Investigations* (*Logische Untersuchungen*) as "theory of knowledge" (*Erkenntnistheorie*),[1] but, in his mature transcendental period that began with *Ideas I* (*Ideen I*; 1913), he reconceived it as "first philosophy," reviving Aristotle's *proté philosophia*, without regard, as he put it, to the sedimented history of the phrase.[2] By this "first philosophy" he did not mean metaphysics or epistemology (neo-Kantianism had made epistemology the "first philosophy"), but rather "a philosophy of beginnings instituting itself in the most radical philosophical self-consciousness."[3]

In 1923, at the very time Husserl was lecturing on *proté philosophia*, Heidegger began composing *Being and Time* (*Sein und Zeit*) as a contribution to phenomenological ontology, radically revising the Greek problematic of being for the contemporary age.[4] As is well known, despite their close personal contacts, Husserl's and Heidegger's projects steadily grew apart in the mid-1920s.[5] Nevertheless, there are strong links between these approaches to philosophy. Both emphasize the need to return to "concrete" experience, getting to the matters themselves. Both are interested in specifying conditions of possibility. Both want to appeal to self-evidence. Both accept the possibility of *Wesensschau*, not as a mystical practice but as attention to what is revealed in all revealing. Both want to anchor conceptuality in preconceptual givenness, to do justice to the world as the backdrop and "horizon of validity" for all experience. Both wanted to have genuine grounding as opposed to merely apparent grounding. Both assume that there is an essence to philosophy itself and that its "primary establishment" (*Urstiftung*) in ancient Greece continues to have significance if one peels back the sedimented history that has accrued to it. Both are involved in a rethinking or deconstruction of the history of philosophy.

But, besides their parallel approaches to phenomenology, is there a deeper philosophical relationship between Husserl's "first philosophy"—the "science of the all," with its search for "ultimate foundation" (*Letztbegründung*) through an account of the genesis and constitution of the "ultimate sense" (*letzter Sinn*), that is, the "sense of being" or "being-sense" (*Seinssinn*) and "validity of being" or "being-validity" (*Seinsgeltung*) of all entities—and Heidegger's inquiry into the "meaning of Being" (*Sinn von Sein*)? To investigate this question, I shall proceed by tracing the parallels between the thematics of these two thinkers in their lecture courses during that period, including their unsuccessful collaborative project on the article on "Phenomenology" for the *Encyclopaedia Britannica*.[6]

1. The Being-Question

According to Heidegger's self-reflections, his entire life's path in philosophy was motivated by the "Being-question" (*die Seinsfrage*),[7] a question that also calls for reflection on the meaning of philosophy itself, provoking complex questions about its historical achievement and essential possibility. Husserl, too, was interested in the meaning of philosophy, especially in the 1920s. His *Erste Philosophie* lecture course (1923–24) opens with an account of the Greek breakthrough to the universal and the ideal in Plato and then proceeds with detailed analyses of the emergence of transcendental philosophy in Descartes, its naturalistic distortion with Locke, and the recovery of the transcendental in Kant.

Husserl, of course, was intent on elaborating his phenomenology in transcendental terms, but he used several different modes of approach into this domain. He is best known for his "Cartesian way" of approaching transcendental phenomenology, portraying it as a radicalized exploration of the true meaning of the Cartesian discovery of the *ego cogito*, especially in the period dating from his 1922 London lectures to his 1929 Paris lectures. Meanwhile, Heidegger, at the same time, was intent precisely on deconstructing that Cartesian legacy, which he diagnosed as bearer of a deep metaphysical residue that he initially located in the Latin transmission of Greek thought but later found at the heart of the Greek experience itself. However, as is now well documented, Husserl's so-called Cartesianism was just one face of a many-sided approach. Equally important as the Cartesian way is the way of thinking about the transcendental field by contrasting it with the psychological domain. In fact, the difference between psychological and transcendental subjectivity is a theme that is common to both the Cartesian way and the way through psychology.

Heidegger, too, was struggling to express his own unique problematic of the meaning of being. In the lectures leading up to *Being and Time*, and in that work itself, Heidegger remains within the framework of the Husserlian legacy of transcendental philosophy, and develops his existential analytic of Dasein specifically within the tension between natural, mundanized subjectivity and transcendental subjectivity. Heidegger thought that Dasein cut across that opposition and offered the beginnings of a solution to the transcendental problematic. Husserl, of course, regarded it as a collapse back into naturalism and anthropologism. What I want to show in this chapter is that, whatever was the precise motivation for Heidegger's long engagement with *die Seinsfrage*, he could not have formulated his question without deep absorption in the central problematic of Husserl's transcendental phenomenology. Heidegger's problem is not the legacy of the Greeks but the manner in which the meaning of everything that appears as such can have its site in a finite, temporal, mundanized existent, Dasein.

The origin of Heidegger's being-question, at least in the manner in which he originally broached it in *Being and Time*, is to be found in Husserl. From the outset of Husserl's career he had been concerned with the conditions that make objective knowledge possible, and was precisely documenting the nature of objectivity in its many varieties, including real being, possible being, and so on. He often speaks of the totality of all things as "being" of "the totality of what is" or "the being of the world,"[8] and he speaks of his project as an attempt to understand the relation between consciousness and the "all." According to the *Cartesian Meditations*, phenomenology proposes to solve the problem of objective being.[9] The central claim of his transcendental phenomenology was that every experience of beings is at the same time an experience of beings as appearing to and correlated with a constituting subjectivity, and that the objects that appear to consciousness are "achievements," "accomplishments," or "performances" (*Leistungen*) of that consciousness. The nature of Husserl's transcendental outlook is well expressed in the *Crisis*:

> As scientists, can we content ourselves with the view that God created the world and human beings within it? . . . The enigma of the creation and that of God himself are essential component parts of positive religion. For the philosopher, however, this, and also the juxtaposition "subjectivity *in* the world as object" and at the same time "conscious subject *for* the world" contain a necessary theoretical question, that of understanding how this is possible.[10]

It was that essential *correlation* between being and site of appearance of being that Heidegger inherited as his central problem. The question of being, as it is posed in Heidegger's 1925 lecture series, *History of the Concept of Time*, which might be considered the "first draft" of *Being and Time*, emerges from a sustained and penetrating critique of Husserl's transcendental phenomenology.[11] In particular, Heidegger makes problematic the being of Husserl's constituting subject. While acknowledging that Husserl was laudably trying to develop a deeper account of subjectivity in his own *Phenomenological Psychology* lecture course of the same semester,[12] which he sees as a Diltheyean project of reviving a personalistic psychology (*History of the Concept of Time*, § 13), he then criticizes Husserl both for neglecting the being-question and even for distorting the grounds that would make it possible to pose that question in a radical way.

Heidegger detected in Husserl, especially in *Ideas I*, an unquestioned presumption drawn from traditional philosophy, specifically, that there existed an essential distinction between material being and the being of consciousness, such that consciousness was "absolute being." As he wrote in 1962:

> Meanwhile "phenomenology" in Husserl's sense was elaborated into a distinctive philosophical position according to a pattern set by Descartes, Kant and Fichte. The historicity of thought remained completely foreign to such a position. . . . The being-question, unfolded in *Being and Time*, parted company with this philosophical position, and that on the basis of what to this day I still consider a more faithful adherence (*Festhaltens*) to the principle of phenomenology.[13]

Despite these emerging disagreements, Heidegger stresses, even as he offers a penetrating critique of Husserl, that "it almost goes without saying that even today I still regard myself as a learner (*als Lernender*) in relation to Husserl."[14] Two years later in *Being and Time* he wrote:

> The following investigation would not have been possible if the ground had not been prepared by Edmund Husserl, with whose *Logical Investigations* phenomenology first emerged. Our comments on the preliminary conception of phenomenology have shown that what is essential in it does not lie in its actuality as a philosophical movement. Higher than actuality stands possibility. We can understand phenomenology only by seizing upon it as a possibility.[15]

In his autobiographical essay "My Way to Phenomenology" Heidegger claimed that what he gained from Husserl and from phenomenology was the practice of "phenomenological seeing."[16] Indeed, both in his explicitly phenomenological decade and in his post-*Kehre* writings, Heidegger frequently explicates his philosophy as a genuine phenomenological seeing in contrast to other superficial conceptions of phenomenology that lay claim to "essential insight" without justification. Thus, in his "Letter to Richardson" of 1962, Heidegger portrays himself as a phenomenologist.[17] Similarly, in a letter to Eugen Fink in 1966, he says that phenomenology "does not refer to a particular direction of philosophy. It names a possibility that continues to exist today, i.e., making it possible for thinking to attain the 'things themselves,' or to put it more clearly, to attain the matter of thinking."[18] As he had written in 1959, "I was trying to think the nature of phenomenology in a more originary manner."[19]

Heidegger struggled with Husserl's phenomenological approach to being right from the start. In the theology faculty of Freiburg University, where Heidegger studied from 1909 to 1911, Husserl's *Logical Investigations* lay on his desk ever since his first semester there.[20] Surely Husserl—a student of Brentano—could shed light on the problem of the underlying unity of the manifold senses of being. Heidegger was drawn to Husserl's endorsement of the objectivity of truth that seemed compatible with scholastic realism, and to the Sixth Logical Investigation with its discussion of categorial intuition that allowed the dimension of "supersensuous" being to appear. In Sixth Investigation, section 44, Husserl explains that the concept of being is not arrived at through reflection on the judgment but is given in the fulfillment of the judgment itself: "the concept of Being can arise only when some being, actual or imaginary, is set before our eyes," and being set before our eyes here involves an intuition broader than sensuous intuition (Sixth Logical Investigation, § 45). The message of the Sixth Investigation is that being appears in a distinct kind of founded judgment.

Part of Heidegger's fascination with the *Investigations* was that Husserl had defended ideal truths, objective senses, and the direct intuitive grasp of nonsensuous categorial entities. But Heidegger was also drawn to Husserl's resolute antinaturalism. Husserl had already rejected psychologism, which in his 1906–7 lecture course on he called the "original sin" of philosophy, the "sin against the Holy Spirit of philosophy."[21] Soon afterward, in *Philosophy as a Rigorous Science* (*Philosophie als strenge Wissenschaft*; 1911) he was attacking the project of the naturalization of consciousness and naturalism in general. He now sought to construe the activity of constituting consciousness in a nonpsychological, nonnaturalistic manner. Heidegger accepted this transcendental antinaturalistic orientation, but he actually thought Husserl retained a commitment to naturalism in his starting point, namely, the natural attitude and its supposedly inherent assumption that humans were to be construed as rational animals (*homo animal rationale*). In Husserl's stratification of attitudes, according to Heidegger: "The *fundamental stratum* is still the *naturally real* (*das Naturwirkliche*) upon which the psychic is built, and upon the psychic the spiritual."[22] Heidegger was never comfortable with Husserl's retention of metaphysically loaded concepts of subject (the Latinized thinking of *to hypokeimenon*) and consciousness, instead of attempting a more unprejudiced description of the being that discloses beings in the being, namely what he would call Dasein. Although, in his "On the Essence of Ground" ("Vom Wesen des Grundes"), Heidegger acknowledges: "If one chooses the title 'subject' for that being that we ourselves in each case are and that we understand as 'Dasein' then we may say that transcendence designates the essence of the subject, that it is the fundamental structure of subjectivity."[23] *Being and Time* would claim that phenomenology required that study of the intentional structures of consciousness needed to be replaced with the more fundamental study of the relation between Dasein and being itself. As Heidegger later wrote: "What occurs for the phenomenology of the acts of consciousness as the self-manifestation of phenomena is thought more originally by Aristotle and in all Greek thinking and existence as *aletheia*, as the unconcealedness of what is present, its being revealed, its showing itself."[24] We shall leave aside the Greek spin on phenomenology, to concentrate on the manner in which Heidegger radicalizes transcendental phenomenology.

Heidegger still followed Husserl's project of explicating the modes of givenness of objectivity in terms of a set of structured and gradated achievements, but now the achievements are attributed to Dasein in its relation to world. In *Being and Time*, he even endorses a kind of transcendental idealism as having an "advantage in principle" over realism: "If what the term 'idealism' says, amounts to the understanding that Being can never be explained by entities but is already that which is 'transcendental' for every entity, then idealism affords the only correct possibility for a philosophical problematic."[25] Of course, idealism is not usually construed as the thesis that being is transcendental for every entity, and indeed Heidegger himself observes that adopting this definition would mean that Aristotle, along with Kant, would be considered idealists. But the point, for Heidegger, is that the meaning of objective being lies beyond or behind those beings, transcendental to them. This transcendental domain has been construed by idealists as "consciousness," but this does not clarify the nature of the region in question. Dasein, on the other hand, with its intrinsic relation to being, offers a chance for clarification.

Interestingly, Husserl himself, when he finally came to grips with *Being and Time*, thought that the root of the disagreement between himself and Heidegger concerned the issue of transcendental philosophy. In his Amsterdam lecture of June 1931 he focuses precisely on the meaning of transcendental philosophy. He points out that the transcendental question can be posed in several ways: "It is the problem of cognition or of consciousness. It is the problem of the possibility of objectively valid science. It is the problem of the possibility of metaphysics—and so on."[26]

But what concerns him in particular is the manner in which being gets rethought as certainty of being (a shift he attributes to Descartes). Transcendental self-reflection involves the new awareness that "a universal belief in being flows through and sustains my entire life."[27] This "constant certitude of being" has up to that point sustained all scientific inquiry. However, the new transcendental science must put this certitude under the *epoché*. Both the whole world, the "totality of entities," and myself as an individual human being are put under suspension. The world becomes world-phenomenon, specifically a stream of experiences: "World in the sense of this universal phenomenon of validity is obviously inseparable from transcendental consciousness."[28] Husserl was the first to articulate the importance of worldhood and the backdrop of horizons that make possible the subject's acts of meaning-intending. The world transcends all experiences and makes them possible and gives them validity by offering a backdrop for the harmonious course of experience. To conceive of a transcendental ego is also always to conceive of a world correlated with it.

Heidegger's discussion of the structures of worldhood, and especially the correlation between Dasein and world such that Dasein can be characterized essentially as "being-in-the-world" (*In-der-Welt-Sein*), is an essential development of the Husserlian theme, but it does so without putting the world in brackets as world-phenomenon. Husserl would react to Heidegger's move by calling it "anthropology," suggesting he had fallen back into naïveté by seeking to ground the world in a finite being who was part of that world, something his own transcendental philosophy had overcome.

Clearly, then, the nature of Heidegger's transcendental phenomenology of the 1920s needs to be explicated by careful comparison with Husserl's project in that very period. In order to make sense of the relation between Husserlian constitution of *Seinssinn* and Heideggerian *Seinsfrage*, I shall first briefly rehearse Husserl's and Heidegger's sense of their respective philosophical missions, and then examine some of their complex interactions in order to situate Heidegger's transcendental philosophy as an extension of Husserl's mature phenomenology.

2. *The Task of Phenomenology*

As Husserl makes clear in his *Erste Philosophie* lectures, the whole purpose of philosophy in its Socratic "primal instituting" (*Urstiftung*) is to achieve the examined life, the life of *Selbstbesinnung*,[29] which is also the life of complete "self-responsibility." In his early Halle and Göttingen years Husserl spoke of this philosophical aim more narrowly as a phenomenological clarification of the conceptual elements, objects, and subjective performances that contribute to the theory and critique of knowledge (*Erkenntnistheorie* and *Erkenntniskritik*) with regard to "fixing" the components of scientific knowledge. His aim was to clarify the epistemology of the statements of scientific knowledge. How do they gain their sense? What grounds their validity? In particular, of course, he was interested in grounding logical claims, but his overall aim was a critique of science as such. But the initial investigations were primarily focused on the nature of objectivity and the kind of warrant held by statements claiming to objective status.

Interestingly, Husserl's analysis of the formal category of object as such led him to develop *formal ontology*, a term inserted into the second edition of the *Investigations* to refer to the pure, a priori theory of the forms of objects as such and their component parts (e.g., the very concepts of "part," "whole," "relation," and so on that allow one to refer to objects at all).[30] Husserl went on to contrast this formal ontology with the various material or regional ontologies that dealt with specific objects (e.g., nature). Formal ontology is always seen by Husserl as the counterpart of logic understood as assertive or apophantic. Formal ontology, however, does not deal with the *experience* of being or with the fundamental *correlation* between consciousness and being; these themes belong to phenomenology, the investigation of the relation between consciousness and being. As Husserl explains in 1911: "If epistemology will nevertheless investigate the problems of the relationship between consciousness and being, it can have before its eyes only being as the correlate of consciousness, as something 'intended' after the manner of consciousness: as perceived, remembered, expected, represented pictorially, imagined, identified, distinguished, believed, opined, evaluated, etc."[31] Being is always "being-for" consciousness. Consciousness, on the other hand, is "absolute being" (and Husserl never wavers from this position), as he put it in *Ideas I*.

Since all concepts have to be traced back to their origins in intuition, must the "sense of being" (*Seinssinn*) too be located in lived experience? Husserl locates the original sense of being in perceptual certainty. Being is given in perception as that which is itself there, with complete certainty. As Husserl writes in his 1924 lecture on Kant:

> [Perception] is what originally makes us conscious of the realities existing for us and "the" world as actually existing. To cancel out all such perception, actual and possible, means, for our total life of consciousness, to cancel out the world as objective sense (*als gegenständlichen Sinn*) and as validating actuality for us (*als uns geltende Wirklichkeit*); it means to remove from all world-thought (in every signification of this word) the original basis of sense and legitimacy (*den ursprünglichen Sinnes- und Rechtsboden*).[32]

In other words, perception is what gives rise to the "being-sense" and the original consciousness of validity. As he writes in his *Passive and Active Synthesis* lectures: "Every normal perception is a consciousness of validity."[33] Building on the primitive certainty or *Urdoxa* of sense perception, Husserl finds more and more layers of being correlated with high-order cognitive acts, including judgments.

The radical doctrine of categorial intuition, which interested Heidegger so much, claims that there are higher levels of givenness beyond the sensory. Being and properties of the object are given in higher-order intuitions, founded on the sensuous. As Heidegger himself explicates in his *History of the Concept of Time* lectures: "Categorial acts are founded acts; in other words, everything categorial ultimately rests on sense intuition."[34] Heidegger comments that a broadened concept of the sensuous is at work here, such that spatiality, for instance, is sensuously apprehended, although not by means of "sense data." Heidegger writes: "*Sensuousness is a formal phenomenological concept* and refers to all material content as it is already given by the subject matters themselves."[35]

For Heidegger, Husserlian phenomenology provided a means for grasping the revelation of being. Furthermore, constitution really meant letting-be-seen: "'*Constituting*' does not mean producing in the sense of making and fabricating; it means letting the entity be seen in its objectivity."[36] It is the transcendental ego that constitutes sense and being, as Husserl put it in the *Cartesian Meditations*:[37] "Transcendence in every form is a within-the-ego, self-constituting being-sense [*Transzendenz in jeder Form ist ein innerhalb des Ego sich konstituierender Seinssinn*]."[38]

Husserl saw his program as tracing the layers of constituted meaning in all aspects of meaningful reality, including not just the actual but every possible world insofar as every such world is correlated with a subjectivity and an actual or possible consciousness. Indeed, phenomenology, carried out with systematic concreteness, is *eo ipso* transcendental idealism, albeit in a fundamentally new sense. He adds that this idealism is not the product of arguments against realism, but rather from close investigations of constituting consciousness in all its possible modalities. Thus he asserts: "*The proof of this idealism is therefore phenomenology itself.* Only someone who misunderstands either the deepest sense of intentional method, or that of transcendental reduction, or perhaps both, can attempt to separate phenomenology from transcendental idealism."[39] Also in 1929 Husserl writes: "The whole of phenomenology is nothing more than scientific self-examination on the part of transcendental subjectivity."[40]

Various claims have been made for how radically Husserl himself interprets the *constitution* of "sense and being" or "being-sense" by transcendental subjectivity. As Fink points out, he does on occasion speak of constitution as *creation*. A. D. Smith has recently defended a particularly strong interpretation of this idealism.[41] I also believe that Husserl intended it in a strong sense. There is no being, no reality, no world, other than those constituted by transcendental subjectivity. To even think of an entity beyond consciousness is a countersense.

Of course, there are complicating factors in interpreting the meaning of this idealism.[42] Husserl explicitly rejected any solipsistic construal of his idealism, and was emphatically neither a Berkeleyan nor a Kantian. His transcendental ego has corporeality, is embodied in the world, is intersubjectively constituted, has practical motivations, and so on. Already, in 1925, he was stressing the complexity of the layered intersubjective life: "The task necessarily arises of descriptively pursuing systematically coherent multiplicities of consciousness which pertain essentially to the cognitively becoming aware of objectivities of every category. Every category of possible objectivities designates an index for a methodic regularity of possible psychic life; every possible real world, a regularity of possible, intersubjective psychic life."[43] Husserl emphasized the intersubjective grounding of objectivity: "Transcendental intersubjectivity is the absolute and only self-sufficient foundation (*Seinsboden*), out of which everything objective (the totality of objectively real entities, but also every objective ideal world) draws its sense and validity."[44] Moreover, especially in the later work, as Dan Zahavi and Natalie Depraz have shown, the Husserlian subject is shot through with the non-egoic, with the "foreign," *das Ich-fremde*, and so on.[45] Just as temporal presence involves and includes absence, and perception has a necessary absent element, so also the ego implies the non-ego. These are difficult themes in the later Husserl but they were already consistently to be found in his lectures and writings between 1915 and 1925, in his Freiburg period generally.

But in all his transcendental discussions, the key point for Husserl is to overcome naïveté and to gain (and sustain) the "absolute attitude" of the transcendental onlooker. The transcendental attitude is to be contrasted with the manner in which we normally live our lives "anonymously" in the natural attitude: "The natural attitude is the form in which the total life of humanity is realized in running its natural, practical course. It was the only form from millennium to millennium, until out of science and philosophy there developed unique motivations for a revolution (*Umwendung*)."[46]

Husserl's genius in part lay in identifying the kinds of attitude that illuminate beings in their specific entitative and senseful status, that is, their *Seinssinn*. The *epoché* and reduction are introduced in order to break the grip of the dominant natural attitude, entwined as it has been since the modern breakthrough of Galileo with the mathematical scientific attitude, in order to grasp the hidden constituting subjectivity at work. To every objectivity there corresponds a set of constituting "acts" (not to be construed in an active sense) and indeed objectivities only come to light when approached through a certain attitude. To being actual there corresponds the attitude of certainty, but there are other modalizations of attitudes that yield objectivities under different modalities (possibility, dubitability, etc.). There are many kinds of attitude (*Einstellung*) but the most prominent are the natural attitude, the personalistic attitude (which humans take to each other and their local and cultural world), the theoretical attitude, the attitude of the formal mathematicizing sciences, the aesthetic attitude, the religious attitude, and so on. An art object only comes to light as such under the aesthetic evaluating attitude, and likewise a tool is only recognized as such under the practical attitude.

With the gaining of the natural attitude, a whole new domain of experience is opened up, and for the time a science of spirit can begin:

> It is my conviction that intentional phenomenology has made of the spirit *qua* spirit for the first time a field of systematic experience and science and has thus brought about the total reorientation (*Umstellung*) of the task of knowledge. The universality of the absolute spirit surrounds everything that exists with an absolute historicity, to which nature as a spiritual structure is subordinated. Intentional phenomenology, and specifically transcendental phenomenology, was first to see the light through its point of departure and its methods. Only through it do we understand, and from the most profound reasons, what naturalistic objectivism is and understand in particular that psychology, because of its naturalism, has to miss entirely the accomplishment, the radical and genuine problem of the life of the spirit.[47]

As Husserl was making these extraordinarily strong claims for phenomenology, Heidegger too was employing phenomenology to solve the central philosophical issue, the meaning of being.

3. Phenomenology and Ontology

Following his mentor Husserl, Heidegger too is "opposed to all free-floating constructions and accidental findings" and to all "pseudo-problems," and wants to secure all claims in a certain kind of "self-evidence."[48] He follows the phenomenological maxim "not to flee from the enigmatic character of phenomena not to explain it away by a violent coup de main of a wild theory but rather to accentuate the puzzlement."[49] Furthermore, phenomenology is a method, and above all not a "standpoint." In fact, as Heidegger puts it in his earliest Freiburg lecture course (1919), to think of phenomenology as a standpoint is the "original sin" of philosophy.[50] Heidegger too is concerned with what Husserl refers to as "the life of spirit" (*Geistesleben*) and his early Freiburg lecture courses extol the phenomenological virtue of "absolute sympathy with life," allowing life to be seen and expressed philosophically without distorting it.[51]

In *Being and Time* Heidegger seeks to reawaken the question of the meaning of being and to do so through a complex phenomenological approach that identifies a particular being—Dasein—and then undertakes a twofold investigation of it by means of an existential analytic of Dasein followed by a rethinking of this with temporality in view. Moreover, phenomenology is the name for the *method* of ontology (*Basic Problems*, § 5). Scientific ontology is nothing but phenomenology, Heidegger says in *History of Time* lectures.[52]

"Phenomenology is always only the name for the procedure of ontology," he says.[53] In his 1927 lecture course *Basic Problems of Phenomenology* he asserts (and emphasizes that at the initial point it remains just an assertion) that "being is the sole and proper theme of philosophy" and hence that "philosophy is ontological": "Philosophy is the theoretical interpretation of being, of being's structure and its possibilities. Philosophy is ontological."[54] Philosophy is to be "universal phenomenological ontology," and it is to be carried out through a hermeneutic of Dasein, which provides the thread to lead philosophical questioning out of the labyrinth.[55]

In *Being and Time*, section 7, Heidegger claims that his own use of the term *ontology* is so "formally broad" there is no point in trying to trace its history: "Since the term 'ontology' is used in this investigation in a sense which is formally broad, any attempt to clarify the method of ontology by tracing its history is automatically ruled out."[56] He makes similar assertions in *The Basic Problems of Phenomenology*: "we take this expression [ontology] in the widest possible sense" (§ 3, p. 11). Because it is new, it has no model to follow:

> When, moreover, we use the term "ontology", we are not talking about some definite philosophical discipline standing in interconnection with others. Here one does not have to measure up to the tasks of some discipline that has been presented beforehand; on the contrary, only in terms of the objective necessities of definite questions and the kind of treatment which the "things themselves" require, can one develop such a discipline.[57]

Ontology must emerge from the phenomenological situation and not by aping any of the existing sciences. Heidegger is claiming then that ontology is a completely new science.

Heidegger's 1925 lectures articulate his sense of phenomenology in quite considerable detail. He discusses Husserl's work at length—not just the *Logical Investigations*, but also *Ideas I*, *Philosophy as Rigorous Science*, and even the unpublished discussions of the personalistic attitude of *Ideas II*. Heidegger traces a very powerful critique of Husserl in these pages, emphasizing the need to inquire more deeply into the being of the subjective. Husserlian intentional description failed because it did not interrogate the sense of the being of the subject and its intentional "acts," and did not link the sense of this subjectivity to transcendence and falling (*Verfallen*). In contrast to this extended discussion, *Being and Time* does not mention intentionality, except in a note where Heidegger promises to show how intentionality is grounded in the ec-static nature of Dasein.[58]

Heidegger in *Being and Time* stresses the importance of Dasein as being-in-the-world. Here he draws heavily on Husserl, who had an awareness of "world" from the beginning. In one sense it is the ultimate horizon, the whole of which everything else is a part (it has this meaning in the Third Logical Investigation). The world in the reduced sense as the world of experiences plays a central role in his transcendental phenomenology. Husserl sees all experience as presuming a world.

Let us consider for a moment Husserl's analysis of world in his 1925 lectures published as *Phenomenological Psychology*, where world-experience and the experienced world become themes for description.[59] According to Husserl, there is always a "pregiven world" as the backdrop of experience.[60] World is the "all-inclusive abiding ground of existence" and the "all-inclusive field for all our activities."[61] It has its own universal, a priori, essential structure,[62] which includes the spatial and the temporal but also much more. The world is always experienced and it is experienced as "one and the same world."[63] It is grasped pre-theoretically and pre-predicatively. Assertions are about it, and thus in a sense it precedes predicative truth. Truth in fact presupposes this world,[64] which is given prior to our activities of questioning, judging, conceiving, theorizing.[65] This world allows a "world truth" to be sought.[66] It is a world spread out before us and receding from us without end.[67] A central—and essentially new—achievement of this work is its characterization of the *Lebenswelt* or life-world in which we find ourselves primarily and most of the time. It is precisely because the scientific worldview has been adopted as the only true worldview that the life-world has become visible for the first time. Moreover, this initial experiential world is not divided into nature and spirit. It is experienced as one totality. It is experienced through the harmonious flow of experiences confirming each other "continually progressing and concordant experience."[68]

Heidegger takes over many aspects of this analysis and it would take too long here to detail the relation between their respective concepts of world. Suffice to say, that Heidegger emphasizes more than Husserl the manner in which Dasein is always involved in falling, that is, being lost in the world.[69] Whereas Husserl sees the understanding of world as giving a new security to the sciences, Heidegger sees it as a way of entering into "existential" discussions concerning inauthentic and authentic ways of living as an individual in the world, either caught in *das Man* or somehow authentically oneself.

Overall, however, in his 1925 lectures Heidegger sees Husserl as beginning from the natural attitude and thus already beginning from a standpoint shot through with traditional metaphysical assumptions. For Heidegger, Husserl's fault is to assume that, in the natural attitude, we "naturally" regard humans as rational animals, as entities in the world. While he regards Husserl's development of the personalistic attitude as a positive improvement on this position, he sees Husserl as actually beginning from a distorted conception of the "natural attitude," in fact from an overly naturalistic reading of the natural attitude. Heidegger's move is to restore to the natural attitude the thickness of its conceptions of human existing, everything that comes under the title Dasein. Husserl falsely assumes that it is "natural" to think of human nature as body and consciousness and so on. This is the Cartesian residue in his thinking. The very starting point for his reorientation (*Umstellung*) remains uninterrogated.

As a result Heidegger thinks it is impossible for Husserl to recover the true sense of humanity in the transcendental attitude, since the transcendental attitude alters the value of everything received in the natural attitude. Heidegger raises a question that he believes is characteristic of the Husserlian project and yet unanswerable in it: "How is it at all possible that this sphere of absolute position, pure consciousness, which is supposed to be separated from every transcendence by an absolute gulf, is at the same time united with reality in the unity of a real human being, who himself occurs as a real object in the world?"[70]

Indeed, this precisely is Husserl's central transcendental question in his mature years. As he himself asks in *Crisis*:

> How can a component part of the world, its human subjectivity, constitute the whole world, namely, constitute it as its intentional formation, one which has always already become what it is and continues to develop, formed by the universal interconnection of intentionally accomplishing subjectivity, while the latter, the subjects appearing in cooperation, are themselves only a partial formation within the total accomplishment?[71]

Both Heidegger and Husserl wrestle with this question, which we might call the fundamental transcendental question. How can that which constitutes the whole be itself a constituted part of that very whole? Husserl sees this as a paradox, but resolves it in terms of two different attitudes—the attitude of "common sense" (he uses the English term), and the attitude of the "disinterested spectator."[72] The way to grasp the question is to apply the *epoché* and reduction, and to remain within them, as Husserl emphasizes in his Amsterdam lectures.

Heidegger's response to this problematic, on the other hand, is to raise the being-question. Heidegger explicates this paradox in terms of Dasein, which both manifests being and is also a being. The distinction then is between beings and being, for Heidegger, between the "ontic" domain of beings and the *ontological* (in Heidegger's new sense) domain of *Sein*, the to-be, the "how" of beings. This "how" had been thought by Husserl as the modes of givenness to constituting subjectivity. Heidegger too starts from this standpoint (in 1925) but soon goes beyond it.

In attempting to address the central paradox of transcendental phenomenology, Husserl was only too aware that he might be heading into the phenomenological equivalent of the medieval theological absurdity of the two kinds of truth. He refers in *Crisis* to the notorious doctrine of "double truth."[73] But, for Husserl, the problem is in fact resolved by the distinction between two attitudes—the natural and the transcendental. Objective truth as such is found only in the natural attitude: "Objective truth belongs exclusively within the attitude of natural human world-life."[74]

Truth, for Husserl, emerges as a practical concern within the world for securing the attitude of certainty against its possible modalizations (into unbelief, etc.). All sciences deal with the objective world and hence are naïve about the productions of transcendental subjectivity. When the subjective correlations are exhibited in the transcendental attitude, we are no longer in the domain of objective truth.

In the reorientation of the *epoché* nothing is lost, none of the interests and ends of world-life, and thus also none of the ends of knowledge. But the essential subjective correlates of all these things are exhibited, and thus the full and true ontic meaning of objective being, and thus of all objective truth, is set forth.[75]

Husserl emphasizes the need to live in the natural attitude in order to make possible the break from it in the transcendental attitude that will grasp intentional life as "accomplishing life" (*als leistendes*).[76] This is precisely what Heidegger seizes on to criticize. If the natural attitude is treated as the outlook of modern philosophy then we have imported prejudices into our discussion. Phenomenology has become unphenomenological, as he will repeatedly say.

The struggles between the competing Husserlian and Heideggerian interpretations of the task of "first philosophy" are nowhere more evident than in the differences between the drafts of the *Encyclopaedia Britannica* article and in the notes Husserl made in his personal copy of *Being and Time*.[77] Both sets of documents reveal a perplexity on the side of Husserl as to what Heidegger meant by fundamental ontology. Where Heidegger speaks of the inquiry into the meaning of being as the most basic and concrete of questions, Husserl agrees, but he comments in the margin that this is a "transcendental-phenomenological question" about the constitutive meaning of being.

In his note at the bottom of *Being and Time*, section 3, Husserl explains that all entities have certain formal ontological properties in common and that every individual being is a concretization of these forms. Husserl is clearly invoking his distinction between formal and material ontologies. In so as there are categories (unity, part/whole, identity, individual, species) that belong to any thing insofar as it is a thing, then these topics belong to formal ontology.

Husserl could only see in Heidegger's transcendental analytic of Dasein an account of human existence in the natural attitude and hence a kind of anthropology. Husserl, however, never does resolve how human beings as entities in the world are at the same time world-constituting. How can the transcendental ego (belonging to no matter what kind of intersubjective community) be mundanized, incarnated, temporalized? Are we not left in Husserl with a "double truth"? Husserl is protected from the consequences of this problem by the *epoché* that separates *Seinssinn* from existence (Dasein in Husserl's sense). Heidegger, on the other hand, by making historically existent Dasein both a transcendental condition for world and at the same time mediating the meaning of being, thinks, at least in *Being and Time*, that he has found a way of solving the transcendental problem. That he would soon be forced to abandon the language of transcendental philosophy and seek an "other thinking that abandons subjectivity" is another story.[78]

CHAPTER 11

The "I Think" and the For-the-Sake-of-Which

Mark Okrent

IN TWO RECENT articles, I argued that one of the early Heidegger's most significant contributions to transcendental philosophy involved a major rethinking of the nature of self-consciousness.[1] "Transcendental self-consciousness" is always understood by Kant to involve a conceptual representation of the act in which a subject conceptually represents an object. Heidegger, on the other hand, argues that, while "the self which the Dasein is, is there somehow in and along with all intentional comportments," the intention directed toward the self is not properly seen as either a representation or as conceptual. Rather, Heidegger suggests, "we understand ourselves and our existence by way of the activities we pursue and the things we take care of."[2] The self is primarily tacitly intended as that "for the sake of which" things matter to us and our activities make sense. For Heidegger, it is only insofar as our interactions with things are implicitly organized in terms of a style of life embodied in such a "for-the-sake-of" that we are capable of using concepts to make judgments concerning objects, or to cognize ourselves as the subject of our experiences.

If, as I have previously argued, Heidegger systematically rethinks the nature of the "I think," this suggests that he must also have rethought the role of the "I think" in transcendental arguments. For Kant, the ability to attach the "I think" to all of my representations is tied up with the ability to form judgments, and this ability in turn is essential for the ability to cognize objects independent of our apprehensions of them, and the capacity to form a coherent, unified experience of an objective world. But Heidegger thinks that it is a mistake to think of the basic form of our self-apprehension in terms of a conceptual representation accompanying our other representations and to think of the activity of judging as the most basic human intentional comportment. Instead, he suggests that there is a self-understanding involved in a distinctively human type of overt, practical activity that is a necessary condition for both the use of concepts in a judgment and the capacity to think the "I think." In this chapter, I discuss the way in which Heidegger constructs a transcendental argument that, first, links practical self-understanding in a "for-the-sake-of" with the ability to intend entities as entities by engaging in certain distinctively human activities, and, second, treats both of these as conditions on the ability to judge and on the capacity to understand oneself in explicitly conceptual terms. Before doing this I briefly summarize the role that Kant gives to the "I think" in his transcendental arguments.

1. Kant on Judgment and the "I Think"

For Kant, "It must be possible for the 'I think' to accompany all my representations; for otherwise something would be represented in me which could not be thought at all, and that is equivalent to saying that the representation would be impossible, or at least would be nothing to me."[3] This assertion, while pithy and memorable, is also unfortunately written in such a way that it is easy to misinterpret. Kant clearly is committed by this statement to the view that the possibility of the "I think" accompanying some representation is necessary for the possibility of that representation being thought as the representation of something. This is what the crucial second clause asserts. It is possible to think of some representation as representing some thing only if it is possible for the "I think" to accompany this representation. But does this imply that for *x* to be a representation of some thing it must be possible for the "I think" to accompany it? That of course depends upon whether or not the possibility of *x* being thought as a representation of *z* is essential to *x* being a representation of *z*. And this seems to be the import of Kant's third clause, where he says that to say that "something represented in me could not be thought" is equivalent to saying that "the representation is impossible." But then he apparently takes this equivalence back in the final, parenthetical clause. According to this final parenthesis, the assertion "representation *x* cannot be thought by me as representing *z*, because I can not affix the 'I think' to it," is *not equivalent* to "*x* representing *z* is impossible, because I can not affix the 'I think' to it," but, rather, to "it (*x*?, *z*?) would be nothing to me if I could not affix the 'I think' to it." And this is clearly a different claim than the stronger claim, seemingly asserted in the second clause, that no object can be represented without the possibility of the "I think." But which of these is Kant's considered opinion on the status and role of the "I think"?

There is excellent reason to believe that the final parenthetical clause governs the whole and that Kant does not equate *x* being a representation of z with the possibility of x being "thought" by me as a representation of z. Indeed, Kant is quite clear, both in the *Critique* and elsewhere, that he believes that it is possible for there to be a representation of z in me of which I am not even conscious, let alone capable of thinking. In the division of types of representations in the Dialectic, for example, Kant distinguishes between the genus "representation" and its species, *perceptio*, or "representation with consciousness."[4] More importantly, in the Jäsche *Lectures on Logic* Kant continues the division by distinguishing between two forms of *perceptio*: to be acquainted (*kennen*) with something, "or to represent something in comparison with other things, both as to sameness and as to difference," and to be acquainted with something with *consciousness*, or *cognition* (*erkennen*). Both of these, Kant tells us, involve intentions directed toward objects, but animals are only acquainted with objects, they do not cognize them. "Animals are acquainted with objects too, but they do not *cognize* them."[5] It is only in the next division that Kant reaches understanding, "to cognize something through the understanding by means of concepts, or to conceive." So, for Kant in 1800 (the date of the Jäsche *Logic*), it is possible for an agent to have a representation *of something*, be conscious of that representation, and even represent that representation in relation to others in respect to sameness and difference, and thus be acquainted with objects, without that agent using concepts or being conscious *that* they are acquainted with objects. And, since in the Jäsche *Logic* Kant uses "to think" as equivalent with "to cognize with concepts,"[6] it is obvious that when he says in the B-Deduction that if it were impossible for the "I think" to accompany a representation x, then x could not be thought by me, this *can't* be equivalent to saying that if it were impossible for the "I think" to accompany x, it would be impossible for x to be a representation of z. For Kant, the possibility of the "I think" is not a necessary condition for representation, or even for acquaintance with objects. If it were, animals could not be acquainted with objects, and, according to the Kant of the late critical period, animals are acquainted with objects.

For what, then, *is* the "I think" necessary? For Kant, it is primarily necessary for two things, both of which are mentioned in the famous statement quoted above: "thinking" a representation as a representation of an object; and a representation, and the object represented by that representation, being something "to" me. But how are we to interpret these?

What does Kant mean when he talks about "something represented in me which is thought"? One of the keys to interpreting this possibility is given in Kant's division of representations in the *Lectures on Logic*. He tells us there that animals, who are incapable of having the "I think" accompany their representations, can be acquainted with objects perceptually, and even represent similarities and differences, but they can't *cognize* objects. To be acquainted with something is to "represent something in comparison with other things, both as to sameness and as to difference." Cognition, on the other hand, Kant says, is being acquainted with something with *consciousness*. The acquaintance side of this division is clear enough. When one is acquainted with an object one represents that object as similar to and different from other objects. When my dog Mac sees other dogs he reacts in similar fashion to all of them but differently in each of those cases than he does when he sees a squirrel. And this gives us reason to believe not only that his representations of the dogs are similar to one another and different from his representations of squirrels, but also that in some sense Mac synthesizes these representations and compares them in regard to their similarities and differences. In Kant's terms, Mac represents the dogs in comparison with the squirrels in respect to sameness and difference. But what, then, does cognition, of which Mac is incapable, add? Kant says that cognition is acquaintance with consciousness. And at first sight this is odd, because an act in which one is acquainted with an object, such as Mac perceiving the difference between a dog and a squirrel, is already itself a conscious representation for Kant. So what can he mean when he says that cognition is being acquainted with something with consciousness?

Although it is not the case that for Kant all conscious states are intentional (he does not appear to take feelings, for example, to be intentional), he does treat many conscious states as having an intentional component. In the division of kinds of representations in the Jäsche *Logic*, for example, he says that the division is "in regard to the objective content" of these representations. That is, acquaintance is different from cognition, and simple perceptual cognition is different from a conceptual cognitive understanding, in respect to *what is represented* in these various states. From this perspective, when Kant speaks of cognition as acquaintance *with consciousness* (his emphasis), *what* is differentially conscious in cognitive states is not the state itself, (both acts of cognition and acts of acquaintance are conscious states), but rather the *content* of those states. That is, Kant is suggesting that the differentia of cognitive acts is that the acts of acquaintance in which the sameness and difference of objects is represented are *themselves* consciously represented in cognitive acts. So, to return to Mac, he represents dogs and squirrels differently (if he didn't he wouldn't be a very successful animal), and he can even distinguish between them when instances of both are present. That is, he can represent something in comparison with other things, both as to sameness and as to difference. But he does not represent that sameness and difference itself *as such*. That is, Mac is incapable of intending *that* he represents dogs and squirrels differently, and that these representations differ from one another in such and such respects. It is for this reason that Mac is incapable of using concepts, and also for this reason that Kant tells us that understanding, or the ability to conceive through concepts, is a *type* of cognition. To have the concept "dog," is at least to be potentially conscious of those respects in which representations of all dogs are similar and the respects in which the representations of all dogs are different from the representations of nondogs.

The distinguishing feature of human representation is not introduced in the Transcendental Deduction through a contrast with animal representation, as it is in the *Lectures on Logic*. Nevertheless, the same differentia is suggested there as in the *Logic*. The B-Deduction begins with the suggestion that the distinguishing "act of spontaneity" of the faculty of the understanding, an act which has "the general title 'synthesis,'" is "the combination of a manifold in general."[7] This way of putting the matter makes it sound as if what is at issue is the act itself of combining or putting together representations. On this reading, however, the act in which my dog combines his representations of another dog and a squirrel in order to compare them would count as an act of understanding, and this can't be right. Fortunately, Kant immediately corrects this misleading impression. For he tells us, first, that it is not the mere combination of representations which is the act of understanding, but the *representation* of the combination, and, second, that what is contained in combination is not merely a manifold and its synthesis, but also *the representation* of the *unity* of the combination or synthesis of a manifold: "of all *representations* combination is the only one which cannot be given through objects." "But the concept of combination includes, besides the concept of the manifold and of its synthesis, also the concept of the unity of the manifold. Combination is the representation of the *synthetic* unity of the manifold. The representation of this unity cannot, therefore, arise out of the combination. On the contrary, it is what, by adding itself to the representation of the manifold, first makes possible the concept of the combination."[8] That is, the understanding combines a manifold in the sense that it represents the manifold as unified in a single representation; it represents the *unity* of what is manifold. Each of our representations of dogs is itself a synthesis or combination of a manifold of different representations. My dog, Mac, insofar as he is acquainted with objects, can have such synthetic representations. Indeed, he can represent two representations of dogs together and note their similarity. But he cannot represent that similarity of representation itself in a single representation by recognizing that both of these synthetic representations have been synthesized in the same way and that they are both instances of the same type of representation, "dog." The representation in which we recognize that Mac is similar to Fido and all other dogs in respect of being a dog is of course the judgment that Mac is a dog. It is for this reason that in the *Logic* Kant explicitly asserts that the distinguishing mark of human cognition is that it is discursive.

It is important to note that for Kant cognition involves two representations that are, in principle, separate and distinct. First, there is no cognition without acquaintance: every cognitive act takes as its object a representation which itself is a synthesis or combination of a variety of other representations. Kant tells us that this is a representation of a type that a mere animal can have. But second, for cognition of a human kind to occur, there must be a second act that involves a second representation: an act in which we represent the unitary character of the act of combination in which we generate the first representation. That is, cognition is acquaintance together with consciousness of the unity of the synthesis of that with which we are acquainted.

In both the A-Deduction and the B-Deduction Kant immediately follows his discussions of the consciousness of the unity of synthesis with the first introduction of the necessity of the unity of apperception. This "I think," which must be capable of accompanying all of my cognitive representations, is itself, for Kant, a representation, a representation which embodies a consciousness of the unity of the synthesis of all that is manifold in my experience. "The synthetic proposition, that all the variety of empirical consciousness must be combined in one single self-consciousness, is the absolutely first and synthetic principle of our thought in general. But it must not be forgotten that the bare representation 'I' in relation to all other representations (the collective unity of which it makes possible) is transcendental consciousness."[9] Indeed, this "I think" is a specific kind of representation, a "thought." "On the other hand, in the transcendental synthesis of the manifold of representations in general, and therefore in the synthetic original unity of apperception, I am conscious of myself, not as I appear to myself, nor as I am in myself, but only that I am. This representation is a *thought*, not an *intuition*."[10] *What* I am conscious of in this thought, this "bare representation 'I,'" is the "unity of synthesis," or combination, of my various representations. Putting this all together, the "I," which must be capable of accompanying all of my representations, is the representation of the unitary act of thinking that relates all of my various representations into a single consciousness or experience.

Kant's line of argument here seems to be as follows. What is distinctive about human cognition is the ability to represent or be conscious of the unifying or combining character of our own mental activity in a single unifying representation. Typically, such a representation itself ultimately involves a concept applied in a judgment to a synthesized manifold; for example, "That is a dog." When one represents in this way, what is represented is the type of synthesizing character of one's own activity. As such, every such representing act, no matter what concept is applied, is also an act of self-representing, an act in which one conceptually represents one's own combining activity. Since it is the synthetic representation of that dog that is conceptually characterized as "dog," and that representation has that character partly in virtue of the character of the synthesizing activity that constituted that complex representation, it is one's own activity that one types when one types a representation as one of a dog. So to be capable of conceptually cognizing something as a dog, one must be capable of conceptually cognizing one's dog representations as one's own representations, in the sense that they are recognized as the product of a certain sort of combining activity on my part. What I have that my dog, Mac, lacks is precisely this ability to be acquainted with objects with consciousness, that is, the reflective capacity to cognize and type my own acts. That which *all* such acts of combination share in common is just that they are all my acts. But insofar as I can cognize conceptually I have the reflective capacity to type my own acts, so I have the ability to conceptually represent, to think, my own acts *as* my own acts. That is, I can conceptually cognize, or think, an object only if the thought "I think" can accompany the act in which I think the object. For Kant, what the "I think" is necessary for is the capacity to judge and to conceptually represent objects by forming discursive judgments about them.

At the same time the possibility of the "I think" is also required if any representation or object is to be anything "to me." Something is something "to me" only if it is recognizable by me as something which *I* am cognizing. That is, for a dog to be something to me I must be able to represent *that* the dog is being thought by me as a dog. But this possibility just *is* the possibility of representing the act in which I intend the dog as my act, that is, the possibility of the "I think" accompanying the cognition of the dog as dog. It is thus analytically true that some thing can be something to me only if I am capable of affixing the "I think" to its representation.

2. *Self-Intention in Heidegger*

The structure of Kant's argument turns on his analysis of the distinctive feature of human mental life. Kant holds that we differ from the other animals in our capacity to cognize objects, rather than merely being perceptually acquainted with them. This cognitive capacity is interpreted by Kant as the human ability to represent the character of our own mental activity, and this root mental activity in turn is understood as the activity of combining or synthesizing our representations in ways that accord with certain rules or instantiate certain patterns. This synthesis itself, "is the mere result of the power of imagination, a blind but indispensable function of the soul."[11] Humans, through our capacity to represent this activity according to its type, or "to bring this synthesis to concepts," are capable of discursive thought, judgment, and logical inference. Since my abilities in these areas are all rooted in my ability to represent the character of my own cognitive activity, and the common feature of all of that activity is that it is *my* activity, *if* I am capable of cognition, in Kant's technical sense, then I am also capable of representing my representations as my representations. That is, a necessary condition on human cognition is our capacity to characterize each of our thoughts as our thoughts.

What does Heidegger think about all of this? How, specifically, does the conceptual cognition of the "I think" enter into Heidegger's transcendental discussions of intentionality? The quick answer to this question is: not much. Heidegger of course accepts that we have the capacity to conceptually intend each of our cognitive acts of recognition or judgment as our own. He is even willing to go further than Kant and to generalize to nonjudgmental, noncognitive acts the formal requirement that all intentional acts directed toward something by a Daseinish intentional agent involve an intention directed toward itself by that agent. ("Formally, it is unassailable to speak of the ego as consciousness of something that is at the same time conscious of itself. . . . To intentionality belongs, not only a self-directing-toward and not only an understanding of the being of the being toward which it is directed, but also the associated unveiling of the self which is comporting itself here.")[12] But at the same time that he asserts the necessity of such self-directed intentionality, he also radically rethinks the character of that self-directedness.

The "I think" that concerns Kant is at once a condition on conceptual representation and itself a conceptual representation, or thought. In Kant, the "I think" is tied up with our ability to reflect and make conceptually present to ourselves the nature of our own cognitive activity. While Heidegger doesn't for a moment doubt that such reflective cognitive intentions are possible, he isn't much interested in them. He isn't interested in the Kantian "I think" because he believes that such reflective conceptual intentions are derivative from a more basic type of self-disclosure, a kind of self-disclosure which itself is a necessary condition on a more basic kind of intentionality than that embodied in discursive, judgmental thought: "The Dasein, as existing, is there for itself, even when the ego does not direct itself to itself in the manner of its own peculiar turning around and turning back, which in phenomenology is called inner perception as contrasted with outer. The self is there for the Dasein itself without reflection and without inner perception, before all reflection."[13]

Just as in Kant the conceptual character of the "I think" is tied up with the cognitive nature of the intentionality for which it is necessary, the character of this nonreflective, noncognitive (in Kant's sense), more basic type of Heideggerian self-directed intention is tied up with the distinctive kind of intentionality for which it is supposed to be necessary. In attempting to describe the character of this nonreflective self-intention, Heidegger appeals to a description of the way in which we intend entities when we pursue ends and care for and about things. Dasein, he tells us, "never finds itself otherwise than in the things themselves, and in fact in those things that daily surround it. It finds itself primarily and constantly in things because, tending them, distressed by them, it always in some way or other rests in things. Each of us is what he pursues and cares for. In everyday terms, we understand ourselves and our existence by way of the activities we pursue and the things we take care of. We understand ourselves by starting from them because the Dasein finds itself primarily in things."[14]

On its surface, this quotation asserts that the primary form of self-directed intentionality is wrapped up in our abilities to "tend" entities, or be distressed by them, or take care of them. There is no doubt, of course, that we *intend* an entity when we tend it or take care of it. I can only "take care" of my computer or be distressed by my fungus-ridden peach tree insofar as I am capable of intending or being directed toward the computer or the tree. Indeed, I can only be engaged with these things in these ways if I intend the computer as a computer or the tree as a tree. My distress for the tree presupposes that I take the tree to be *diseased*, that is, as a tree of a certain sort that is failing to satisfy the norms appropriate to that sort. And I can care for the computer only if I take it to be a computer. But these truisms lead to two puzzles. First, just how is a *self-directed* intention involved in these intentional comportments? And second, given that being distressed by a tree or taking care of a computer seem to involve treating the tree as a tree and the computer as a computer, why does Heidegger think that such intentional acts are *nonreflective*, or noncognitions, in Kant's sense? We will approach the answer to the first question by considering the second.

We can begin to answer this question if we remind ourselves that even in Kant it is not quite true that the ability to intend a tree as a tree, or a dog as a dog, depends upon the intentional capacity to judge that the tree is a tree by forming a conceptual representation of a tree. For Kant, animals, such as my dog, Mac, can be acquainted with trees as trees and dogs as dogs in the sense that they can compare these objects in respect to similarity and difference, even though they are incapable of conceptually recognizing and judging that some tree is a *tree*, that is, that it conforms to the concept of a tree. It is only because Mac, and we, have an imagination that has the blind power of representing dogs according to the schema of doghood that we, but not Mac, can recognize that we are intending dogs as dogs. So, perhaps surprisingly, when Heidegger in this passage suggests that there is a precognitive, prejudgmental ability to intend entities as belonging to kinds, for example in being distressed by things or taking care of them, his assertion is simply orthodox Kant.

Heidegger is also an orthodox Kantian in a second important respect. Kant, and Heidegger, believe that there is a significant intentional divide between animals and humans, although they locate this divide in different distinctions.

For Kant, as we have seen, it doesn't follow from the fact that Mac can intend another dog in a doggy way that Mac can recognize that what he is doing is intending a dog as a dog. And failing that ability, Mac can never be rational and think, or act, out of a recognition of principle. Heidegger, of course, also denies animals these Kantian, rational capacities. But, importantly, he also denies them a second, prior, intentional capacity, of which Kant does not speak. Humans, who are Dasein, are in such a way as to be "in a world." Animals, at most, are "world poor." What capacity for intentional content does "being-in-the-world" track?

According to a familiar list, Heidegger says that beings who are in the world are capable of the following intentional comportments, and entities that are not in-the-world, such as animals, are not capable of these kinds of comportments: "Working on something with something, producing something, cultivating and caring for something, putting something to use, employing something for something."[15] Notice two things about this list. First, all of these intentional comportments are practical rather than judgmental or cognitive. When one produces something, or cultivates and cares for something, or employs something for something, one engages in an overt practical activity that has some teleological point. Second, included in this list of practical intentional comportments is "cultivating and caring for something," and "caring for something" is precisely what, in another context, Heidegger specifies as the locus of human self-directed intentionality. "Each of us is what he pursues and cares for. In everyday terms, we understand ourselves and our existence by way of the activities we pursue and the things we take care of."

In what sense are these kinds of overt practical intentional performances characteristic of human intentionality? Surely animals are capable of acting in order to achieve practical ends, aren't they? Well, yes and no. They are, of course, capable of acting so as to attain ends that they require in order to stay alive. But most animals are surely *incapable* of the specific *kinds* of practical intentional performances which are included in Heidegger's list of the modes of "being-in." I cultivate and care for my peach tree; my dog, Mac, is incapable of such action. I work on my garden with a shovel; Mac is incapable of doing so. I employ alcohol for disinfecting the saw I use to prune my diseased tree; Mac cannot employ something for something. All of these varieties of practical comportment essentially involve a particular way of interacting with objects. In each of these activities both the objects which we use and the objects which we use them on seem to be typed in a determinate way. In each of these cases the overt, practical, intentional activity tacitly involves intending an entity or entities as fulfilling or potentially fulfilling some job classification or other, as "in order to" satisfy some instrumental role. One can't employ alcohol for disinfecting unless one can intend something *as* a disinfectant, that is, as an entity to be used in order to kill fungus on a tool or organism. One can't cultivate and care for a peach tree unless one intends the seedling to be cultivated into a fruit-bearing tree, that is, as something for producing, or in order to produce, fruit. I can't use this entity as a tool which is a shovel unless I can intend it as to be used in order to accomplish a certain kind of task, the task of digging holes in the ground.

So, for Heidegger, insofar as Dasein is being in the world, Dasein is capable of certain types of overt intentional performances, such as cultivating and caring for something, or employing something for something, and these types of performances all involve intending something as "in order to" fulfill some job classification or other. To intend something *as* "in order to" satisfy some job classification is, for Heidegger, just to intend it as a piece of equipment or as ready-to-hand.[16] Heidegger thinks, wrongly as it turns out, that only humans can intend the ready-to-hand as ready-to-hand. But, formally, it is a necessary condition on the possibility of an entity being Dasein that it is always intending entities as ready-to-hand. "Dasein always assigns itself from a 'for-the-sake-of-which' to the 'with-which' of an involvement; that is to say, to the extent that it is, it always lets entities be encountered as ready-to-hand."[17]

This ability to intend things as belonging to or adhering to equipmental types, as ready-to-hand, provides the base step for all of Heidegger's transcendental arguments. Just as Kant raises the question of what else we must intend and in what other ways must we be capable of intending if we are to be able to intend entities by conceptually cognizing them in judgment, Heidegger raises the question of what else and in what other ways we must be capable of intending if we are to be able to intend entities as ready-to-hand. And, just as Kant in turn argues that the ability to conceptually cognize objects in judgments is necessary for the ability to intend a single unified world of possible experience or empirical knowledge, Heidegger argues that the ability to intend entities as ready-to-hand is necessary for a variety of other kinds of intentional comportments. Most notably, he argues that the ability to intend entities as equipment, together with all of the other types of intentional comportments that are implicated in this intentional accomplishment, are necessary for the possibility of those types of intentions which Kant associates with the ability to reflectively cognize. In the remainder of this chapter I will briefly lay out the overall structure of Heidegger's transcendental argument, paying special attention to the role and nature of Heidegger's replacement for transcendental apperception, the "for-the-sake-of-which."

Heidegger asserts that there are three salient necessary conditions on intending a tool as a tool. That is, he holds that any agent that can intend a tool as a tool must also intend in these other ways. In the order I will treat them here these conditions are: (1) One can not intend anything as belonging to an in-order-to type unless one also intends other entities as belonging to other in-order-to types. (2) One can not intend anything as belonging to an "in-order-to" type unless one also intends what it is for something to belong to some in-order-to type. (3) One can not intend anything as belonging to an "in-order-to" type unless one also intends oneself as "that for the sake of which" one engages in the activity in which one engages. This last, self-directed, type of intention plays the same structural role in Heidegger's thought that the "I think" does in Kant.

First, Heidegger holds that all intentions directed toward the ready-to-hand as ready-to-hand are holistic. One cannot intend anything as belonging to an in-order-to type unless one also intends other entities as belonging to other in-order-to types. "Taken strictly, there is no such thing as *an* equipment. To the being of any equipment there always belongs a totality of equipment, in which it can be the equipment it is. . . . Equipment—in accordance with its equipmentality—always is *in terms of* [*aus*] its belonging to other equipment."[18] That is, Heidegger holds that when I reach for my alcohol in order to disinfect the blade of my saw so that I don't infect other parts of the peach tree or other trees, by the very nature of the case that very act involves not merely intending the alcohol as a disinfectant but also involves intending the saw as an instrument for pruning, the rag as an instrument for wiping, the tree as in order to bear fruit, and so on. His reasons for asserting this have to do with the overtly teleological character of the order of the "in-order-to" and the fact that all teleological determinations are holistic in just this way. What something is in order to accomplish is something that itself is only determinate in terms of other in-order-to roles.

Heidegger also holds that (2) one intends any entity as in-order-to only if one also intends what it is for something to belong to some in-order-to type.

> Whenever we let there be an involvement with something in something beforehand, our doing so is grounded in our understanding such things as letting something be involved, and such things as the "with-which" and "in-which" of involvements. Anything of this sort, and anything else that is basic for it, such as the "towards-this" as that in which there is an involvement, or such as the "for-the-sake-of-which" to which every "towards-which" ultimately goes back—all of these must be disclosed beforehand with a certain intelligibility.[19]

That is, Heidegger asserts that when we, say, employ the alcohol as a disinfectant, we must in some sense intend not merely the alcohol, but also what it is for something to be properly employed to achieve some specified end. And, since to tacitly intend this one must also have some tacit understanding of the form of the holistic structures in terms of which anything can be in-order-to, in intending the alcohol as disinfectant I am also intending "world," or "that wherein Dasein understands itself beforehand in the mode of assigning itself."[20]

Heidegger insists, explicitly and often, on the necessity of one being able to intend the world and its structure if one is to intend an entity as equipment or as ready-to-hand. The argument turns, once again, on the holistic character of the order of the ready-to-hand. Heidegger asserts, plausibly, that it is a mistake to think of a ready-to-hand entity as just an individual whose identity conditions turn on spatial and temporal continuity, an individual that happens to be such that it can be used in a certain way. Broken tools can't be used as they are "in order to be" used, and not everything that can be used in a certain way counts as belonging to a tool type. Rather, in the case of equipment, that there is some unified individual at all to be intended is constituted precisely by what it is to be used for. The identity and individuation conditions on ready-to-hand entities are themselves "in-order-to" determinations. "The specific *thisness* of a piece of equipment, its *individuation*, if we take the word in a completely formal sense, is not determined primarily by space and time in the sense that it appears in a determinate space and time position. Instead, what determines a piece of equipment as an individual is in each instance its equipmental character and equipmental contexture."[21]

According to Heidegger, then, not all spatially and temporally continuous or connected masses constitute individuals, and not all individual tools are spatially and temporally continuous and connected masses. A Band-Aid affixed to a severed hand is not an individual of any order and a set of bookends can be a single tool. It is that an entity is to be used in order to accomplish some task, then, that constitutes the entity as a single equipmental entity. But, as the end of this quote hints, no tool can have an equipmental character, an "in-order-to" role, apart from belonging to an equipmental contexture, a context of mutually supporting and sustaining teleologically organized roles. This "belonging to" such a context, however, is no fact about the individual tool independent of *being intended as* to be intended as belonging to such a context.[22] When instantiated in action, rather than judgment, such "being intended as belonging to an equipmental contexture" is always embodied in some ongoing, integrated pattern or schema of behavior by an agent in which the agent employs a whole series of tools from a given tool chest in order to accomplish ends that are characteristic of the use of that tool chest. What I do with the alcohol when I rub down my blade with a rag counts as employing the alcohol as a disinfectant only within the pattern of activity that constitutes my gardening. This ongoing, integrated pattern or schema of behavior by an agent in which the agent employs a whole series of tools from a given tool chest, in order to accomplish ends that are characteristic of the use of that tool chest, *displays* an understanding of how things and activities can be fit together in order to accomplish ends. It is *itself* an intentional act, an act that amounts to an intentional prejudgmental understanding of the holistic structures in terms of which anything can be in-order-to. Since an intention directed toward a given piece of equipment as a piece of equipment can only occur as part of such an ongoing set of activities, it is a necessary condition on intending a ready-to-hand entity that one also intend, indeed understand, the structure of relations that constitute a world or equipmental context in which tools are.

This characteristic Heideggerian assertion, that the *structure* of the equipmental context in which tools function "must be disclosed beforehand with a certain intelligibility," is the key to understanding Heidegger's claims regarding the role of self-directed intentionality. For, Heidegger holds, it is part of the structure of the world that every such context is anchored by some "that for the sake of which," some "potentiality for being" Dasein itself, which provides the point of the context. "In understanding a context of relations such as we have mentioned, Dasein has assigned itself to an 'in order to', and it has done so in terms of a potentiality-for-being for the sake of which it itself is."[23] The thought is simply this. Every teleological process is organized to realize some end. As Aristotle taught, this end can be of one of two types. Either, as in building, the end is such that when it is attained the process ceases. Or, as in living, the end is attained only if the process continues. In the latter case, all that occurs in the process, respiration, digestion, and so forth, is for the sake of the continuation of the process; although the act of respiration is in order to oxygenate the blood, oxygenation of the blood is for the sake of the life of the organism. Now, the typically human pattern of tool-using behavior that constitutes our primary kind of intentional comportment toward tools as tools is of the second type. Gardening is a way of acting which uses particular tools in particular prescribed ways in order to attain characteristic kinds of goals. While one gardens, that is, while one engages in these kinds of behavior, for these ends with these tools, in order to produce fruit and flowers, one acts so as to produce fruit and flowers only if one is a gardener, that is, only if one intends oneself as a gardener and intends the world as gardeners do. My dog acts as dogs act, but humans act as gardeners act, or shoemakers, or professors. So every act of gardening is, Heidegger believes, an implicit affirmation of oneself as a certain type of person, a gardener. I garden if, and only if, I understand myself as a gardener, and I engage in gardening acts for the sake of my being a gardener. I garden so that, or for the sake of, my being a gardener, that is, for the sake of the continuation of my gardening activity. Being a Dasein in the way of being a gardener is, as Kant puts it, an end in itself.

Heidegger thus argues that human activity is distinctive in that the patterns of activity and intentionality embodied in that activity have themselves as ends, as well as having external ends. And, as such, any agent that acts in these ways does so for the sake of being a kind of agent, realizing a possible way of being Dasein. To see the world as a philosopher does, and to act with the tools of his trade as philosophers do, is *itself* to act for the sake of being a philosopher and intend oneself *as* a philosopher. This is Heidegger's third necessary condition on an agent intending a tool as a tool. One can intend a tool as a tool only if, in caring for and cultivating things, in being distressed by them, or employing them for something, one intends oneself by way of the activities we pursue, as that for the sake of which we pursue them.

Kant argues that the possibility of the "I think" accompanying every act of cognition is a necessary condition on acts of conceptual cognition, or thought. In an exactly parallel manner, Heidegger argues that *if* an agent is capable of being in the world, of intending entities as tools that are to be used according to some equipmental type, *then* that agent also, thereby, intends herself as that for the sake of which her world, or the equipmental contexture to which she "assigns" herself, is organized. That is, Heidegger argues that the fact of the "for-the-sake-of-which" is a necessary condition on the possibility of intending a tool as a tool.

But Kant doesn't merely argue that the possibility of the "I think" is necessary for cognition. He also argues that cognition, and with it the possibility of the "I think," is itself necessary *for* several other kinds of intentional performance, most notably including intentions directed toward a coherent world of possible experience. Similarly, for Heidegger, the ability to intend equipment as equipment, and the coordinated ability to intend oneself as that for the sake of which one acts, are necessary for other kinds of intentional performance, most notably including precisely those types of intentions that Kant treats as basic to human intentionality, cognition, and the possibility of the "I think."

That Heidegger holds that intending entities within an equipmental contexture, and thus being-in-the-world and intending oneself as the for-the-sake-of-which of the world, is necessary for cognition in Kant's sense, judgment, and the possibility of the "I think," is displayed by the priority that he accords to intentions directed toward the ready-to-hand over those directed toward the extant, or present-at-hand. Present-at-hand entities are those entities whose individuation conditions are such that they turn on spatial and temporal position, connectedness, and continuity, as well as causal powers. They are the ordinary substances that have been taken to be the basic entities since Aristotle. That intentions directed toward the extant are to be associated with intentions directed toward objects, in Kant's sense, and thus with cognition and judgment, is indicated by Heidegger's analysis of intentions directed toward the extant. For, he tells us, intentions directed toward the extant are actualized only in and through the act of *assertion*.

If this entity [e.g., a hammer] becomes the "object" of an assertion, then as soon as we begin this assertion, there is already a change-over in the fore-having. Something ready-to-hand with which we have to do or perform something, turns into something "about which" the assertion that points it out is made. . . . This leveling of the primordial "as" of circumspective interpretation to the "as" with which presence-at-hand is given a definite character is the specialty of assertion.[24]

And assertion, for Heidegger, is "a pointing out which gives something a definite character and which communicates."[25] So one intends an extant entity insofar as one makes an assertion about it, and one makes an assertion about it when one communicates that that entity has some definite character, that is, when one communicates that it is of some definite type. To point out that some entity is of some definite type, is to make a judgment about that entity. So, to intend the extant as the extant is to make a judgment concerning it. As, for Kant, objects as objects are the objects of judgment, Kant's objects of possible cognition are just Heidegger's extant entities.

Heidegger has a different theory of judgment from Kant. And for that reason there are important differences between Kant's understanding of cognitive intentions directed toward objects and Heidegger's understanding of intentions directed toward the present-at-hand. In particular, early Heidegger's emphasis on, and interpretation of, assertion embodies a modification of Kant. The fact that for Heidegger an assertion is always a pointing out or exhibition of that about which it is an assertion indicates that that about which the assertion is made must already have been intentionally given *prior* to the assertion. That is, for Heidegger, all judgment presupposes a prior intention directed toward the *entity* that is referred to in the assertion. Now, in Kant, judgment is always theoretically understood in terms of representation. *What* I intend when I judge is my own representation, and it is only by representing that representation as my own and as belonging to some type, that is, by making a judgment about *it*, that it becomes possible for me to cognitively represent. Heidegger, on the other hand, does not accept Kant's representational theory of intentionality. The cross-over, the transcendence of intentionality toward an entity other than myself, must, he suggests, have already occurred prior to my forming a judgment concerning that entity. If I didn't already intend an *entity* prior to my judging concerning it, the judgment could never be an intention directed toward *that entity*.

Assertion does not as such primarily unveil; instead, it is always, in its sense, already related to something antecedently given as unveiled. . . . Some being must be antecedently given as unveiled in order to serve as the possible about-which of an assertion. But so far as a being is antecedently given for a Dasein it has . . . the character of being within the world. Intentional comportment in the sense of assertion about something is founded in its ontological structure in the basic constitution of Dasein which we described as being-in-the-world.[26]

This analysis of judgment as assertion thus indicates the nature of the priority that Heidegger accords to intentions directed toward the ready-to-hand over those directed toward the present-at-hand. The way in which Heidegger often asserts this priority makes it seem as if the priority is a genetic one: one first intends an entity as ready-to-hand and then only later does one intend it as a substance or object. But this is misleading, at best. Rather, the priority is a transcendental priority: any agent capable of intending entities as continuing substances with properties must also be capable of intending entities as ready-to-hand or as useful for realizing some end.

The analysis of judgment as assertion also indicates the nature of Heidegger's argument in favor of the claim that being in the world, and thus intending oneself as the for-the-sake-of of an equipmental totality, is a necessary condition on Kantian style cognition, judgment, and the possibility of the "I think." In outline, the argument runs as follows. The act of judging about, or the typing of, objects is properly seen as the act of forming assertions about them. Since making an assertion about an object is essentially reflectively pointing something out or typing *that object*, that is, recognizing that *what is intended* shares features with other intended entities, and not reflectively recognizing that our *intentions directed toward* those entities share features, one can make assertions concerning those entities only if the entities are intended in some way other than through the act of judging them. Entities are primarily intended as entities only in our circumspective, coping activity that implicitly treats entities as typed by the in-order-to roles specified by the equipmental context in which we live. So, unless one were capable of intending things as ready-to-hand by being-in-the-world, one would be incapable of forming judgments, and thus incapable of cognition, in Kant's sense, or of conceptually attaching the "I think" to one's thoughts.

This transcendental argument sketch is clearly problematic in several different ways. Most obviously, to fill in the sketch one would need to show both that "assertion as such does not primarily unveil" and that entities as such can only be intended within the intentional structure which Heidegger calls "being-in-the-world." And it is anything but clear that there is anything in the Heideggerian corpus that is adequate to these argumentative tasks. It strikes me that there is a more promising strategy for reaching Heidegger's conclusion from his premises than the one which Heidegger himself mostly pursues. For, arguably, the ability to use an articulate language is a necessary condition on the possibility of making discursive judgments. So, if one can support the plausible thesis that language itself is a tool chest of specialized tool types, it would follow from Heidegger's transcendental discussion of the conditions on intending equipment as equipment that no agent could make explicit judgments unless they were also Dasein, or being-in-the-world.

Acknowledging that Heidegger is not much interested in this strategy, however, does not detract from the originality of the early Heidegger's transcendental project. For that project amounts to the attempt to place the entire *Kantian* transcendental project, with its emphasis on the centrality of the reflective act of typing our own mental activity, within a broader intentional context. For Heidegger, that intentional context is provided by a manner of coping with the world which is distinctively human, required for Kantian cognition, and does not require the ability to make conceptual judgments regarding one's own mental activity. Heidegger's name for this kind of intentional comportment is "being-in-the-world," and it involves the ability to intend oneself as a certain type of agent by intending entities within the world as to-be-used in determinate ways to achieve determinate ends.

CHAPTER 12

Heidegger's "Scandal of Philosophy"

THE PROBLEM OF THE 'DING AN SICH' IN 'BEING AND TIME'

Herman Philipse

Like Carnap, Moore, and Wittgenstein, Heidegger developed a debunking strategy with regard to the problem of the external world. As he said, the "scandal of philosophy" is not that a proof of the external world has yet to be given, but rather that such proofs are expected and attempted again and again. Heidegger's hermeneutic ontology of human existence (Dasein) purported to show that the problem of the external world has no sense at all. However, Being and Time *(*Sein und Zeit; *1927) is not only a hermeneutic ontology but also a treatise in transcendental philosophy, and transcendental philosophy after Kant has been haunted by the problem of the Ding an sich (thing in itself). Does Heidegger's debunking strategy succeed in avoiding this latter problem, which is nothing but a Kantian version of the problem of the external world? And is Heidegger's strategy viable from a philosophical point of view?*

1. The Problem of the 'Ding an sich'

According to one of Immanuel Kant's most celebrated quotes, it remains a "scandal of philosophy . . . that the existence of the things outside us must be accepted merely on faith, and that if anyone thinks good to doubt their existence, we are unable to counter this doubt by any satisfactory proof."[1] Kant claimed to have remedied this philosophical embarrassment by giving a stringent demonstration of the existence of external reality. But the import of his proof, which he staged as a "Refutation of Idealism," is restricted to things in the phenomenal world, which are constituted by, and are ontologically dependent upon, transcendental subjectivity.[2] In order to avoid the conclusion that human transcendental subjectivity creates the world and so equals the Divinity, Kant had to assume a "world" in another sense, which he called the *Ding an sich*, that exists independently of the transcendental subject. This hypothesis explains the passive aspect of human experience by postulating that the world *an sich* impinges on our sense organs and causes a multiplicity of sensations in us.[3] Clearly, then, Kant did not completely succeed in removing the scandal of philosophy by proving the existence of the external world, because he did not provide a proof of the existence of the *Ding an sich*.

It has been argued by many authors, the first of whom was Friedrich Heinrich Jacobi (1743–1819), that Kant *could* not provide such a proof. In order to explain how a priori propositions such as the axioms of Euclidean geometry can be informative about the external world ("synthetic"), Kant contended that the subjective cognitive structures that enable us to know these propositions a priori are also constitutive of (entities in) the phenomenal world, and that it is this phenomenal world which is the object of mathematics, physics, and all other empirical knowledge. Accordingly, we know a priori that the phenomenal world is Euclidean and obeys the principle of causality, for example. From this transcendental theory it follows, however, that we cannot state any truths by applying synthetic a priori propositions or the categories to the world as it is in itself (*an sich*). What is more, we cannot know anything whatsoever about the world in itself, because all knowledge is based upon synthetic a priori principles. If this is so, how can Kant claim that the world in itself is causally responsible for the input of our transcendental cognitive system?[4] Is causality not one of the twelve categories, and is the field of application of the categories not restricted to the phenomenal world? Indeed, how can Kant even say that a *Ding an sich* exists? "Existence" (Dasein, in Kant's sense) also is a category.

It seems, then, that the hypothesis of a *Ding an sich* contradicts Kant's transcendental theory, so that Kant could not argue for that hypothesis on the basis of his philosophy. And yet, without this hypothesis, no one would accept the transcendental theory in the first place.[5] Thus, instead of being solved by Kant once and for all, the traditional problem of the external world merely transmuted into the problem of the *Ding an sich*, and this problem continued to haunt Kantianism throughout the nineteenth century. Many different solutions were proposed by authors such as Jacobi (naïve sentimental realism), Fries (1773–1843; psychological Kantianism), and Reinhold (1758–1823; neutral monism or syncretism), but none of them could escape from the fundamental paradox that transcendental philosophy both requires and excludes the hypothesis of a *Ding an sich*. In his

Kritik der theoretischen Philosophie (*Critique of Theoretical Philosophy*), of 1801, Gottlob Ernst Schulze (1761–1833) argued that any attempt to transcend the limits of possible experience by a transcendental philosophy is condemned by this very same transcendental philosophy.[6] As a result, authors such as Salomon Maimon (1754–1800), Sigismund Beck (1761–1840), and Fichte (1762–1814) came to the conclusion that the very notion of a *Ding an sich* is an "impossible concept."[7] By transforming the notion of a *Ding an sich* in various ways, they paved the road to the embarrassing conclusion that Kant had tried to avoid, the idealist doctrine that ultimately our transcendental subjectivity is identical with the Divinity. Thus, the development of transcendental philosophy culminated in Eckhartian mysticism and German idealism. The problem of the external world was eliminated by the arbitrary decision that the world is not external. What we call the world is but an aspect of our, that is, God's mind.

When after Hegel's death German philosophy sobered up from these idealist speculations, and started to take seriously the impressive advances in the natural sciences, it was landed again in the intellectual predicament of the philosophers of the scientific revolution. The problem of the external world, which was raised by these philosophers because of their analysis of matter and perception, regained its position at the center of the philosophical stage. A great many solutions were tried out, such as the hypothetical scientific realism of Herbart (1776–1841) and Brentano (1838–1917); the transcendental realism of Eduard von Hartmann (1842–1906); the phenomenalism of positivists such as Mach; and, later on, Edmund Husserl's transcendental idealism. According to a number of authors, such as von Hartmann and Husserl, the problem of the external world is the central problem of epistemology. Moreover, epistemology acquired the basic role of first philosophy, for its task was to investigate the most fundamental assumption that underlies all empirical sciences, namely that there is an external world which exists independently of the human mind.[8] No solution to the problem of the external world gained general acceptance, so that Kant's scandal continued to torment philosophers. In this respect, German philosophy from Herbart to the neo-Kantians is a replay of the development from Descartes and Locke to Kant, and no essentially new doctrines emerged.

2. *Debunking Strategies*

This historical background explains the fact that during the first half of the twentieth century philosophers started to doubt the very legitimacy of the problem of the external world. Was the issue a meaningful problem at all, which had to be solved by a philosophical theory or "proof"? Husserl, for example, maintained in 1907 and 1913 that the philosopher should not attempt to argue for the existence of the external world; his task was to describe phenomenologically the transcendental correlation between mental acts and their intentional correlates. Yet Husserl's elimination of the problem suffers from a defect similar to that of Fichte's philosophy, for at the transcendental level Husserl held that the world as a whole is ontologically dependent on transcendental subjectivity.[9]

A different strategy for debunking the problem was proposed by G. E. Moore in 1925 and 1939. Moore did not dispute that one has to prove the existence of the external world, but he believed that such proofs were so easy that no intricate philosophy was needed to provide them. It would suffice to hold up one's hands, for example, and to say, pointing to each hand in turn, "Here is one hand," and "Here is another," a procedure which allegedly amounts to a "perfectly rigorous" proof of the existence of external things.[10] But Moore's defense of common sense is unconvincing, for it is open to a double charge. On the one hand, proofs of the external world à la Moore do not make sense within the framework of common sense, as Wittgenstein argued in *On Certainty*. On the other hand, Moore's proofs are an *ignoratio elenchi* if they are meant to address the philosophical arguments for external world skepticism, which are typically based upon a scientific analysis of matter and sense perception.

Whereas Moore attempted to defuse the problem of the external world from the point of view of common sense, Rudolf Carnap tried to eliminate it from a scientific and empiricist perspective. Carnap argued in 1928 that statements cannot be meaningful in the sense of having a factual content unless experiential conditions can be indicated under which they are to be called true and under which they are to be called false.[11] The controversy between the philosophical solutions to the problem of the external world, such as idealism and realism, is in principle not open to a settlement by experiential methods. It follows that these solutions do not have, though they may seem to have, factual content, and are meaningless from the point of view of scientific method. Carnap's dismissal of the external world issue as a pseudoproblem survived his liberalization of the empirical meaning criterion in his later works. In 1950, Carnap argued that the problem is an illegitimate confusion between on the one hand questions of existence internal to a linguistic framework, which can be settled by empirical investigations, and on the other hand external questions about the pragmatic efficiency of such a framework.[12]

If we write off Moore's attempt to diffuse the problem of the external world as superficial because it does not address the arguments for external world skepticism, we will pass the same verdict on Carnap's strategy. Although Carnap is correct in his diagnosis that the problem is meaningless from a scientific point of view, because in principle it cannot be settled by experiential methods, his claim that this result eliminates the problem is illicit. Indeed, Carnap's early work strongly suggests the problem of the external world. In *Aufbau*, Carnap justifies his choice of the "autopsychological" basis for his constitutional system by the demand that the system reflect the epistemic order of objects. In other words, he holds the view that our knowledge of physical objects is based upon subjective experiences. The fact that Carnap wants to "bracket" (in Husserl's sense) the question of the objective reality of these experiences at this stage of *Aufbau* shows that it arises naturally at that point. Bracketing the problem of the external world, that is, exercising a phenomenological "withholding of judgment," neither answers nor eliminates it.[13]

It is the objective of this chapter to determine whether Martin Heidegger's strategy in *Being and Time* for disposing of the scandal of philosophy is more successful than those of Carnap and Moore. Like Husserl, Carnap, and Wittgenstein, but unlike Moore, Heidegger held that any attempt to prove the existence of the external world is misguided. The reason is this: "The question of whether there is a world at all and whether its being can be proved, makes no sense if it is raised by *Dasein* as Being-in-the-world; and who else would raise it?"[14] Hence, having criticized Kant's proof of the external world, Heidegger declares that the "scandal of philosophy" is not that this proof has yet to be given, but *that such proofs are expected and attempted again and again*."[15] Why does Heidegger think that the problem of the external world does not make sense? And why is it questionable whether Heidegger's strategy for eliminating the problem succeeds?

3. Heidegger's Diagnosis: A Preliminary Sketch

In the introduction to section 43 of *Being and Time*, Heidegger says that four different questions are mixed up in the problem of the external world: "(1) whether any entities which supposedly 'transcend our consciousness' *are* at all; (2) whether this reality of the 'external world' can be adequately *proved*; (3) to what extent this entity, if it is real, can be known in its being-in-itself; (4) what the sense [*Sinn*] of this entity, reality, signifies in general."[16] In the first two questions there is a further ambiguity. Are they concerned with the "world" in the sense of entities *in* the world (*innerweltliches Seiendes*) or with "world" in the sense of *that within which* these entities supposedly are?[17]

The first task of the philosopher is to clarify these questions. This is why Heidegger states in section 43a that the fourth question is the most fundamental one.[18] He argues for two theses: first, that what "reality" means, as the ontological sense of entities in the world, cannot be elucidated without an adequate ontological analysis of what is supposedly transcended by these real entities, to wit, human subjectivity.[19] And second, that an adequate analysis of human existence shows that questions (1) to (3) are meaningless as they stand. In short, Heidegger claims in his second thesis that the ontological analysis of Dasein in the two published divisions of *Being and Time* exposes the problem of the external world as a meaningless issue. A brief summary of some main points will indicate why Heidegger thinks that this is the case.

Heidegger defines Dasein as "the being that we ourselves are."[20] It is a central question of *Being and Time* in terms of which categories we should try to understand ourselves ontologically. According to Heidegger, traditional philosophy from the Greeks to our times applied categories to human existence that were originally derived from nonhuman domains, such as artifacts (*Hergestelltheit*) or other inanimate objects. Since these categories allegedly are inadequate for understanding our human mode of existence and its temporal structure, Heidegger sets himself a double task: a "destruction" of traditional categories by showing why they are inadequate, and a "construction" of a system of new categories for ontological self-understanding, the so-called *existentialia*.[21] In developing these existentialia, we should start from the way we understand ourselves implicitly in everyday life (*Alltäglichkeit*) and, using the method of hermeneutic phenomenology, attempt to explicate conceptually the structural features of our everyday human existence. This task is difficult because, as Heidegger says, we are constantly tempted to understand ourselves in terms of the things in the world we relate to, such as artifacts and inanimate objects.[22] Although Dasein is "ontically nearest" to itself, it is "ontologically furthest removed" from itself.[23]

One of Heidegger's existentialia is particularly pertinent to the problem of the external world, and, like the other existentialia, it is developed by reflecting on features of everyday life. It is a striking characteristic of our everyday existence that whenever we try to specify who or what we are, we do so in terms of the "world." We say, for instance, that we are from a determinate country, that we have a job in a specific firm or institution, that we live in a particular town, that we are a son or daughter of so-and-so, and so on. Indeed, it is impossible to specify otherwise who we are, because who we are is deeply determined by the way we are practically involved in the world. On the ontological level of existentialia, Heidegger expresses this feature by saying that Dasein is "being-in-the-world," and Division One of *Being and Time* consists largely of an exploration of this fundamental existentiale and its various aspects. "Being-in," for instance, does not refer to a spatial relationship of two inanimate things but expresses our familiarity with the world in which we are involved and in terms of which we understand ourselves.

It follows that, being who we are, it is logically impossible for us to doubt the existence of the world. Such a doubt is meaningless if uttered by us, because, in understanding who we ourselves are, we inevitably refer to the world. As Heidegger says, the problem of the external world "makes no sense if it is raised by *Dasein* as Being-in-the-world; and who else would raise it?"[24] Hence, "The problem of reality in the sense of the question whether there is an external world and whether such a world can be proved, turns out to be an impossible one, not because its consequences lead to inextricable impasses, but because the very entity which serves as its theme, is one which, as it were, repudiates any such formulation of the question."[25] In Wittgenstein's terminology, one might say that there is an internal relation between Dasein and world, so that it cannot make sense for us to doubt the existence of the world. And where doubting does not make sense, there is no room for proofs of the existence of the external world either. Once we articulate a more adequate ontology of Dasein, that is, of our everyday existence in the world, we see that the problem of the external world cannot make sense. It follows that ontology, and not epistemology (defined as the discipline that deals with the problem of the external world), is the fundamental philosophical discipline.[26]

To the extent that I have depicted it so far, Heidegger's strategy for eliminating the problem of the external world by an ontology of Dasein bears striking resemblances with, but also interesting differences from, the strategies of Moore and Carnap. The perspective in which Heidegger views the problem, that of everyday life (*Alltäglichkeit*), resembles Moore's perspective of common sense, although in contrast to Moore, Heidegger explores in depth what this perspective consists in. Yet in another respect Heidegger contrasts favorably with Moore. Like the later Wittgenstein (*On Certainty*), but unlike Moore, Heidegger holds that within the perspective of ordinary life there is no room for proofs of the external world, because doubting its existence does not make sense.

As far as Carnap is concerned, it seems at first sight that the difference between his strategy and Heidegger's could not be greater, for Carnap approaches the problem from the point of view of scientific method, whereas Heidegger prefers the perspective of ordinary life. Heidegger would have agreed with Carnap that the problem of the external world is not a meaningful scientific question, but he would have argued that this insight is superficial and does not remove the problem. In order to eliminate it, we have to analyze ontologically the very sense in which we may be said to exist and the sense of "world" and "reality."

Yet there is a striking resemblance between Heidegger and the later Carnap at this very point. Both Heidegger (1927) and Carnap (1950) make a distinction between empirical questions of existence, concerned with particular entities, and a global framework without which such questions do not have a determinate meaning. In Carnap's case, global frameworks are linguistic and optional. We may choose different linguistic frameworks at will, using considerations of practical expediency. For Heidegger, however, the encompassing framework of the "world" is prelinguistic and always already there: it is the background or horizon of all our choices and not itself an option. Here again, Heidegger is closer to Wittgenstein than to Carnap. In *On Certainty*, Wittgenstein argues that we cannot meaningfully doubt propositions that express the bedrock of all our language games. This bedrock is not optional, because it belongs to our human form of life.

Using the distinction between on the one hand the world as a background or framework and on the other hand entities in the world (*innerweltliche Seiende*), we may now summarize as follows Heidegger's view on the scandal of philosophy. The problem of the external world concerns either entities in the world or the world as a framework. In the first case, the problem of the external world is not a philosophical question. With regard to many particular entities in the world we may wonder whether they exist, but this is an empirical and not a philosophical issue, which has to be settled by experiential methods.[27] In the second case, of the world as a framework, the problem does not make sense, because Dasein and the world form one unitary phenomenon: Dasein is being-in-the-world. "World" here means not the totality of entities or the totality of facts but "that '*wherein*' a factical *Dasein* as such 'lives.'"[28] The world in this sense is a meaningful structure of referential and functional relations (*Bezugszusammenhang*) between equipment, work, institutions, infrastructure, and so on, without which humans and nonhuman things could not show up for us as that what they are. On the one hand, this structure cannot be without Dasein, because all its referential relations are informed ultimately by a "for-the-sake-of" (*Worum-willen*) that is Dasein itself. On the other hand, Dasein cannot be without world, because it is always involved in it and interprets itself in its terms.[29]

We may conclude that Heidegger's strategy for debunking the problem of the external world is superior to the strategies of Carnap and Moore, since Heidegger combines the virtues of their accounts while avoiding some of the weaknesses. This does not imply, however, that Heidegger's strategy is a viable one. In order to reach a decision on this matter, two kinds of considerations are required. On the one hand, there are several problems of interpretation to be settled. On the other hand, we must evaluate philosophically the strategy we attribute to Heidegger. Although these two kinds of considerations are different, and even though interpretation must precede evaluation, philosophical reflection is relevant to matters of interpretation because interpretations have to be maximally "charitable." In the next section, I identify four problem areas pertaining to the interpretation of Heidegger's strategy. Can the problems of these areas be solved by an interpretation that attributes to Heidegger a consistent and viable philosophical strategy?

4. Problems and Method of Interpretation

Heidegger's strategy for debunking the problem of the external world on the basis of an ontology of Dasein is questionable because of a fundamental ambiguity in the very notion of Dasein, and, indeed, in the "question of being" that informs *Being and Time.* In one sense, the question of being aims at developing regional ontologies, such as the ontologies of nature, of Dasein, of life, or of space-time, and so on, by spelling out fundamental concepts for articulating these regions.[30] In the context of regional ontology, Heidegger means by "being" the particular mode of being of entities belonging to a specific ontological region. Since Dasein is characterized by self-interpretation, the method of the regional ontology of Dasein is the method of hermeneutic phenomenology. In my *Heidegger's Philosophy of Being* (1998), I called this the "phenomenologico-hermeneutical leitmotif" in the question of being.

In a second sense, the question of being is a transcendental question. Heidegger holds that the being (*Sein*) of entities is determined by Dasein's understanding of being (*Seinsverständnis*), and he compares the "philosophical phenomenon" of being with Kantian transcendental structures.[31] In the context of this "transcendental theme," Heidegger means by being a holistic transcendental framework that is somehow constitutive for the way in which entities appear to us, and he holds that being in this sense depends upon Dasein, that is, upon Dasein's understanding of being.

The fact that the ontological analysis of Dasein is both a regional ontology and a transcendental philosophy renders the notion of Dasein ambiguous. Dasein not only is "the being that we ourselves are," as Heidegger says in section 2 of *Being and Time*, but Dasein also is the transcendental agent *in* us.[32] Furthermore, whereas Dasein in the sense of regional ontology is merely one ontological region among others, Dasein in the sense of transcendental philosophy is unique and more fundamental than any other ontological region, because it somehow constitutes these other regions. Accordingly, the transcendental philosophy of Dasein develops "the conditions for the possibility of any ontological investigation."[33]

We might say that the phenomenologico-hermeneutical leitmotif in the question of being is its pole of plurality, because it aims at articulating the many senses in which "being" is said (there are many ontological regions), whereas the transcendental leitmotif is its pole of unity, because all notions of "being" are transcendentally reducible to Dasein's understanding of being (*Seinsverständnis*). Hence, Heidegger's question of being has a bipolar structure similar to Aristotle's question of being.[34] If this is correct, there is one global interpretative issue that should be resolved if we want to assess the philosophical viability of Heidegger's debunking strategy. Does Heidegger want to show that the problem of the external world is meaningless by a *regional ontology* of Dasein, by a *transcendental philosophy* of Dasein, or by both? More in particular, one might distinguish four areas of interpretative problems:

A. One cannot doubt that there are transcendental arguments in *Being and Time*. According to Heidegger, the "Being" (*Sein*) of things depends upon Dasein's "understanding of the Being" (*Seinsverständnis*) of things.[35] In other words, the "subjective" conditions for understanding being, such as the originary temporality of Dasein, are also "objective" conditions for being. In the past, all such transcendental theories turned out to imply a specific variety of the problem of the external world: the problem of the *Ding an sich* (section 1, above). We may wonder how Heidegger can be a transcendental philosopher and also claim that he eliminates this problem (instead of providing some solution to it). How should we interpret Heidegger's attempt to reconcile the "no problem" view with the "transcendental" view? Does Heidegger succeed in reconciling them?

B. The first problem area condenses, as it were, into a number of passages in the text of *Being and Time*, which David Cerbone has aptly called "puzzle passages."[36] Here are two of them:

(1) Being (not entities) is something which "there is" only insofar as truth is. And truth *is* only insofar as and as long as Dasein is.[37]
(2) Entities *are*, quite independently of the experience by which they are disclosed, the acquaintance in which they are discovered, and the grasping in which their nature is ascertained. But Being "is" only in the understanding of those entities to whose being something like an understanding of Being belongs.[38]

In these puzzle passages, Heidegger tries to reconcile some version of "entity-realism" with some version of "being-idealism" (being "is" only in the understanding by Dasein).[39] But how is that possible, if "being" is defined as "that which determines entities as entities, that on the basis of which entities are already understood, however we may elucidate them in detail"?[40] The solutions of Kant and Husserl consisted in a combination of empirical realism regarding entities and transcendental idealism regarding constitutive structures ("being"). However, both solutions implied that empirical entities are transcendentally constituted, so that, on the transcendental level, there is entity idealism with regard to empirical entities. Furthermore, both solutions raised the problem of the *Ding an sich*, the existence of which was affirmed by Kant and denied by Husserl.[41] What solution does Heidegger propose? How can Heidegger reconcile his solution with his claim that the problem of the external world is meaningless?

C. In section 3, above, I argued that Heidegger's strategy for debunking the problem of the external world is superior to the strategies of Carnap and Moore. However, this apology for Heidegger is seriously incomplete. We saw that both Moore and Carnap failed to address the reasons for external world skepticism, reasons which derive predominantly from a scientific analysis of matter and perception. Does Heidegger fare better in this respect, so that his analysis is superior on this point as well? In section 43a of *Being and Time* there is a passage in which Heidegger diagnoses the source of external world skepticism as follows:

> Our task is not to prove that and how there is an "external world," but to point out why Dasein, as being-in-the-world, has the tendency first to annul "epistemologically" the "external world" in order to prove it afterward. The cause (*Grund*) of this lies in Dasein's falling and in the way in which the primary understanding of Being has been diverted to Being as occurrentness—a diversion which is motivated by that falling itself.[42]

But this passage is not sufficiently clear. In particular, it is unclear why Heidegger thinks that what he calls Dasein's falling (*Verfallen*) is the cause (*Grund*) of external world skepticism, and why analyzing this cause will refute the arguments for external world skepticism. An interpretation of Heidegger's strategy for debunking the problem of the external world has to clarify this point.

D. A final area of difficulties consists of Heidegger's pronouncements on the *Ding an sich* in *Being and Time*. Within the global horizon or framework of the world, Heidegger distinguishes between a number of more determinate frameworks in terms of which we may interpret the entities that we encounter.[43] Two of these frameworks are discussed in *Being and Time*, the framework of being ready-to-hand or being serviceable (*zuhanden*) and the framework of being present-to-hand, extant, being occurrent, or being present (*vorhanden*). Other frameworks are merely mentioned, such as the framework of nature as that "which 'stirs and strives', which assails us and enthralls us as landscape."[44] Now Heidegger writes repeatedly in italics that "*Readiness-to-hand is the way in which entities as they are 'in themselves' are determined ontologico-categorially*."[45] This is surprising, for in the Kantian tradition, entities are said to be *an sich* if they are ontologically independent with regard to the (transcendental) subject, whereas equipment and other entities that are ready-to-hand (*zuhanden*) are implausible candidates for this position. Why, then, does Heidegger claim that readiness-to-hand (*Zuhandenheit*) is the way things are *an sich*? The fact that the relevant statements are italicized proves their importance for the interpretation of *Being and Time*.

Since the text of *Being and Time* is unclear at many crucial points, substantial interpretations of Heidegger's strategy for debunking the problem of the external world will be underdetermined by the texts. For this reason we must evaluate the existing interpretations by a comparative analysis and inquire to what extent they satisfy a number of criteria for theory-choice. With regard to the interpretation of philosophical texts, the two most important criteria for theory-choice are: (1) the criterion of historical textual adequacy, and (2) the criterion of philosophical fecundity. Is it possible to develop an interpretation of Heidegger's strategy that solves the problems of areas A–D, above, and that is both textually adequate in an historically plausible way and philosophically fruitful?

5. *Recent Interpretations: Being Idealism*

Most recent interpretations of the way in which Heidegger deals with the problem of the external world in *Being and Time* focus on area B, the puzzle passages. How are we to interpret and reconcile the "being idealism" and the "entity realism" affirmed in these texts? Let me begin by sketching the space of possible solutions.

According to (a) a minimalist reading of "being idealism," Heideggerian "being" is just the meaning or significance that we humans attribute to entities; it is what entities are understood *as*. A maximalist reading (b) would interpret Heideggerian "being" as an entity-constitutive transcendental framework à la Kant and Husserl, a position that I call "strong transcendentalism." Between (a) and (b), there is an intermediate interpretation (c), according to which "being" is a transcendental framework which is not constitutive of entities but only of that "as what" entities are encountered. Let me call this view "weak transcendentalism."

With regard to "entity realism," readings (b) and (c) of "being idealism" invite us to make a distinction between an empirical and a transcendental point of view. We may then interpret Heidegger's entity realism either (m) on the empirical level (empirical realism) or (n) on the transcendental level (transcendental realism), or both. Even if we do not make this distinction, we have a choice between (o) restricting entity realism to occurrent (*Vorhanden*) entities or (p) interpreting it more generally. If we opt for (m) empirical entity realism, we may regard questions concerning entities at the transcendental level as either (q) meaningful or (r) meaningless.

In order to produce a complete interpretation of the puzzle passages, we have to combine one element of (a–c) with more than one element of (m–r). Some combinations are clearly unsatisfactory. For example, if one unites (b) with (m), (o), and (q), Heidegger would be faced with the traditional problem of the *Ding an sich*, whereas he claims to have shown that this problem is senseless. We are investigating whether it is possible to develop a complete interpretation that explains all relevant texts and is philosophically interesting in itself.

Apart from the two puzzle passages I quoted, there is a third one, which seems to exclude both transcendental realism (n) and transcendental idealism concerning entities:

(3) Of course only as long as Dasein *is* (that is, only as long as an understanding of being is ontically possible), "is there" being. When Dasein does not exist, "independence" "is" not either, nor "is" the "in itself." In such a case this sort of thing can be neither understood nor not understood. In such a case even entities within-the-world can neither be discovered nor lie hidden. *In such a case* it cannot be said that entities are, nor can it be said that they are not. But *now*, as long as there is an understanding of Being and therefore an understanding of occurrentness, it can indeed be said that *in this case* entities will still continue to be.[46]

In this passage, Heidegger seems to rule out transcendental entity realism because he states that the independence of entities with regard to Dasein is itself dependent upon Dasein, and that there is no "in itself" without Dasein. As Cerbone says, "this passage has the effect of nesting the independence claim within a broader claim of dependence, thereby undercutting a straightforwardly realistic understanding of entities."[47] But of course, the passage also seems to exclude transcendental idealism with regard to entities. For Heidegger says, "*In such a case* it cannot be said that entities are, nor can it be said that they are not." I shall come back to the issue of transcendental entity realism later on (sections 7 and 9). Let me first focus on two interpretative problems that are somewhat easier to solve: the problems of being idealism and of empirical entity realism.

With regard to being idealism, the minimalist interpretation (a) has been defended by Dorothea Frede, among others. "If a thing's being consists in its *meaning*, then it only has a being when there is someone for whom this *is* its meaning."[48] Although she does not explicitly make a distinction between the empirical and the transcendental level, she restricts entity realism to occurrent (*vorhanden*) entities (o): *we* interpret these entities *as* existing independently from us.[49] This explains why the "independence" of entities depends on Dasein. As she says, "with things ready-at-hand it is different," for they "lose their ontological status as soon as there is nobody who could make use of their practical meaningfulness."[50] Furthermore, Frede endorses a variety of (r). Heidegger could reject the demand for proofs of the external world because "things have an 'in themselves' only if there is some understanding within which they are what they are. The question what they are apart from this meaning turns out . . . to be senseless."[51]

William Blattner correctly objects to minimalist interpretations of being idealism such as Frede's that they trivialize Heidegger's transcendental arguments, so that they fail for problem area A. Interpretation (a) makes Heidegger's being idealism true by redefinition. If one defines "being" as "a thing's meaning" (Frede) or as a thing's "intelligibility to us" (Olafson),[52] and if one assumes, plausibly, that we humans give meaning to things, it is trivially true that being depends on Dasein. Such an interpretation is both philosophically sterile, because it trivializes Heidegger's being idealism, and textually inadequate. For although interpretation (a) seems to fit Heidegger's definition of "being" as "that in terms of which entities are already understood," Heidegger also defines "being" as "that which determines entities as entities."[53] Furthermore, Heidegger explicitly rejects the view that an entity's being ready-at-hand should be conceived of as a "subjective colouring" given to some world-stuff that is already there in itself.[54]

Should we then opt for interpretation (b) of being idealism, the maximalist view that *entities* are constituted by transcendental frameworks? According to this view, shared by Kant and Husserl, the most fundamental link between consciousness and entities in the world is perception. In perception, the transcendental subject constitutes empirical entities out of its own subjective sensations. Whereas Kant stipulated a *Ding an sich* in order to account for the passive aspect of perception at the transcendental level, Husserl held that this notion of a *Ding an sich* is meaningless, although in 1913 he speculated about God as a theological principle that might explain the order of sensations in transcendental consciousness.[55] In other words, whereas Kant was a transcendental realist concerning entities (although he was a transcendental idealist with regard to space and time), Husserl was, like Berkeley, a transcendental idealist concerning entities (with the exception of God and, indeed, other minds).[56]

Clearly, versions of strong transcendentalism are inadequate as an interpretation of *Being and Time,* although they do imply empirical realism with regard to entities in the world. In the first place, Heidegger explicitly denies that perceptual knowledge is the fundamental link between the world and ourselves. According to his analysis of Dasein as being-in-the-world, perceptual knowledge, and, indeed, knowledge in general, is a secondary, "founded" mode of access to innerworldly things. "All access to such entities is founded ontologically upon the basic structure of *Dasein,* being-in-the-world," Heidegger says, summarizing his analysis.[57] It follows that our being-in-the-world can never be explained in terms of the perceptual relation. In the second place, Heidegger rejects transcendental idealism if it "signifies tracing back every entity to a subject or consciousness . . . " but this is precisely what strong transcendentalism does.[58] Finally, it is unclear how strong transcendentalism can avoid the problem of the external world, whereas Heidegger claims that he succeeds in eliminating the problem as meaningless.

I conclude that we should interpret Heidegger's being idealism in sense (c), weak transcendentalism. Within the context of the transcendental leitmotif, Heideggerian "being" in *Being and Time* is a transcendental framework that is not constitutive of entities but *only of that "as what" entities are encountered*.[59] Many authors adopt this interpretation, such as Blattner (1994, 1999), Dreyfus (1991), Mulhall (1996), and Philipse (1998).

6. Recent Interpretations: Empirical Entity Realism

These authors may still differ on two issues. First, they may have different views on what Heidegger's conception of a transcendental framework amounts to. A Heideggerian transcendental framework cannot be a mere conceptual scheme in the sense of a set of rules for using words, because Heidegger holds that the world as that in which we are involved is meaningful independently from language. World is characterized by holistic significance (*Bedeutsamkeit*) and language can be used for articulating pre-existing meanings: "To meanings, words accrue."[60] This is a major difference between Heidegger and Wittgenstein. For Wittgenstein, words have meaning because of the way in which they are used, so that there can be no meaning without standard uses of words, although Wittgenstein also stresses that language games cannot be understood apart from forms of life.

Second, weak transcendentalism as an interpretation of being idealism may be combined with various interpretations of Heidegger's entity realism. What does Heidegger mean when he says that "entities are, quite independently of the experience by which they are disclosed . . . " (puzzle passage [2])? If we focus on puzzle passage (3), which nests the independence claim within a deeper dependence of Dasein ("When *Dasein* does not exist, 'independence' 'is' not either . . . "), it is plausible to interpret the independence of entities with regard to Dasein as a feature attributed to entities *within* a particular transcendental framework ([m], empirical realism). Whereas Mulhall holds (p) that Dasein encounters *both* occurrent *and* ready-to-hand things "as phenomena which exist independently of its encounters with them," most authors (Blattner, Dreyfus, Frede, Schatzki) restrict this independence to the framework of occurrentness (o).[61] Which of these two conflicting views is correct as an interpretation of *Being and Time*?

At first sight, neither the text of puzzle passage (3) nor its context in section 43c permits us to answer this question with certainty. Although Heidegger links the characteristic of independence with the notion of reality, he distinguishes between a wider and a narrower sense of "reality" in the first paragraph of section 43c. In the wider sense, reality is the mode of being of all nonhuman entities in the world, either occurrent or ready-to-hand. In the narrower and more traditional sense, reality is the mode of being of occurrent entities only.[62] Since Heidegger does not tell us in which of these two senses he is going to use the word "reality" in the remainder of section 43c, it may seem that both interpretation (p) and interpretation (o) are permitted by the text of *Being and Time*.

One cannot argue that one of these apparently permitted interpretations is more charitable than the other because it attributes a philosophically superior opinion to Heidegger. The reason is that Heidegger's notions of occurrentness (*Vorhandenheit*), readiness-to-hand (*Zuhandenheit*), and independence are too ill-defined for constructing a satisfactory philosophical view. For example, Heidegger does not distinguish between things accidentally used as tools (one picks up a stone in order to throw it at a dog) and tools as artifacts (a hammer). The stone is both dependent on Dasein and independent from Dasein. On the one hand, it is dependent because it becomes a tool when it is picked up and loses its status as a tool again when it is thrown away. On the other hand it is independent because humans did not produce it and because it may continue to be after all humans have perished. The hammer also is both dependent and independent with regard to Dasein, but in a somewhat different sense. It is dependent in the sense that it has been made on purpose as an artifact in which its function is inscribed, so to say, and because it fits in with a referential totality of functions (of nails, wood, etc.). If humans did not exist, hammers would not exist either. But the hammer is also independent because it continues to exist and to be ready for use even when nobody is aware of its existence; indeed it may continue to exist when all humans have died.[63]

Yet a more careful reading of section 43 in the context of *Being and Time* as a whole justifies interpretation (o), which restricts to occurrent things Heidegger's "realism" with regard to entities said to be "independent" from Dasein. There are three textual arguments for this interpretation. First, Heidegger starts section 43b by declaring that "nothing else is meant by" the term "reality" than things occurrent (*vorhanden*) within-the-world.[64] Because puzzle passage (3) follows Heidegger's ruminations on the notion of reality, it is plausible to read it as concerned primarily with occurrent things. Second, Heidegger intimates in section 43a that the notion of "independence" is associated with the notion of reality.[65] Combining these two points, one comes to the conclusion that Heidegger links the notion of "independence" to the notion of occurrence. Finally, the last sentence of puzzle passage (3) relates independence from Dasein, in the sense of continuing to be there without Dasein, explicitly to Dasein's understanding of occurrentness: "But *now*, as long as there is an understanding of Being and therefore an understanding of occurrentness, it can indeed be said that *then* [to wit, when Dasein does not exist] entities will still continue to be."[66]

The most important point is, however, that according to puzzle passage (3), this independence from Dasein depends itself upon Dasein: "When *Dasein* does not exist, 'independence' 'is' not either, nor 'is' the 'in itself.'" In other words, the independence of entities with regard to Dasein is a characteristic which depends upon a transcendental framework. Only because occurrent entities are encountered within such a framework can they be encountered *as* independent from us. The entity realism Heidegger defends in puzzle passage (3) is an *empirical* realism concerning occurrent entities. But what about realism at the transcendental level? Is Heidegger also a transcendental realist or is he a transcendental agnostic with regard to entities? Whereas puzzle passage (3) seems to exclude transcendental realism, puzzle passage (2) seems to affirm it.[67]

7. The Transcendental Standpoint

The most sophisticated interpretation of what we can say at the transcendental level has been proposed by William Blattner, who focuses on puzzle passage (3). As I mentioned already, Blattner restricts Heidegger's entity realism at the empirical level to occurrent entities.[68] With regard to the transcendental level in (3), he distinguishes between a trivial and a more substantial interpretation (a "weak" and a "strong" reading, as he calls it) of the following clause from (3): "When *Dasein* does not exist, 'independence' 'is' not either, nor 'is' the 'in itself.' In such a case this sort of thing can be neither understood nor not understood. In such a case even entities within-the-world can neither be discovered nor lie hidden. *In such a case* it cannot be said that entities are, nor can it be said that they are not." According to the trivial reading, Heidegger here specifies what is the case *under* the circumstances of our nonexistence. It is trivially true that without Dasein nothing can be related to Dasein as independent or dependent, as understood or not understood, as discovered or hidden, and that without Dasein there is no speech. Blattner rejects this reading not only because it is trivial but also because it leaves Heidegger without an interesting transcendental argument for the dependence of being on Dasein. But what is Blattner's more substantive interpretation?

Blattner claims that Heidegger in this passage says something *of* the circumstances of Dasein's nonexistence. These circumstances annul the general human framework or "human standpoint" without which questions of dependence or independence, understanding or nonunderstanding, discovery or hiddenness, and existence or nonexistence do not make sense. Because they annul this general framework, we cannot even ask, at the transcendental level, whether entities exist or whether they are independent from Dasein. At the transcendental level, no answer to these questions can have a truth value, so that Heidegger is neither a transcendental realist nor a transcendental idealist about entities. In other words, because being, in the sense of the holistic transcendental framework, depends on Dasein (being idealism), and because being is "that which determines entities as entities," the assumption of the absence of Dasein implies that questions concerning entities must lack a determinate answer.

Blattner explains his interpretation with reference to the standard account of presuppositions. It is senseless to ask "Who is the president of England?" because this question presupposes, mistakenly, that in England a specific political framework is in place, the framework of the presidential system. Similarly, all questions about existence and (in)dependence of entities would presuppose a maximally global framework, the human framework or "world." We descend to the transcendental level if we discover this framework and wonder what can be said about entities if it is not in place. According to Blattner, Heidegger claims that at this level, nothing whatsoever can be said about the (in)dependence or (non)existence of entities.

But why does Heidegger think that there is such a global framework that depends on Dasein? Why is he a transcendental idealist concerning being? According to Blattner, the basic premise of Heidegger's transcendental argument is that without Dasein, there would be no time (temporal idealism). Furthermore, because the very being of entities has a temporal structure or sense, being also depends upon Dasein. Temporal idealism implies transcendental idealism about being. And transcendental idealism about being implies that at the transcendental level there is a failure of bivalence if questions concerning the (non)existence and (in)dependence of entities are raised apart from the human framework. Heidegger's being idealism does not result from a mere redefinition of "being," as Dorothea Frede holds, but is the conclusion of a substantial transcendental argument.

Blattner's interpretation elegantly solves the central problem of this chapter, the issue of how Heidegger could reconcile a variety of transcendental philosophy with his view that the philosophical problem of the external world is meaningless (problem areas A and B). Supposing that the problem is concerned with entities and not with the world as a holistic transcendental framework, we might locate it either at the empirical or at the transcendental level, depending on whether it presupposes or suspends the set of transcendental conditions. At the empirical level, the problem boils down to the question of whether specific occurrent entities really exist, but this is a purely empirical issue, to be settled by empirical investigations. Here, we can say that many occurrent entities will continue to exist even when the human race will have died out (puzzle passage [3]). At the transcendental level, however, the conditions under which questions of existence make sense are suspended, so that answers to these questions lack bivalence and are senseless. At this level, the level of the *Ding an sich*, we cannot meaningfully say that entities exist (or do not exist) and will continue to exist (or will not continue to exist) when there is no Dasein. Heidegger rejects the traditional notion of a *Ding an sich*, as did his teacher Husserl, since it does not make sense to speculate about the question of how things are apart from the transcendental framework that is presupposed by all questions concerning any thing whatsoever.

Let us assume, for the moment, that Blattner's interpretation is optimally adequate with regard to the text of *Being and Time* (although it does not explain problem areas C and D), and raise the issue as to whether Heidegger's doctrine, so interpreted, is tenable from a philosophical point of view. Among the four objections against his interpretation that Blattner discusses in his 1994 article, there is one that he announces as "a further and more far reaching challenge, one to the very idea that Heidegger could think that such a transcendental standpoint is coherent or conceivable."[69] Since "Heidegger insists that all understanding takes place in the context of an involvement in the world," one might conclude that "the detached, uninvolved perspective of the transcendental standpoint is simply impossible." If this is correct, Blattner says, Heidegger's implicit claim that at the transcendental level statements about entities lack bivalence "turns out to be a disappointing consequence of a more general and debilitating failure of the transcendental standpoint as I have described it."[70] Indeed, if Heidegger's transcendental philosophy excludes that we may adopt a transcendental standpoint, his strategy of eliminating the problem of the *Ding an sich* by first adopting the transcendental standpoint and then limiting what can be said from that standpoint cannot make sense.

Both in his 1994 article and in his 1999 book, Blattner admits that "the general thrust of this objection is correct," although "one can say something from the transcendental standpoint."[71] That is, we can exploit the consequences of the assumption that there is no Dasein. These consequences are that in that case there is no being, in the sense of a holistic transcendental framework, and that questions concerning the existence or nonexistence of entities do not make sense. In the article, but, surprisingly, not in the book, Blattner elaborates this answer by distinguishing between two senses of the expression "transcendental standpoint." On the one hand, (1) the transcendental standpoint is the point of view one occupies when one asks after the conditions for the possibility of (a priori) knowledge. From this standpoint, one allegedly discovers that there is a holistic transcendental framework which determines entities as entities and which depends upon Dasein. On the other hand, (2) one might also call "transcendental standpoint" the point of view one tries to occupy by asking what things are like independently of the holistic transcendental framework (the question of the *Ding an sich* in the Kantian sense). Strictly speaking, one cannot occupy the transcendental standpoint in this latter sense, because the question one attempts to ask is meaningless.[72]

However, by distinguishing between these two kinds of transcendental standpoint Blattner fails to take the sting out of the philosophical objection. In my 1998 book, I argued, with reference to Davidson's article "On the Very Idea of a Conceptual Scheme," that the notion of a *comprehensive* transcendental framework is incoherent because, if the framework is really comprehensive, we cannot specify *what* is framed by the framework. And if we cannot specify what is framed by the framework, the notion of a framework has no clear sense either.[73] Applying Davidson's argument to Heidegger as interpreted by Blattner, we come to the conclusion that if we cannot make meaningful statements about entities from the transcendental standpoint in the second sense (2), we cannot make meaningful statements about the comprehensive transcendental scheme from the transcendental standpoint in the first sense (1) either. This result confirms Gottlob Ernst Schulze's verdict according to which any attempt to transcend the limits of possible experience by a transcendental philosophy is condemned by this very same transcendental philosophy. Can one avoid this verdict, which shipwrecks Heidegger's alleged strategy of debunking the problem of the external world, by means of a transcendental philosophy?[74]

8. Readiness-to-Hand as Being 'an Sich'

A radical tactic for avoiding the verdict is to do away with transcendental philosophy. One might deny that there are transcendental arguments in *Being and Time* and reject the distinction between the empirical and the transcendental standpoint as an interpretation of puzzle passage (3). One simply stresses what Heidegger says about Dasein or being-in-the-world as a unitary phenomenon and explains puzzle passage (3) as saying that our understanding of (occurrent) entities as independent from us humans "cannot be detached from our fundamental way of being, namely being-in-the-world." This is the interpretation preferred by David Cerbone and by Theodore R. Schatzki.[75] But it is clearly unsatisfactory because it fails for problem area A.

For this reason, we must try out more moderate methods, which purport to rescue some kind of transcendental scheme from the Davidsonian objection. Since the Davidsonian objection holds against the very idea of *comprehensive* transcendental schemes only, we must try to restrict the scope of Heidegger's transcendental frameworks and make room for the possibility of encountering entities apart from specific transcendental schemes, or, at least, for the possibility of establishing identity conditions for entities across different transcendental frameworks. I shall now discuss two of such more moderate methods or interpretations, which both have an anchorage in Heideggerian texts. Both of these interpretations hold that, according to Heidegger, we are able to know or at least encounter things as they are in themselves (*an sich*), apart from transcendental schemes. What they differ about is the nature of things as they are in themselves. Let us call them the thesis of the primacy of readiness-to-hand (*Zuhandenheit*) and the thesis of the primacy of occurrentness (*Vorhandenheit*), respectively.

The textual anchorage of the first interpretation consists of those passages in *Being and Time* where Heidegger says, in italics, that "*Readiness-to-hand is the way in which entities as they are 'in themselves' are determined onto-logico-categorially*" (see problem area D). Heidegger puts the expression *an sich* in quotes because the point of these passages is not to contrast the way things are in themselves with the way things are for us. Heidegger's point is rather that the way things are for us primarily, that is, as the colorful and serviceable things of everyday life in the everyday world, things which are meaningful to us within the horizon of the world, *precisely is* the way things are in themselves. As we have seen, with regard to things in the world so conceived it is not meaningful for Dasein to raise the problem of the external world, because Dasein defines itself in terms of these things. The idea that Dasein might be what it is and at the same time exist *without* its everyday world is simply incoherent. But if this is so, why and how did the problem of the external world arise in the first place?

Heidegger's answer to this question is provided by the text I quoted in problem area C: "the cause of this lies in *Dasein*'s falling and in the way in which the primary understanding of Being has been diverted to Being as occurrentness [*Vorhandenheit*]—a diversion which is motivated by that falling itself." Heidegger argues both in *Being and Time* and in his lecture course on Kant of the winter semester 1935–36, published in 1962 as *What Is a Thing?* (*Die Frage nach dem Ding?*), that during the scientific revolution a new metaphysical view of nature became dominant, according to which nature is a mathematical multiplicity of entities that lack many of the features which we attribute to them in everyday life, such as colors and other secondary qualities, or meaningfulness. Although Heidegger does not spell out the connection between this metaphysical view and external world skepticism, it is easy to see how the new metaphysics of nature gave rise to the problem of the external world. For reasons of succinctness I use Wilfrid Sellars's terminology and call this new metaphysics of nature the "scientific image" of the world, whereas the "manifest image" is our view of the world as it manifests itself in daily life.

The philosophers of the scientific revolution argued (1) that the scientific image is incompatible with the manifest image because material entities as conceived of by the new physics lack secondary qualities such as colors, smells, hot or cold, and so forth. This *incompatibility thesis* raises a problem concerning the ontological priority of these images. If one accepts (2) the thesis that the scientific image is ontologically adequate and primary, a problem concerning perception results: what is the status of the colors, sounds, and smells that we perceive, if they are not really there in physical nature? The philosophers of the scientific revolution resolved this issue by endorsing (3) the subjectivity thesis: perceived secondary properties are "impressions in the mind," caused by physical stimuli, and in perception these impressions are projected onto the world by a mental mechanism of projection. In things as they are in themselves, secondary properties are merely dispositions to cause the relevant impressions in perceivers. Generalizing this projective theory of perception, philosophers were faced with the problem of the external world: how can the perceiving subject know that its impressions are really caused by a physical world which exists independently from the subject, if, in perception, it only has access to its own impressions and not to the physical world as it is in itself? Paradoxically, then, the new scientific image of the physical world motivated skeptical doubts concerning the very existence of that physical world. Kant did not resolve this issue. He merely made it more complex by arguing that the things we perceive are phenomenal objects transcendentally constituted by applying various unifying transcendental forms to the multiplicity of impressions.

If external world skepticism is essentially based upon (1) the incompatibility thesis and (2) the ontological primacy of the scientific image, one might debunk the problem of the external world by demolishing either (1) or (2). Whereas Gilbert Ryle opted for the first strategy in chapter 5 of *Dilemmas*, called "The World of Science and the Everyday World,"[76] Heidegger may be seen as someone who accepted (1), but rejected (2) by arguing that the *everyday* world is ontologically primary. As Heidegger says, "*Readiness-to-hand is the way in which entities as they are 'in themselves' are determined ontologico-categorially*." This second strategy can only succeed, however, if one holds that the physical view of the world is not forced upon us by factual empirical discoveries. This is precisely what Heidegger argues both in 1927 and in 1935–36. According to section 69b of *Being and Time*, scientific facts can be ascertained only on the basis of a transcendental scheme projected upon nature. "In principle, there are no 'bare facts,'" because "only 'in the light' of a nature which has been projected in this manner a 'fact' can be found and set up for an experiment regulated and delimited in terms of this projection."[77]

In *What Is a Thing?* Heidegger concludes from a similar argument that the scientific image of the world is optional. He says that his lectures aim at preparing a decision (*Entscheidung*) concerning the question of whether science (*die Wissenschaft*) really is the measure for knowledge (*das Wissen*).[78] This decision might liberate us "from that which imprisons us most and makes us unfree in our experience and definition of things," that is, from "modern science of nature, to the extent that it has become . . . a general form of thought."[79] However, arguing that the scientific image is *optional* does not suffice to ensure the success of Heidegger's debunking strategy. Heidegger has to show as well that the scientific image is *inadequate* as an ontology of the world, as he argues in his critique of the Cartesian ontology of matter as *res extensa*, which is the most explicit version of the scientific image projected during the scientific revolution. In section 21 of *Being and Time*, Heidegger says that the Cartesian doctrine not only is ontologically defective (*eine ontologische Fehlbestimmung der Welt*), but also has led Descartes "to *pass over* [*überspringen*] both the phenomenon of the world and the Being of those entities within-the-world which are proximally ready-to-hand."[80]

How does this interpretation of Heidegger's debunking strategy avoid the Davidsonian objection? And how can Heidegger be a neo-Kantian transcendental philosopher and yet dismiss the problem of the external world as meaningless? Like Kant, Heidegger assumes in *Being and Time* that modern physics is based upon a transcendental structure that is synthetic a priori and that is a condition for the possibility of constituting scientific facts. In contradistinction to Kant, however, Heidegger holds that this transcendental structure is an optional projection (*Entwurf*), which is projected upon things *that are already accessible to us as they are in themselves*, to wit, as ready-to-hand (*zuhanden*). For instance, it is this hammer that we reinterpret in a scientific framework as an occurrent (*vorhanden*) object, a corporeal thing subject to the law of gravity.[81] If the very same things that are seen as occurrent within the framework of modern physics were already accessible beforehand, as they really are, that is, as the serviceable and meaningful things of ordinary life, the Davidsonian critique, that the idea of a comprehensive conceptual framework is meaningless because it excludes our articulating *what* is framed by the framework, is inapplicable.

If we so restrict the transcendental leitmotif to the foundations of physics, and hold that the metaphysical framework of the scientific image is a secondary and optional ontological framework projected upon things that are already accessible as they are *an sich*, it is easy to see how Heidegger on the one hand can be a transcendental philosopher and on the other hand can avoid the problem of the external world, or the problem of the *Ding an sich*. For this problem is meaningless if raised by Dasein in the everyday world, the world as it really is. The problem of the external world arises only on the basis of the projected framework of *Vorhandenheit*, to wit, the scientific image. But as soon as the phenomenologist discovers that this projected framework is ontologically defective because it passes over (*überspringt*) the world as it really is, he grasps that the problem of the external world is a philosophical delusion. Spelling out the phenomenologico-hermeneutic leitmotif, Heidegger shows why the problem of the external world cannot arise in ordinary life. The transcendental leitmotif is then used for showing the ontological irrelevance of the context in which the problem *does* arise, the context of science.

It is only if we misinterpret the world and, consequently, our own ontological constitution, by elevating the scientific image to the position of the true ontology, that we will take the problem of the external world seriously. This kind of inauthentic interpretation of Dasein and the world is one form of what Heidegger calls Dasein's falling (*Verfallen*), the tendency of Dasein to ignore its real nature and to overlook its most authentic possibilities. As Heidegger says, "the cause [*Grund*] of this [i.e., of raising the problem of the external world] lies in *Dasein*'s falling and in the way in which the primary understanding of Being has been diverted to Being as occurrentness [*Vorhandenheit*]—a diversion which is motivated by that falling itself."[82]

9. Angst and Transcendental Realism

The thesis of the primacy of readiness-to-hand (*Zuhandenheit*), spelled out in section 8 as an interpretation of *Being and Time*, has a number of undisputable advantages. First, it elegantly solves the interpretative problems of areas C and D. Second, it links up *Being and Time* both with Heidegger's earliest writings, not contained in the collected works, in which he defended Catholic orthodoxy against individualism and against the scientific conception of the world, and with later works, such as the essay on "The Question Concerning Technology" ("Die Frage nach der Technik").[83] Finally, it clearly shows the extent to which Heidegger and Kant shared the philosophical strategy of limiting the ontological import of science to a phenomenal world in order to make room for authentic morality, meaningfulness, and religion in a world *an sich*. Unfortunately, however, there are serious philosophical and textual drawbacks to this interpretation.

From a philosophical point of view, one might dispute Heidegger's doctrine that scientific facts depend upon an optional metaphysical framework. Is the idea that science essentially has metaphysical presuppositions, which are a priori and cannot be tested empirically, not part of an outdated foundationalist view of science?[84] Can one not reject dubious forms of scientistic metaphysics and yet use the best scientific theories now available as a clue to constructing a scientific picture of the world by a consilience of inductions, so to say? According to this line of criticism, we should reject Heidegger's views if the interpretation of section 8 is historically adequate.

The problems of textual adequacy are not less serious. The interpretation of section 8 can avoid the Davidsonian critique of transcendental schemes only if the way in which things are "in themselves," that is, as ready-to-hand, is not in its turn determined by a comprehensive transcendental scheme, the framework of the everyday world. But Heidegger seems to think that the everyday world *is* such a transcendental framework, and not a mere "horizon" in Husserl's sense. For he uses again and again Kantian phrases when he characterizes what he calls the phenomenon of world. He says, for instance, that "the worldhood of the world provides the *basis* on which such entities [to wit: *innerweltlich Zuhandenes*] can be discovered in the first place as they are 'substantially' 'in themselves,'" and he speaks of an "'a priori' letting-something-be-involved," which is "the condition for the possibility of encountering anything ready-to-hand."[85]

Even more seriously, it seems that Heidegger holds that, in order to be interpreted as ready-to-hand (*zuhanden*), things have to be already there (*vorhanden*). Having written in italics that being ready-to-hand is the way things are in themselves ontologically, he continues as follows: "Yet 'there is' something ready-to-hand only on the basis of something occurrent [*Vorhandenem*]. Does it follow, however, granting this thesis for the nonce, that readiness-to-hand is ontologically founded upon occurrentness?"[86]

Perhaps it is possible to interpret these last lines as stating the position of Heidegger's opponent, a position Heidegger is going to refute later on. But what is worrisome is that there are similar passages elsewhere, which seem to conjure up the specter of the traditional problem of the *Ding an sich*. These passages would refute Blattner's interpretation of the transcendental point of view, according to which one cannot discuss or encounter entities apart from transcendental schemes. Many authors have drawn our attention to such passages and Blattner discusses one of them. This is the passage on "world-entry" from the lecture course *The Metaphysical Foundations of Logic* (*Metaphysische Anfangsgründe der Logik im Ausgang von Leibniz*; 1928), where Heidegger says: "World-entry and its happening is the presupposition not for occurrent entities first becoming occurrent entities and coming into what manifests itself to us as their occurrentness and which we understand as such, but rather, merely for occurrent entities announcing themselves precisely in their not needing world-entry with respect to their own being."[87] Heidegger seems to say here that occurrent (*vorhanden*) entities as such exist independently from the meaningful "world" which is inseparably bound up with Dasein, and, indeed, independently from all transcendental schemes.[88]

Blattner's reaction to this passage in his (1999) book is somewhat surprising. He holds that the passage conflicts not only with his interpretation but also with the literal text of *Sein und Zeit*, that is, with puzzle passage

(3). Blattner says: "However one reads it, p. 212 of *Being and Time* literally states that independence (occurrentness) neither is nor is not, when *Dasein* does not exist, and also that occurrent entities then neither are nor are not."[89] The problem with Blattner's reaction is, that as far as entities are concerned, Heidegger does not state this on that page. What Heidegger says is, rather, "When *Dasein* does not exist . . . it cannot *be said* that entities are, nor can it *be said* that they are not."[90] From the facts that when Dasein does not exist it cannot be *said* that entities are and that it cannot be *said* that entities are not, it does not follow that in that case entities neither are nor are not. Could it be that, according to Heidegger, there is some kind of transcendental access to entities as they are apart from any transcendental scheme, an access that leaves us speechless and yet *shows* that *at the transcendental level* entities exist independently from Dasein and would be there even if Dasein were not around?

If that were the case, Heidegger could claim on the one hand that without Dasein, that is, without a transcendental framework, neither can it be *said* that entities are nor can it be *said* that entities are not, and on the other hand describe by means of a formal indication (*formale Anzeige*) a situation in which entities show up for us even though no transcendental framework determines *as what* they show up for us. In such a situation, it would be revealed that entities are there (*vorhanden*) without any framework whatsoever, even though they can only be apprehended *as* something of some kind (for instance, *as* independent from us) within a transcendental framework. The Davidsonian objection would be avoided, not because we can *say* what entities are apart from an all-encompassing transcendental scheme, but because we can *show* that they are there apart from all such schemes. Even though Heidegger is a transcendental idealist about being, he would be a transcendental realist about entities.

One might suggest that this is part of what Heidegger attempts to show in section 40 of *Being and Time*, the section on the fundamental mood of anxiety or *Angst*.[91] In contradistinction to fear, *Angst* is not related to a particular entity within the world. "In anxiety what is environmentally ready-to-hand sinks away, and so, in general, do entities within-the-world."[92] Although the entities are still there, they are completely depleted from their familiar everyday significance: "Nothing which is ready-to-hand or occurrent within the world functions as that in the face of which anxiety is anxious. Here the totality of involvements of the ready-to-hand and the occurrent discovered within-the-world, is, as such, of no consequence; it collapses into itself; the world has the character of completely lacking significance."[93] Yet, Heidegger says, "Being-anxious discloses, primordially and directly, the world as world."[94] So it seems that Heidegger is here discussing the very phenomenon we are looking for. Because in *Angst*, the framework of the world stops determining *as what* entities appear to us, the framework as such is revealed apart from the entities, and the entities are simply there, undetermined by the framework, devoid of their familiar significance, revealed in their "full but heretofore concealed strangeness as what is radically other."[95] Heidegger's description of *Angst* may be interpreted as showing, then, that he is a transcendental realist concerning entities.[96] In *Angst*, "the original openness of entities as such arises: that they are entities—and not nothing."[97]

This interpretation of section 40 is compatible with puzzle-passage (3) because in *Angst* we are speechless. Since the world completely lacks significance, speech (*Sprache*) is impossible, for according to Heidegger speech articulates a pre-existing significance. As Heidegger says in his inaugural lecture *What Is Metaphysics?* (*Was ist Metaphysik?*), of 1929, "Anxiety robs us of speech. Because beings as a whole slip away, so that just the nothing crowds round, in the face of anxiety all utterance of the 'is' falls silent."[98] Blattner is correct in stressing that if the transcendental framework does not determine *as what* entities show up for us, it cannot *be said* that entities are, nor can it *be said* that they are not. This is what puzzle passage (3) affirms. But the experience of *Angst* shows that even in this case entities are still there, albeit without having any significance for us. Hence, Blattner is mistaken in concluding from puzzle passage (3) that, according to Heidegger, in the absence of a transcendental framework "entities then neither are nor are not."

Attributing transcendental realism to Heidegger explains puzzle passage (2): "Entities *are*, quite independently of the experience by which they are disclosed, the acquaintance in which they are discovered, and the grasping in which their nature is ascertained. But Being 'is' only in the understanding of those entities to whose being something like an understanding of Being belongs."[99] This passage does not refer to occurrent entities only, as is clear from the context in section 39 of *Being and Time*. It refers to all entities, whether they are occurrent or ready-to-hand. One might read it as a straightforward expression of transcendental realism concerning entities.

This reading of Heidegger as a transcendental realist is compatible with his debunking strategy concerning the problem of the external world on condition that we do not confuse Heidegger's transcendental realism with scientific realism. In the grip of anxiety, Dasein has no reason whatsoever to doubt whether the meaningless entities it is confronted by really exist. On the contrary, in the experience of *Angst* these entities obtrude themselves upon us in their "full but heretofore concealed strangeness as what is radically other." The problem of the external world arises only within the transcendental framework of the scientific image, and the ontological adequacy of that framework is denied by Heidegger (section 8, above). Within the transcendental framework of science, we may be scientific realists in the sense of empirical realists. But at the transcendental level, the experience of

Angst reveals that entities are already there apart from any transcendental framework, as "the original ground-possibility of both the presentness-at-hand of the theoretical object of science and the readiness-to-hand of the equipment of everyday praxis."[100]

For this reason, it is surprising that some interpreters have attributed to Heidegger a robust form of *scientific* realism, robust in the sense that it is not limited to an empirical realism in the sense of transcendental philosophy. Dreyfus and Spinosa argue, for example, that "although Heidegger pioneered the deflationary realist account of the everyday, he sought to establish a robust realist account of science."[101] In order to substantiate this claim, the authors draw attention to Heidegger's descriptions of the phenomena of *Angst* and of the reinterpretation of tools such as a hammer as an object of science. But to the extent that Heidegger's descriptions can be interpreted as *scientific* realism, it is the empirical realism argued for by Blattner and others. Dreyfus and Spinosa admit as much when they write that "he [Heidegger] has no account of how the meaningless beings revealed by breakdown [and anxiety] can serve as data for science."[102] Even if the authors are right in arguing that Heidegger would, in principle, have (some of) the conceptual resources for developing a robust (transcendental) scientific realism, nothing could be further removed from Heidegger's real intentions, as his critique of scientistic ontologies shows (section 8, above).

10. Conclusions

Having explored some of the complexities of Heidegger's debunking strategy with regard to the problem of the external world, we may now attempt to answer the central question of this chapter: did Heidegger develop a viable strategy, by consistently combining phenomenological analysis with transcendental philosophy? Did he successfully reconcile the "no problem" view with a transcendental view?

In order to obtain consistency, we have to distinguish between three levels of analysis in *Being and Time* and between four different meanings of the notion of occurrentness (*Vorhandenheit*).

1. At the most superficial level of analysis, that of empirical realism with regard to scientific entities, things in the world are interpreted as occurrent (*vorhanden*) within the framework of a specific transcendental scheme. It is at this level that the problem of the external world is generated by a scientific metaphysics of nature. Heidegger does not attempt to solve the problem at this level. Rather, he eliminates it by arguing that the scientific level of analysis *as a whole* is ontologically defective, because it passes over

(*überspringt*) the real phenomenon of the "world." A scientific analysis of natural entities merely decontextualizes entities *that were already given* at a more fundamental level, that is, at level (2).

2. At this more fundamental level, the phenomenological analysis of everyday life reveals that Dasein cannot exist without its world, because it is essentially being-in-the-world. Entities in the everyday world are in themselves (*an sich*) ready-to-hand (*zuhanden*), so that the "reality" of these entities cannot be understood without reference to Dasein, whereas Dasein defines itself in terms of, and hence cannot be understood without, these entities in the world. At this level of analysis, the problem of the external world does not make sense, and it is discovered that the problem arises only within a projected transcendental framework, the framework of science.
3. At an even more fundamental level, revealed in the fundamental mood of *Angst*, it is discovered that the world as a comprehensive referential structure is also a transcendental scheme, and that entities are there (*vorhanden*) apart from all transcendental schemes, in their "full but heretofore concealed strangeness as what is radically other." Since at this level entities cannot be interpreted *as* something, because the structure of significance (*Bedeutsamkeit*) has collapsed, we cannot *say* anything about entities at this level, apart from saying that they are there in their radical otherness. Heidegger is a transcendental realist, and not a transcendental agnostic, as Blattner has argued.[103]

Although Kant could not consistently adopt the hypothesis of a *Ding an sich* at level (3), because he was a strong transcendentalist (interpretation [b] of section 5, above), Heidegger can put forward the phenomenological thesis of transcendental realism without inconsistency, because he is a weak transcendentalist with regard to being (interpretation [c]), and because he holds that one can experience things at the transcendental level in *Angst*. In other words, Heidegger escapes by means of his analysis of *Angst* from Schulze's verdict that any attempt to transcend the limits of possible experience by a transcendental philosophy is condemned by this very same transcendental philosophy. At the transcendental level (3), things are occurrent (*vorhanden*), but the problem of the external world does not arise, as we saw above.

We may say that relative to empirical level (1), level (2) is a transcendental level, and that relative to level (2), level (3) is a transcendental level, the ultimate transcendental level. Heidegger is a "realist" at all levels, but his "realism" does not have the same meaning as the various realisms that allegedly solve the problem of the external world. At levels (1) and (2), Heidegger holds that "along with *Dasein* as Being-in-the-world, entities within-the-world have in each case already been disclosed." "This existential-ontological assertion seems to accord with the thesis of realism that the external world is really occurrent," because it does not deny or doubt that entities are occurrent. But the agreement is a "merely doxographical" one, for Heidegger's "realism" at all levels presupposes the ontology of Dasein, which shows that the problem of the external world is meaningless.[104]

In contradistinction to the term *zuhanden*, the word *vorhanden* is not a Heideggerian archaism or neologism.[105] This may explain the fact that Heidegger uses the term *vorhanden* ("occurrent") loosely and in a number of different senses. In the widest sense, it just means "being there," and in this sense even Dasein is *vorhanden*.[106] In a second sense, which is somewhat more restricted, everything except Dasein is *vorhanden*, as we discover in the fundamental mood of *Angst*.[107] Third, Heidegger uses the word *vorhanden* for things as they show up within the world even if they do not fit into the framework of *Vorhandenheit* in the fourth and narrowest sense. So he says, for instance, that "not all occurrentness is the occurrentness of things. The 'nature' that 'envelops' us consists of course of entities-in-the-world, but it exhibits neither the mode of Being of readiness-to-hand nor that of occurrentness in the sense of 'natural entities.'"[108] Fourth, *Vorhandenheit* is the particular transcendental framework within which things show up for us as merely there, devoid of practical significance. This is Heidegger's technical and narrowest sense of the term *vorhanden*. Sometimes, but not always, he differentiates between this fourth sense of *Vorhandenheit* and a scientific way of envisaging things. In section 69b of *Being and Time*, for instance, Heidegger wonders whether "a scientific attitude has already constituted itself only because, instead of deliberating circumspectively about something ready-to-hand, we 'take' it as something occurrent."[109]

Although Heidegger's strategy for debunking the problem of the external world can be made consistent in this manner, one may doubt whether it is philosophically fruitful. Those who consider *Being and Time* as an indispensable antidote to the dominance of scientific thought in our culture, will welcome Heidegger's ontological disqualification of science. But those who hold with Quine, Dreyfus, and Spinosa, the Churchlands, and many others, that scientific thought is the best access to things as they are in themselves, will reject this disqualification. Since the ontological disqualification of science is the crucial move in Heidegger's debunking strategy, the latter party will have to develop another attitude vis-à-vis the problem of the external world. One may either propose a solution to it or argue that one should accept the best scientific theories without endorsing the scientistic metaphysics that generated the problem in the first place.[110]

CHAPTER 13

Necessary Conditions for the Possibility of What Isn't

HEIDEGGER ON FAILED MEANING

Robert B. Pippin

1. Being as a "MacGuffin"

In his famous interviews with François Truffaut, Alfred Hitchcock insisted that while many of his thrillers concerned some piece of information or object around which swirled all the intrigue and energy of the film, it didn't matter if that object was never identified, that it could even turn out to be nothing at all, of no serious importance in itself.[1] Borrowing from some Kipling stories, he called such an elusive object of attention a "MacGuffin," and went on to say, "My best MacGuffin, and by that I mean the emptiest, the most nonexistent, and the most absurd, is the one we used in *North by Northwest*. . . . Here, you see, the MacGuffin has been boiled down to its purest expression: nothing at all."[2] In 1987, the great intellectual historian Hans Blumenberg, in a supremely backhanded compliment, noted the effectiveness of Heidegger's "question about the meaning of Being" in functioning in just this Hitchcockean way. In a clever rejoinder to Heidegger, Blumenberg titled his article, "Das Sein—Ein MacGuffin," thereby deliberately invoking Hitchcock's own description of the MacGuffin, "boiled down to its purest expression: nothing at all."[3]

The cleverness of this invocation of the nothingness of the Heideggerian MacGuffin, *Sein*, derives from the enormous if infamous and elusive importance that Heidegger himself ascribes to "the nothing," *das Nichts*. The appeals to *das Nichts* and *die Nichtigkeit* occur just when *Being and Time* begins to indicate how we should understand the meaning of Dasein's very being *as*, in a way, "nothing at all." Here is Heidegger from Division Two of *Being and Time*.

> Care itself, in its very essence, is permeated (*durchsetzt*) with nullity (*Nichtigkeit*) through and through. Thus "care"—Dasein's Being—means, as thrown projection, Being-the-basis-of-a-nullity (and this being-the-basis is itself null) [*Das nichtige Grundsein einer Nichtigkeit*]. This means that Dasein as such is guilty, if our formally existential definition of "guilt" as "Being-the-basis-of-a-nullity" is indeed correct.[4]

Blumenberg is suggesting in effect, with King Lear, that "nothing comes from nothing," and that Heidegger's picture of Dasein's *Angst*-ridden realization of its own nullity should be taken as a revelation about the emptiness and misleading quality of the question (or worse, of Heidegger's fanciful analysis), not as the manifestation of the existential abyss. The idea is clearly that while the creation of the expectation of a "comprehensive meaning" (an unnecessary and artificial requirement in Blumenberg's view) is vital to the possibility of the Heideggerian narration of a person's life (or in Heidegger's terms vital to being able to "temporalize" (*zeitigen*) temporality, the supreme "condition" of meaningfulness), and while the intimation of a profoundly elusive, almost necessarily *absent* meaning may best of all fulfill a dramatic need (something that preserves what Heidegger calls a complete *Unabgeschlossenheit*, un-closedness, incompleteness, in Dasein's existence), at some point such an expectation is more a dramatic trick than anything else. The "meaning of Being expectation" is already such a trick, Blumenberg suggests, and is *in reality* nothing at all, in the ordinary not Heideggerian sense of "there's nothing to it."

This is a bit of a cheap shot, not as cheap as Carnap's famous swipes in "The Elimination of Metaphysics Through Logical Analysis of Language,"[5] but unfair nonetheless. However, understanding just why it is unfair, and how the appeal to *das Nichts* functions in Heidegger's early philosophy, and especially why the question opens up for Heidegger distinctly philosophical issues (not issues of psychological health, historical diagnosis, social theory, or literary mood), will require several steps.

2. *The Question of Being*

First, it is important to stress that Heidegger's understanding of the *Seinsfrage* is that it is directed toward what he frequently calls the "meaning of Being" (*Sinn des Seins*).[6] A typical programmatic statement in *Being and Time*, "Basically, all ontology . . . remains blind and perverted from its ownmost aim, if it has not already first clarified the meaning of being, and conceived this clarification as its fundamental task."[7] In his 1936–37 Nietzsche lectures Heidegger characterizes the "decisive question" at the end of Western philosophy as "the question about the meaning of Being, not only about the

Being of beings"; and, he goes on, "'meaning' (*Sinn*) is thereby delimited in its concept as that whence and on the basis of which Being in general as such can be revealed and come into truth (*in die Wahrheit kommen*)."[8] This seems pretty clearly to say that the "clarification" spoken of in *Being and Time* was of the "possibility" of the meaning of being at all, rather than any direct answer to the question.[9] It is hard to exaggerate the scope of this question as Heidegger understands it, since it seems to cover the intelligibility, deep existential familiarity, of someone uttering noises at me, of ink marks on a page, of having to make breakfast, seeing that someone is angry with me, or facing a decision about whether to volunteer for a mission. The issue, he keeps stressing, is not what there is, what the basic kinds are, or even (as in the *Introduction to Metaphysics*) why there is something and not nothing.[10] The question concerns the very possibility of intelligibility at all, how it is that sense can ever be made of anything, that there could be a *Lichtung*, a clearing or lighting or *Unverborgenheit* that "happens," such that a "sense" of being is possible.[11]

Now a formulation like "whence and on the basis of which Being in general as such *can* be revealed and come into truth," since it looks very much like a question about the "conditions necessary" for the possibility of any "meaning of Being," seems a project in the tradition of transcendental philosophy, or part of a post-Kantian heritage. Despite his protestations in *Grundprobleme* that his own concept of transcendental truth "does not coincide without further ado with the Kantian,"[12] and his criticism of *Being and Time* in the Nietzsche lectures as too transcendental in the Kantian sense,[13] Heidegger certainly takes up what seems the language of transcendental philosophy. "By 'existentiality' we understand the state of Being that is *constitutive* for those entities that exist."[14] The hermeneutic of Dasein becomes a hermeneutic "in the sense of working out the *conditions* on which the *possibility* of any ontological investigation depends."[15] And most directly: "But in significance [*Bedeutsamkeit*] itself, with which Dasein is always familiar, there lurks the ontological condition which makes it possible for Dasein, as something which understands and interprets, to disclose such things as 'significances' [*Bedeutungen*]; upon these in turn is founded the Being of words and language."[16] There is even what has sounded to some like transcendental idealist language: "Dasein only has meaning. . . . Hence only Dasein can be meaningful (*sinnvoll*) or meaningless (*sinnlos*)."[17] "Only as long as Dasein is (that is only as long as an understanding of Being is ontically possible), 'is there' Being."[18] And even: "All truth is relative to Dasein's being."[19] Heidegger is certainly clear that in such passages he is not talking about phenomenalism or subjective idealism. Even though "Reality is referred back to the phenomenon of care," this does *not* mean that "only when Dasein exists and as long as Dasein exists, can the Real be as that which in itself it is."[20] Or,

"Being (not entities) is dependent upon the understanding of Being; that is to say, Reality (not the Real) is dependent upon care."[21] And all commentators on Heidegger can cite his famous realism in section 44. "What is to be demonstrated is not an agreement of knowing with its object, still less of the psychical with the physical; but neither is it an agreement between 'contents of consciousness' among themselves. What is to be demonstrated is solely the being-uncovered [*Entdeckt-sein*] of the entity itself—that entity in the *how* of its uncoveredness."[22] It is clear from the literature on this issue in Heidegger that passages with such realist and such idealist implications, such transcendental and more traditionally ontological implications, could be produced at great length. The talk of "dependence" still, though, at least suggests some sort of a "dependence of sense," if not existence dependence, in the roughly transcendental or "condition for the possibility" meaning.[23] Such "uncovering" or disclosedness as discussed above obviously can't happen without us (although that does not mean it happens to or for us in any straightforward sense, and since the phenomena Heidegger is interested in are "hidden," his version of phenomenology is also a hermeneutics),[24] and nothing Heidegger says in section 44 undermines or contradicts the dependence claim in general. (The entity *in* its uncoveredness, or being *in* its disclosedness, is not the entity "itself," or being, directly apprehended; there is a "how" of uncoveredness; a distinct event of disclosedness. Or, it seems natural to frame the issue as John Haugeland has: that ontological disclosedness is a condition for the possibility of comportment toward entities as entities, of ontic truth.)[25]

In terms of Heidegger's project, though, we can see straightaway both what the first question would be if his enterprise were to be considered transcendental, and that the absence of any concern for such a question already reveals that he conceives of his project somewhat differently. The question would be: why should Dasein's requirements for intelligibility—what being could come to mean for Dasein—have anything to do with "the intelligibles" as such, with what being *could* possibly mean? There is no immediately obvious reason not to believe, with Nietzsche, that what we count as intelligibility is the perspectival expression of the will to power, or with Foucault that there are no power-neutral accounts of such sense making.[26] (Indeed, in his famous *Abbau*, Heidegger himself makes similar claims about the "hybris" and subjectivism of all metaphysics.) Or, suppose: *as far as we can make it out*, Dasein must be understood as "ontologically unique." Is this because we lack the intellectual resources to understand Dasein as, say, a sophisticated machine, or, despite appearances, as ontologically continuous with other mammals, or because Dasein in itself cannot *be* such an object or such a kind, and this is so in a way not dependent on what we could make sense of?

The direct answer to such questions would be what Kant called a transcendental deduction, and so a demonstration that the "conditions for the possibility of experience" are, *must* be, "at the same time the conditions for the possibility of objects of experience" (that what "we" require for being to have meaning is what is required for being itself to have any possible meaning). But such a deduction in anything like its Kantian form would require an appeal to pure forms of intuition or something analogous (something outside "the space of the conceptual," or outside the requirements of the subject, yet accessible to philosophy) and (to make a very long story very, very short) by the middle of the nineteenth century, such an appeal had become largely moot, and there is no indication of such a strategy in *Being and Time*.[27]

The absence of that or any analogous argument form in *Being and Time* suggests something like the approach already manifest in Hegel, but which in Heidegger results from his famous break with Husserlian phenomenology. That is, we begin from an original denial of any possible separability of conceptual and material, intuitional elements in any philosophical account of experience in the first place and so an insistence that we did not *need* to cross any divide between "*our* conditions for intelligibility" and "*the* intelligible," and do not need to deduce how our requirements for intelligibility might be said to "fit" what we are independently given. The question itself should be rejected, not answered.[28] In fact, in his Davos encounter with Cassirer and in his *Kant and the Problem of Metaphysics* (*Kant und das Problem der Metaphysik*) shortly thereafter, Heidegger presses his account of the finitude of Dasein—the absence of a formal point of view from which to secure any sort of philosophical necessity, even transcendental necessity—to the point of transforming Kant's *Critique* into his own existential analytic. (Of course, Heidegger's name for his version of the inseparability thesis is *in-der-Welt-sein*, being-in-the-world, or, eventually, *Geschichtlichkeit*, historicality.)

There is, for example, no argument by Heidegger that purports to investigate what a meaningful engagement with entities and others would be like, were there *not* some comprehensive "horizon" of significance, or some orientation from the meaning of Dasein's being, and thereby to try to show that such a putative situation is not really possible. He does not do this because he does not consider the relation between such a comprehensive horizon and determinate intelligibility as that between necessary condition and conditioned, a fact that is dramatically manifest in the possibility that the existential function of such a comprehensive horizon can pass into "forgetfulness" (without any ontic "senselessness").[29]

And we should keep in mind our main topic: in Heidegger's account we are headed toward some sort of claim that whatever conditions we might establish, they can, in some way, fail. "Care" is the meaning of the being of

Dasein, and the entire interrelational structure of the world of Care can fail so catastrophically that Dasein will appear not as the world-embedded, open-to-meaning, engaged agent in a shared world that it is, but, all at once as it were, the null basis of a nullity. (Or, to anticipate an even more radical challenge: Dasein is, at the same time, both.) Wherever Heidegger's Kantian talk might lead us, we have to keep in mind how bizarre it would sound to refer to some sort of "breakdown" in the constitutive-conditioning function of the experience-enabling categories of causality or substance.

But where does this leave us with respect to our question: what *sort* of question is the *Seinsfrage* and how might one go about answering it? It is not, we should now conclude, a transcendental question in Kant's sense (of the sort that might require a deduction), and Heidegger seems to adopt the "inseparability" thesis about subject and object, concept and intuition, Dasein and world, but (to make another very long story very short) without the phenomenological reduction, bracketing, and abstracting that might lead us back to a claim of Husserlian philosophical necessity.[30] So we seem left without any distinctly philosophical claims, except negative ones. We might be tempted to conclude that, if Dasein *is*, in some radical sense, thrown projection, always already embedded in its world, if any possible meaning of being is existential in just this sense, then there is nothing to say about *what it is to be so thrown* except insofar as any such answer is "attested" in the experience of such subjects, in a historical world, at a time.

There is a sense in which, properly understood, making such a claim *is* what fundamental ontology consists in. But everything comes down to "properly understood," and we are therewith in the vicinity of one of Heidegger's deepest anxieties: that this radical doctrine of finitude, a finitude that makes the adoption of a transcendental interpretation of Heidegger quite misleading, will be misinterpreted as the invitation to a historicist philosophical anthropology, a *mere* hermeneutics of what being *has come to mean*; radical only in that considerations of how anything *could* come to mean are included *within* the hermeneutic, not treated independently, *prior* (that is, transcendentally). Another of his anxieties also lurks in this area: that he is an "existentialist," for whom the horrible truth about the "meaninglessness" or "absurdity" of Dasein's existence is *too* horrible to face, it provokes despair, and so on. I think Heidegger is right that both characterizations are inaccurate.

That is, both transcendentalist and existentialist interpretations are hard to make consistent with the fact that Heidegger is manifestly not talking about the finitude and mortality and self-obscuring characteristics of Dasein on the one hand, and on the other hand some considerably more than finite capacity on the part of philosophy to set out the necessary conditions always required for anything to make sense for such a finite being, or to state the "real" truth about Dasein's "absurd" existence. Finitude, the consequences of Heidegger's criticism of standard logic, of Husserlian phenomenology and Kantian transcendentalism, and eventually of all metaphysics, is primarily a critique, one might even say an attack, *on philosophy itself*, not a reminder that we all die and are afraid of that or cannot face the absurdity of our lives.[31] (As early as 1920 Heidegger was writing, "We philosophize, not in order to show that we need a philosophy, but instead precisely to show that we do not need one.")[32] Avoiding though the transcendental or historicist anthropology or existentialist interpretations has everything to do with the radicality of Heidegger's account of *das Nichts*, to which I now turn.

3. Being and the Nothing

Heidegger presents an existential analytic that is proposed as preliminary, a stalking horse such that progress in understanding the meaning of Dasein's being could be *the* decisive step in understanding any *Sinn des Seins* ("meaning of being") for Dasein. Again, this approach creates a transcendental temptation, as if we are looking for Dasein's conditions of sense, conditions that will set the horizon for the possibility of all sense (even though still "for Dasein"). But I want to suggest that the Dasein analytic is privileged because it is *exemplary* (exemplary of how the meaning of being "happens"), *not transcendental* in this sense (not constitutive of any possible meaning, as if "necessary conditions" have been found). To see how this works, we need to remind ourselves briefly of the drama that makes *Being and Time* so riveting.

The catchphrase associated with Heidegger and Sartre, "existence precedes essence," amounts, minimally, to a denial that any distinctively human "way of life" could be said to have an anthropologically fixed, or essential, or socially "assigned" nature.[33] Rather, one existence is always in a kind of suspended state, everywhere oriented and "lived forward" by some prediscursive understanding of and commitment to a "meaning of one's being" that cannot have something like a resolution or totality or a fixed "grounding" in the usual sense.[34]

And, Heidegger notes, Dasein can "decide its existence by taking hold *or* neglecting."[35] In the historical world Heidegger interprets (that is, our world), it is the latter that mostly manifests how Dasein is at issue for itself, by neglecting in some way the call of conscience, calling one back to oneself as a concernful being-in-the-world, living a life only by "taking up the reins," only by *leading* one's life, but constantly "falling," lost in the concerns of *das Man*, attempting to avoid the claims of such a requirement. Dasein's being is said to "lie hidden," but in a way such that that "hiddenness also belongs to what thus shows itself."[36] And in the most dialectical expression, the *Ich* or I can exist as "not-I," in the mode of having lost *Ichheit* ("I-ness"), or *is* only by having lost itself (*Selbstverlorenheit*).[37] (And it is already important to note, contra the "existentialist" reading: this does not mean a simple falling away from an authentic selfhood, to which we may resolutely return. The point is the more radical claim that the "Ich's" capacity to exist as *Selbstverlorenheit* "is" what it is to be an "I" at all. Achieving some sort of stable "Ichheit" would be to cease to be an "Ich.")

This account sets the stage for the sort of philosophical question about meaning Heidegger wants to pose. For the question he wants to ask is not a skeptical one (either about other minds, the external world, or the very possibility of a distinction between knowing and not-knowing at all), and not an idealist worry (what the relation is between the conditions for our understanding the meaning of our being and what being could be), and not an ethical one (how Dasein can remain "true" to itself), but a different question: what could meaning—"fundamentally," preeminently the meaning of being—*be, such that it could fail, utterly, and in a way absolutely fail*? This sort of orientation (examining the nature of significance, meaningfulness in our engagements with others and the world, by taking our bearings from a breakdown in meaningful practices) had been methodologically prominent from the very first accounts of being-in-the-world. The "worldly" character of the world itself (*Weltlichkeit*), not just aspects of the world or items in the world, is announced by, perhaps even consists in, such breakdowns as "conspicuousness" (*Auffallen*), "obtrusiveness" (*Aufdringlichkeit*), and "obstinacy" (*Aufsässigkeit*), each a kind of "break" (*Bruch*) in the referential contexts within which *Zuhandenheit* makes the kinds of sense it does. No regressive transcendental argument to necessary conditions of sense is involved in such a making-manifest; Heidegger is appealing instead to the phenomenological evidence of "attestation" (*Bezeugung*), what "shows itself" *in* such experiences of breakdown *as having been at work*.

Moreover the sort of significance Heidegger is interested in as a matter of fundamental ontology is hardly limited to the dealings and engagements involved in the equipmental world of sense. Dasein's being is, "fundamentally ontologically," care, its "circumspection" always "concernful." The meaningfulness of its engagements with objects and others involves a layered relation of ends, "for the sakes of which" (*Worumwillen*) in Heidegger's nominalization.[38] Even if the directedness and normative commitments that, as Dreyfus notes,[39] sustain our comportment in the world "non-robotically" are not self-referential mental states, this directedness is *sustained*, which is evident when that sustaining fails, when, in the simplest sense, care fails: when we cannot care. That is, the accounts of everyday significance and of the meaningfulness of being are treated as matters of mattering. The prethematic ontological horizon of sense "held open" by Dasein is a horizon of mattering, with saliences of significance and ordered relations of importance always at issue if not directly "pointed at" or aimed at or consciously attended to, in such engagements. It can be best seen as that sort of sense, mattering, when we experience the distinctiveness of its failure, something Heidegger first begins to describe in his account of anxiety.

There he begins to explore this unusual "*logos* of mattering" with a remark that is not given the usual headline treatment but is astonishing nonetheless. For Heidegger notes an experience rarely treated before Kierkegaard's thinking on despair, and rarely treated anywhere as being of such consequence. "The totality of involvements [*Bewandtnisganzheit*] of the ready-to-hand and the present-at-hand discovered within the world is, as such, of no consequence [*ohne Belang*]; it collapses into itself; the world has the character of completely lacking significance [*die Welt hat den Charakter völliger Unbedeutsamkeit*]."[40] Is such a thought even thinkable? *Complete* insignificance? The *totality* of involvements of the *Zuhanden* and *Vorhanden* "collapses into itself"? It is not until Heidegger revisits in Division Two the issues here introduced that both the existential dimensions of such an experience and its importance for fundamental ontology emerge. Having noted that any full account of the meaning of Dasein's being must take account of Dasein as possibly a totality or whole, Heidegger argues that Dasein can never be such a whole, but its own total significance can come into view by being toward its end, indeed an ending that constantly threatens Dasein's very being. He asks, "How is it existentially possible for this constant threat to be genuinely disclosed? All understanding is accompanied by state-of-mind. Dasein's mood brings it face-to-face with the thrownness of its 'that it is there.' But the state of mind which can hold open the utter and constant threat to itself arising from Dasein's ownmost individualized being is anxiety."[41] This is the preparation for Heidegger's extraordinary account of "freedom towards death" and his summary account of care as "shot through" with *Nichtigkeit*, and Dasein being the null basis of a nothingness.

Heidegger at this point allows himself a no doubt deliberately comic understatement when he then notes, "the ontological meaning of the notness [*Nichtheit*] of this existential nothingness is still obscure."[42] But what he tries to stress throughout his extended account of conscience, care, guilt, and authenticity is the radicality of the failure of meaning provoked by the conflict between any sense-making, care-ful engagement, and defeat of such attempts in the face of the absoluteness of one's death. What he describes is a collapse of significance that allows us to see that what had "kept up" such a structure of significance was "nothing" but our caring to keep it in place, a care originating and failing in utter contingency. The unincorporability of one's death into this structure of significance, or of mattering, the impossibility that death could mean anything, brings into experiential prominence the contingency of care itself, the escape or flight from such a nullity without which leading an existence, temporalizing a time, would not be possible. His claim seems to be that the experience of the constant impendingness of one's death can "block" in some way the practical projection into the future that amounts to the work of sustaining meaning for Dasein. Such an experience does not cause such a breakdown, nor is it merely the occasion for such a reaction. Heidegger must mean that the sustaining of such meaning requires the fulfilling of an existential condition, a sense of futurity, a being-toward-an-end, that the absoluteness and arbitrariness of death calls into question ("calls" as the call of conscience). The idea is not that death itself is unintelligible or absurd, but what being-toward death calls into question reveals that what it means to be Dasein is to be able to fail to be a "concernful," circumspective "site" of meaning, and that the succeeding and failing cannot be a part of Dasein's project, cannot be assigned to it as a task, a work. (This begins the difference with Hegel, whose position I want later to bring in as a contrast.)

A short time later, in his lecture course of 1929–30, Heidegger focuses on a *Stimmung* that reveals a failure or collapse of meaning that is intuitively clearer but less intuitively connected with responsive action or redemption. He notes as an ontological phenomenon the possibility of "deep boredom" (*tiefe Langeweile*). The "emptiness" evinced in such a profound or deep boredom (*die langweilende Leere*) is not the sort one can will or argue oneself out of, not the sort of orientation one can control.[43] (It should be stressed here that Heidegger's variations in appeals to various "Stimmungen," or moods, attunements, means that his analysis is not restricted to any particular experience of *death*. He is looking for paradigmatic cases where the whole interrelated practical structure of care can, "on its own" as it were, fail; and then to ask what such meaning must be that it could fail.)

And of course Heidegger is not trying to say that the fact of one's inevitable death gives one a *reason* to lose faith in the worth or point of one's projects and goals. In the first place the character of the significance or meaning he takes to be threatened is, in his terms, "prior" to any belief or project. What fails is care, and this precisely not for any reason. (One must already care about reasons for that to be a possibility, and in that case the mattering of reasons would not fail.) It fails because nothing matters in isolation from whatever else matters, and Heidegger thinks there must be some primordial horizon of significance for such care to be sustained (the kind of primordial horizon that comes into view when the problem of Dasein's totality is in question). What is important in this context is that the practical implication of this failure is what Heidegger calls "guilt," an owning up both to the radical contingency of one's thrownness and the inescapability of an ever threatening death, as well as to the practical necessity, in acting at all, of fleeing in some way from such nullity, of "erring" in the ontological sense in order to be, in order to "stretch one's existence along in time." This incompatibility is not a rational inconsistency or a failure to be rational enough. We are simply not "in charge" of whether care fails or not, or how to think our way into or out of such an experience. "This 'Being-a-basis' means never to have power over one's ownmost being from the ground up. This 'not' belongs to the existential meaning of thrownness."[44] And, "being-guilty is more primordial than any knowledge of it."[45]

This is the predecessor account for all attempts—eventually Carnap's too—to tame or moderate the existential and ontological challenge of not-being.[46] But our own not-being, is not *another way for us to be*, we *are* not something other than alive when we are dead. Death is also not a natural completion, or ripeness, or the lack or privation of life in a material body; it is not—existentially, with respect to Dasein's experience of the meaning of its being—even a factual "event" to be expected and has its role in such a meaning question only by our "being-toward" it. And, as Heidegger never tires of saying, the ontological problem of not-being cannot be reduced to the problem of a logical operator, the paradigmatic form of treating not-being as otherness; not this being, but *thereby some other being* or some other possible point in logical space. This is the sense of the famous passage from *What Is Metaphysics?* (*Was ist Metaphysik?*) that so enraged Carnap:

> Does the nothing exist only because the not, i.e. negation exists? Or is it the other way around? Do negation and the not exist only because the nothing exists? . . . We assert: the nothing is prior to the not and the negation. . . . Where do we seek the nothing? How do we find the nothing? . . . Anxiety reveals the nothing. That for which and because of which we were anxious was "really" nothing. Indeed: the nothing itself—as such—was present. . . . What about this nothing?—The nothing itself nothings.[47]

(Even here, it is important to stress, Heidegger is tying this so-called "reference to the Nothing" to anxiety, or the failure of possible "projection." He is always referring, I think, to the unique Dasein-possibility—failed "lived meaning"—not to any metaphysical nonmeaning.) Death, Heidegger is suggesting, is not simply the negation of life, other than life (but some other state of being). For Dasein qua Dasein (not qua biological organism) is always "dying,"[48] always in a way "at" its end, and for it, ceasing to be is an absolute nothingness, the meaning of which cannot captured by the negation operation applied to "life." Heidegger goes to an extreme formulation to try to suggest that such radical not-being cannot be domesticated by us, is not the result of what we do to ourselves, bring about in some psychological sense—his infamous phrase is "the nothing itself nothings"—but his contrast is clear enough.[49]

From a Heideggerian point of view, in other words, when Creon and Antigone in Sophocles' play are arguing over what is to be done with Polyneices' body, when the audience is made aware of the utter difference between Polyneices and the thing now rotting thing outside the city walls, they are enacting what they must enact in order to live, even though both "mediations," both appeals to the Penates on the one hand and the city's requirements on the other, are attempts to reclaim, within a logic of mattering, what cannot make sense in this way; both represent in ways typical of such human flight a refusal to allow Polyneices to die. There is no way to continue to stretch along into the future the world that had Polyneices in it. He is not in it at all; he is nothing; and when in some contingent way the structure of care fails to continue such redemption, the character of such an attempt, its ultimate *Nichtigkeit*, becomes unavoidable.

Such a failure of meaning is radical in ways now more familiar from modern literature.[50] When Bartleby the Scrivener stops working, and "prefers not to," what is "uncanny" (in exactly the Heideggerian sense) about his story is that the failure of meaning he suffers is not in the name of what his form of life lacks, what it should have; not in the name of any absence or privation, any "other than what now is." The failure of meaning appears to be complete, not a response to the failure of humanism, of justice, not a response to the brutality of wage labor and so forth. Bartleby has in effect no "everyday" psychology (none Melville gives as relevant), no beliefs or aspirations, no reasons. Mattering just "fails" in the way it can (the way it can fundamentally in anxious being-toward-death), *in the way that reveals the utter contingency and fragility of it succeeding when it does.* Its happening or not happening *is* the event of truth (the occasion for living "in truth"). The "disturbance" that Bartleby provokes in his colleagues is very much as if he is the presence of death among then, the "uncanniest" of guests. In the same way that the nihilistic culmination of metaphysics reveals something about the nature of metaphysics as such, and is not a contingent event—philosophers losing faith in metaphysics—so too in the existential situation it is the radicality of this failure of meaning that reveals what is most essential about such meaning (that it can so fail). Any partial or determinate failure (of the kind central to Hegel's account of conceptual and social change, for example) amounts merely to an extension of sense-making practices and so blocks any radical reflection on their possibility. ("Only by the anticipation of death is every accidental and 'provisional' possibility driven out.")[51]

But there are no determinate conditions *necessary* for care to succeed, to be sustained, for anything to matter, such that to call the call of conscience, anxiety, and being-toward-death a threat to the existential satisfaction of transcendental conditions is to obscure the point Heidegger is trying to make.[52] There is no way that being-in-the-world can be isolated from its historical incarnations so that we might isolate "conditions" necessary for the *pragmata* of the world to make the sort of determinate practical sense they occasionally do. Heidegger's accounts of involvement, comportment, falling, and so forth are both (1) primordial elements of how things have come to make sense in a historical world (such that the gradual transformation of such a world into one wherein a predatory technological subject confronts material stuff for its mundane purposes is not a failure or breakdown of sense, but the contingent transformation of the horizon of ontological meaning), and (2) preparatory to the account of the *failure* of such a way of things mattering when the call of conscience and its attendant anxiety bring the practical structure of care crashing down. Again, Kantian or transcendental conditions cannot "fail." That is the whole point of the case for their necessity. The Heideggerian elements of practical sense making can ultimately fail or even be permanently forgotten. That is the whole point of saying that Care is shot through with *Nightigkeit* and is the null basis of a nullity. This failure, occasioned by the "threat" to meaning posed by one's ever-impending death, is not a failure "as yet" to make the proper sense of what seems without sense.[53] There is no horrible fate that we are too fearful or too finite to make sense of. The failure Heidegger is trying to account for is not a failure to "make sense" of death, but an occasion in which the failure to make sense of, be able to sustain reflectively, sense making itself "happens."

This situation, I have claimed, is an exemplary, not a transcendental, account. Of what is it exemplary? In existential terms (in Heidegger's sense of existential) it exemplifies the occasion requiring either an "authentic" or "inauthentic" response, an issue that would require several volumes to discuss appropriately. But the basic direction of the book's analysis suggests the obvious answer: what is exemplified is the temporal character of being, that being is time, the truth of the meaning of being historical, a matter of *Geschichtlichkeit*. I close with some brief remarks about that sort of claim and temporality itself.

4. Time and Historicality

I have said that for Heidegger mattering can just "fail," and in a way that reveals the utter contingency and fragility of it succeeding when it does, so that meaning happening or not happening *is* the event of truth (the occasion for living "in truth," in the acknowledgment of this finitude or in flight from it).

There is another way to put this point, once we take in Heidegger's most comprehensive account of care, his way of making the point cited earlier—that care must be sustained to function as care, stretched along into the future. Heidegger's formulation is that "temporality [*Zeitlichkeit*] reveals itself as the meaning of authentic care,"[54] and the "primordial unity of the structure of care lies in temporality." This is the opening to what he calls "a more primordial insight into the temporalization structure of temporality, which reveals itself as the historicality [*Geschichtlichkeit*] of Dasein."[55] This distinctive historicality (or historicity as it is now more frequently translated) is stressed by Heidegger in a way not entirely clear in the Macquarrie-Robinson translation.

> The movement [actually this is another neologism, more like "moved-ness" or "motility," *Bewegtheit*] of existence is not the motion [*Bewegung*] of something present-at-hand. It is definable in terms of the way *Dasein* stretches along [*aus der Ersteckung des Daseins*]. The specific movement [*Bewegtheit*] in which Dasein is stretched along and stretches itself along, we call its happening [*Geschehen*, "historizing" by Macquarrie and Robinson].[56]

However valuable it is to draw attention to the etymological connections between *Geschehen* and *Geschichte*, it is crucial that the translation capture the sense of contingency connoted by *Geschehen*, and especially regrettable that the translators often make *Geschehen* a verb when Heidegger uses it as a noun, suggesting just the opposite of what Heidegger wants to suggest—the mere "happenstance," let us say, of meaning as a temporalizing, care-ful engagement, and the happenstance of its failure.[57] So the summary claim that he makes should be, "This is how we designate Dasein's primordial happening [*ursprüngliche Geschehen*], lying in its authentic resoluteness, and in which Dasein hands itself down to itself, free for death, in a possibility which it has inherited and yet has chosen."[58]

There is a lot packed into such claims, but the basic dimensions of the case attributed to Heidegger are visible. What is meaning such that it can fail? Finite, contingent; a *Geschehen*, distinctively temporal, in a way a kind of event, *Er-eignis* (or "e-vent" as it is sometimes translated to capture Heidegger's hyphen), which can happen *to* us, or not, cannot be redeemed or reflectively grounded by philosophy.

This *Geschehen* quality also differentiates Heidegger's position from that other Southwest German philosopher, and that can be a final way to make the Heideggerian point. I quote from the preface to Hegel's *Phenomenology of Spirit* (*Phänomenologie des Geistes*):

> But the life of Spirit is not the life that shrinks from death and keeps itself untouched by devastation, but rather the life that endures it and maintains itself in it. It wins its truth only when, in utter dismemberment [*Zerrissenheit*], it finds itself. . . .

Spirit is this power only by looking the negative in the face, and tarrying with it. This tarrying [*Verweilen*] with the negative is the magical power [*Zauberkraft*] that converts it into being.[59]

This claim is possible in Hegel's account because such instances of failure, breakdowns in a form of life as a whole, "utter dismemberment," are precisely *not* mere "happenings" or events, and so not instances of radical non-being. As he notes in the introduction,

Thus consciousness suffers this violence at its own hands: it spoils its own limited satisfaction. When consciousness feels this violence, its anxiety may well make it retreat from the truth and strive to hold on to what it is in danger of losing. But it can find no peace. If it wishes to remain in a state of unthinking inertia, then thought troubles its thoughtlessness, and its own unrest disturbs its inertia.[60]

There is of course no such "magical power" for Heidegger, and this because spirit does not suffer the violence of death "at its own hands," such that some way can be found to reconstruct the subjective purposiveness inherent in so suffering, in bringing about such suffering (the purposiveness necessarily assumed if this self-inflicted suffering is to count as a deed). From Hegel's (or perhaps from Adorno's) point of view, the Heideggerian experience of death *as* (now, for us) radical not-being, *as* unintegratable in any way with Dasein's projected meaning, *is* "something we have done to ourselves," itself can be made sense of, given the historical situation of late modernity, or late industrial capitalism, and so forth. From Heidegger's point of view, on the other hand, Hegelian death remains Christian; the tarrying of which Hegel spoke is possible because of a faith in "resurrection," and the ultimacy of death in our experience is not being faced authentically, but clearly avoided. It is as if Hegel cannot help giving away his dodge and his own uncertainty with that revealing (most un-Hegelian) word or Freudian slip, *Zauberkraft*, "magical power."

But, contrary to many interpretations of Hegel, these remarks by him show that Hegel does not treat the failure of some community to sustain a practical "directedness" as a mark of some *ultimately* in-principle *overcomeable* finitude. For, only as long as there is such "violence suffered at its own hands" *is* there *Geist*. According to Hegel there is a narrative ("rational") structure to our coming to this realization, but *this* is the realization we are coming to (i.e., just the opposite of the jejune invocations of Hegel as announcing the end of history or a complete "closed" systematicity).[61] But, as I have been suggesting, this realization (otherwise known as "Absolute Knowledge") cannot itself be a Heideggerian "happening" since the realization that only in such "failure" is there success (success at being *Geist*) is historically an achievement like no other, is what makes what Heidegger calls the "revealing and concealing" process *itself* manifest. This is why Hegel treats the final problem of reconciliation in the *Phenomenology* (*Versöhnung*) as "forgiveness" (*Verzeihung*), forgiveness not at being "merely" human but grounded in the realization of being "absolutely" human.

Stated this way, matters between the Baden and the Schwabian are left pretty much at a standoff. But Heidegger reminds us that philosophy is "the opposite of all comfort and assurance," "the highest uncertainty," and maintains itself "in authentic questionableness." So perhaps an unresolved standoff, an ending that is not an end, is a good place to close.

CHAPTER 14

Projection and Purposiveness

HEIDEGGER'S KANT AND THE TEMPORALIZATION OF JUDGMENT

Rachel Zuckert

HEIDEGGER'S KANT interpretation is, as he admits, "violent," not meant to be scholarly exegesis, but to understand the path of Kant's thought "better than" Kant did himself.[1] This turns out, perhaps predictably, to mean reading Kant's project in the *Critique of Pure Reason* as anticipatory of Heidegger's own project in *Being and Time*—it is an attempt to "lay the ground" for metaphysics through an analysis of human understanding of being—and as (ultimately) a failure at such a project. For, Heidegger argues, Kant too narrowly defines being as the being of "extant" objects or of nature and (correspondingly) did not investigate deeply enough the "subjectivity of the subject."[2] This "reading" of Kant may appear—and has appeared to many Kantians—a highly dubious one: from a neo-Kantian point of view, for example, Heidegger's characterization of Kant's project as "ontology,"[3] is from the first inconsistent with the enterprise of Kant's transcendental philosophy, which (on this view) is at its heart epistemology, not concerned to establish ontological truths, but only "epistemic conditions," that is, the forms and justifications for our knowledge.[4]

Such a dismissal seems, however, premature, since Heidegger's reading is, somehow, both compelling and unsettling as a reading *of Kant*. And if one construes Kant's own transcendental project in a broader, but (I suggest) nonetheless faithful, way—as an investigation into the necessary conditions for the possibility of experience[5]—Heidegger's interpretation may be read not simply as a translation of Kant's claims into his own language and philosophical concerns, but as an exercise in transcendental philosophy, indeed as a challenge to Kant, namely, that he has failed properly to identify the conditions for the possibility of experience.[6] Specifically, Heidegger may be said to argue (contra Kant) that there is a more fundamental condition for the possibility of experience than Kant's categorial principles or synthetic a priori judgment(s)—the projective unity of the subject's transcendental, imaginative synthesis, and the unity of time itself. Thus, Heidegger argues, we must "temporalize" Kant's account of the transcendental subject and of its characteristic cognitive activity, synthesis.

Or so I shall suggest here, beginning with an overview of Heidegger's Kant interpretation, before turning to articulate the challenges that Heidegger poses to Kant, the philosophical "stakes" of such challenges, and some, preliminary reflections concerning possible Kantian responses. In such a short chapter, I cannot, of course, adjudicate this Kant-Heidegger debate; rather, I aim more modestly to reformulate Heidegger's interpretation as comprising such a debate, and to identify the core lines of argument that divide Kant and Heidegger over the necessary conditions for the possibility of experience. I shall suggest that this debate is best formulated to concern Kant's distinction (and Heidegger's rejection thereof) between reflective and determinative judgment. Thus, like Cassirer, I shall suggest that Heidegger's Kant interpretation concerns the *Critique of Pure Reason* decontextualized from Kant's larger philosophical system;[7] unlike Cassirer, I shall suggest that Heidegger's account of subjective, projective "judging" reads the doctrines of the *Critique of Judgment* (concerning reflective judgment) "back" into the *Critique of Pure Reason* (account of determinative judgment), thus occluding the systematic place, or attempting to undermine the specific concerns, of the *Critique of Pure Reason* within Kant's system.

1. Heidegger's Reading of Kant: Interpretation as Confrontation

Heidegger's Kant interpretation comprises, most generally, a transformation of Kant's project through rereading Kant's guiding question in the *Critique of Pure Reason* concerning whether and how synthetic a priori judgments can be justified. Heidegger frames his conception of Kant's project by arguing that Kant's understanding of the human knower as "finite"—by contrast to God's infinite intellect—serves as Kant's key premise, from which Kant draws his claim that human knowledge comprises two, also finite, cognitive faculties, sensibility and understanding.[8] As finite knowers, that is, as knowers dependent upon objects beyond or outside of us, human beings require "receptive" intuition. And because we must thus "receive" intuitions of objects, we require "spontaneous" (active) discursive thinking, that is, conceptual rules for the unification and "determination" of these intuitions. Thinking is, thus, in "service" to intuition, the main source of experience or knowledge of objects, "presenting" such objects to us or allowing us to encounter them.

In the *Critique of Pure Reason*, Kant then—on Heidegger's reading—attempts to "reveal" the ways in which human beings attain knowledge of appearances, through the interaction of these two, distinct cognitive faculties in (transcendental) judgment or the act of synthesis (or, more specifically, through the a priori synthesis of the a priori intuitions [space and time] and concepts [the categories] that "enables" all empirical synthesis of particular objects).[9] Kant's question concerning the possibility of metaphysics (or of synthetic a priori judgments) is to be understood as: *How* is it possible for human beings to know objects? Or, specifically, *how* can human beings judge, namely synthesize or determine, intuitions to comprise unified objects?[10] Not surprisingly, Heidegger then takes the schematism—Kant's sketchy answer to this question (via the schemata of the imagination)—to be the central chapter of the *Critique of Pure Reason.*

Heidegger's emphases upon human (cognitive) finitude in Kant's project, and on Kant's consequent understanding of human knowers' experience as grounded upon activities of synthesis, understood as the union of understanding and sensibility, do reflect one of Kant's most basic doctrines concerning human cognition (famously: intuitions without concepts are blind, concepts without intuitions are empty). Likewise, in the Transcendental Deductions, Kant explains the possibility of the synthetic a priori principles and justifies the a priori categories as applicable to objects of experience, by arguing that they function as rules for transcendental synthesis, which is necessary for the possibility of (unified) experience. Kant even occasionally uses the contrast between divine and human intellect explicitly to ground his claims that human knowledge comprises both intuition and *discursive* thinking, and (therefore) that the "schematic" character of judgment, namely, our need to *apply* rules to intuitions (or universals to particulars), is characteristic of human knowledge.[11]

Heidegger's reading seems, then, not to be (particularly) transformative. But Heidegger does, hereby, *de*emphasize another central aspect of Kant's project: the *quaestio juris*, or Kant's description of his project as a *justification* of certain synthetic, a priori propositions (judgments in a narrower, propositional sense), including, most famously, the causal principle, "Every event has a cause." (This story of Kant's formulation of the *Critique of Pure Reason* project—his "awakening" from "dogmatic slumber" by Hume—is familiar, and I will not rehash it here.)[12] Heidegger recognizes that he is deemphasizing Kant's justificatory question, but argues that once Kant has revealed the categories (in their schematized form) *to be* necessary conditions for the possibility of experience, Kant has thereby also answered the *quaestio juris.*[13] We may *justifiably* claim that objects of experience conform to the categorial principles because such principles make experience possible, are "always already" appropriate to any object we could experience.

Thus: *a* "problem" of synthetic "judgment" is, indeed, central to the *Critique of Pure Reason*, on Heidegger's reading, though it is not the justificatory problem Kant poses, but an "ontological" problem concerning the possibility of the act of transcendental judgment, how we may synthesize intuitions as determined by concepts. Correspondingly, Heidegger argues that Kant's "subjective deduction" of the categories—the argument that categorial synthesis is necessary for the possibility of experience—is itself sufficient to answer Kant's most important question, while the "objective" deduction—to establish that the categories constitute the nature of objectivity, or objecthood (and are, thus, justifiably applied to objects)—is pleonastic.

In concert with his reformulation of Kant's project, from a justificatory to a "revelatory" one, Heidegger transforms Kant's conception of the a priori, an epistemological, evidentiary term, into a characterization of our manner and activity of apprehending objects, namely, as that which we understand "in advance" or "beforehand," that which we "anticipate" in empirical judgments, or in our "pre-ontological understanding" (everyday practical engagement with the world).[14] This gloss on *a priori* is, of course, suitably etymological for Heidegger, but it also plays a philosophical role in securing terminologically (as it were in advance) Heidegger's "temporalizing" interpretation of Kant's views, to which I now turn.

On Heidegger's reading, Kant's project itself is not to be understood as a justification of a priori claims already formulated in scientific investigation,[15] but as disclosing structures that are "always already" functioning within experience, that "enable" our more specific apprehension of particular objects, but do so "pre-ontologically," that is, as implicit, unconceptualized, or unarticulated. Kant *himself* is, then, engaged in "ontology," understood as the "objectification," "thematization," or conceptualization of this "pre-ontological" (Heideggerian) understanding;[16] he is "transforming the pre-ontological understanding of being into an explicit ontological understanding."[17] Kant's project is, then, itself temporalized, that is, explicitly "situated" as arising out of everyday experience, and as itself, an activity of conceptualization, retrospectively articulating that which has already been anticipated "in advance."[18]

This translation of the a priori into the "in advance" is also central to Heidegger's temporalized interpretation of Kant's doctrine of transcendental judgmental synthesis. Heidegger argues that the Kantian transcendental synthesis ought to be understood not (primarily) as a conceptually guided act of the understanding applying concepts or principles to intuited objects (as Kant understands it), but as a projective, anticipatory act of the productive imagination, an act that constitutes "in advance" the horizon within which beings (objects) may be "encountered."[19] This activity of the transcendental imagination is, Heidegger suggests, identical to time (as originary temporality) and to transcendental subjectivity itself. Thus, famously, Heidegger claims that Kant "shrinks back" from the conclusion to which his investigation should lead, namely that the transcendental imagination is the "common root" of Kant's two primary cognitive faculties, intuition and understanding.[20]

Heidegger argues for the implicit primacy of the imagination over the understanding in Kant's account of transcendental synthesis by emphasizing the centrality of the schematism (a function of the imagination, on Kant's view) in Kant's project. The imagination is the solution to (Heidegger's) Kant's central "problem of judgment," namely, how the two basic elements of knowledge may be combined in judgment, despite their utterly distinctive natures: the imagination "gives" content to the categories (and order to intuitions) by "bringing" intuitions to the unities of the understanding. This combination is accomplished, Kant himself argues, through the imagination's relation to time: the imagination mediates between the categories and intuitions by producing schemata or interpretations of the categories as forms or structures of objective time, thereby explaining how the categories may be applied to (combined with) intuitions, which must all be presented in time, the "pure form" of all intuitions.[21]

Consonantly with his emphasis upon the "subjective" rather than "objective" deduction (on the abilities of the subject necessary for the possibility of experience, not on the necessary character of objecthood or objectivity as such), Heidegger reads the schematism primarily as providing an account of the imagination as a faculty that allows us to unite understanding (thought) and sensibility. The imagination is our ability to "give" ourselves that which is not given, to "present" that which is not "present," or (in other words) is "spontaneous intuiting," or "intuitive creativity." The imagination thus shares the characteristics of the two other faculties, and serves to mediate between them, and it does so because of its unique relationship to time, its "presentation" of that which is not "present."[22] Specifically, our imaginative, anticipatory grasp of the future is that which "guides" and unifies the given intuitions, the past and the present, into one synthesis, and thereby makes conceptual "determination" of such intuitions, and indeed unified experience, possible.[23] Heidegger identifies "original temporality" itself, in turn, as the ultimate source of unity in this imaginative synthesis: the imagination's anticipatory synthesizing is unified because *time* itself is so unified, because past, present, and future are "aspects" of the one time that grounds the unity of experience.[24] Thus, Heidegger argues, the a priori transcendental synthesis of intuitions—guided (on Kant's view) by the categories—is fundamentally an imaginative synthesis, an anticipatory act of synthesis.[25]

Unlike Heidegger's reformulation of Kant's guiding question, this interpretation of Kant's *answer* to that question is markedly "violent," at odds even with Kant's A edition "subjective deduction," that is, the account of threefold syntheses necessary for the possibility of experience, on which Heidegger draws. For Heidegger's interpretation inverts the roles of the categories and of time in Kant's account. Kant argues that in order for experience to be possible, we must (imaginatively) synthesize a manifold of intuitions in "apprehension"; in order, in turn, for such apprehension to be possible, we must "reproduce" intuitions (by imagination), and in order (finally) to be able to reproduce intuitions, we must have a concept or rule by which we could "recognize" the (reproduced) intuitions as the same or indeed *re*-produce the same intuition at all.[26] The progressive "in order to's" and "musts" here are (in part) responses *to* a problem generated *by* time: we cannot apprehend a manifold (as such) without reproduction because intuition (distinguished solely by its occurrence at a moment in time) is an "absolute unity" undifferentiated into a manifold. Nor can we "reproduce" without conceptual guidance, for intuitions simply qua occurrent at a time are not distinguishable or reproducible as the "same," for each moment of time is indistinguishable as such from any other. More broadly, Kant's arguments in the Analytic of Principles turn on the claim that we cannot perceive time itself; therefore, Kant argues, we require the categorial principles in order to generate a coherent time order. In other words, Kant does indeed take thinking to be in "service to" intuition (specifically) *as* structures of (objective) time, and argues that only as such structures do the categories have objective "reality" (content or meaning), as Heidegger stresses, but Kant likewise argues that intuition (here, the pure intuition of time) is unintelligible ("blind") without such conceptual determination.

As is well known, Heidegger's counterclaim is that Kant here misunderstands the nature of time, as the mere, objective time of a "succession of nows," and fails to recognize the "originary temporality" that characterizes subjective existence.[27] The categorial principles may be structures of objective time (as Kant contends) but they are—more basically—dependent upon the subject's imaginative projection (they operate as unities "in advance") and thus emerge from the unified structure of imagination as unified, original temporality.[28]

Heidegger's violent "interpretation" is, then, a challenge to Kant, for it threatens to undermine Kant's central, demonstrative aims, that is, to show that the categories are necessary for the possibility of experience, and (therefore) that the synthetic a priori judgments employing such categories are justifiable claims concerning objects of experience. For if temporality (or the subject) is itself, and can constitute within experience, a "unity of the manifold," then Kant's argument in the deductions proves otiose, since in that case the unity of experience does not, solely or originally, derive from and require the categorial rules of synthesis.[29] The categories may, on this view, apply justifiably to (some) experience, as Kant wants to argue, but only as "thin" articulations of unities thereof; they are not necessary for—nor universally true of—*all* experience.[30] Likewise, the grounding of such categorial claims on the nature of the existentially, originally temporal subject would be anathema to Kant: such a substantive, metaphysical claim concerning the "noumenal" or "supersensible" nature of the subject would violate Kant's critical limitations on our abilities to know a priori.

From the Heideggerian point of view this debate has parallel (though positively put) consequences as well: if Heidegger shows that such temporal anticipation grounds the unity and possibility of categorial thought or synthesis of objects, Heidegger can then argue, as he does, that Kant has (wrongly) identified nature, or objects, as "extant," as the sole type of objects we may experience, and that he has identified only those categories that are necessary to comprehend this type of object. If the categories are only "thin" articulations of a more "primordial" unity of experience (grounded in the activities of the imagination, and in time), it may well be that human beings could approach beings from other perspectives, according to other anticipatory, pre-ontological understandings of being. More generally, such a move, as Heidegger celebratorily announces, promises a "new and radical philosophical grounding of logic,"[31] a rejection of the traditional philosophical identification of being with *logos* (here the categories, or most basic concepts for thought), by recognizing the dependence of such *logos* upon existence and time.[32] But Kant "shrank back."

2. *A First Reflection*

Despite the "violence" of Heidegger's reading, and the challenges it presents, several things can, I think, be said in its favor, from a broadly Kantian point of view. First, Heidegger is right in identifying the odd character of Kant's transcendental "judgmental" synthesis. Such synthesis is not, on Kant's view, simply predicative or an establishment of purely conceptual relationships. Kant argues, of course, that synthetic judgment must (in order to be synthetic, not analytic) "advance beyond" concepts, must "relate" to an intuitively given object.[33] Such judgment can be construed (still) as predicative or propositional, distinctive (from analytic judgment) only in that it requires different justification, that is, a connection in the object. But Kant's argument that (our apprehension of) this very connection *within* the object is grounded *itself* upon a "judgmental" synthesis renders Kant's conception of judgmental synthesis a very different (in Heidegger's terms, "veritative") sort of synthesis indeed: one that unifies (or institutes relations among) a manifold of *intuitions*, and therefore one that is not, at the very least, exhaustively rendered in propositional form.[34] As Heidegger emphasizes, Kant argues that "general logic," and the corresponding (predicative) definition of judgment (a ruled governed relation between two concepts) is distinct, even derivative, from a more fundamental form of judging described by "transcendental logic" (the "logic of truth") wherein we do not relate concepts to one another but determine objects (intuitions) by concepts. Thus Kant is, perhaps, not as far as his terminology (of "judgment") might suggest from questioning the foundational role of *logos* in knowledge or the understanding of being(s).[35]

Second, Heidegger here provides an interesting, unusual response to a long-standing problem posed by Kant's transcendental psychology, specifically by his accounts of synthesis. On Kant's account, time is an a priori form of intuition, and thus forms phenomena alone, and the *objective* time order governing experience and objects is constituted by the subject's transcendental activities of synthesis. The transcendental subject who engages in these activities is, however, to be considered separately from time; and indeed *as* the agent whose activities determine the objective time order, must be "prior" to, not determined by, this time order. Synthesis, however, at least sounds like an activity; it is, thus, difficult to conceive of it as nontemporal.

The two standard responses to this problem are both (in different ways, and with differing severity) reductive. Scholars such as Paul Guyer and Patricia Kitcher propose that Kant's accounts of synthesis be understood as describing empirically occurring psychological activities; thus such activities are not mysterious atemporal activities, but, rather, events (of a particular kind) in time. This view seems, however, a deeply reductive characterization of Kant, for, on this interpretation, Kantian philosophy must be understood as an episode in the history of empirical psychology. But according to Kant, empirical psychology and its explanations of its object (the mind) are themselves governed by the categorial principles, and thus must presuppose, but cannot explain or nonreductively instantiate, the categorial synthesis (nor, on Kant's view, would empirical psychology carried out entirely a priori be methodologically acceptable).

On the other hand, scholars such as Henry Allison and P. F. Strawson construe Kant's claims about synthesis as purely logical claims, articulating the normative constraints on how we may conceive of objects or ourselves. The atemporality of the transcendental subject simply means that the subject can (indeed must) conceive of itself and of objects in the "space of reasons," rather than in the order of causes. This line of interpretation is clearly reconstructive, at odds with Kant's presentation of synthesis as an *activity*. More importantly, however, this interpretation raises difficulties concerning whether or how such normative constraints, rules, or reasons function in actual human experience and judgment.[36] This interpretation, then, seems reductive (though less problematically so); it is not clear in what sense this transcendental subject (or its concepts) can be said to be who we actually are, to provide an account of what it is like to be a subject of experience, to have a first-person "point of view." Nor is it clear, on this view, how (or that) categorial judgment is to be grounded in its purchase upon (as necessary condition for) *actual* experience. (Such difficulties are, as has been frequently argued, exacerbated when one turns to consider Kant's conception of the transcendental subject as moral, free agent.)

By contrast to these two proposals, Heidegger's proposal that the transcendental subject is constituted by an alternative, originary temporality might allow one to understand the transcendental subject, coherently and nonreductively, as an agent engaged in synthesis or judgment, and as an experiencing subject. But one can also argue that such activity is a precondition for, and "prior" to, the "constitution" of an objective time order as the "succession of 'nows'" (provided, of course, that originary temporality can be coherently understood).

Thus, for both well and ill, there is a great deal at stake in Heidegger's temporalizing "reading" of Kant: Heidegger not only threatens Kant's demonstrative aims, the necessity of the categories (*logos*) for experience, and violates Kant's theoretical humility, but also proffers an account of the judging, synthesizing subject that may suit a Kantian's antireductive inclinations. But now we may ask: Does Heidegger give us reason so to conceive of the subject, to unseat the reign of *logos*, to transcend critical limitations, or to yield to such inclinations? Why should we, that is, "leap forward" to originary temporality?

3. Stalemate?

As we have seen, Heidegger himself emphasizes the schematism question—how we may synthesize intuitions according to conceptual rules or unite the understanding with sensibility—as the central problem of the *Critique of Pure Reason* and as the main reason for identifying the imagination as the "root" of the two main faculties, or for understanding the subject as characterized by originary temporality. The schematism question is potentially a troubling one for Kant, as was also found to be the case by the neo-Kantians and German Idealists (who both respond by eliminating, in differing ways, Kant's dualism concerning the sources of cognition). But I am not sure that this problem, in its more pressing forms, is addressed by Heidegger's proposal that the subject (and, derivatively, its rules of judging) should be understood as itself temporal. For the question is how intuitions may be construed, rightly, as objects, or how to judge that these intuitions—and not those—are to be unified, or properly subsumed to the categories.[37] The subject's own temporal status does not, it would seem, make this easier to understand. And Heidegger's response to the question concerning correct application suggests as much, for it seems little different (and no more or less persuasive) than Kant's own. Heidegger writes:

> "Faculty of rules," . . . means: to hold before us in advance the represented unities which give direction to every possible unification that is represented. These unities (. . . categories) which are represented as regulative, however, *must not only have learned to play their part based on their proper affinity*, but this affinity must itself also be grasped comprehensively in advance in a lasting unity *through a still more anticipatory pro-posing* of them.[38]

Thus, Heidegger's solution to the question of correct application is simply a gesture toward the "affinity" of concepts to intuitively presented materials.

But in the second emphasized passage above, Heidegger is also asking (I think more promisingly) what a subject must be "like" in order to *be* rule-following, and suggests that such rule-following *presupposes* that the subject is anticipatory, or future-directed (or, in more proper Heideggerian language perhaps, such rule-following presupposes "existence" rather than being).[39] Unlike Heidegger's claim that the imagination (and its schemata) is necessary for the application of the categories to intuitions—which Kant does not deny, but himself argues—this line of argument would promote Heidegger's strongest claim, contra Kant, that imaginative projection is foundational, a necessary condition or "root" for the categories or our ability to formulate and follow rules. And perhaps indeed rule-following requires or constitutively *is* a stance of anticipatory temporality, not appropriately characterized either in terms of objective temporality (mere succession governed by causal law) or as atemporal.

As suggested in the title of this section, this line of argument might seem, however, to lead to a stalemate between Heidegger and Kant. For Kant would, of course, reply to this suggestion that only because we can follow rules can we take such a projective, anticipatory stance, or employ the "productive imagination" to anticipate or project a unified time order and world in "advance" of particular, individual experiences.[40] It is, precisely, the universality of categorial rules (their application to numerous, temporally distinct instances) and our ability to employ such rules that allows us to "anticipate" nonpresent (future) order in the world or states of affairs.

Apart from the general suggestion here that Kant perhaps illicitly privileges epistemological over ontological conditions (why should rules count as conditions, while the nature of the subject does not?), Heidegger does, at least implicitly, provide broadly epistemological grounds to reject this claim (that such projection could be grounded upon concepts) expressed most clearly in his temporalization of Kant's project itself (as an act of conceptualization or "thematization"): in order to be following concepts or rules (or for these to be the "basis" for synthesis or judgment), Heidegger suggests, we must be conscious of such concepts as such. And just as Kant's project must be understood as a "conceptualization" of the "preconceptual," so too must the applicability of the categorial principles to experience be a (mere) conceptualized by-product of a more "original," preconceptual, imaginative projection.

In some sense, Heidegger must be right: if Kant claims that the categories or the principles employing them are necessary conditions for the possibility of experience, that they articulate the ultimately judgmental, synthetic character of experience for all subjects, at all times, these principles must be understood as "pre-ontological," implicit, rather than explicit, principles of judgment and experience. (Even those of us who have read the *Critique of Pure Reason*, and thus are explicitly conscious of the categories, schemata, and principles, do not, consciously or explicitly, engage in judgment or synthesis to generate our experience.) This implicit status of synthetic a priori judgments is, indeed, consistent with Kant's view of the (justified) a priori as the form or "constitutive" structure of experience, which entails that one may need to engage in considerable analysis (or, as Kant puts it, "sifting") of experience to generate explicit formulations of "pure" a priori principles. The familiarity, or obviousness, of the principles—once formulated—might then reflect, as Heidegger suggests, a recognition of that which we have "pre-ontologically," always already understood.

Do such considerations entail Heidegger's more radical suggestion that Kant's principles not only render explicit that which is implicit, but *conceptualize* a pre*conceptual* "understanding," or (thereby or therefore) that one ought to understand the experience-constituting activity of synthesis, and the subject engaged in such synthesis, as characterized by "originary" temporality? It seems not: Kant's explicit principles may be taken, rather, as articulating a priori commitments that are, indeed, *implicit* in ordinary empirical judgments or experience, as *conceptual*. For, one might suggest, the categories comprise implicit *conceptual* content (or, in Kant's terms, "marks") in empirical *concepts*. Thus in Kant's famous examples, "The sun shines, and the stone is warm," and "The sun warms the stone," the category of quality might be "part" of the conceptual content of "warm," as might the category, cause, comprise a component of "event" or "process" (in "warm*ing*"). More broadly, since concepts are rules or functions by which we categorize, unify, or determine (judge) appearances, on Kant's view, these categories might—as syntax does, for natural language users—operate as rules within or governing behavior (here empirical judgment, but also imaginative projection). As applied and applicable universally, and as unifying, such rules perform the function of concepts, even if the subject is not conscious of this function.

From a Kantian point of view, then, Heidegger's position appears to be based on an assumption that concepts (categories) must be explicitly such "for" the judging subject, in order so to function in a subject's experience, and therefore might be said to betray an inappropriately Cartesian presumption concerning the transparency of subjectivity and conceptual thought. From a Heideggerian point of view, Kant helps himself to a very broad conception of concepts (or rule-following), thus ("in advance") cementing the foundational status of rules, concepts, or *logos*, and precluding the questions Heidegger (like Wittgenstein) wishes to raise concerning the degree to which practical competence (or behavior responsive to norms) can be characterized as a form of (explicit-)rule-following.

Thus the Heidegger-Kant debate might be formulated in these terms: Does rule-following depend upon temporal anticipation, or vice versa? Does the imagination "ground" the categories' function as rules to unify experience, or does it merely "execute" the norms given by such categories? Does practical competence (in empirical judging or "pre-ontological understanding") ground rules and make explicit rule-following possible, or do rules govern or define such practices? These are real questions, but arguments for them turn (as I have just suggested) on almost question-begging conceptions of rules on either side; certainly the considerations Heidegger raises here against Kant are not weighty enough to press Kant into accepting a radically metaphysical (from a Kantian point of view) conception of the judging subject.

Heidegger also argues, however, that the imagination is the "root" of the categories by providing an alternative "Metaphysical Deduction" (the account of the origin of the categories) to the one that Kant himself provides. This line of argument is, I shall suggest, a better, more unequivocal case for taking anticipatory temporality to be independent of, and indeed a precondition for, categorially determined synthesis or conceptually governed judgment. It also, as I shall argue, suggests a more precise and tractable reformulation of the Kant-Heidegger debate, as one concerning the relationship between reflective and determinative judgment.

4. A Reformulation: The Necessity (or Not) of Determinative Judgment

On Kant's view, the categories are a priori concepts; they are not innate, however, but are generated by the understanding. In the Metaphysical Deduction, Kant argues (specifically) that the categories are so generated from the forms of judgment elaborated in general logic. Heidegger rejects this account because (he argues) the categories are rules of ("veritative") synthesis of the intuitive manifold and cannot, therefore, be derived from the ("predicative") functions of judgmental unification in general logic, which concern merely unification of concepts, independent of "reference" to an object or intuitions.[41] Heidegger suggests that the categories are (rather) generated through two cognitive activities, both described (by Kant) as acts of "reflection": the activity of empirical concept formation, and the act of self-understanding wherein one brings one's mental activities and their functions (here the first kind of reflection) to self-consciousness. Because empirical concept formation is synthesizing judgment of the intuitively given, Heidegger argues, it can be the origin for the categories as synthetic functions of intuitions.[42] And (Kant's account of) empirical concept formation shows that this "origin" is, indeed, an act of imaginative anticipation; thus not only is imaginative anticipation possible without categorial guidance, but the categories themselves derive (depend upon) such imaginative anticipation as their origin.

Kant describes empirical concept formation as follows:

To make concepts out of representations one must . . . be able to *compare, to reflect,* and *to abstract,* for these three logical operations of the understanding are the essential and universal conditions for generation of every concept whatsoever. I see, e.g., a spruce, a willow, and a linden. By first comparing these objects with one another I note that they are different from one another in regard to the trunk, the branches, the leaves, etc.; but next I reflect on that which they have in common among themselves, trunk, branches, and leaves themselves, and I abstract from the quantity, the figure, etc. of these; thus I acquire the concept of a tree.[43]

Heidegger reads this description (plausibly) as providing an account of the anticipatory activity of judgment, in which we (must) hold before ourselves a unity "in advance," in order to perform the comparison, discrimination, and abstraction that will then allow us to conceptualize that very unity:

Of these three acts [comparison, reflection, and abstraction], reflection has a crucial and leading role. . . . For prior to everything else there is an advance bringing into view that in reference to which an intuitively extant many is to be noted as different. What is different in its possible difference [for example, differently arranged branches] gets determined only on the basis of this unifying one of agreement [having branches of some sort], so that on the basis of reflection we can explicitly disregard "the respect in which given representations are different." . . . Reflection is situated in the anticipatory bringing into view that with regard to which the many should be compared.[44]

This activity of reflection is, as Kant's example suggests, the activity of *empirical* concept formation; but Heidegger takes Kant's claim that it is the "essential condition" for the generation of "any" concept at Kant's word, and argues that this activity generates the categories (a priori concepts) as well. The categories, Heidegger suggests, are conceptualized articulations of the unifying functions or relations (e.g., genus and species/differentia, and disjunction) *implicit* or "held in advance" in empirical concept formation (or, in Kant's terms, they are "representations" of the unifying functions of consciousness).[45] Such explicit representations of these functions of unifying are brought to consciousness (made explicit) by "reflection" in the second sense, understanding of one's own cognitive activities. Thus the categories are what is implicit "in advance" in reflective concept formation, an activity itself "temporal" in Heidegger's "originary" sense, as governed by, and directed toward, a future, anticipated unity.

Kant does not explicitly hold the Heideggerian view concerning empirical concept formation, but he may well suggest such a view in his *Critique of Judgment* account of "reflective" judgment—including empirical concept formation—as ruled by the principle of "purposiveness."[46] Kant defines "reflective" judgment—by contrast to "determinative" judgment (the judgment with which the *Critique of Pure Reason* is concerned)—as judgment in which we are not "guided by" a concept or rule in judging, nor do we "determine" an object thereby; rather, we "seek" the universal (that might, later, be used to determine objects).[47] This judgmental activity is, then, not (fully) conceptually guided by definition, and it does indeed "aim" at conceptualization of the preconceptual (sensations or empirical particulars as such). And because we seek empirical concepts, the governing unities of objects we seek here cannot, unlike the categories, be gleaned from our judgmental activities themselves. This is, indeed, what one might call a "transcendental" definition of the empirical: that which we do not, cannot, determine a priori, that to which we must be "open" or "responsible."

"Reflective" judgment is thus unifying without (prior) conceptual determination, but on Kant's view it cannot, merely, be intuitive apprehension without principled guidance, for such apprehension would be mere "groping," potentially overwhelmed by undifferentiated, chaotic sense experience. And indeed reflective judgment does have its own "principle": the principle of "purposiveness." Kant characterizes this principle and its role in empirical concept formation as follows: in attempting to form empirical concepts, we must presuppose that nature is "purposive" for us, that it coheres with our cognitive aims.[48] This formulation does not suggest that purposiveness has anything to do with Heidegger's projective temporality, but Kant also understands purposiveness to be "directedness" by or toward a purpose and uses it to characterize the act of reflective judging itself.[49] As such, it bears considerable similarity to Heidegger's anticipatory projection: reflective judging is structured as "directedness toward" a (not given) purpose (here, the empirical concept of this sort of object), or is a unification unified by its own aims at unification or anticipation of unity. Kant's characterization of *aesthetic* reflective judgment (the judging "solely" governed by the principle of purposiveness) bears striking similarities to Heidegger's account of imaginative synthesis: in such judging, Kant argues, we are not guided by concepts; rather, the imagination "unintentionally" or "purposively without a purpose" apprehends the object as a unity of the manifold.[50]

In the *Critique of Judgment*, Kant provides, moreover, strictly "subjective" deductions for this principle and act of judging, as (merely) "subjective conditions" for the possibility of experience. Reflective judging—and its principle, purposiveness—are not "determinative" of objects; reflective judging comprises, precisely, an openness to objects in their empirical character, not a determination of them. But such judging is a "subjective condition" for experience: if we cannot form empirical concepts, we would, Kant argues (plausibly), be incapable of any coherent experience.[51] Thus, on the Kantian as on the Heideggerian view, we must be able to transform the preconceptual into the conceptual.

Perhaps, then, Kant's account of reflective judgment in the *Critique of Judgment* vindicates Heidegger's reading of Kant: though Kant does not articulate the "original temporality" of the judging subject, Kant himself identifies "purely subjective" conditions for the possibility of experience, which comprise something like an anticipatory, non-conceptually guided grasp of the unity of the object.[52] And Heidegger suggests so: he cites paragraph 59 of the *Critique of Judgment* as confirmation of his views concerning Kant's conception of transcendental imagination and subjectivity,[53] a passage in which Kant (strikingly) argues that insofar as reflective, aesthetic judging is purposive (end-directed, though without a conceptually specified end) it not only "symbolizes" our capacity for moral self-legislation (of ends), but also reveals the *supersensible* nature of the subject.[54]

But Heidegger's reading of Kant is not, I suggest, completely vindicated here, specifically Heidegger's suggestions that the recognition of such anticipatorily temporal subjectivity will undermine the status of the categories or discursive thought. For Kant gives Heidegger's purely subjective "deduction" a systematic *place*: the subjective principle of purposiveness does not override, but complements, the *objective* a priori principles as (subjective *and* objective) conditions for the possibility of experience; and it governs our experience and knowledge of *empirical* nature in particular. Kant's contrast between determinative and reflective judgment is a distinction between two sorts of subjective conditions for the possibility of experience: the conditions for the possibility of (our knowledge of) *universal* and necessary, lawful order in the world and the conditions for the possibility of (our knowledge of) *contingent* (empirical, particular, and diversified) order. Thus Kant may admit that the categorial principles are not necessary conditions for any unity of experience or unification of the manifold, but argue that we require a priori rules for *necessary* order in nature or the *necessary* unity of objects as such. Kant indeed suggests just such a role for the categories in the A-Deduction: "We find that our thought of the relation of all knowledge to its object carries with it an element of necessity; the object is viewed as that which prevents our modes of knowledge from being haphazard or arbitrary."[55] Since all "necessity, without exception, is grounded in a transcendental condition,"[56] *this* (necessary) unity "is impossible if the intuition cannot be generated in accordance with a rule by means . . . [to make] the reproduction of the manifold a priori necessary."[57] Objectivity (object-hood) as such is a unification of the manifold that "resists" our arbitrary construal; the categories constitute such unity precisely in their function as a priori rules.

If one places Kant's arguments in the *Critique of Pure Reason* in the context of his systematic consideration of judgment, the debate between Kant and Heidegger may be reformulated, then, not to concern the question how *any* (synthetic) unity in experience is possible, but the question whether—even if all concepts (unities) ultimately originate in reflective judging—we must engage in *determinative*, as well as reflective, judgment for experience to be possible, whether we must not only imaginatively anticipate but *also* engage in conceptually determined or rule-governed synthesis. Correspondingly, Heidegger's reading of the *Critique of Pure Reason* might be seen as a transformation of a priori determinative judgment *into* reflective judgment, thus eliding these two conditions, proposing that the sole a priori conditions for the possibility of experience are conditions for the apprehension of *contingent* order.[58] This elision is corroborated by Heidegger's striking deletion of "necessity" terms (including "laws" or "lawfulness") in his characterization of Kant's project, as compared to the pervasiveness of such terms in Kant's text (which pervasiveness the Kant-responding-to-Hume line of interpretation emphasizes).

Again, Heidegger's deletion is not coincidental: the necessary *content* of a priori determinative judgments is necessary for the possibility of experience, on Kant's view, because it grounds a distinction between the "merely subjective" and the objective construed as independent-of-or-resistant-to-the-subject.[59] On Heidegger's view, the categorial rules function, then, to generate a falsifying, or at least highly derivative, self-conception as separate from objects, not as transcending itself toward the world, a metaphysical view of subjects (Heidegger contends) simply presupposed, on the Kantian view, as fundamental.[60]

The questions that divide Kant and Heidegger may, therefore, be more precisely characterized, in Kantian terms, as follows: Must we be able to formulate specifically necessary and universal claims in order to have experience? Must we be able to distinguish our "subjective" experiences from objects of experience proper, in order to have self-conscious experience? Or, in Heideggerian terms: Must we conceive of objects as "merely" present at hand? And, if so, must we come to such a conception through conceptual rules of necessary or normative import, rather than through "breakdown" or anxiety?[61] Or, in terms of Heidegger's Kant interpretation: for experience to be possible, we may indeed require intentional objects recognized as different from or "against" ourselves (as "objects" or *Gegenstände*). Is, as Heidegger suggests, intuitive "givenness" (and our reflective openness thereto) enough to comprise the "againstness" of the intentional object—or must we, as Kant contends, employ conceptual determination in order to render (or conceive) an object *as* such, as "over against" us?

These questions are, of course, too large to be addressed here. In conclusion, I shall simply note that we can now see the (meta)philosophical significance of Heidegger's reformulation of Kant's question concerning a priori synthetic judgment, with which I began, and that this leaves us with a final question that weighs, perhaps, in Kant's favor.[62] For the necessary and universal "content" of the categorial principles is, on Kant's view, the "sign" that such principles are known a priori (if known at all), and this therefore provides the impetus to a strictly philosophical project, as opposed to naturalist or psychological explanations for the origins of such propositions. Or, that is, such principles raise a *quaestio juris*. Heidegger's dismissal of the *quaestio juris* as pleonastic (in favor of "straight" investigation or "revelation" of the subjective conditions for the possibility of experience), is, as we can now see, quite consistent with his deletion of Kant's concerns with (logical and [meta]physical) necessity, and with his assimilation of determinative to reflective judgment. But this dismissal might also be something like kicking away the ladder. For why should one engage in this transcendental investigation of the nature of subjectivity if there is no "clue" that a priori, subjectively contributed concepts *do* function in experience? Or: if, as on both Kant's and Heidegger's views, the philosopher's task is to articulate the a priori "forms" that ground experience, how is one to "sift out" the a priori, properly philosophical claims from purely empirical facts about human beings? Necessity functions as such a "clue" for Kant. And from *within* the transcendental framework, motivated and justified by the *quaestio juris*, Kant can *then* suggest that explaining the possibility of empirical knowledge might require a "purposive" conception of subjectivity (in its reflective judging), a conception of subjectivity (I have suggested) that Heidegger greatly expands and reads back into the *Critique of Pure Reason*. What, however, functions as such a "clue" for Heidegger or for Heidegger's Kant?

REFERENCE MATTER

Notes

In the present volume, whether in endnotes or in the text of the chapters themselves, citations from *Being and Time* will refer to the John Macquarrie and Edward Robinson translation (New York: Harper and Row, 1962), unless a chapter author prefers the translation by Joan Stambaugh (Albany: State University of New York Press, 1997), which will be noted separately. The corresponding pages in *Sein und Zeit* will be from the Niemeyer edition of 1993. The citations will give the English page number first, followed by the German pagination (again, unless indicated otherwise).

CHAPTER 1: INTRODUCTION

1. There is an existing literature, of course, on Heidegger's relation to Kant, which includes, in English, Charles Sherover, *Heidegger, Kant, and Time* (Bloomington: Indiana University Press, 1971); Frank Schalow, *The Renewal of the Kant-Heidegger Dialogue* (New York: State University of New York Press, 1992); and Martin Weatherstone, *Heidegger's Interpretation of Kant* (London: Palgrave, 2003). This is an area that is still relatively undeveloped, though it is receiving increasing attention. Indeed, the work of several contributors to this volume, including that of William Blattner, Daniel O. Dahlstrom, and Robert B. Pippin, has been particularly important in this respect. Heidegger's relation to the wider transcendental tradition has also attracted some attention. Manfred Brelage's pioneering *Studien zur Transzendentalphilosophie* (Berlin: de Gruyter, 1965) explores the relation between Heidegger and the transcendental logic of the neo-Kantians; and Carl-Friedrich Gethmann's *Verstehen und Auslegung: Das Methodenproblem in der Philosophie Martin Heideggers* (Bonn: Bouvier, 1974) remains an indispensable treatment of the transcendental elements in Heidegger's thought. For a more recent effort see Steven Crowell, *Husserl, Heidegger, and the Space of Meaning: Paths Toward Transcendental Phenomenology* (Evanston, IL: Northwestern University Press, 2001).

2. Suspicion of the idea of the transcendental within English-speaking thought undoubtedly goes back to the association between that notion and idealist philosophy. However, two seminal papers—Barry Stroud, "Transcendental Arguments," *Journal of Philosophy* 65 (1968): 241–56; and Stephan Körner, "The Impossibility of Transcendental Arguments," *Monist* 51 (1967): 317–31—have been extremely influential in advancing similarly negative assessments of the viability of transcendental

modes of reasoning (although in Stroud's case, this has also gone hand-in-hand with a recognition of the importance of the issues such arguments are intended to address).

3. A more developed version of this way of understanding the idea of the transcendental appears in Jeff Malpas, "The Transcendental Circle," *Australasian Journal of Philosophy* 75 (1997): 1–20.

4. Recent discussion of this issue in English and German can be usefully tracked in three collections: *Transcendental Arguments and Science*, ed. Peter Bieri, Rolf-Peter Horstman, and Lorenz Krüger (Dordrecht: Reidel, 1979); *Bedingungen der Möglichkeit: "Transcendental Arguments" und transzendentales Denken*, ed. Eva Shaper and Wilhelm Vossenkuhl (Stuttgart: Klett-Cotta, 1984); and *Transcendental Arguments: Problems and Prospects*, ed. Robert Stern (Oxford: Oxford University Press, 1999).

5. The relevant texts can be found as appendices 3 and 4 in Martin Heidegger, *Kant and the Problem of Metaphysics*, 5th ed., trans. Richard Taft (Bloomington: Indiana University Press, 1997), pp. 191–207.

6. In addition to the article by Stroud, cited in note 2, above, see Moltke S. Gram, "Transcendental Arguments," *Nous* 5 (1972): 15–26; and Anthony Brueckner, "Transcendental Arguments I," *Nous* 17 (1983): 551–75.

CHAPTER 2: ONTOLOGY, THE A PRIORI, AND THE PRIMACY OF PRACTICE

1. "Early philosophy" refers principally to *Being and Time* (*Sein und Zeit*), but also to *The Basic Problems of Phenomenology* (*Die Grundprobleme der Phänomenologie*); *Phenomenological Interpretation of Kant's "Critique of Pure Reason"* (*Phänomenologische Interpretation von Kants "Kritik der reinen Vernunft"*); and other lectures from the mid- to late 1920s.

2. William Blattner, "Is Heidegger a Representationalist?" *Philosophical Topics* 27 (1999): 179–204; "Laying the Ground for Metaphysics: Heidegger's Appropriation of Kant," in *The Cambridge Companion to Heidegger*, ed. Charles Guignon, 149–76, 2nd ed. (Cambridge: Cambridge University Press, 2003); and "The Primacy of Practice and Assertoric Truth: Dewey and Heidegger," in *Heidegger, Authenticity and Modernity: Essays in Honor of Hubert L. Dreyfus*, ed. Mark Wrathall and Jeff Malpas, vol. 1, 231–49 (Cambridge, MA: MIT Press, 2000).

3. *Die Grundprobleme der Phänomenologie*, ed. Friedrich-Wilhelm von Herrmann, *Gesamtausgabe*, vol. 24 (Frankfurt am Main: Klostermann, 1975), p. 15.

4. Theodore Kisiel, *The Genesis of Heidegger's "Being and Time"* (Berkeley and Los Angeles: University of California Press, 1993).

5. In what follows I shall make two controversial translation choices. First, I shall render *Erkenntnis* as "cognition." This diverges from Macquarrie and Robinson's "standard" translation of *Being and Time*, in which they use "knowing" instead. My choice reflects recent practice among translators of Kant, such as Paul Guyer and Allen Wood in their translation of *The Critique of Pure Reason* (which is not, however, the one I shall use below). One indirect advantage of my way of rendering Heidegger is that we can distinguish between the general "problem of cognition" under discussion in § 13 of *Being and Time* and the more focused problem of the "provability of the external world" in § 43a. I suggest that Heidegger means to ap-

ply the strategy of § 13 to the issues of § 43a; they are not, however, exactly the same problem. Second, I shall render *Vernehmen* as "taking-in" or "taking-as," rather than "perception," as Macquarrie and Robinson do. This makes better sense of the flow of argument in the crucial paragraph from p. 61 to p. 62 of *Sein und Zeit*, as I shall argue below. (See Immanuel Kant, *Critique of Pure Reason*, trans. Paul Guyer and Allen Wood [Cambridge: Cambridge University Press, 1997]; and Martin Heidegger, *Being and Time*, trans. John Macquarrie and Edward Robinson [New York: Harper and Row, 1962].) In what follows, all translations from *Sein und Zeit* are my own unless otherwise noted.

6. Specifically, Heidegger characterizes interpretation as a "development" (*Ausbildung*) of understanding. See Heidegger, *Being and Time*, p. 188/148.

7. Ibid., p. 89/62.

8. Ibid., p. 189/149.

9. Ibid., p. 385/336.

10. Ibid., p. 183/143.

11. Ibid., pp. 188–89/148–49.

12. *Die Grundprobleme der Phänomenologie*, p. 440.

13. Hubert Dreyfus, *Being-in-the-World: A Commentary on Heidegger's "Being and Time," Division I* (Cambridge, MA: MIT Press, 1991).

14. *Being and Time*, p. 99/69.

15. Ibid., p. 89/62.

16. Dreyfus, *Being-in-the-World*, p. 5; my emphasis.

17. Note, as well, that on this construal the role of the concept of interpretation in the § 13 argumentation becomes unclear.

18. There is the one reference to "mathematical functionalization" on p. 122/88, but that is about it.

19. *Being and Time*, p. 189/149.

20. Ibid., p. 191/150.

21. Ibid.

22. Ibid.

23. I would actually want to dispute this assimilation on Heidegger's part, but that does not matter here. See Blattner, "Is Heidegger a Representationalist?" for some suggestions along these lines.

24. *Being and Time*, p. 189/149, quoted in part above.

25. Immanuel Kant, *Critique of Pure Reason*, trans. Norman Kemp Smith (London: Macmillan, 1968), A79/B104–5.

26. There is some confusion in the text surrounding this implication. I have tried to resolve it in Blattner, "Is Heidegger a Representationalist?"

27. *Being and Time*, p. 89/62.

28. Ibid., p. 183/143, quoted above.

29. As I begin to argue in Blattner, "Primacy of Practice and Assertoric Truth," Heidegger understands practice differently than does Dewey, and for this reason, Heidegger does not accept anything like the classical pragmatist account of truth. It would, thus, be highly misleading to characterize Heidegger as a pragmatist, even if there are certain important affinities between the early Heidegger and Dewey.

30. *Being and Time*, pp. 30–31/10–11.

31. *Phenomenological Interpretation of Kant's "Critique of Pure Reason,"* trans. Parvis Emad and Kenneth Maly (Bloomington: Indiana University Press, 1997), p. 25.

32. In Blattner, "Laying the Ground."

33. In light of the first section of this chapter, this formulation might be confusing. *Understanding* in Kant refers to a conceptually articulated act, whereas in *Being and Time* it refers to a preconceptual activity. Thus, Kantian understanding is a form of Heideggerian interpretation. Understanding in *Being and Time* corresponds better with Kant's "pure productive imagination," at least as interpreted by Heidegger.

34. Blattner, "Laying the Ground."

35. *Phenomenological Interpretation of Kant's "Critique of Pure Reason,"* p. 187.

36. I here restate Heidegger's analysis of the "threefold synthesis" in the A-Deduction, Kant, *Critique of Pure Reason*, A98–104. See Heidegger, *Phänomenologische Interpretation von Kants "Kritik der reinen Vernunft,"* ed. Ingtraud Görland, *Gesamtausgabe*, vol. 25 (Frankfurt am Main: Klostermann, 1977), § 24. It is obviously modeled upon Husserl's analysis of time-consciousness, the published version of which Heidegger edited during the period in which he was mulling over Kant. See Edmund Husserl, *The Phenomenology of Internal Time-Consciousness*, ed. Martin Heidegger, trans. James S. Churchill (Bloomington: Indiana University Press, 1964).

37. *Phenomenological Interpretation of Kant's "Critique of Pure Reason,"* p. 247.

38. I have, in any case, gone into this in considerable detail in my William Blattner, *Heidegger's Temporal Idealism* (Cambridge: Cambridge University Press, 1999).

39. Kant, *Critique of Pure Reason*, A11–12/B25.

40. *Die Grundprobleme der Phänomenologie*, p. 15.

41. Ibid., pp. 12–13.

42. Ibid., p. 28.

43. *Being and Time*, p. 414/363. In § 69b of *Being and Time*, from which the last sentence is drawn, there is ambiguity about whether objectification consummates the "change-over" from the available to the occurrent, or whether objectification is a more basic process. Heidegger writes, "The scientific projection of entities that we somehow already encounter allows their sort of being to be explicitly understood, so much so, in fact, that the possible paths to a pure discovery of intraworldly entities become manifest. We call the whole of this projecting, including the articulation of the understanding of being, the delineation of the material region (*Sachgebiet*), and the sketching out of the appropriate conceptuality that belongs to the entities, *thematizing*" (Heidegger, *Being and Time*, p. 414/363). The reference to the "pure discovery" of entities, that is, to the experience of the occurrent, suggests that the stronger reading of thematizing, as the process through which entities become shorn of context. It may well be, however, that the reference here to pure discovery is an artifact of the context in which it is used, the context in which Heidegger is discussing precisely the origin of natural science. By "thematizing" and "objectifying," therefore, Heidegger might simply have in mind the development of understanding into interpretation. Following this suggestion, "objectifying" refers to the process whereby something is made amenable to conceptualization, becomes available for cognition and interpretation in the broadest sense. This suggestion fits well with the use of "thematizing" in *Basic Problems*, for surely whatever else he might

want to say, Heidegger does not mean to indicate that phenomenology somehow makes being occurrent. That would be a category error of the rankest sort, a violation of the Ontological Difference. Rather, phenomenology is the science in which being becomes salient, explicit, available for interpretation. Further, as I will indicate below, reading "thematizing" and "objectifying" the way I do here also explains why *all* interpretation is thematic, as Heidegger says in § 32.

44. *Being and Time*, p. 62/37.

45. The worry I am highlighting here, it should be noted, is not the tension between description and interpretation, between transparency and construal, that many readers have found in *Being and Time*. Even if we could understand how a "direct presentation" (ibid., p. 59/35) of being could at the same time be an interpretation reflecting the "obvious, undiscussed assumptions of the interpreter" (ibid., p. 192/150), we still would not be any closer to seeing how a preconceptual condition for the possibility of conceptualization could be conceptualized.

46. Nor is, I believe, "formal indication." Kisiel makes much out of formal indication as a potential solution to the problem and thereby places a heavy burden on the few references to formal indication in *Being and Time*. As with hermeneutics, however, "formal indication" is merely a name for the problem, not a solution.

47. Kisiel, *Genesis of Heidegger's "Being and Time."*

48. *Towards the Definition of Philosophy* (trans. Ted Sadler [London: Continuum, 2002]), is a translation of Martin Heidegger, *Zur Bestimmung der Philosophie*, ed. Bernd Heimbüchel, *Gesamtausgabe*, vol. 56–57, 2nd ed. (Frankfurt am Main: Klostermann, 1999). These volumes comprise Heidegger's lectures from the war emergency and summer semesters of 1919.

49. In *one* sense, Husserl's principle is not even a principle: "If by a principle one were to understand a theoretical proposition, this designation would not be fitting" (Heidegger, *Towards the Definition of Philosophy*, p. 92).

50. Ibid., pp. 92–93.

51. Ibid., p. 93.

52. Ibid.

53. Ibid., quoted above.

54. Steven Crowell, "Heidegger's Phenomenological Decade," *Man and World* 28, no. 4 (1995): 435–48.

55. And that means giving up on phenomenology as well. The Kant lectures are perhaps, then, the close of Heidegger's "phenomenological decade," the close not just in the sense of ending, and not so much a consummation as a collapse.

56. "What Is Metaphysics?" (*Basic Writings*, ed. David Farrell Krell, pp. 89–110, rev. and exp. ed. [New York: HarperCollins, 1993]) is a translation of Martin Heidegger, "Was ist Metaphysik?"

57. Martin Heidegger, "Time and Being," in *On Time and Being*, trans. Joan Stambaugh (New York: Harper and Row, 1972), p. 24.

58. Herman Philipse, *Heidegger's Philosophy of Being: A Critical Interpretation* (Princeton, NJ: Princeton University Press, 1998).

59. I would like to thank the participants of the conference on which this volume is based, Heidegger and Transcendental Philosophy (Rice University, Houston, April 2003), as well as the participants of the Fifth Annual Meeting of the International Society for Phenomenological Studies (Asilomar, CA, July 2003), all of whom

listened and responded to an earlier version of this argument. I would like to thank especially the editors of this volume, Steve Crowell and Jeff Malpas.

CHAPTER 3: HEIDEGGER ON KANT ON TRANSCENDENCE

1. *Kritik der reinen Vernunft*, in *Kant's gesammelte Schriften*, ed. Royal Prussian [later German] Academy of Sciences, vol. 3 (Berlin: Georg Reimer [later Walter de Gruyter], 1900–), A84/B116.
2. Ibid., p. A89/B122.
3. *Phänomenologische Interpretation von Kants "Kritik der reinen Vernunft,"* ed. Ingtraud Görland, *Gesamtausgabe*, vol. 25 (Frankfurt am Main: Klostermann, 1977), p. 309. All translations are author's unless otherwise stated.
4. *Kant und das Problem der Metaphysik* (Frankfurt am Main: Klostermann, 1951), pp. 68ff.
5. *Phänomenologische Interpretation*, pp. 372ff.
6. Ibid., p. 384.
7. Ibid., p. 315.
8. *Kant und das Problem der Metaphysik*, Vorwort.
9. *Phänomenologische Interpretation*, p. 3.
10. Ibid.
11. *Kant und das Problem der Metaphysik*, p. 25.
12. *Die Grundprobleme der Phänomenologie*, ed. Friedrich-Wilhelm von Herrmann, *Gesamtausgabe*, vol. 24 (Frankfurt am Main: Klostermann, 1975), p. 177.
13. *Being and Time*, p. 367/319.
14. *Kant und das Problem der Metaphysik*, pp. 21–22, 174.
15. Ibid., pp. 21–22.
16. *Phänomenologische Interpretation*, p. 321.
17. Ibid., p. 320.
18. Ibid., p. 322.
19. Ibid., p. 319.
20. Ibid., p. 312.
21. Ibid., p. 316.
22. Ibid., p. 314.
23. Ibid.
24. Ibid., p. 315.
25. Ibid., 319.
26. Ibid., p. 308.
27. *Kritik der reinen Vernunft*, A85/B117.
28. *Phänomenologische Interpretation*, p. 311.
29. Ibid., p. 400.
30. *Kritik der reinen Vernunft*, A111.
31. *Phänomenologische Interpretation*, pp. 330ff.
32. Ibid., p. 315.
33. Ibid.
34. Ibid.
35. Ibid., p. 331; see also *Kant und das Problem der Metaphysik*, p. 151.
36. *Phänomenologische Interpretation*, p. 324.
37. Ibid., p. 333.
38. Ibid., p. 373; *Kritik der reinen Vernunft*, A341/B399ff.
39. *Kritik der reinen Vernunft*, A115; *Kant und das Problem der Metaphysik*, p. 126.

40. *Kritik der reinen Vernunft*, A118; *Phänomenologische Interpretation*, p. 410.
41. *Kritik der reinen Vernunft*, A15/B29.
42. *Kant und das Problem der Metaphysik*, p. 147.
43. *Phänomenologische Interpretation*, p. 376.
44. Ibid., pp. 408–9.
45. Ibid., p. 12.
46. John Locke, *An Essay Concerning Human Understanding* (Chicago: Regnery, 1956), p. 17.
47. *Kritik der reinen Vernunft*, A50/B47.
48. Ibid., A50/B47; cf. A147/B242.
49. Ibid., A104.
50. Ibid., B3.
51. Ibid., Bxiv.
52. Ibid., A369.
53. Ibid., B136.
54. See Edmund Husserl, *Ideas Pertaining to a Pure Phenomenology and to a Phenomenological Philosophy: First Book*, trans. F. Kersten (The Hague: Nijhoff, 1983), § 62.
55. See Edmund Husserl, *The Crisis of European Sciences and Transcendental Phenomenology: An Introduction to Phenomenological Philosophy*, trans David Carr (Evanston, IL: Northwestern University Press, 1970), § 30.
56. Edmund Husserl, *Cartesian Meditations: An Introduction to Phenomenology*, trans Dorion Cairns (The Hague: Nijhoff, 1969), p. 26.

CHAPTER 4: CONSCIENCE AND REASON

1. Immanuel Kant, *Critique of Pure Reason*, trans. Norman Kemp Smith (London: Macmillan, 1968), p. 96; *Kritik der reinen Vernunft*, in *Kant's gesammelte Schriften*, ed. Royal Prussian [later German] Academy of Sciences, vol. 3 (Berlin: Georg Reimer [later Walter de Gruyter], 1900–), A56/B80.
2. Ibid., p. 100; A63/B87.
3. See, for one instance, Martin Heidegger, *Metaphysical Foundations of Logic*, trans. Michael Heim (Bloomington: Indiana University Press, 1984), p. 134: "We must . . . make intentionality itself into a problem."
4. Evidence for the first construal can be found at Martin Heidegger, *Being and Time*, p. 224/180, while evidence for the second construal can be found on the immediately following page of Heidegger's text. Future references to *Being and Time* will be inserted into the text at the appropriate point. In this chapter I have generally followed the Macquarrie and Robinson translation, but I will modify the translation as I see fit, without comment.
5. Martin Heidegger, "The Word of Nietzsche: 'God is Dead,'" in *The Question Concerning Technology and Other Essays*, trans. William Lovitt (New York: Harper and Row, 1977), p. 112.
6. Ernst Tugendhat, *Der Wahrheitsbegriff bei Husserl und Heidegger* (Berlin: de Gruyter, 1967), p. 329. Translations from Tugendhat are mine.
7. Ibid., p. 351.
8. On constitutive rules, see John Haugeland, "Truth and Rule-Following," in *Having Thought: Essays in the Metaphysics of Mind*, by John Haugeland (Cambridge MA: Harvard University Press, 1998), pp. 303–61.

9. This Wittgensteinian reading has been most forcefully elaborated by Hubert Dreyfus, *Being-in-the-World: A Commentary on Heidegger's "Being and Time," Division I* (Cambridge, MA: MIT Press, 1991).

10. Robert B. Pippin, "On Being Anti-Cartesian: Hegel, Heidegger, Subjectivity and Sociality," in *Idealism as Modernism: Hegelian Variations*, by Robert B. Pippin (Cambridge: Cambridge University Press, 1997), p. 381.

11. Ibid., pp. 382, 388.

12. Robert B. Pippin, "Heideggerian Historicity and Metaphysical Politics," in *Idealism as Modernism: Hegelian Variations*, by Robert B. Pippin (Cambridge: Cambridge University Press, 1997), p. 410.

13. Pippin, "On Being Anti-Cartesian," pp. 386–87; 378.

14. Ibid., pp. 386–87; 390.

15. Pippin, "Heideggerian Historicity," p. 404.

16. Ibid., p. 410.

17. Ernst Tugendhat, "Wir sind nicht fest gedrahtet: Heideggers 'Man' und die Tiefdimension der Gründe," in *Aufsätze, 1992–2000* (Frankfurt am Main: Suhrkamp, 2001), p. 150. Following Tom Scanlon, Tugendhat defines a "reason" as "something that speaks for something," where the latter "something" is almost always "a judgment or an intention or an action" (p. 143). All translations from Tugendhat's essay are mine.

18. Tugendhat, "Heideggers 'Man'," p. 144.

19. Ibid., p. 158.

20. Ibid., pp. 149–50.

21. Ibid., p. 157.

22. Ibid., p. 159.

23. Ibid., p. 160.

24. Ernst Tugendhat, *Self-Consciousness and Self-Determination*, trans. Paul Stern (Cambridge, MA: MIT Press, 1986), p. 215.

25. Ibid., p. 217.

26. Tugendhat, "Heideggers 'Man,'" p. 151.

27. There are a number of ambiguities in these passages. I here provide the German for comparison: "Das Selbst, das als solches den Grund seiner selbst zu legen hat, kann dessen *nie* mächtig werden und hat doch existierend das Grundsein zu übernehmen." "*Nicht durch* es selbst, sondern *an* es selbst *entlassen* aus dem Grunde, um *als dieser* zu sein. Das Dasein ist nicht insofern selbst der Grund seines Seins, als dieser aus eigenem Entwurf erst entspringt, wohl aber ist es als Selbstsein das *Sein* des Grundes. Dieser ist immer nur Grund eines Seienden, dessen Sein das Grundsein zu übernehmen hat" (*Being and Time*, p. 377/284; 378/285).

28. Carl-Friedrich Gethmann, *Verstehen und Auslegung: Das Methodenproblem in der Philosophie Martin Heideggers* (Bonn: Bouvier, 1974), p. 141. All translations from this book are mine.

29. Ibid., p. 208.

30. Ibid., pp. 222, 227–28, recognizes that Heidegger owes us an account of "how something like principles lie in the *Seinsvollzug des Daseins*." Unlike most commentators, however, he sees that Heidegger provides the beginning of such an account in the chapter on conscience and guilt, even if there are "gaps between the fundamental-ontological phenomenon of being-guilty and the principle of reason as a

transcendental-ontological principle" that can "be closed only through an interpretive further-thinking of the text."

31. In Gethmann's terms, "the meaning of grounding [*Begründung*; justification] is first of all co-given through the *Existenz* of the ground itself." *Verstehen und Auslegung*, p. 233.

32. T. M. Scanlon, *What We Owe to Each Other* (Cambridge, MA: Harvard University Press, 1998), p. 17. Scanlon actually writes that a reason is something that "counts in favor" of something, which Tugendhat renders as "etwas, was für etwas spricht." Tugendhat, "Heideggers 'Man,'" p. 143. My reasons for preferring to translate back from the German will become obvious in the argument that follows.

33. It is tricky to specify just what this "speaking for" something amounts to, but it will involve a norm that governs a kind of success or failure. A reason might speak for something by answering the question of why it should be that way, thus being oriented toward the norm of the Good. Or it might be taken as evidence for *believing* something, in which case it is oriented toward the norm of the True. A "justifying" reason is not simply a cause, which might bring something about but cannot speak for it.

34. Cristina Lafont, *Heidegger, Language, and World-Disclosure* (Cambridge: Cambridge University Press, 2000), pp. 1–84, has shown that such pre-predicative involvements are not prelinguistic, but she argues that the Humboldtian role Heidegger ascribes to language—as an essentially historical linguistic milieu that provides the *unhintergehbar* horizon of all intelligibility—leads back to a version of Tugendhat's criticism. Because Heidegger holds that "entities are in no way accessible without an understanding of being," he is trapped in a "linguistic idealism" that leaves no room for a transhistorical normativity of reason, no possibility that the norms prevalent within a certain historical "disclosure" could be *rationally* criticized or called into question, since all criticism and questioning depend on them. But the force of such objections can be assessed only if one has first provided an adequate ontological account of reason and reasoning. Here I argue only that the necessary ontological account must begin with the notion of conscience, which is a mode of discourse that is *not* bound to the Humboldtian historical linguistic milieu and offers different access to the problem of critique.

35. I would argue that the following elements of a phenomenology of deliberation hold regarding moral deliberation as well, but to show this would require a separate essay.

36. Bernard Williams, *Ethics and the Limits of Philosophy* (Cambridge, MA: Harvard University Press, 1985), p. 68, argues that "practical deliberation is in every case first-personal, and the first-person is not derivative or naturally replaced by *anyone*." But Heidegger would respond that though the first-person is not derivative, "the self of everyday Dasein"—including the self who deliberates—"is the *one-self*" (*Being and Time*, p. 167/129); that is, already understands itself in typical ways and so, in a sense, as "anyone." It is true, as Williams argues, that "the *I* of reflective practical deliberation is not required to take the result of anyone else's properly conducted deliberation as a datum" (*Ethics and the Limits of Philosophy*, p. 69), but it nevertheless remains, in Heidegger's terms, "dispersed into the 'One'" and its way of interpreting

the situation (*Being and Time*, p. 167/129). For an account of how a genuine first-person is distinguished from the one-self see Steven Crowell, "Subjectivity: Locating the First-Person in *Being and Time*," *Inquiry* 44 (2001): 433–54.

37. Martin Heidegger, "What Is Metaphysics?" in *Basic Writings*, ed. David Farrell Krell, rev. and exp. ed. (New York: HarperCollins, 1993), p. 103.

38. Ibid., p. 101.

39. William Blattner, "The Concept of Death in *Being and Time*," *Man and World* 27 (1994): 49–70.

40. John Haugeland, "Truth and Finitude: Heidegger's Transcendental Existentialism," in *Heidegger, Authenticity, and Modernity*, ed. Mark Wrathall and Jeff Malpas (Cambridge, MA: MIT Press, 2000), p. 65.

41. Heidegger, *Metaphysical Foundations of Logic*, p. 11.

42. Hans-Georg Gadamer, "Rhetorik, Hermeneutik, Ideologiekritik," in *Gesammelte Werke* (Tübingen: J. C. B. Mohr, 1993), 2: 247.

43. Dreyfus, *Being-in-the-World*.

44. This is, of course, something of an idealization. It is only in fully "mindless" coping that the analogy between natural causes and factic social norms is fully compelling. Everyday life, as Heidegger recognizes, exhibits intermediate forms in which, in my ongoing practical engagement in some task, I am responsive to the normative demands on me *as* normative. But this raises the question of how to *account* for such responsiveness, and I argue below that Heidegger gives such an account in terms of conscience as "taking over being-a-ground."

45. Martin Heidegger, "On the Essence of Ground," *Pathmarks*, ed. William McNeill (Cambridge: Cambridge University Press, 1998), p. 106. Hereafter, cited as EG.

46. Heidegger goes on to criticize what becomes of this situation in Plato when the *epekeina* gets translated into a "realm of Ideas" and so our relation to world becomes "*noein, intuitus*, as an apprehending that is no longer mediated, as 'reason'" (EG, p. 125). This negative dismissal of "reason"—in scare quotes—is thoroughly typical of Heidegger and demands an account, one that I hope to provide on another occasion.

47. Haugeland, "Truth and Rule-Following," pp. 340ff. It follows that resolve or commitment cannot itself be rationally grounded: I can give reasons for committing myself to something, but those reasons will be normative only to the extent that I have *already* committed myself to them. As Haugeland puts it, "the governing or normative 'authority' of an existential commitment comes from nowhere other than itself, and it is brought to bear in no way other than by its own exercise" (p. 341). When Heidegger says that "only the resolution itself can give the answer" to the question of "what it is to resolve upon" (*Being and Time*, p. 345/298), this is not a rejection of deliberation but a description of its ontological condition.

48. This should not be taken to mean that entities cannot show up unless I give some reason for them propositionally. Rather, "what" beings are and "how" they are *demands* such a practice of "referral." Ontic truth in the sense of the "truth of things"—the self-showing of beings as they are in themselves—depends on Dasein's practical dealings with them, in which constitutive standards are in play. *What* a thing is, and *how* it is, thus depend on these standards, which have the *structure* of reasons: this is a hammer *because* it serves thus and so, is produced thus and so, and

so on. But then, to *say* what and how beings are is always to imply a reference to these standards and this, when made explicit, *is* to refer them to their grounds, that is, to give reasons. This is just another way of saying that disposition and understanding alone are not enough to account for intentionality; for "ontic truth"—something *as* something—some relation to "discourse" or language (in this case, the possibility of offering constitutive standards as "reasons") is also necessary.

49. I would like to thank those who criticized this paper, both at Rice University and at the Fifth Annual Meeting of the International Society for Phenomenological Studies at Asilomar, California, July 2003—in particular Cristina Lafont, Mark Wrathall, Mark Okrent, William Blattner, and Robert Pippin. I have not been able to do full justice to their criticisms, but my thinking on this topic, if not the chapter itself, has been vastly improved by them.

CHAPTER 5: TRANSCENDENTAL TRUTH

1. *Being and Time*, p. 269/226. All translations are by the author unless otherwise noted.

2. Some examples: Da-sein is said to be "the ontic condition of the possibility of discovering entities within the world at all" (*Being and Time*, p. 121/88); not only Dasein, but the manner of being of every other sort of entity is disclosed in view of "the conditions of its possibility" (ibid., p. 184/145); the structure of care is "the condition of the possibility" of existing authentically in an "anticipatory resoluteness" (ibid., p. 365/317); the original time is "the condition of the possibility" of the everyday experience of time (ibid., pp. 381ff./332ff.); a mode of the timing is "the existential condition of the possibility" of relevance (ibid., p. 404/353).

3. See the oft-quoted remark by Martin Heidegger at the end of his lectures in the winter semester of 1927–28, published as *Phänomenologische Interpretation von Kants "Kritik der reinen Vernunft,"* ed. Ingtraud Görland, *Gesamtausgabe*, vol. 25 (Frankfurt am Main: Klostermann, 1977), p. 41: "Some years ago, as I studied the *Critique of Pure Reason* anew and read it against the backdrop of Husserl's phenomenology, it is as though scales fell from my eyes, as it were, and Kant became for me an essential confirmation of the rightness of the path on which I searched." On Heidegger's Kantian turn in the 1920s, also see John van Buren, *The Young Heidegger: Rumor of the Hidden King* (Bloomington: Indiana University Press, 1994); Theodore Kisiel, *The Genesis of Heidegger's "Being and Time"* (Berkeley and Los Angeles: University of California Press, 1993); and Daniel O. Dahlstrom, "Heidegger's Kantian Turn: Notes to His Commentary of the *Kritik der reinen Vernunft*," *Review of Metaphysics* 45, no. 2 (December 1991): 329–61.

4. Martin Heidegger, *Beiträge zur Philosophie (Vom Ereignis)*, ed. Friedrich-Wilhelm von Herrmann, *Gesamtausgabe*, vol. 65 (Frankfurt am Main: Klostermann, 1989), pp. 305, 351, 372.

5. In *Besinnung*, Heidegger lists the following treatments of truth: (1) his 1930 address, "On the Essence of Truth," together with the interpretation of Plato's allegory of the cave in lectures of 1931–32; (2) his 1935 Freiburg address, "On the Origin of the Work of Art"; (3) his 1936 Frankfurt address by the same title; (4) his 1937–38 lectures "On the Essence of Truth"; (5) his 1938 address "The Grounding of the

Modern Picture of the World by Means of Metaphysics"; (6) his remarks in the second volume of the lectures on Nietzsche, focusing on *Untimely Considerations*, § 6: truth and correctness, lesson 1938–39; (7) his 1939 lectures on Nietzsche (*Will to Power*, bk. 3: "The Will to Power as Knowledge"); (8) his 1936 *Contributions to Philosophy*, the section on grounding; (9) his lecture on Aristotle's *Physics*, bk. 1, in the first trimester of 1940. See Martin Heidegger, *Besinnung*, ed. Friedrich-Wilhelm von Herrmann, *Gesamtausgabe*, vol. 66 (Frankfurt am Main: Klostermann, 1997), p. 107. To this list we can add the discussion in *Besinnung* itself (ibid., pp. 107–23, 259 ["Die Irre"], 313–18), the "Letter on 'Humanism'" ("Brief über den 'Humanismus'") and passages at the end of "Hegel and the Greeks" ("Hegel und die Griechen"); for the latter two works, see Martin Heidegger, *Wegmarken*, ed. Friedrich-Wilhelm von Herrmann, 2nd exp. ed. (Frankfurt am Main: Klostermann, 1978), pp. 311–60, 432–38.

6. Ermst Tugendhat, *Der Wahrheitsbegriff bei Husserl und Heidegger* (Berlin: de Gruyter, 1967), p. 364.

7. Ernst Tugendhat, "Heideggers Idee der Wahrheit," in *Heidegger*, ed. Otto Pöggeler, 2nd ed. (Cologne: Kiepenheuer and Witsch, 1970), pp. 296, 398. For criticisms similar to those made by Tugendhat, see Karl Jaspers *Notizen zu Martin Heidegger*, ed. Hans Saner (Munich: Piper, 1978), pp. 78ff., 119ff., 129, 172, 223; and Karl Löwith, "Wahrheit und Geschichtlichkeit," in *Truth and Historicity*, ed. Hans-Georg Gadamer (The Hague: Nijhoff, 1972), p. 20.

8. Both retractions are to be found in Martin Heidegger, *Zur Sache des Denkens*, 2nd ed. (Tübingen: Niemeyer, 1976), pp. 77ff.; as for the claim about the essential transformation, see Martin Heidegger, *Der Ursprung des Kunstwerkes* (Stuttgart: Reclam, 1960), 48ff.; *Wegmarken*, pp. 221, 228–36; *Beiträge*, p. 216; and Martin Heidegger, *Vom Wesen der Wahrheit: Zu Platons Höhlengleichnis und Theätet*, ed. Hermann Mörchen, *Gesamtausgabe*, vol. 34 (Frankfurt am Main: Klostermann, 1988), pp. 17, 131–44.

9. Karl-Otto Apel, "Regulative Ideas or Truth-Happening? An Attempt to Answer the Question of the Conditions of the Possibility of Valid Understanding," in *The Philosophy of Hans-Georg Gadamer*, ed. Lewis Edwin Hahn (Chicago: Open Court, 1996), p. 72.

10. Of course, one might argue that he should have retracted as much and that Apel's reading and, for that matter, Tugendhat's criticisms are generous since they both suggest how Heidegger's analysis might be salvaged. But even if we might be inclined to make this argument, its trenchancy turns on answering the second question posed in this chapter.

11. *Beiträge*, p. 216. The story related here is an abbreviated form of that given by Heidegger on the same page of *Beiträge*. Because Plato has a sense that what it means to be is not completely filled by the account of ideas, he attempts to take the step beyond (*epekeina tes ousias*) beings. But because his questioning is directed at beings and not being itself, he can only determine that dimension beyond beings in terms of a relation to human beings. Thus, the good (*agathon*) surfaces, not as a deeper understanding of beingness and beings, but as the evaluation of them (ibid., pp. 209ff.).

12. Heidegger actually mentions five senses; I omit here the fifth sense of transcendence, so-called metaphysical transcendence, only for the sake of the economy

of the exposition. Metaphysical transcendence refers to any movement beyond familiar and reliable entities to something else, as typified by the leading, metaphysical question (what is the entity?), the answer to which requires looking away from the entity itself; cf. ibid., p. 218.

13. Ibid., pp. 252ff., 93ff.; in this connection, see note 3 above.

14. Ibid., p. 2. Despite these criticisms in the *Beiträge*, Heidegger does not seem to think that the ontological difference has completely outlived its usefulness; for a positive take on it, see ibid., pp. 258, 287.

15. See Heidegger's criticism of the misleading way that thrownness is characterized in *Being and Time*; *Beiträge*, p. 318.

16. Ibid., p. 251; see, too, pp. 254, 262.

17. Immanuel Kant, *Critique of Pure Reason*, trans. Norman Kemp Smith (London: Macmillan, 1968), A598/B626.

18. David Hume, *A Treatise of Human Nature*, ed. L. A. Selby-Bigge, 2nd ed., Peter Nidditch (Oxford: Clarendon, 1978), pp. 94ff.: "But as 'tis certain there is a great difference betwixt the simple conception of the existence of an object, and the belief of it, and as this difference lies not in the parts or composition of the idea, which we conceive; it follows, that it must lie in the *manner*, in which we conceive it." Gottlob Frege, *Begriffschrift und andere Aufsätze*, ed. Ignacio Angelelli, 2nd ed. (Darmstadt: Wissenschaftliche Buchgesellschaft, 1971), § 2, pp. 1ff.: "Wenn man den kleinen senkrechten Strich am linken Ende des wagerechten *fortläßt*, so soll dies das Urtheil in eine *blosse Vorstellungsverbindung* verwandeln, von welcher der Schreibende nicht ausdrückt, ob er ihr Wahrheit zuerkenne oder nicht [If one *leaves off* the small, vertical stroke an the left end of the horizontal one, then this is supposed to transform the judgment into a *mere combination of representations*, regarding which the writer does not express whether he attributes truth to it or not]."

19. *Zur Sache des Denkens*, p. 75.

20. *Sein und Zeit*, p. 220; see, too, Martin Heidegger, *Vom Wesen der Wahrheit* (Frankfurt am Main: Klostermann, 1949), p. 12.

21. *Zur Sache des Denkens*, p. 76.

CHAPTER 6: THE DESCENT OF THE 'LOGOS'

1. Thomas Aquinas, *Questiones disputatae de veritate*, qu. 1, art. 1.

2. *Being and Time*, p. 270/227.

3. Friedrich Nietzsche, "Über Wahrheit und Lüge im aussermoralischen Sinne," *Kritische Studienausgabe*, ed. Giorgio Colli und Mazzino Montinari, vol. 1 (Munich: Deutscher Taschenbuch, 1980), p. 875; "On Truth and Lies in a Nonmoral Sense," in *Philosophy and Truth: Selections from Nietzsche's Notebooks of the Early 1870s*, trans. and ed. Daniel Breazeale (Atlantic Highlands, NJ: Humanities Press, 1979), p. 79.

4. *Being and Time*, p. 272/229.

5. Ibid., p. 204/161.

6. See Steven Crowell, *Husserl, Heidegger, and the Space of Meaning: Paths Toward Transcendental Phenomenology* (Evanston, IL: Northwestern University Press, 2001).

7. Heidegger, review of *Autorität und Freiheit: Betrachtungen zum Kulturproblem der Kirche* (1910), by Friedrich Wilhelm Förster, in Martin Heidegger, *Reden und andere*

Zeugnisse eines Lebensweges, ed. Hermann Heidegger, *Gesamtausgabe*, vol. 16 (Frankfurt am Main: Klostermann, 2000), p. 8. All translations are the author's unless otherwise noted.

8. Hugo Ott, *Martin Heidegger: Unterwegs zu seiner Biographie* (Frankfurt an Main: Campus, 1988), p. 65.

9. Review of Förster, *Reden und andere Zeugnisse*, p. 8; Ott, *Martin Heidegger*, pp. 63–64.

10. Review of Förster, *Reden und andere Zeugnisse*, p. 7.

11. Martin Heidegger, "Nur Noch ein Gott Kann Uns Retten," *Der Spiegel* 23 (1976): 193–219; trans. "'Only a God Can Save Us': The *Spiegel* Interview (1966)," trans. William J. Richardson, in *Heidegger: The Man and the Thinker*, ed. Thomas Sheehan (Chicago: Precedent, n.d.), pp. 45–67.

12. *Being and Time*, p. 443/391.

13. "Zur philosophischen Orientierung für Akademiker," p. 11.

14. Ibid.

15. Ibid.

16. Ibid.

17. Ibid., p. 12.

18. Such an insistence on *Eigenentwicklung* has to call into question all talk of the *Befehlscharakter* of church dogma and Dieter Thomä's claim that such questioning came only much later. Already in 1910 Heidegger's relationship to the Church was not untroubled. See Dieter Thomä, *Die Zeit des Selbst und die Zeit danach: Zur Kritik der Textgeschichte Martin Heideggers* (Frankfurt am Main: Suhrkamp, 1990), p. 39.

19. "Zur philosophischen Orientierung für Akademiker," p. 12.

20. Ibid.

21. "Per mortem ad vitam: Gedanken über Jörgensens 'Lebenslüge und Lebenswahrheit'" (1910), in *Reden und andere Zeugnisse*, p. 5.

22. Review of Förster, *Reden und andere Zeugnisse*, p. 7.

23. In *Being and Time* Heidegger connects such a strengthening with authentic being unto death: "But the phenomenon of this authentic potentiality-for-Being also opens our eyes for the constancy of the Self in the sense of its having achieved some sort of position" (p. 369/322). But leaping over the world, such constancy is in principle incapable of providing the required orientation. See Harries, "Death and Utopia: Towards a Critique of the Ethics of Satisfaction," *Research in Phenomenology* 7 (1977): 138–52.

24. "Neuere Forschungen über Logik," in *Frühe Schriften (1912–1916)*, ed. Friedrich-Wilhelm von Herrmann, *Gesamtausgabe*, vol. 1 (Frankfurt am Main: Klostermann, 1978), p. 23.

25. Thomä, *Die Zeit des Selbst*, p. 42.

26. Heidegger, *Die Lehre vom Urteil im Psychologismus*, in *Frühe Schriften (1912–1916)*, *Gesamtausgabe*, vol. 1, p. 88.

27. Heidegger, "Phänomenologie und Theologie," in *Wegmarken*, ed. Friedrich-Wilhelm von Herrmann, *Gesamtausgabe*, vol. 9 (Frankfurt am Main: Klostermann, 1979), p. 51.

28. Ibid., p. 53.

29. Ibid., p. 66.

30. Ibid., p. 6.

31. "Davoser Disputation zwischen Ernst Cassirer und Martin Heidegger," in *Kant und das Problem der Metaphysik*, ed. Friedrich-Wilhelm von Herrmann, *Gesamtausgabe*, vol. 3 (Frankfurt am Main: Klostermann, 1976), p. 277.

32. Ibid., p. 278.

33. Ibid., p. 285.

34. Ibid.

35. Ibid., p. 286.

36. Ibid., p. 276.

37. *Being and Time*, p. 74/49.

38. Ibid.; trans. of original Latin, p. 74/49, n. viii.

39. Ibid., p. 75/49, n. ix; trans. of original German.

40. "Davoser Disputation," p. 282.

41. Martin Heideger, "The Rectorial Address," trans. Lisa Harries, in *Martin Heidegger and National Socialism*, ed. Günther Neske and Emil Kettering (New York: Paragon, 1990), pp. 6–7.

42. "Davoser Disputation," p. 286.

43. Ibid.

44. Ibid., p. 287.

45. Immanuel Kant, *Critique of Judgment*, trans. Werner S. Pluhar (Indianapolis: Hackett, 1987), para. 26, p. 111.

46. Ibid., p. 111.

47. *Being and Time*, p. 289/245.

48. Ibid., p. 353/305.

49. Ibid., p. 369/322.

50. Ibid., p. 367/320.

51. "On Truth and Lies," p. 84.

52. Kant, *Critique of Pure Reason*, trans. Norman Kemp Smith (London: Macmillan, 1968), A235–36/B294–95.

53. "On Truth and Lies," p. 82.

54. Ibid., p. 87.

55. Ibid., p. 88.

56. *Being and Time*, p. 101/71.

57. Martin Heidegger, *Sein und Zeit*, ed. Friedrich-Wilhelm von Herrmann, *Gesamtausgabe*, vol. 2 (Frankfurt am Main: Klostermann, 1977), p. 96.

58. *Being and Time*, p. 101/71.

59. "Der Ursprung des Kunstwerkes," in *Holzwege* (Frankfurt am Main: Klostermann, 1972), pp. 7–68; here p. 36; "The Origin of the Work of Art," in Martin Heidegger, *Poetry, Language, Thought*, trans. Albert Hofstadter (New York: Harper and Row, 1971), pp. 17–87; here p. 47.

60. Martin Heidegger, " . . . dichterisch wohnet der Mensch . . . ," in *Vorträge und Aufsätze*, ed. Friedrich-Wilhelm von Herrmann, *Gesamtausgabe*, vol. 7 (Frankfurt am Main: Klostermann, 2000), p. 200. Poem from Hölderlin's fragment "In himmlische Bläue."

61. Martin Heidegger, "Hölderlin und das Wesen der Dichtung," in *Erläuterungen zu Hölderlins Dichtung*, ed. Friedrich-Wilhelm von Herrmann, *Gesamtausgabe*, vol. 4 (Frankfurt am Main: Klostermann, 1996), p. 41.

62. Ibid., p. 45.

63. " . . . dichterisch wohnet der Mensch . . . ," p. 151.

64. Kant, *Kritik der Urteilskraft*, in *Kants gesammelte Schriften*, ed. Royal Prussian [later German] Academy of Sciences, vol. 5 (Berlin: Georg Reimer [later Walter de Gruyter], 1900–), "Einleitung" and paras. 49, 57, and 59.

65. "Aus einem Gespräch von der Sprache," in *Unterwegs zur Sprache*, ed. Friedrich-Wilhelm von Herrmann, *Gesamtausgabe*, vol. 12 (Frankfurt am Main: Klostermann, 1985), p. 91.

66. *Einführung in die Metaphysik*, ed. Petra Jaeger, *Gesamtausgabe*, vol. 40 (Frankfurt am Main: Klostermann, 1983), pp. 143, 141.

67. Ibid., p. 143.

68. Ibid., p. 91.

69. Ibid., p. 139.

70. *Being and Time*, p. 204/161.

CHAPTER 7: LETTING BE

1. *Being and Time*, pp. 117ff./84ff. All translations are the author's unless otherwise noted.

2. Ibid., p. 154/118.

3. *The Basic Problems of Phenomenology*, trans. Albert Hofstadter (Bloomington: Indiana University Press, 1982), § 11b.

4. *Being and Time*, p. 414/363.

5. Ibid., p. 255/212.

6. Ibid., p. 269/226.

7. Ibid., p. 269/227.

CHAPTER 8: HEIDEGGER AND THE SYNTHETIC A PRIORI

1. Theodor Kisiel, *The Genesis of Heidegger's "Being and Time"* (Berkeley and Los Angeles: University of California Press, 1993), p. 408.

2. *Phenomenological Interpretation of Kant's "Critique of Pure Reason,"* trans. Parvis Emad and Kenneth Maly (Bloomington: Indiana University Press, 1997), p. 289.

3. Here I will not focus on how Heidegger's hermeneutic idealism is in turn rooted in his temporal idealism. On the latter see the excellent analysis of William Blattner in his book *Heidegger's Temporal Idealism* (Cambridge: Cambridge University Press, 1999). I basically agree with Blattner's account of Heidegger's temporal idealism, but I think that such an account needs to be complemented with an analysis of the hermeneutic idealism that Heidegger derives from it in order to understand the specific features that he ascribes to our experience, as well as the reasons for his strong apriorism. In my view Heidegger's hermeneutic idealism is the key to understanding why he sees himself justified in inferring from his temporal idealism the "aggressively anti-empirical" understanding of science as being based on an a priori foundation, as Blattner ascribes to him in his article "Laying the Ground for Metaphysics: Heidegger's Appropriation of Kant" (in *The Cambridge Companion to Heidegger*, ed. Charles Guignon, 2nd ed. [Cambridge: Cambridge University Press, 2006], pp. 149–76). I surely agree with Blattner's claim that Heidegger has in fact not earned the right to such a view, but in my opinion this can only be shown through a critical analysis of Heidegger's arguments in support of his hermeneutic idealism, as I try to do here.

4. Right at the beginning of his lectures Heidegger makes it clear that the synthetic a priori is Kant's crucial discovery, that it concerns the understanding of being or ontological knowledge, and that it is the fundamental problem of the *Critique of Pure Reason*: "The fundamental discovery of Kant consists in the realization that these peculiar kinds of knowledge—the preontological understanding of the being of entities and all ontological knowledge—are such as to contain an extension of the knowledge of entities while remaining nonetheless a knowledge which is free from experience and pure. Synthetic judgments a priori are knowledge of this kind.

But for Kant this discovery is not the result of his investigation, but its beginning. How are such judgments possible? The inquiry into the ground of the possibility of ontological knowledge constitutes the fundamental question of the *Critique of Pure Reason*" (*Phenomenological Interpretations*, p. 35).

5. Ibid., p. 38; emphasis in original.

6. In *What Is a Thing?* (trans. W. B. Barton, Jr., and Vera Deutsch [Chicago: Regnery, 1967]), Heidegger makes the following remark about Kant's principle: "Whoever understands this principle understands Kant's *Critique of Pure Reason*. Whoever understand this . . . masters a fundamental condition [*Grundstellung*] of our historical existence, which we can neither avoid, leap over, nor deny in any way" (p. 183).

7. *Being and Time*, pp. 25–26/6. Here I agree with Blattner's claim, in "Is Heidegger a Kantian Idealist?" (*Inquiry* 37 [1994]: 185–201), that Heidegger's equation of these two senses of being constitutes a substantive, idealist thesis and is not just the expression of a convention or definition of the term "being" as meaning merely "intelligibility for Dasein." I also agree with Blattner's analysis of the parallelism between Kant's and Heidegger's attempts at combining idealism and realism. However, I think that his analysis could be made clearer by paying attention to Heidegger's distinction between "being" in the sense of *existence* and "being" in the sense of *essence*. See notes 10 and 11.

8. *Being and Time*, p. 251/208.

9. Ibid., 26/6. As he explains it in *The Metaphysical Foundations of Logic*: "Because being 'is' not, and thus is never along with other beings, there is no proper sense at all or legitimacy in asking what the being of beings in themselves is. . . . We always know only beings, but never being as such a being. This becomes clear from the nature of transcendence and the ontological difference." *Metaphysical Foundations of Logic* (*Metaphysische Anfangsgründe der Logik*), trans. Michael Heim (Bloomington: Indiana University Press, 1984), p. 153.

10. Heidegger remarks in *Being and Time*: "With Dasein's factical existence, entities within-the-world are already encountered too. The fact *that* such entities are discovered along with Dasein's own "there" of existence, is not left to Dasein's discretion. Only *what* it discovers and discloses on occasion, in *what* direction it does so, *how* and *how far* it does so—only these are matters for Dasein's freedom, even if always within the limitations of its thrownness" (*Being and Time*, p. 417/366).

11. Here I share Herman Philipse's impression, when he remarks, in *Heidegger's Philosophy of Being: A Critical Interpretation* (Princeton, NJ: Princeton University Press, 1998), that "probably there is no interpretation of Heidegger's transcendental theory that is compatible with all texts" (p. 433). This seems especially compelling in light of the question that Philipse poses, namely, how is it that entities do not depend on Dasein, if their being depends on Dasein and the relation of "depending on" is transitive? But, precisely in light of this question, I find Philipse's interpretation of Heidegger as a transdencental realist to be much more problematic than any of the idealist alternatives. Regardless of its tenability, Heidegger's way of avoiding the problem that Philipse's question poses is through the sharp distinction between essence and existence. This is what makes the relation "depending on" intransitive. For it implies that two entirely different dependencies are at issue: the essence of entities depends on Dasein, whereas their existence does not. Accordingly, the most

one can claim is *that* entities exist independently of Dasein, not *what* entities there are. For "there is no proper sense at all or legitimacy in asking what is the being of entities-in-themselves" (*Metaphysical Foundations of Logic*, p. 153). If this is the case, though, the claim that entities exist independently of Dasein entails only a commitment to the (ontologically very weak) claim that *something or other* exists, but it cannot entail what transcendental realism requires: a commitment to the existence of specific entities with specific essences. As Heidegger makes clear in his discussion of idealism and realism in *Being and Time*, the truth of idealism lies precisely in recognizing that distinguishing some entities from others requires a prior projection of their being, and that such a projection is dependent on Dasein. Of course, that Heidegger would like to be a (consistent) idealist does not mean that he succeeds (even in his own terms). But, in my opinion, the inconsistencies that one may find in some passages are due to the very instability of his hermeneutic idealism and not to any attempt (or any temptation) on his part to defend a transcendental realism. As he makes crystal clear in *Being and Time*, "in realism there is a lack of ontological understanding" (p. 251/207), for "realism tries to explain reality ontically by real connections of interaction between things that are real" (ibid.). This is why, in his opinion, "as compared with realism, idealism . . . has an advantage in principle," and, provided it does not misunderstand itself in psychological terms, "idealism affords the only correct possibility for a philosophical problematic" (ibid.).

12. Here I follow Henry Allison's interpretation of Kant's transcendental idealism as the logical consequence of accepting Kant's claims about the epistemic conditions of human experience (see *Kant's Transcendental Idealism* [New Haven, CT: Yale University Press, 1983], pp. 10ff.). Similarly, I see Heidegger's hermeneutic idealism as the logical consequence of accepting Heidegger's claims about the hermeneutic conditions of human experience.

13. *Kant and the Problem of Metaphysics*, trans. Richard Taft, 4th ed. (Bloomington: Indiana University Press, 1990), pp. 8–9.

14. In *Being and Time* Heidegger defines the structure of the "always already" as "a perfect tense *a priori*, which characterizes the kind of being belonging to Dasein itself" (p. 117/85), and equates it with Kant's transcendental a priori without further theoretical explanation. In his personal copy of the book, Heidegger explains the "prior" character of the projection in the following terms: "'Prior' in this ontological sense is called 'a priori' in Latin and *proteron te phusei* in Greek (Aristotle, *Physics* A I). . . . Not something that is ontically past, but rather *that which is in each case earlier*, that to which we will point back in the question concerning entities as such; instead of 'a priori perfect', it could also be called an 'ontological' or 'transcendental' perfect (cf. Kant's Doctrine of the Schematism)" (*Sein und Zeit*, "Randbermerkungen," pp. 441–42, 85b. The reference here is to the German edition alone, as the Randbermerkungen do not appear in the English translation.

15. Ibid., p. 264.

16. Ibid., p. 265.

17. See ibid., p. 414.

18. W. V. O. Quine, *Theories and Things* (Cambridge, MA: Harvard University Press, 1981), p. 102. Needless to say, the coincidence between Quine and Heidegger suggested here concerns exclusively the acceptance of the maxim (i.e., their com-

mon conviction that it is meaningless to purport to refer to entities whose conditions of identity one cannot possibly indicate). This acceptance, in turn, commits both authors to the assumption that "meaning determines reference within each fixed ontology," to put it in Quine's terms (in "The Elusiveness of Reference," in *Sprache, Theorie und Wirklichkeit*, ed. Michael Sukale [Frankfurt: Lang, 1990], p. 22). However, with regard to the further issues that follow from this acceptance (such as which criteria of identity or principles of individuation are acceptable, etc.), their views are indeed extremely different.

19. *The Essence of Truth: On Plato's Cave Allegory and Theaetetus*, trans. Ted Sadler (London: Continuum, 2005), pp. 1–2; my italics. Similarly, Heidegger explains in *What Is a Thing?* "If we become acquainted with this rifle or even a determinate model of rifle, we do not learn for the first time what a weapon is. Rather, we already know this in advance and must know it, otherwise we could not at all *perceive the rifle as such.* When we know in advance what a weapon is, and only then, does what we see lying before us become *visible* in that which it is" (p. 72). In order to focus on the strongest, that is, most charitable interpretation of Heidegger's claim, I disregard here the extent to which in Heidegger's opinion our understanding of the being of entities determines any possible experience of those entities. Examples can be found in most of Heidegger's works. In *Being and Time*, Heidegger claims that "entities can be *experienced* 'factually' only when being is already understood" (*Being and Time*, p. 363/315; my italics). Along the same lines, in *Basic Questions of Philosophy* (trans. Richard Rojcewicz and André Schuwer [Bloomington: Indiana University Press, 1994]), he explains: "Ever in accordance with how we gather [*erblicken*] essence and to what extent we do so, we are also able to experience and to determine what is particular about things. That which stands in view in advance, and how it thus stands, *decides* what we *in fact* see in each particular case" (p. 65; my italics). In *What Is a Thing?* Heidegger makes explicit his view that our preunderstanding determines our perception in the following terms: "What we call hypothesis in science is the first step toward an essentially different, conceptual representation as over against mere perceptions. *Experience does not arise 'empirically' from perception, but rather is enabled metaphysically: through a new, anticipatory conceptual representation peculiar to what is given*" (pp. 139–40; my italics).

20. Here I use the expression *for us* in order to make explicit the weak reading that Heidegger always suggests, when he tries to convince us of the trivially correct nature of his claim. The expression that Heidegger uses is *as such*. This expression is more ambiguous, for it admits of both a "realist" and a "hermeneutic" interpretation. But to the extent that one can read it in the latter sense (i.e., as a shorthand of the expression *as so understood*) Heidegger's claim may still be seen as trivially correct: our understanding of what entities are determines what these entities are as such (i.e., as so understood). A very clear example of this use of the expression can be found in *Phenomenological Interpretation of Kant's "Critique of Pure Reason,"* where Heidegger explains: "It is in dealing with things that we understand, from the very outset, what something like a tool or things for use generally mean. We do not develop this understanding in the course of use. On the contrary, we must already understand ahead of time something like tool and tool-character, in order to set about using a certain tool. . . . In the same way we always already understand in advance

what the power of nature means and *only in the light of this pre-understanding of nature's power can a specific force of nature as such overwhelm us*" (p. 22; my italics). Here it is pretty clear that we *must* interpret the expression *as such* in the hermeneutic sense of *as so understood*. Otherwise we would not get a more or less trivial claim, but a patently false one. However, even if we grant Heidegger the weak reading, I think that his view is wrong nonetheless. See next note.

21. Here I agree with Philipse's claim in *Heidegger's Philosophy of Being* that Heidegger's position is a variety of weak transcendentalism. This is certainly correct to the extent that Heidegger does not accept Husserl's transcendental idealism; that is, Heidegger's claims about the *being* of entities are supposed to concern only their *essence* and not their *existence*. However, my assessment of what makes Heidegger's weak transcendentalism nontrivial varies from Philipse's. According to Philipse, Heidegger's acceptance of meaning holism is what gives a Kantian flavor to Heidegger's position and distinguishes it from "the trivial view that humans give significance to pre-existing things." However, meaning holism seems perfectly compatible with the trivial view. Moreover, to the extent that it only concerns the question of how we give significance to things (namely, in a holistic rather than in an atomistic way), it is hard to see what is specifically Kantian about it. For it does not seem to have any bearing on the issue whether our experience of entities is *determined* by our *prior* understanding of their being. In my opinion, the Kantian flavor of the latter claim has a different origin, namely, Heidegger's assumption that meaning determines reference. Only the combination of meaning holism with this further claim renders Heidegger's view of our experience as determined by a holistic and prior understanding of being incompatible with the trivial view. But precisely in light of this incompatibility Heidegger's hermeneutic idealism cannot be seen as weak in the sense of trivially correct. Far from trivial, its correctness essentially depends on the correctness of the assumption that meaning determines reference. I certainly agree that the hermeneutic reasons that Heidegger provides to support his view are meant to reduce it to the apparently trivial claim that our understanding of what entities are determines what these entities are for us. But this claim is not as trivial as it may sound. In fact, I think that it is false. For an essential component of our understanding of what entities are is precisely that they may be different from what and how we understand them as being. This trivial view is anchored in our use of designating expressions as directly referential (i.e., in the fact that, contrary to Heidegger's assumption, the meaning of the designative expressions we use does not determine their reference). I develop this argument at greater length in chapter 4 of my book *Heidegger, Language, and World-Disclosure* (Cambridge: Cambridge University Press, 2000).

22. *Being and Time*, p. 194/152.

23. Needless to say, for Heidegger the circle of understanding is not merely a fact about philological interpretation, but "the expression of the existential *fore-structure* of Dasein itself" (ibid., p. 195/152). Moreover, Heidegger is confident that he will be able to trace the fore-structure of understanding back to Dasein's originary temporality (see ibid., § 69, p. 360/312).

24. *Basic Problems of Phenomenology*, trans. Albert Hofstadter (Bloomington: Indiana University Press, 1982), p. 72.

25. *Einleitung in die Philosophie*, ed. Otto Saame and Ina Saame-Speidel, *Gesamtausgabe*, vol. 27 (Frankfurt am Main: Klostermann, 2001), pp. 222–23. Along the same lines, in *Phenomenological Interpretation of Kant's "Critique of Pure Reason,"* he explains: "The genesis of a science originates in the objectification of a realm of beings, that is, in the development of an understanding of the constitution of the being of the respective beings. . . . Through objectification, i.e., through opening up the ontological constitution, science first obtains a basis and a ground and circumscribes its field of investigation at the same time" (pp. 20 and 23).

26. See *What Is a thing?* pp. 49–82, esp. pp. 70–73. I offer a much more detailed analysis of this text in chapter 5 of my *Heidegger, Language, and World-Disclosure*.

27. In *What Is a Thing?* Heidegger explains:

> Regarding what the object is in accordance with its objective essence, we must always already have a material knowledge, according to Kant a synthetic knowledge, in advance, a priori. Without synthetic judgments a priori, objects could never stand over against us as such, objects toward which we "then" direct ourselves, i.e. in special investigations and inquiries, and to which we constantly appeal. Synthetic judgments a priori are already asserted in all scientific judgments. They are pre-judgments in a genuine and necessary sense. . . . There is no presuppositionless science because the essence of science consists in such presupposing, in such pre-judgments about the object. (p. 180)

28. *Kant and the Problem of Metaphysics*, pp. 11–14.

29. *Being and Time*, p. 414/362–63.

30. For a clear illustration of the extent to which Heidegger feels justified in keeping this feature of Kant's transcendental idealism after its hermeneutic transformation, see the example he discusses in *Basic Questions of Philosophy* (pp. 59–60) to support his claim that perception cannot contradict our preunderstanding.

31. *What Is a Thing?* p. 90.

32. *Basic Questions*, pp. 52–53; my italics.

33. *What Is a Thing?* pp. 78–79; my italics.

34. *Being and Time*, p. 269/226.

35. As Heidegger remarks in his lectures of the summer semester of 1934, *Logik: Die Frage nach der Wahrheit* (ed. Walter Biemel, *Gesamtausgabe*, vol. 21 [Frankfurt am Main: Klostermann, 1995]), "there is no absolute truth for us" (p. 36). Earlier in his lectures of the winter semester of 1923–24, *Einführung in die phänomenologische Forschung* (ed. Friedrich-Wilhelm von Herrmann, *Gesamtausgabe*, vol. 17 [Frankfurt am Main: Klostermann, 1994]), he already indicates that "it could well be that the idea of absolute validity is meaningless" (p. 96).

36. For a very illuminating account of Putnam's conception of the contextually a priori, see Axel Mueller, *Referenz und Fallibilismus* (Berlin: de Gruyter, 2001), pp. 106–36.

37. "Rethinking Mathematical Necessity," in *Words and Life*, by Hilary Putnam, ed. James Conant (Cambridge, MA: Harvard University Press, 1994), pp. 255–56.

38. As will soon become clear, in contradistinction to Heidegger, the other traditional feature of the notion of apriority, namely, that a priori statements are necessarily true and thus cannot turn out to be false, will not be preserved in Putnam's approach.

39. "'Two Dogmas' Revisited," in *Realism and Reason: Philosophical Papers*, by Hilary Putnam, vol. 3 (Cambridge: Cambridge University Press, 1983), p. 95.

40. "Rethinking Mathematical Necessity," pp. 255–56.

41. Ibid., p. 251.

42. "It Ain't Necessarily So," in *Mathematics, Matter, and Method: Philosophical Papers, by Hilary Putnam, vol. 1* (Cambridge, MA: Cambridge University Press, 1975), p. 240.

43. On this point see Gary Ebbs, "Putnam and the Contextually A Priori," in *The Philosophy of Hilary Putnam*, ed. Lewis E. Hahn and Randall E. Auxier (La Salle, IL: Open Court, forthcoming). In "Rethinking Mathematical Necessity," Putnam points at some terminological corrections he would introduce if he were to rewrite "It Ain't Necessarily So" in order to avoid possible misunderstandings: "If I were writing 'It Ain't Necessarily So' today, I would alter the terminology somewhat. Since it seems odd to call statements which are false 'necessary' (even if one adds 'relative to the body of knowledge B'), I would say '*quasi*-necessary relative to body of knowledge B.' Since a 'body of knowledge', in the sense in which I used the term, can contain (what turn out later to be) false statements, I would replace 'body of knowledge' with 'conceptual scheme'" (p. 251).

44. It should be clear that Heidegger incorporates this feature of the traditional conception of apriority into his interpretation of the ontological difference, according to which there is an absolute (and permanent) distinction between ontic and ontological knowledge.

45. Putnam's argument against such an empiricist approach is basically that "to identify 'empirical' and 'synthetic' is to lose a useful distinction" ("Rethinking Mathematical Necessity," p. 251). In "'Two Dogmas' Revisited" he explains his argument more in detail:

> Giving up the idea that there are any absolutely a priori statements requires us to also give up the correlative idea (at least it was correlative for the empiricists) that a posteriori statements . . . are always and at all times "empirical" in the sense that they have specifiable confirming experiences and specifiable disconfirming experiences. Euclidean geometry was always revisable in the sense that no justifiable canon of scientific inquiry *forbade* the construction of an alternative geometry; but it was not always "empirical" in the sense of having an alternative that good scientists could actually conceive. (p. 95)

46. Putnam discusses here only one of the possible lines of argument to support the view that a priori and a posteriori are permanent statuses of statements, namely, the positivist's strategy of assimilating the "synthetic a priori" status to the status of "analytic in virtue of the meaning of the terms." Another line of argument, though, would be to claim that if something turns out to be empirically false, it cannot have been a priori precisely for that reason (by definition, so to speak). In the example discussed by Putnam this argument would first require distinguishing between pure and applied geometry and then claiming that the latter belongs to the (a posteriori) empirical sciences and not to (a priori) mathematics. On the basis of this distinction it would be possible to argue that what turned out to be false as a consequence of the acceptance of Einstein's theory was not Euclidean geometry, as such, but only a

specific theory of space that belongs to the empirical sciences, namely, that the geometrical structure of physical space is Euclidean (Jerrold J. Katz follows this line of argument in *Realistic Rationalism* [Cambridge, MA: MIT Press, 1997], pp. 49ff.). The problematic consequence of this proposal is, as Quine expresses it, that "it puts . . . geometry qua interpreted theory of space, outside mathematics altogether" ("Carnap and Logical Truth," in *The Ways of Paradox and Other Essays*, by W. V. O. Quine [New York: Random House, 1966], p. 117). Putnam refers to this interpretative alternative very briefly with the following remark: "Unless one accepts the ridiculous claim that what seemed a priori was only the *conditional* statement that *if* Euclid's axioms, *then* Euclid's theorems (I think that this is what Quine calls 'disinterpreting' geometry in 'Carnap and Logical Truth'), then one must admit that the key propositions of Euclidean geometry were *interpreted* propositions . . . and these interpreted propositions were methodologically immune from revision (prior to the invention of rival theory)" ("'Two Dogmas' Revisited," p. 94).

47. "It Ain't Necessarily So," p. 248.

48. See *What Is a Thing?* pp. 66–95.

49. In fact, Heidegger not only claims that the Aristotelian approach did not turn out to be empirically false; in addition, he claims that it is actually "more true" than the modern approach inaugurated by Newton. In *Basic Questions of Philosophy*, he explains that modern science is "*not a whit more true* than Greek science. *On the contrary, it is much more untrue*, since it remains completely bound up with its methodology, and for all its discoveries it lets that which is actually the object of these discoveries slip away: nature, the relation of human beings to it, and their attitude within it" (p. 53; my italics).

50. In his *History of the Concept of Time: Prolegomena* (trans. Theodore Kisiel [Bloomington: Indiana University Press, 1985]), Heidegger claims that "all of geometry as such is proof of the existence of a material apriori" (p. 101). As is well known, "material apriori" is Husserl's term for synthetic a priori knowledge (see his *Ideen zu einer reinen Phänomenologie und phänomenologischen Philosophie*, *Husserliana*, vol. 3 [The Hague: Nijhoff, 1976], § 16). In his so far published work, Heidegger never discusses the issue of non-Euclidean geometries, nor is there any evidence that he ever came to doubt that the knowledge of geometry is synthetic a priori.

51. "It Ain't Necessarily So," p. 240.

52. Ibid.; emphasis in original.

53. Ibid., pp. 240–41.

54. Of course, Putnam's attack is targeted toward the logical positivist attempt to get rid of the synthetic a priori status of statements, by first interpreting such statements as meaning postulates and subsequently reducing their alleged synthetic status to the status of "analytic in virtue of the meaning of the terms" (i.e., true by linguistic convention). On the similarities and differences between this attempt and Heidegger's, see chapter 5 of my *Heidegger, Language, and World-Disclosure*.

55. Heidegger makes this view explicit in *The Basic Problems of Phenomenology*, when he explains that a prior projection of an understanding of the being of entities as equipment is what makes possible to individuate any specific equipmental entity as such:

Equipment is encountered always within an equipmental contexture. Each single piece of equipment carries this contexture along with it, and it is *this* equipment only with regard to that contexture. The specific *thisness* of a piece of equipment, its *individuation*, if we take the word in a completely formal sense, is not determined primarily by space and time in the sense that it appears in a determinate space- and time-position. Instead, what determines a piece of equipment as an individual is its equipmental character and equipmental contexture. . . . A being of the nature of equipment is thus encountered as the being that it *is in itself* if and when we understand beforehand the following: functionality, functionality relations, functionality totality. . . . [That is,] if we have already beforehand *projected this entity upon functionality relation*." (pp. 292–93; italics in original)

I am grateful to Mark Okrent for pointing me to that passage.

56. Although Putnam always sticks to the term *realism* in order to characterize his philosophical approach, given the drastic transformations that this approach has suffered throughout the years, the exact sense of his realism is not always clear. However, that "transcendental idealism" is not one of these possible senses is an explicit claim of Putnam's. In his "Replies" (*Philosophical Topics* 20 [1992]), he writes: "Like Strawson, I believe that there is much insight in Kant's critical philosophy, insight that we can inherit and restate; but Kant's 'transcendental idealism' is not part of that insight" (p. 366).

57. Putnam explains this view with an example from physics as well:

"Momentum is not the product of mass and velocity" once had no sense; but it is part of Einstein's achievement that the sense he gave those words seems now inevitable. We "translate" old physics texts homophonically, for the most part; certainly we "translate" momentum homophonically. We do not say that the word "momentum" used not to refer, or used to refer to a quantity that was not conserved; rather we say that the old theory was wrong in thinking that momentum was exactly *mv*. And we believe that wise proponents of the old theory would have accepted our correction had they known what we know. ("Rethinking Metaphysical Necessity," p. 257)

58. In "Rethinking Metaphysical Necessity," Putnam makes clear that this criterion for the distinction between contextually a priori and a posteriori statements should not be interpreted in psychological terms:

I would further emphasize the nonpsychological character of the distinction by pointing out that the question is not a mere question of what some people can imagine or not imagine; it is a question of what, given a conceptual scheme, one knows how to falsify or at least disconfirm. Prior to Lobachevski, Riemann, and others, no one knew how to disconfirm Euclidean geometry, or even knew if anything could disconfirm it. . . . I do believe that this distinction, the distinction between what is necessary and what is empirical relative to a conceptual scheme, is worth studying even if (or especially if) it is not a species of analytic-synthetic distinction." (pp. 251–52)

CHAPTER 9: HEIDEGGER'S TOPOLOGY OF BEING

1. Letter (1802), in *Hymns and Fragments*, trans. Richard Sieburth (Princeton, NJ: Princeton University Press, 1984). The larger passage of which this is a part is dis-

cussed by Heidegger in "Hölderlin's Heaven and Earth," *Elucidations of Hölderlin's Poetry*, trans. Keith Hoeller (New York: Humanity Books, 2000), pp. 175–207.

2. See Gadamer, "Reflections on my Philosophical Journey," in *The Philosophy of Hans-Georg Gadamer*, ed. Lewis Edwin Hahn, Library of Living Philosophers 24 (Chicago: Open Court, 1997), p. 47.

3. "The Origin of the Work of Art," in *Poetry, Language, Thought*, trans. Albert Hofstadter (New York: Harper and Row, 1971), pp. 41–43.

4. *Ontology: The Hermeneutics of Facticity*, trans. John van Buren (Bloomington: Indiana University Press, 1999), p. 5.

5. Ibid., p. 68.

6. Ibid., p. 62.

7. Ibid., p. 69.

8. Donald Davidson, "Three Varieties of Knowledge," in *A. J. Ayer: Memorial Essays*, ed. A. Phillips Griffiths, Royal Institute of Philosophy Supplement 30 (Cambridge: Cambridge University Press, 1991), pp. 153–66.

9. *Being and Time*, pp. 105/74–75.

10. I have argued elsewhere that just such a circular structure characterizes the transcendental. See my "The Transcendental Circle," *Australasian Journal of Philosophy* 75 (1997): 1–20.

11. Heidegger, *Zollikon Seminars: Protocols, Conversations, Letters*, trans. Franz Mayr and Richard Askay (Evanston, IL: Northwestern University Press, 2001), p. 115.

12. *Being and Time*, p. 170/130.

13. "Martin Heidegger: 75 Years," in *Heidegger's Ways*, trans. John W. Stanley (Albany: State University of New York Press, 1994), p. 17.

14. See my discussion of this idea in *Place and Experience: A Philosophical Topography* (Cambridge: Cambridge University Press, 1992).

15. This conception of the transcendental is one that I have developed elsewhere, notably in "The Transcendental Circle"; but see also "From the Transcendental to the Topological," in *From Kant to Davidson: Philosophy and the Idea of the Transcendental*, ed. Jeff Malpas (London: Routledge, 2002), pp. 80–86.

16. In "Kehre and Ereignis: A Prolegomenon to *Introduction to Metaphysics*," in *A Companion to Heidegger's "Introduction to Metaphysics,"* ed. Richard Polt and Gregory Fried (New Haven, CT: Yale University Press, 2001), pp. 3–16, Thomas Sheehan argues that the "Turning" (*Kehre*) refers to the turning in thinking that is tied up with the *Ereignis* and not to the change (*Wendung*) that occurred historically in Heidegger's thinking between 1930 and 1936. Sheehan's point is well-taken, but it seems to me that it gives too much emphasis to the difference here and not enough to the way in which the change in Heidegger's thinking is itself an instance of the turning in thinking as such. The ambiguity that obtains here is one that recurs in a number of places in Heidegger's discussion of these matters and of which Heidegger would seem to be well aware.

17. See "Letter on 'Humanism,'" trans. Frank A. Capuzzi, in *Pathmarks*, ed. William McNeill (Cambridge: Cambridge University Press, 1998), p. 256. Also *Seminare*, ed. Curd Ochwadt, *Gesamtausgabe*, vol. 15 (Frankfurt am Main: Klostermann, 1986), p. 366.

18. "Letter on 'Humanism,'" p. 256; *Being and Time*, p. 38/68.

19. "Letter on 'Humanism,'" p. 257.

20. *The Metaphysical Foundations of Logic*, trans. Michael Heim (Bloomington: Indiana University Press, 1984), pp. 160 and 165–66. Compare:

> Transcendence means surpassing [*Übersteig*]. . . . Transcendence in the terminological sense to be clarified and demonstrated means something that properly pertains to human Dasein . . . it belongs to human Dasein as the fundamental constitution of this being, one that occurs prior to all comportment. . . . If one chooses the title of "subject" for that being that we ourselves in each case are and that we understand as "Dasein", then we may say that transcendence designates the essence of the subject, that it is the fundamental structure of subjectivity. . . . We name *world* that *toward which* Dasein as such transcends, and shall now determine transcendence as *being-in-the-world*.

"On the Essence of Ground," in *Pathmarks*, pp. 108–9.

21. The focus on transcendence, but understood specifically in relation to the problem of "world," is also a central preoccupation in Heidegger's work in the period of the late 1920s, including *The Metaphysical Foundations of Logic* (*Metaphysische Anfangsgründe der Logik*; 1928) and *The Fundamental Concepts of Metaphysics* (*Die Grundbegriffe der Metaphysik*; from 1929–30).

22. As Heidegger notes in *The Principle of Reason*, trans. Reginald Lilly (Bloomington: Indiana University Press, 1996): "Kant names 'transcendent' that which lies beyond the limits of human experience, not insofar as it surpasses objects in the direction of their objectness; rather insofar as its surpasses objects along with their objectness—and this without sufficient warrant, namely, without the possibility of being founded" (p. 78).

23. See ibid.

24. Preface to *Kant and the Problem of Metaphysics*, trans. Richard Taft, 4th ed. (Bloomington: Indiana University Press, 1990), p. xv.

25. *Contributions to Philosophy (from Enowning)*, trans. Parvis Emad and Kenneth Maly (Bloomington: Indiana University Press, 1999), § 199, p. 226.

26. Ibid., § 172, p. 208.

27. "In *Contributions*, Heidegger speaks of 'Da-sein' with a hyphen, which indicates a shift in his notion of Dasein as he conceived it in *Being and Time*. Da-sein now designates not primarily the essence of human being but rather the open middle of the truth of beyng as enowning." Daniela Vallega-Neu, "Poietic Saying," in *Companion to Heidegger's Contributions to Philosophy*, ed. Charles E. Scott, Susan M. Scoenbohm, Daniela Vallega-Neu, and Alejandro Vallega (Bloomington: Indiana University Press, 2001), p. 73. See *Contributions to Philosophy*, §§ 190–91.

28. *Contributions to Philosophy*, § 200, p. 227.

29. Ibid., § 191, p. 219.

30. Ibid., § 7, p. 19.

31. "The Way in the Turn," in *Heidegger's Ways*, pp. 129–30.

32. "The End of Philosophy and the Task of Thinking," in *On Time and Being*, trans. Joan Stambaugh (New York: Harper and Row, 1972), p. 73 (first published in 1964).

33. See, once again, "From the Transcendental to the Topological." Heidegger is perhaps the only thinker in whose work the idea of topology is made explicit in terms that directly address the idea of *topos*. However, I would argue that such a topology is also a central element in the work of a number of key thinkers. See, for instance, my discussions of the work of Donald Davidson in papers such as "Locating Interpretation: The Topography of Understanding in Heidegger and Davidson," *Philosophical Topics* 27 (1999): 129–48.

34. "Building Dwelling Thinking," in *Poetry, Language, Thought*, pp. 152–53.

35. Of course, both "Homecoming" ("Heimkunft") and "Remembrance" ("Andenken") name poems by Hölderlin that are the focus for separate lectures by Heidegger. See "Homecoming/To Kindred Ones" and "Remembrance," in *Elucidations of Hölderlin's Poetry*, pp. 23–50 and 101–74. On remembrance see also Heidegger, *Basic Concepts*, trans. Gary E. Aylesworth (Bloomington: Indiana University Press, 1993), pp. 54ff.

36. "Conversation on a Country Path," in *Discourse on Thinking*, trans. John M. Anderson and E. Hans Freund (New York: Harper and Row, 1966), p. 66.

37. "Hölderlin's Heaven and Earth," p. 188.

38. There is some indication of this in *Beiträge zur Philosophie (Vom Ereignis)*, ed. Friedrich-Wilhelm von Herrmann, *Gesamtausgabe*, vol. 65 (Frankfurt am Main: Klostermann, 1989), § 266, pp. 327–30. The relation between identity and difference is, of course, a major theme in the two lectures contained in Heidegger, *Identity and Difference*, trans. Joan Stambaugh (Chicago: University of Chicago Press, 2001).

39. Heidegger, "Cézanne," in *Aus der Erfahrung des Denkens, 1910–1976*, ed. Hermann Heidegger, *Gesamtausgabe*, vol. 13 (Frankfurt am Main: Klostermann, 2002), p. 223.

40. "Seminar in Le Thor 1969," in *Seminare*, p. 344.

41. "Letter on 'Humanism,'" p. 253.

42. *Parmenides*, trans. André Schuwer and Richard Rojcewicz (Bloomington: Indiana University Press, 1992), p. 149.

43. In the "Letter on 'Humanism,'" Heidegger writes:

> In the lecture on Hölderlin's elegy "Homecoming" (1943) [the] . . . nearness "of" being, which the Da of Dasein . . . is called the "homeland". The word is thought here in an essential sense, not patriotically or nationalistically, but in terms of the history of being. The essence of homeland, however, is also mentioned with the intention of thinking the homelessness of contemporary human beings from the essence of being's history. . . . Homelessness . . . consists in the abandonment of beings by being. Homelessness is the symptom of the oblivion of being. (p. 258)

CHAPTER 10: HEIDEGGER'S TRANSCENDENTAL PHENOMENOLOGY

1. Edmund Husserl, *Logische Untersuchungen*, vol. 1, *Prolegomena zur reinen Logik*, text of the 1st and 2nd ed., ed. E. Holenstein, *Husserliana*, vol. 18 (The Hague: Nijhoff, 1975); and *Logische Untersuchungen*, vol. 2, *Untersuchungen zur Phänomenologie und Theorie der Erkenntnis*, ed. Ursula Panzer, *Husserliana*, vol. 19 (Dordrecht: Kluwer, 1984); trans. J. N. Findlay, *Logical Investigations*, 2 vols., rev. ed. with a new introduction by Dermot Moran (London: Routledge, 2001).

2. Husserl, *Erste Philosophie (1923–24), Erster Teil: Kritische Ideengeschichte*, ed. R. Boehm, *Husserliana*, vol. 7 (The Hague: Nijhoff, 1965) (hereafter *Hua*, 7); and *Erste Philosophie (1923–24), Zweiter Teil: Theorie der phänomenologischen Reduktion*, ed. R. Boehm, *Husserliana*, vol. 8 (The Hague: Nijhoff, 1965). The reference here is to *Hua*, 7: 3.

3. *Hua*, 7: 6.

4. Martin Heidegger, *Sein und Zeit*, 17th ed. (Tübingen: Niemeyer, 1993). The English translation used here is John Macquarrie and Edward Robinson, *Being and Time* (New York: Harper and Row, 1962).

5. The growing tension between Husserl and Heidegger is well documented in Thomas Sheehan, "Husserl and Heidegger: The Making and Unmaking of Their Relationship," in *Psychological and Transcendental Phenomenology and the Confrontation with Heidegger (1927–31)*, by Edmund Husserl, trans. Thomas Sheehan and Richard E. Palmer, in Husserl Collected Works 6 (Dordrecht: Kluwer, 1997), pp. 1–32.

6. The drafts of these cooperative attempts at writing the *Encyclopaedia Britannica* article (1927–28) are translated in Edmund Husserl, *Psychological and Transcendental Phenomenology*, pp. 35–196.

7. Heidegger's self-interpretation here has been challenged in Steven Crowell, *Husserl, Heidegger, and the Space of Meaning: Paths Toward Transcendental Phenomenology* (Evanston, IL: Northwestern University Press, 2001). I do not intend to discuss this issue here, except to agree with Crowell that Heidegger is as occupied with the meaning of philosophy as he is with the meaning of being.

8. Husserl, *Die Krisis der europäischen Wissenschaften und die transzendentale Phänomenologie: Eine Einleitung in die phänomenologische Philosophie*, ed. Walter Biemel, *Husserliana*, vol. 6 (The Hague: Nijhoff, 1962) (hereafter *Hua*, 6), p. 184; trans. David Carr, *The Crisis of European Sciences and Transcendental Phenomenology: An Introduction to Phenomenological Philosophy* (Evanston, IL: Northwestern University Press, 1970), p. 180.

9. Husserl, *Cartesianische Meditationen und Pariser Vorträge*, ed. Stephan Strasser, *Husserliana*, vol. 1 (The Hague: Nijhoff, 1950) (hereafter *Hua*, 1), p. 121; trans. Dorion Cairns, *Cartesian Meditations: An Introduction to Phenomenology* (The Hague: Nijhoff, 1967), p. 89.

10. Husserl, *Crisis*, § 53, pp. 180–81; *Hua*, 6: 184.

11. Martin Heidegger, *Prolegomena zur Geschichte des Zeitbegriffs*, ed. Petra Jaeger, *Gesamtausgabe*, vol. 20 (Frankfurt am Main: Klostermann, 1994) (hereafter *GA*, 20); trans. Theodore Kisiel, *History of the Concept of Time: Prolegomena* (Bloomington: Indiana University Press, 1985).

12. Husserl, *Phänomenologische Psychologie: Vorlesungen Sommersemester 1925*, ed. Walter Biemel, *Husserliana*, vol. 9 (The Hague: Nijhoff, 1968) (hereafter *Hua*, 9); trans. J. Scanlon, *Phenomenological Psychology: Lectures, Summer Semester 1925* (The Hague: Nijhoff, 1977).

13. Heidegger, "Letter to Richardson," preface to William J. Richardson, *Heidegger: Through Phenomenology to Thought* (The Hague: Nijhoff, 1963), pp. xiv–xv.

14. Heidegger, *History of the Concept of Time*, p. 121; *GA*, 20: 168.

15. *Being and Time*, pp. 62–63/38.

16. Heidegger, "My Way to Phenomenology," in *On Time and Being*, trans. Joan Stambaugh, (New York: Harper and Row, 1972), p. 78 (trans. modified).

17. Heidegger, preface to Richardson, *Through Phenomenology to Thought*, pp. x–xi.

18. Heidegger, "For Eugen Fink on His Sixtieth Birthday," in *The Fundamental Concepts of Metaphysics: World, Finitude, Solitude*, trans. William McNeill and Nicholas Walker (Bloomington: Indiana University Press, 1995), p. 367.

19. Heidegger, *Unterwegs zur Sprache* (Pfullingen: Neske, 1959); trans. Peter D. Hertz, *On the Way to Language* (New York: Harper and Row, 1982), p. 9.

20. Heidegger, "My Way to Phenomenology," p. 74.

21. Husserl, *Einleitung in die Logik und Erkenntnistheorie: Vorlesungen, 1906/07*, ed. Ullrich Melle, *Husserliana*, vol. 24 (Dordrecht: Kluwer, 1985), p. 176.

22. Heidegger, *History of the Concept of Time*, § 13, p. 124; *GA*, 20: 172.

23. Heidegger, "On the Essence of Ground," trans. William McNeill, in *Pathmarks*, ed. William McNeill (Cambridge: Cambridge University Press, 1998), p. 108.

24. "My Way to Phenomenology," p. 79.

25. *Being and Time*, p. 251/208.

26. Husserl, "Phenomenology and Anthropology," in *Psychological and Transcendental Phenomenology*, p. 486; *Aufsätze und Vorträge, 1922–37*, ed. T. Nenon H. R. Sepp, *Husserliana*, vol. 27 (The Hague: Kluwer, 1988) (hereafter *Hua*, 27), 168.

27. Ibid., p. 490; *Hua*, 27: 169.

28. Ibid., p. 492; *Hua*, 27: 171.

29. *Hua*, 7: 9.

30. See especially, Husserl, *Logical Investigations*, 1: 310, 2: 3.

31. Husserl, "Philosophy as a Rigorous Science," in *Edmund Husserl: Phenomenology and the Crisis of Philosophy*, trans. Quentin Lauer (New York: Harper and Row, 1964), p. 89.

32. Husserl, "Kant and the Idea of Transcendental Philosophy," trans. Ted E. Klein and William E. Pohl, *Southwestern Journal of Philosophy* 5 (Fall 1974): 26 (trans. modified); *Hua*, 7: 251.

33. Husserl, *Analysen zur passiven Synthesis: Aus Vorlesungs- und Forschungsmanuskripten (1918–1926)*, ed. M. Fleischer, *Husserliana*, vol. 11 (Dordrecht: Kluwer, 1988), p. 33; trans. Anthony J. Steinbock, *Analyses Concerning Passive and Active Synthesis: Lectures on Transcendental Logic*, Husserl Collected Works 9 (Dordrecht: Kluwer, 2001), p. 71.

34. Heidegger, *History of the Concept of Time*, p. 69; *GA*, 20: 94.

35. Ibid., p. 70; *GA*, 20: 95–96.

36. Ibid., p. 71; *GA*, 20: 97.

37. "Bereich der transzendentalen Subjectivität als der Sinn und Sein konstituierenden"; *Cartesian Meditations*, § 41, p. 84; *Hua*, 1: 117.

38. *Cartesian Meditations*, § 41, p. 84; my trans.

39. Ibid., § 41, p. 86; *Hua*, 1: 119; emphasis in original.

40. Husserl, *Formale und transzendentale Logik: Versuch einer Kritik der logischen Vernunft*, ed. Paul Janssen, *Husserliana*, vol. 17 (The Hague: Nijhoff, 1974), p. 280; trans. Dorion Cairns, *Formal and Transcendental Logic* (The Hague: Nijhoff, 1978), § 104, p. 273.

41. See A. D. Smith, *Husserl and the Cartesian Meditations* (London: Routledge, 2003).

42. For a discussion of the nature of Husserl's transcendental idealism, see Dermot Moran, "Making Sense: Husserl's Phenomenology as Transcendental Idealism,"

in *From Kant to Davidson: Philosophy and the Idea of the Transcendental*, ed. Jeff Malpas, Routledge Studies in Twentieth-Century Philosophy (London: Routledge, 2003), pp. 48–74.

43. Husserl, *Phenomenological Psychology*, p. 34; *Hua*, 9: 47.

44. *Hua*, 9: 344.

45. See Dan Zahavi, *Husserl and Transcendental Intersubjectivity*, trans. Elizabeth A. Behnke (Athens: Ohio University Press, 2001); and his *Husserl's Phenomenology* (Stanford, CA: Stanford University Press, 2003); Natalie Depraz, *Transcendance et incarnation: Le Statut de l'intersubjectivité comme altérité à soi chez Husserl* (Paris: Vrin, 1995).

46. *Hua*, 7: 244.

47. Husserl, *Crisis*, pp. 298–99; *Hua*, 6: 346–47.

48. *Being and Time* § 7, p. 50/28.

49. Heidegger, *The Basic Problems of Phenomenology*, trans. Albert Hofstadter (Bloomington: Indiana University Press, 1982), § 9, p. 69.

50. Heidegger, *Zur Bestimmung der Philosophie*, ed. Bernd Heimbüchel, *Gesamtausgabe*, vols. 56–57, 2nd ed. (Frankfurt: Klostermann, 1999), p. 110; "The Idea of Philosophy and the Problem of Worldview," in *Towards the Definition of Philosophy*, trans. Ted Sadler (London: Continuum, 2002), p. 93.

51. Heidegger, "The Idea of Philosophy and the Problem of Worldview," p. 92.

52. Heidegger, *History of the Concept of Time*, p. 72; *GA*, 20: 98.

53. Heidegger, "Phenomenology and Theology," trans. James G. Hart and John C. Maraldo, in *Pathmarks*, p. 53.

54. Heidegger, *The Basic Problems of Phenomenology*, § 3, p. 11.

55. *Being and Time*, p. 487/436.

56. Ibid., § 7, p. 49/27.

57. Ibid.

58. Heidegger, *Being and Time*, § 69, p. 498n33/363n1.

59. *Hua*, 9: 64.

60. *Hua*, 9: § 6.

61. *Hua*, 9: 74.

62. *Hua*, 9: 57.

63. *Hua*, 9: 5.

64. *Hua*, 9: 58.

65. *Hua*, 9: 61.

66. *Hua*, 9: 63.

67. *Hua*, 9: 62.

68. *Hua*, 9: 56.

69. *Being and Time*, 264–65/222.

70. Heidegger, *History of the Concept of Time*, § 10, p. 101; *GA*, 20: 139.

71. Husserl, *Crisis*, § 53, p. 179; *Hua*, 6: 183.

72. Ibid.

73. Ibid., p. 175; *Hua*, 6: 178.

74. Ibid., § 52, p. 176; *Hua*, 6: 179.

75. Ibid.

76. Ibid., p. 177; *Hua*, 6: 181.

77. These notes have been edited by Roland Breeur, "Randbemerkungen Husserls zu Heideggers *Sein und Zeit* und *Kant und das Problem der Metaphysik*," *Husserl Studies* 11 (1994): 3–63; newly edited and translated by Thomas Sheehan, "Husserl's Marginal Remarks in Martin Heidegger, Being and Time," in Husserl, *Psychological and Transcendental Phenomenology*, pp. 258–422.

78. Heidegger, "Letter on 'Humanism,'" trans. Frank A. Capuzzi, in *Pathmarks*, p. 249.

CHAPTER 11: THE "I THINK" AND THE FOR-THE-SAKE-OF-WHICH

1. See Mark Okrent, "Heidegger and Korsgaard on Human Reflection," *Philosophical Topics* 27, no. 2 (Fall 1999): 47–76; and "Intending the Intender; or, Why Heidegger Isn't Davidson," in *Heidegger, Authenticity, and Modernity: Papers Presented in Honor of Hubert Dreyfus*, ed. Jeff Malpas and Mark Wrathall (Cambridge, MA: MIT Press, 2000), pp. 279–301.

2. Martin Heidegger, *The Basic Problems of Phenomenology*, trans. Albert Hofstadter (Bloomington: University of Indiana Press, 1982), p. 159.

3. Immanuel Kant, *Critique of Pure Reason*, trans. Norman Kemp Smith (London: Macmillan, 1968), B131.

4. Ibid., A320/B376.

5. Kant, *Lectures on Logic*, ed. J. M. Young (Cambridge: Cambridge University Press, 1992), pp. 569–70.

6. Cf. ibid., p. 564.

7. Kant, *Critique of Pure Reason*, B130.

8. Ibid., B130–31.

9. Ibid., A117n.

10. Ibid., B157. It is interesting that Kant chooses to characterize the "I think" as a *Denken* rather than as a concept or a judgment.

11. Ibid., A78/B103.

12. Heidegger, *Basic Problems of Phenomenology*, p. 158.

13. Ibid., p. 159.

14. Ibid.

15. Heidegger, *History of the Concept of Time: Prolegomena*, trans. Theodore Kisiel (Bloomington: Indiana University Press, 1985), p. 159.

16. Cf., e.g., *Basic Problems of Phenomenology*, p. 292.

17. *Being and Time*, p. 119/86.

18. Ibid., p. 97/68.

19. Ibid., pp. 118–19/85–86.

20. Ibid., p. 119/86.

21. Heidegger, *Basic Problems of Phenomenology*, p. 292.

22. While there are holistic conditions on a set of behaviors constituting a set of intentions to employ tools in certain ways, conditions that include the general suitability of most of the tools for the purposes to which they are to be put, these conditions are "charity" considerations on the system of behavior as a whole, not conditions that must be met by any given tool.

23. Heidegger, *Being and Time*, p. 119/86.

24. Ibid., pp. 200–201/157–58.

25. Ibid., p. 199/156.

26. Heidegger, *Basic Problems of Phenomenology*, p. 208.

CHAPTER 12: HEIDEGGER'S "SCANDAL OF PHILOSOPHY"

1. Kant, *Kritik der reinen Vernunft* (Hamburg: Meiner, 1976), B39–41: "so bleibt es immer ein Skandal der Philosophie und allgemeinen Menschenvernunft, das Dasein der Dinge außer uns (von denen wir doch den ganzen Stoff zu Erkenntnissen selbst für unseren inneren Sinn her haben) bloß auf *Glauben* annehmen zu müssen, und, wenn es jemand einfällt es zu bezweifeln, ihm keinen genugtuenden Beweis entgegenstellen zu können."

2. Ibid., B274–79.

3. In order to avoid the internal contradiction which this interpretation implies (see next paragraph in the main text), most present-day interpreters of Kant give a different reading of Kant's notion of a *Ding an sich*. But I believe that the interpretation in the main text is historically adequate.

4. For instance, Kant, *Kritik der reinen Vernunft*, A494/B522: "Das sinnliche Anschauungsvermögen ist eigentlich nur eine Rezeptivität, auf gewisse Weise mit Vorstellungen affiziert zu werden. . . . Die nichtsinnliche Ursache dieser Vorstellungen ist uns gänzlich unbekannt, und diese können wir daher nicht als Objekt anschauen; denn dergleichen Gegenstand würde weder im Raume, noch in der Zeit (als bloßen Bedingungen der sinnlichen Vorrstellung) vorgestellt werden müssen, ohne welche Bedingungen wir uns gar keine Anschauung denken können [The faculty of sensible intuition is strictly only a receptivity, a capacity of being affected in a certain manner with representations. . . . The nonsensible cause of these representations is completely unknown to us, and cannot therefore be intuited by us as object. For such an object would have to be represented as neither in space nor in time (these being merely conditions of sensible representation), and apart from such conditions we cannot think any intuition]."

5. Cf. Friedrich Heinrich Jacobi, "Beylage über den transscendentalen Idealismus" (1815), in *David Hume über den Glauben oder Idealismus und Realismus: Ein Gespräch*, in *Friedrich Heinrich Jacobi's Werke*, ed. Friedrich Roth, vol. 2 (Leipzig: Gerhard Fleischer d. Jüng, 1812–25), p. 304.

6. Gottlob Ernst Schulze, *Kritik der theoretischen Philosophie* (Hamburg: Bohn, 1801), pp. 549ff. Cf. also Schulze, *Aenesidemus oder über die Fundamente der von dem Herrn Professor Reinhold in Jena gelieferten Elementar-Philosophie* (1792), ed. Manfred Frank (Hamburg: Meiner, 1996), pp. 24, 56–57, 103–4, 127ff., 196–200, and 294–310.

7. Cf. Salomon Maimon, *Versuch einer Transscendentalphilosophie* (1790) (Darmstadt: Wissenschaftliche Buchgesellschaft, 1963), pp. 419ff. References are to the 1790 pagination.

8. Eduard von Hartmann, *Kritische Grundlegung des Transcendentalen Realismus* (Berlin: Carl Duncker, 1875), p. 171: "Die Erkenntnistheorie . . . liefert . . . einerseits der Metaphysik, andererseits der Naturwissenschaft eine gesicherte Basis, auf der diese Disciplinen weiterbauen können [The Theory of Knowledge delivers, on the one hand to metaphysics and on the other to natural science, a secure basis on which these disciplines can build further]"; von Hartmann, *Grundriß der Erkenntnislehre* (Bad Sachsa im Harz: Hermann Haacke, 1907), p. 12: "So verstanden, ist die Philosophie Erkenntnislehre oder philosophia prima, oder auch Wissenschaftslehre [So understood, Philosophy is theory of knowledge or first philosophy, but also theory of science]"; Edmund Husserl, *Logische Untersuchungen* (Halle a.S.: Niemeyer, 1900 and 1901 [= ed. A]; Tübingen: Niemeyer, 1913 and 1921 [= ed. B]), B2/1, p. 21; Husserl, "Bericht über deutsche Schriften zur Logik in den Jahren 1895–99, Erster Artikel," *Archiv für systematische Philosophie* 9 (1903): 120; Husserl, *Erste Philosophie (1923–24), Zweiter Teil: Theorie der phänomenologischen Reduktion*, ed. R. Boehm, *Husserliana*, vol. 8 (The Hague: Nijhoff, 1965), pp. xvi–xix.

9. See Herman Philipse, "Transcendental Idealism," in *The Cambridge Companion to Husserl*, ed. Barry Smith and David Woodruff Smith (Cambridge: Cambridge University Press, 1995), pp. 239–322.

10. G. E. Moore, "A Defence of Common Sense" (1925), in *Philosophical Papers* (London: George Allen and Unwin, 1959), pp. 32–59; and "Proof of an External World" (1939), in *Philosophical Papers*, pp. 127–50.

11. Rudolf Carnap, *Scheinprobleme in der Philosophie: Das Fremdpsychische und der Realismusstreit* (Berlin: Weltkreis, 1928).

12. Carnap, "Empiricism, Semantics, and Ontology," in *Meaning and Necessity*, by Rudolf Carnap, 2nd ed. (Chicago: University of Chicago Press, 1956), pp. 205–29.

13. Carnap, *Der logische Aufbau der Welt* (Berlin: Weltkreis, 1928), § 64.

14. *Being and Time*, pp. 246–47/202: "Die Frage, ob überhaupt eine Welt sei und ob deren Sein bewiesen werden könne, ist als Frage, die das *Dasein* als In-der-Welt-sein stellt—und wer anders sollte sie stellen?—ohne Sinn." *Being and Time* trans. modified in the quote ("being" not with an initial upper case).

15. Ibid., p. 249/205: "Der 'Skandal der Philosophie' besteht nicht darin, daß dieser Beweis bislang noch aussteht, sondern *darin, daß solche Beweise immer wieder erwartet und versucht werden*" (Heidegger's italics; *Being and Time* trans. modified).

16. Ibid., pp. 245–46/201: "Unter dem Titel 'Realitätsproblem' vermengen sich verschiedene Fragen: 1. ob das vermeintlich 'bewußtseinstranszendente' Seiende überhaupt *sei*; 2. ob diese Realität der 'Außenwelt' zureichend *bewiesen* werden könne; 3. inwieweit dieses Seiende, wenn es real ist, in seinem An-sich-sein zu erkennen sei; 4. was der Sinn dieses Seienden, Realität, überhaupt bedeute" (Heidegger's italics; *Being and Time* trans. modified).

17. Ibid., p. 247/202: "Überdies bleibt sie mit einer Doppeldeutigkeit behaftet. Welt als das Worin des In-Seins und 'Welt' als innerweltliches Seiendes."

18. Ibid., p. 246/202: "In der Ordnung der aufgezählten Fragen nach der Realität ist die ontologische, was Realität überhaupt bedeute, die erste."

19. Ibid.: "Die Möglichkeit der zureichenden ontologischen Analyse der Realität hängt daran, wie weit das, *wovon* Unabhängigkeit bestehen soll, *was* transzendiert werden soll, *selbst* hinsichtlich seines *Seins* geklärt ist."

20. Ibid., p. 27/7: "Dieses Seiende, das wir selbst je sind . . . fassen wir terminologisch als *Dasein*."

21. Cf. *Sein und Zeit*, §§ 5–6.

22. Ibid., p. 36/15: "Das Dasein hat vielmehr gemäß einer zu ihm gehörigen Seinsart die Tendenz, das eigene Sein aus *dem* Seienden her zu verstehen, zu dem es sich wesenhaft ständig und zunächst verhält, aus der 'Welt'" (Heidegger's italics).

23. Cf. ibid.: "Das Dasein ist zwar ontisch nicht nur nahe oder gar das nächste—wir *sind* es sogar je selbst. Trotzdem oder gerade deshalb ist es ontologisch das Fernste" (Heidegger's italics).

24. See note 14.

25. *Being and Time*, p. 250/206: "Das 'Realitätsproblem' im Sinne der Frage, ob eine Außenwelt vorhanden und ob sie beweisbar sei, erweist sich als ein unmögliches, nicht weil es in der Konsequenz zu unaustragbaren Aporien führt, sondern weil das Seiende selbst, das in diesem Problem im Thema steht, eine solche Fragestellung gleichsam ablehnt" (trans. modified).

26. Cf. ibid., p. 252/208: "Die Diskussion der unausgesprochenen Voraussetzungen der nur 'erkenntnistheoretischen' Lösungsversuche des Realitätsproblems zeigt, daß es in die existenziale Analytik des Daseins als ontologisches Problem zurückgenommen werden muß."

27. Cf. ibid., p. 247/203: "Allerdings kann gerade das innerweltliche Seiende im Sinne des Realen, nur Vorhandenen noch verdeckt bleiben. Entdeckbar jedoch ist auch Reales nur auf dem Grunde einer schon erschlossenen Welt. Und nur auf diesem Grunde kann Reales auch *verborgen* bleiben."

28. Ibid., p. 93/65: "das, '*worin*' ein faktisches Dasein als dieses 'lebt'" (Heidegger's italics).

29. Heidegger is less explicit than Wittgenstein, in *On Certainty*, about the fact that such a global framework presupposes the existence of many entities, so that it does not make sense to doubt the existence of these entities either. I assume, however, that Heidegger would agree with Wittgenstein on this point.

30. Cf. ibid., § 3, p. 29/9: "Das All des Seienden kann nach seinen verschiedenen Bezirken zum Feld einer Freilegung und Umgrenzung bestimmter Sachgebiete werden. Diese ihrerseits, z. B. Geschichte, Natur, Raum, Leben, Dasein, Sprache und dgl. lassen sich in entsprechenden wissenschaftlichen Untersuchungen zu Gegenständen thematisieren."

31. Ibid., p. 54/31.

32. It is no accident that Heidegger consistently speaks of "Dasein im Menschen" in his first book on Kant, of 1929, *Kant und das Problem der Metaphysik* (4th ed., Frankfurt am Main: Klostermann, 1973).

33. Ibid., *Being and Time*, p. 62/37: "Bedingungen der Möglichkeit jeder ontologischen Untersuchung" (trans. modified).

34. See Herman Philipse, *Heidegger's Philosophy of Being: A Critical Interpretation* (Princeton, NJ: Princeton University Press, 1998), §§ 6–9 and 13, for a development of this interpretation.

35. Cf. ibid., pp. 122–23, for the structure and details of Heidegger's transcendental arguments. Cf. also Mark Okrent, *Heidegger's Pragmatism: Understanding, Being, and the Critique of Metaphysics* (Ithaca, NY: Cornell University Press, 1988); William Blattner, *Heidegger's Temporal Idealism* (Cambridge: Cambridge University Press, 1999).

36. David R. Cerbone, "World, World-Entry, and Realism in Early Heidegger," *Inquiry 38* (1995): 401.

37. Ibid., p. 272/230: "Sein—nicht Seiendes—'gibt es' nur, sofern Wahrheit ist. Und sie *ist* nur sofern und solange Dasein ist" (Heidegger's italics).

38. Ibid., p. 228/183: "Seiendes *ist* unabhängig von Erfahrung, Kenntnis und Erfassen, wodurch es erschlossen, entdeckt und bestimmt wird. Sein aber 'ist' nur im Verstehen des Seienden, zu dessen Sein so etwas wie Seinsverständnis gehört" (Heidegger's italics). Of course, the genitive *des Seienden* is a *genitivus subjectivus* and refers to *Dasein*.

39. Of course, Heidegger uses *idealism* in a particular sense. Cf. ibid., p. 251/208: "Besagt der Titel Idealismus soviel wie Verständnis dessen, daß Sein nie durch Seiendes erklärbar, sondern für jedes Seiende je schon das 'Transzendentale' ist, dann liegt im Idealismus die einzige und rechte Möglichkeit philosophischer Problematik."

40. Ibid., pp. 25–26/6: "das Sein, das, was Seiendes als Seiendes bestimmt, das, woraufhin Seiendes, mag es wie immer erörtert werden, je schon verstanden ist" (trans. modified).

41. Husserl denies the possibility of a *Ding an sich* in the traditional sense but he also redefines the very notion of a *Ding an sich*. Cf. Philipse, "Transcendental Idealism."

42. *Being and Time*, p. 250/206: "Zu beweisen ist nicht, daß und wie eine 'Außenwelt' vorhanden ist, sondern aufzuweisen ist, warum das Dasein als In-der-Welt-sein die Tendenz hat, die 'Außenwelt' zunächst 'erkenntnistheoretisch' in Nichtigkeit zu begraben, um sie dann erst zu beweisen. Der Grund dafür liegt im Verfallen des Daseins und der darin motivierten Verlegung des primären Seinsverständnisses auf das Sein als Vorhandenheit" (trans. modified).

43. Cf. ibid., p. 254/211: "*alle* Seinsmodi des innerweltlichen Seienden sind ontologisch in der Weltlichkeit der Welt und damit im Phänomen des In-der-Welt-seins fundiert" (Heidegger's italics).

44. Ibid., p. 100/70: "die Natur als das, was 'webt und strebt', uns überfällt, als Landschaft gefangen nimmt." Cf. ibid., p. 254/211: "Die 'Natur', die uns 'umfängt', ist zwar innerweltliches Seiendes, zeigt aber weder die Seinsart des Zuhandenen noch des Vorhandenen in der Weise der 'Naturdinglichkeit.'"

45. Ibid., p. 101/71: "*Zuhandenheit ist die ontologisch-kategoriale Bestimmung von Seiendem, wie es 'an sich' ist*" (Heidegger's italics, trans. modified); cf. *Being and Time*, pp. 103–6, 120–21, 140–41/74, 75–76, 87, 106.

46. *Being and Time*, p. 255/212: "Allerdings nur solange Dasein *ist*, das heißt die ontische Möglichkeit von Seinsverständnis, 'gibt es' Sein. Wenn Dasein nicht existiert, dann 'ist' auch nicht 'Unabhängigkeit' und 'ist' auch nicht 'An-sich'. Dergleichen ist dann weder verstehbar noch unverstehbar. Dann ist auch innerweltliches Seiendes weder entdeckbar, noch kann es in Verborgenheit liegen. *Dann* kann weder gesagt werden, daß Seiendes sei, noch daß es nicht sei. Es kann *jetzt* wohl, solange Seinsverständnis ist und damit Verständnis von Vorhandenheit, gesagt werden, daß *dann* Seiendes noch weiterhin sein wird" (Heidegger's italics, trans. modified).

47. Cerbone, "World, World-Entry, and Realism," p. 402.

48. Dorothea Frede, "Heidegger and the Scandal of Philosophy," in *Human Nature and Natural Knowledge*, ed. A. Donagan, A. N. Perovich, and M. V. Wedin (Dordecht: Reidel, 1986), p. 141.

49. Ibid., p. 143: "since the things' occurrence, as *we* understand occurrence, does not depend on our noticing or using them."

50. Ibid., p. 142.

51. Ibid.

52. Frederick Olafson, *Heidegger and the Philosophy of Mind* (New Haven, CT: Yale University Press, 1987), p. xvii.

53. Blattner, "Is Heidegger a Kantian Idealist?" in *Inquiry* 37 (1994): 188–89. Cf. Philipse, *Heidegger's Philosophy of Being*, pp. 142–44.

54. *Being and Time*, p. 101/71: "sie darf jedoch nicht als bloßer Auffassungscharakter verstanden werden, als würden dem zunächst begegnenden 'Seienden' solche 'Aspekte' aufgeredet, als würde ein zunächst an sich vorhandener Weltstoff in dieser Weise 'subjektiv gefärbt.'" Heidegger argues here against Husserl, Rickert, Nicolaï Hartmann, and others.

55. Husserl, *Ideen zu einer reinen Phänomenologie und phänomenologischen Philosophie*, *Husserliana*, vol. 3 (The Hague: Nijhoff, 1976), § 51, "Anmerkung." Cf. Philipse, "Transcendental Idealism."

56. Cf. Philipse, "Transcendental Idealism," for a defence of this interpretation.

57. *Being and Time*, p. 246/202: "Aller Zugang zu solchem Seienden ist ontologisch fundiert in der Grundverfassung des Daseins, dem In-der-Welt-sein" (trans. modified).

58. Ibid., pp. 251–52/208: "Bedeutet Idealismus die Rückführung alles Seienden auf ein Subjekt oder Bewußtsein, die sich nur dadurch auszeichnen, daß sie in ihrem Sein *unbestimmt* bleiben und höchstens negativ als 'undinglich' charakterisiert werden, dann ist dieser Idealismus methodisch nicht weniger naiv als der grobschlächtigste Realismus" (Heidegger's italics). I read this passage as giving *two* reasons for rejecting traditional transcendental idealism.

59. Remember, however, that this is only one of the two leitmotifs in the question of being in *Being and Time*.

60. *Being and Time*, p. 204/161: "Den Bedeutungen wachsen Worte zu." Cf. ibid., § 18.

61. Stephen Mulhall, *Heidegger and "Being and Time"* (London: Routledge, 1996), p. 98. His example is a table. Cf. Frede, "Heidegger and the Scandal of Philosophy"; Hubert Dreyfus, *Being-in-the-World: A Commentary on Heidegger's "Being and Time," Division I* (Cambridge, MA: MIT Press, 1991), p. 257; Cerbone, "World, World-Entry, and Realism"; and Theodore R. Schatzki, "Early Heidegger on Being, the Clearing, and Realism," in *Heidegger: A Critical Reader*, ed. Hubert Dreyfus and Harrison Hall (Oxford: Blackwell, 1992), p. 93; Blattner, "Is Heidegger a Kantian Idealist?"

62. *Being and Time*, p. 254/211: "Realität ist als ontologischer Titel auf innerweltliches Seiendes bezogen. Dient er zur Bezeichnung dieser Seinsart überhaupt, dann fungieren Zuhandenheit und Vorhandenheit als Modi der Realität. Läßt man aber diesem Wort seine überlieferte Bedeutung, dann meint es das Sein im Sinne der puren Dingvorhandenheit."

63. Cf. Mulhall, *Heidegger and "Being and Time,"* p. 98: "Dasein encounters material things as phenomena which exist independently of its encounters with them. Part of what we mean when we claim to see a table in the room is that we are seeing something which was there before we entered the room and which will continue to be there after we leave." Cf. also Blattner, "Is Heidegger a Kantian Idealist?" note 3.

64. *Being and Time*, p. 252/209: "Wenn der Titel Realität das Sein des innerweltlich vorhandenen Seienden (res) meint—und nichts anderes wird darunter verstanden."

65. Ibid., p. 246/202: "sofern zu Realität der Charakter des An-sich und der Unabhängigkeit gehört."

66. Ibid., p. 255/212: "Es kann *jetzt* wohl, solange Seinsverständnis ist und damit Verständnis von Vorhandenheit, gesagt werden, daß *dann* Seiendes noch weiterhin sein wird" (trans. modified).

67. In my *Heidegger's Philosophy of Being*, pp. 432–433n258, I stressed the difference between these two passages.

68. Blattner, "Is Heidegger a Kantian Idealist?" p. 186.

69. Ibid., p. 195, objection (D). In Blattner, *Heidegger's Temporal Idealism*, this is objection (C), on p. 248.

70. Blattner, "Is Heidegger a Kantian Idealist?" p. 195; Blattner, *Heidegger's Temporal Idealism*, pp. 248–49.

71. Blattner, "Is Heidegger a Kantian Idealist?" p. 195; Blattner, *Heidegger's Temporal Idealism*, p. 249.

72. This is not exactly what Blattner says in "Is Heidegger a Kantian Idealist?" p. 196. What he says is: "As with Kant's transcendental standpoint in sense (2), we can only say something negative from within it, in this case, that being 'is' not." But that was not at all what one attempted to say from standpoint (2). The discovery that "being" depends upon Dasein rather belongs to transcendental standpoint (1).

73. Philipse, *Heidegger's Philosophy of Being*, pp. 303–5 and 326–27.

74. It shipwrecks, for instance, also McDowell's attempt in *Mind and World*. See Philipse, "Should We Be Kantians?" in *Ratio: An International Journal of Analytic Philosophy* 13 (2000): 239–55; and 14 (2001): 33–55.

75. Cerbone, "World, World-Entry, and Realism," pp. 416, and §§ 3–4 as a whole; and Schatzki, "Early Heidegger on Being," pp. 95–96.

76. Gilbert Ryle, *Dilemmas* (Cambridge: Cambridge University Press, 1964).

77. *Being and Time*, p. 414/362: "es gibt grundsätzlich keine 'bloßen Tatsachen'"; "Erst 'im Licht' einer dergestalt entworfenen Natur kann so etwas wie eine 'Tatsache' gefunden und für einen aus dem Entwurf regulativ umgrenzten Versuch angesetzt werden" (trans. modified).

78. *What Is a Thing?* (*Die Frage nach dem Ding?*) (Chicago: Henry Regnery, 1967), p. 10: "We want to participate in the preparation of a decision: Is science the measure of knowledge, or is there a knowledge in which the ground and limit of science and thus its genuine effectiveness are determined?"

79. Ibid., p. 38: "was uns am meisten gefangen hält und in der Erfahrung und Bestimmung der Dinge unfrei macht. Es ist die neuzeitliche Naturwissenschaft, sofern sie nach gewissen Grundzügen zu einer allgemeinen Denkform geworden ist."

80. *Being and Time*, p. 128/95: "daß *Descartes* nicht etwa nur eine ontologische Fehlbestimmung der Welt gibt, sondern daß seine Interpretation und deren Fundamente dazu führten, das Phänomen der Welt sowohl wie das Sein des zunächst zuhandenen innerweltlichen Seienden zu *überspringen*" (Heidegger's italics). Cf. *Being and Time*, p. 93/65: "A glance at previous ontology shows that if one fails to see being-in-the-world as a state of dasein, the phenomenon of worldhood likewise gets passed over" (Heidegger's italics). Cf. also *Being and Time*, pp. 133–34/100.

81. See *Being and Time*, p. 412/360–61: "das vorliegende Seiende, das wir umsichtig schon als Hammer kennen, hat ein Gewicht, das heißt die 'Eigenschaft' der Schwere. . . . Das nunmehr Gesichtete eignet nicht dem Hammer als Werkzeug, sondern als Körperding, das dem Gesetz der Schwere unterliegt."

82. See note 42.

83. See for a description of the papers Heidegger published as a young student of theology in *Der Akademiker*, Hugo Ott, *Martin Heidegger: Unterwegs zu seiner Biographie* (Frankfurt am Main: Campus, 1988), pp. 62–66.

84. Unless one is an orthodox follower of Thomas Kuhn.

85. *Being and Time*, p. 122/88: "daß auf dem Grunde von Weltlichkeit der Welt dieses Seiende in seinem 'substanziellen' 'An-sich' allererst entdeckbar ist"; and ibid., p. 117/85: "Dieses 'apriorische' Bewendenlassen ist die Bedingung der Möglichkeit dafür, daß Zuhandenes begegnet."

86. Ibid., p. 101/71: "Aber Zuhandenes 'gibt es' doch nur auf dem Grunde von Vorhandenem. Folgt aber—diese These einmal zugestanden—hieraus, daß Zuhandenheit ontologisch in Vorhandenheit fundiert ist?" (trans. modified).

87. *Metaphysical Foundations of Logic*, trans. Michael Heim (Bloomington: Indiana University Press, 1984), p. 195: "World-entry and its occurrence is the presupposition *not* for extant things to become first extant and enter into that which manifests itself to us as its extantness and which we understand as such. Rather world-entry and its occurrence is solely the presupposition for extant things announcing themselves in their not requiring world-entry regarding their own being." This text is also discussed by Cerbone, in "World, World-Entry, and Realism."

88. Another passage is *Metaphysical Foundations of Logic*, p. 156, where Heidegger says that the factical existence of Dasein "presupposes the factical extantness of nature[*faktische Vorhandensein*]." Cf. Steven Crowell, "Metaphysics, Metontology, and the End of *Being and Time*," *Philosophy and Phenomenological Research* 60 (2000): 321, for a discussion of this passage.

89. Blattner, *Heidegger's Temporal Idealism*, p. 250, referring to *Being and Time*, p. 255/212.

90. See note 46.

91. See Joseph P. Fell, "The Familiar and the Strange: On the Limits of Praxis in Early Heidegger," in *Heidegger: A Critical Reader*, ed. Hubert Dreyfus and Harrison Hall (Oxford: Blackwell, 1992), pp. 65–80.

92. *Being and Time*, p. 232/187: "In der Angst versinkt das umweltlich Zuhandene, überhaupt das innerweltlich Seiende."

93. Ibid., p. 231/186: "Nichts von dem, was innerhalb der Welt zuhanden und vorhanden ist, fungiert als das, wovor die Angst sich ängstet. Die innerweltlich entdeckte Bewandtnisganzheit des Zuhandenen und Vorhandenen ist als solche überhaupt ohne Belang. Sie sinkt in sich zusammen."

94. Ibid., p. 232/187: "Das Sichängsten erschließt ürsprünglich und direkt die Welt als Welt."

95. Cf. "What Is Metaphysics?" (*Was ist Metaphysik?*), in *Pathmarks*, ed. William McNeill (Cambridge: Cambridge University Press, 1998), p. 33: "Das Seiende wird doch durch die Angst nicht vernichtet, um so das Nichts übrig zu lassen"; and p. 90: "Nihilation . . . manifests . . . beings in their full but heretofore concealed strangeness as what is radically."

96. I do not agree, then, with the interpretation of Hubert Dreyfus and Charles Spinosa in "Coping with Things-in-Themselves: A Practice-Based Phenomenological Argument for Realism," *Inquiry* 42 (1999), on what Heidegger says on Angst: "What the phenomenon of strangeness revealed in total breakdown supports is the sparer claim that *we can make sense* of nature as independent of our coping practices" (p. 55). What Heidegger says is that in *Angst* we cannot make sense of entities at all.

97. *Was ist Metaphysik?* p. 34; Martin Heidegger, *Basic Writings*, ed. David Farrell Krell, rev. and exp. ed. (New York: HarperCollins, 1993), p. 103: "In der hellen Nacht des Nichts der Angst ersteht erst die ursprüngliche Offenheit des Seienden als einen solchen: daß es Seiendes ist—und nicht Nichts" (trans. modified).

98. *Was ist Metaphysik?* p. 32; *Basic Writings*, p. 101: "Die Angst verschlägt uns das Wort. Weil das Seiende im Ganzen entgleitet und so gerade das Nichts andrängt, schweigt im Angesicht seiner jedes 'Ist'-Sagen."

99. See note 38.

100. Fell, "The Familiar and the Strange," p. 70.

101. Dreyfus and Spinosa, "Coping with Things-in-Themselves," p. 50.

102. Ibid., p. 56.

103. It seems that Heidegger in his lectures *Metaphysical Foundations of Logic* (*Metaphysische Anfangsgründe der Logik*), of 1928, wanted to develop an ontology of nature ("metontology") which spells out transcendental realism. Crowell, in "Metaphysics, Metontology," argues correctly that this type of transcendental realism would be incompatible with the transcendental philosophy of *Being and Time*: "To suggest that Dasein's understanding of being presupposes the factical extantness of nature thus implies a shift toward a transcendental realistic perspective which is not just supplemental to, but *inconsistent* with, the phenomenological project" (p. 325). Crowell indeed thinks that "*Being and Time* is finally inconsistent on the issue" (ibid., note 44).

104. See *Being and Time*, p. 251/207: "Mit dem Dasein als In-der-Welt-sein ist innerweltliches Seiendes je schon erschlossen. Diese existenzial-ontologische Aussage scheint mit der These des Realismus übereinzukommen, daß die Außenwelt real vorhanden sei," and so on. (trans. modified).

105. In fact, *zuhanden* is an archaism, and meant in one's hands or near to one's hands. In Swiss German, *zuhanden* is used as *zu Händen* in German. *Es ist mir zuhanden gekommen* means the same as *Es ist mir in die Hände gekommen* in German (I acquired it accidentally). *Zuhanden* also means being near, easily accessible, ready to be grasped.

106. See *Die Grundbegriffe der Metaphysik: Welt, Endlichkeit, Einsamkeit*, *Gesamtausgabe*, vols. 29–30 (Frankfurt am Main: Klostermann, 1983), pp. 398–400; and Fell, "The Familiar and the Strange," p. 71.

107. Cf. Fell, "The Familiar and the Strange," p. 71.

108. *Being and Time*, p. 254/211: "Aber nicht jede Vorhandenheit ist Dingvorhandenheit. Die 'Natur', die uns 'umfängt', ist zwar innerweltliches Seiendes, zeigt aber weder die Seinsart des Zuhandenen noch des Vorhandenen in der Weise der 'Naturdinglichkeit'" (trans. modified).

109. Ibid., p. 412–13/361: "Aber konstituiert sich dadurch, daß wir, statt Zuhandenes umsichtig zu überlegen, es als Vorhandenes 'auffassen', schon ein wissenschaftliches Verhalten?" (trans. modified).

110. An example of the latter approach is P. M. S. Hacker, *Appearance and Reality: A Philosophical Investigation into Perception and Perceptual Qualities* (Oxford: Blackwell, 1987).

CHAPTER 13: HEIDEGGER ON FAILED MEANING

1. In fact, Hitchcock came to realize the mystery, intensity, and tension of a narrative greatly increased if such a presence could also remain an absence.

2. François Truffaut, *Hitchcock* (New York: Simon and Schuster, 1985), p. 139.

3. "Das Sein—Ein MacGuffin," *Frankfurter Allgemeine Zeitung*, May 27, 1987, p. 35.

4. *Being and Time*, p. 331/285.

5. Rudolf Carnap, "The Elimination of Metaphysics Through Logical Analysis of Language," in *Logical Positivism*, ed. A. J. Ayer (New York: Free Press, 1959), pp. 60–81.

6. I realize that I am here taking a side in a dispute with many facets. But Heidegger seems to me pretty consistent about this, and critics like Tugendhat are off-base when they charge Heidegger with equivocating between asking about the meaning of being and asking about the meaning of the word, being. However, I need to charge ahead if I am to get to the issue of interest. See Ernst Tugendhat, *Self-Consciousness and Self-Determination*, trans. Paul Stern (Cambridge, MA: MIT Press, 1986), pp. 147–48. The most comprehensive and convincing refutation of Tugendhat's overall interpretation is in Daniel O. Dahlstrom, *Heidegger's Concept of Truth* (Cambridge: Cambridge University Press, 2001). See also chapter 5 of Stanley Rosen, *The Question of Being: A Reversal of Heidegger* (New Haven, CT: Yale University Press, 1993), pp. 176–211.

7. *Being and Time*, p. 31/11.

8. Martin Heidegger, *Nietzsche*, vol. 1 (Pfüllingen: Neske, 1961), p. 26.

9. That any such meaning must be a "temporal" meaning is an answer to such a possibility question not to a question about being itself. Indeed, as we shall see, Heidegger's main thesis is that there cannot be such a latter answer and that is why the answer to the first question is as it is.

10. Martin Heidegger, *Introduction to Metaphysics*, trans. Gregory Fried and Richard Polt (New Haven, CT: Yale University Press, 2000), p. 19.

11. Now immediately we have to state such claims carefully. Heidegger is clear that he considers the great initiating moment of post-Platonic Greek metaphysics—the resolution that "to be" was "to be intelligible," to be determinate (delimited by determinate form)—to be in fact a hybristic "resolve," the beginning of Western metaphysics as the imposition of subjective requirements for intelligibility, and so an orientation that obscured to the point of forgetting the "being process" itself, the "happening" or eventually historical character of the meaning of being, and so the intertwined relation between being and nothing, between meaning and darkness, nonmeaning. But it is clear that it is meaningfulness itself that is at issue in Heidegger's project, what could be object of any understanding, what could somehow mark the basic difference between "meaningfully being" at all, and absent, or what I want to discuss later as failed, meaning.

12. Martin Heidegger, *Grundprobleme der Phänomenologie*, ed. Friedrich-Wilhelm von Herrmann, in *Gesamtausgabe*, vol. 24 (Frankfurt am Main: Klostermann, 1975), p. 460.

13. *Nietzsche*, 2: 415.

14. *Being and Time*, p. 33/13.

15. Ibid., p. 62/37.

16. Ibid., p. 121/87.

17. Ibid., p. 193/151.

18. Ibid., p. 255/212.

19. Ibid., p. 270/227.

20. Ibid., p. 255/212.

21. Ibid.

22. Ibid., p. 261/218. The same point is made if, following Dahlstrom and in a different way, Haugeland (see below, note 25), we note the limited, ontic frame for

"uncoveredness" in the above passage and note that by the time of *Being and Time*, the fundamental happening of truth occurs as "disclosedness" (*Erschlossenheit*). Dahlstrom, *Heidegger's Concept of Truth*, pp. 389–90.

23. This is the sense in which Robert Brandom argues that, say, the only grip the notion of a particular might have for us consists in our understanding the role of singular terms in language. Cf. "Holism and Idealism in Hegel's *Phenomenology*," in *Tales of the Mighty Dead: Historical Essays in the Metaphysics of Intentionality* (Cambridge, MA: Harvard University Press, 2002), pp. 194ff.

24. I think that Taylor Carmen is right about this in *Heidegger's Analytic: Interpretation, Discourse and Authenticity in "Being and Time"* (Cambridge: Cambridge University Press, 2003).

25. John Haugeland, "Truth and Finitude: Heidegger's Transcendental Existentialism," in *Heidegger, Authenticity, and Modernity: Essays in Honor of Hubert Dreyfus*, ed. Mark Wrathall and Jeff Malpas, vol. 1 (Cambridge, MA: MIT Press, 2000), p. 57. For reasons that will soon become apparent, I don't agree with Haugeland that something like the basic laws of physics, constituting what is to count as a physical object, could be an example of Heideggerian disclosedness. For an influential treatment of Heidegger as "still transcendental," in a way continuous with Husserl, see Ernst Tugendhat, *Der Wahrheitsbegriff bei Husserl und Heidegger* (Berlin: de Gruyter, 1967).

26. This is the sort of question that emerges for any transcendental account that tries to isolate "that without which" some undeniable feature of our experience or language, like the difference between the succession of representations and the representation or succession, or the possible re-identifiability of particulars, would be impossible. Even in Strawson's "austere" version of the Kantian project, as delimiting the bounds of sense, the question of the status of his results and so the problem of "verificationism," was raised immediately; especially by Barry Stroud, "Transcendental Arguments," in *The First Critique*, ed. T. Penelhum and J. MacIntosh (Belmont, CA: Wadsworth, 1969), pp. 54–69; and Richard Rorty, "Strawson's Objectivity Argument," *Review of Metaphysics*, 24 (1970): 207–44.

27. See the very helpful account in Michael Friedman, *A Parting of the Ways: Carnap, Cassirer, and Heidegger* (Chicago: Open Court, 2000). See also chapter 1 of Theodore Kisiel, *The Genesis of Heidegger's "Bring and Time"* (Berkeley and Los Angeles: University of California Press, 1993); Daniel O. Dahlstrom, "Heidegger's Kantian Turn: Notes to His Commentary of the *Kritik der reinen Vernunft*," *Review of Metaphysics* 45, no. 2 (December 1991): 329–61; and Steven Crowell, "Lask, Heidegger, and the Homelessness of Logic," *Journal of the British Society for Phenomenology* 23, no. 3 (October 1991): 222–39.

28. Cf. *Being and Time*: "But subject and object do not coincide with Dasein and the world" (p. 87/60). Without Dasein, there can be entities but no "meaning of being" question. Speculating about the meaning of being "in itself" is like speculating about what objects could be said to be like, were we to abstract from *any* way in which we could know such objects.

29. This issue leads into complicated territory. Heidegger insists that, just as a mode of presence for some meaning can *be* its hiddenness, living in the forgetfulness of the meaning of being is still *ontologically distinctive*, the question is still present

by virtue of its absence. Much more would have to be said about this to counter the impression that Heidegger is stacking the deck against objections to his claim that Dasein "is" ontological. But it remains a problem for any "transcendental account." See Haugeland in "Truth and Finitude," p. 47, where one must cite both Heidegger's claim that the question of being has been forgotten (no disclosure goes on), and that such disclosure is a "condition of the possibility of *any* comportment towards entities as entities" (my emphasis). There are similar paradoxes elsewhere. Haugeland wants to treat Heideggerian fallenness as analogous to what Kuhn calls normality in science. But, for Kuhn, this tenacious hold of normality is, as Haugeland notes, *a good thing*. It requires a persistent attempt to solve problems, not give up on them. But we are "lost" in the "they," not merely going on as they do. Haugeland himself notes on the next page that as publicness functions in Heidegger it has a "tendency to disguise and forget anxiety," the disclosive state that can call us back to ourselves. All such paradoxes stem from the unusual sort of "failure" Heidegger wants to account for.

30. If there really is such an inseparability then we can only quite artificially isolate condition and conditioned. Each "side" is so determined in respect to the other ("meaning" and "that without which meaning is impossible") that we are smack in the middle of Heidegger's circle, not the realm of transcendental necessity. Thus, when Heidegger invokes transcendental terminology, there is usually some qualification. At *Being and Time*, p. 65/41, "a priori" gets scare quotes; when, at p. 78/53, he says freely that being-in-the-world is a "necessary a priori constituent [*Verfassung*] of Dasein," he tosses it off as if it were a mere preliminary observation and "not by a large measure sufficient" to fully determine the being of Dasein.

31. Compare this telling remark from the 1929–30 *Fundamental Concepts of Metaphysics: World, Finitude, Solitude*, trans. William McNeill and Nicholas Walker (Bloomington: Indiana University Press, 1995), pp. 1–2:

> What if it were a prejudice that metaphysics is a fixed and secure discipline, and an illusion that philosophy is a science that can be taught and learned? . . . Is all this talk of philosophy being the absolute science a delusion? Not just because the individual or some school never achieves this end, but because positing the end is itself fundamentally an error and a misunderstanding of the innermost essence of philosophy. Philosophy as absolute science—a lofty, unsurpassable ideal. So it seems. And yet perhaps even judging philosophy according to the idea of science is the most disastrous debasement of its innermost essence.

Die Grundbegriffe der Metaphysik: Welt, Endlichkeit, Einsamkeit, ed. Otto Saame and Ina Saame-Speidel, *Gesamtausgabe*, vols. 29–30 (Frankfurt: Klostermann, 1983), p. 2.

32. *Phänomenologie der Anschauung und des Ausdrucks*, ed. Claudius Strube, *Gesamtausgabe*, vol. 59 (Frankfurt am Main: Klostermann, 1993), p. 91. Quoted by Dahlstrom, "Heidegger's Kantian Turn," p. 385. Note his qualification in the footnote.

33. "Way of life": to invoke Haugeland's comprehensive term of art for Dasein in his "Dasein's Disclosedness," in *Heidegger: A Critical Reader*, ed. Hubert Dreyfus and Harrison Hall (Oxford: Blackwell, 1992), p. 35.

34. In this, Heidegger is closer than he knows to the Kantian and post-Kantian tradition, once one breaks free from Heidegger's Cartesian interpretation. Begin-

ning especially with Kant's moral philosophy, "person," despite the surface grammar, is in no sense a substantive or metaphysical category but in some way or other a practical achievement, and the attribution of the notion to an other is an ascription not a description. As Fichte would say, the I posits itself; as Hegel would say, *Geist* is a "result of itself." The somewhat confusing but very important point here is that being a subject means being able to fail to be one, something that already tells us a lot about the uniquely practical, not metaphysical, status of subjectivity in the post-Kantian tradition. See my "Naturalness and Mindedness: Hegel's Compatibilism," *European Journal of Philosophy* 7, no. 2 (1999): 194–212; and "Fichte's Alleged One-Sided, Subjective, Psychological Idealism," in *The Reception of Kant's Critical Philosophy: Fichte, Schelling and Hegel*, ed. Sally Sedgwick (Cambridge: Cambridge University Press, 2000).

35. *Being and Time*, p. 33/12.

36. Ibid. p. 59/35.

37. Ibid., p. 152/116.

38. Ibid., p. 97/68; p. 109/78; pp. 117–20/85–87.

39. Hubert Dreyfus, *Being-in-the-World: A Commentary on Heidegger's "Being and Time," Division I* (Cambridge, MA: MIT Press, 1992), p. 68.

40. *Being and Time*, p. 231/186.

41. Ibid., p. 310/265–66.

42. Ibid., p. 331/285.

43. *Die Grundbegriffe der Metaphysick*, pp. 244 and 248. These lectures are filled with references to the economic and social global crisis of 1929, and make clearer how Heidegger understood the political implications of his account of the meaning of being. They thus give a chilling sense of the kind of desperation that can be produced if one believes oneself to be in such a situation. See Gregory Fried's interesting study, *Heidegger's Polemos: From Being to Politics* (New Haven, CT: Yale University Press, 2000).

44. *Being and Time*, p. 330/284.

45. Ibid., p. 332/286. The radicality and extreme difficulty of the claim that the primordial meaning of Dasein's being is disclosed in the collapse of meaning, in such a primordial meaning just *being* the possibility of collapse or failure of meaning, are related to what Heidegger says about the nature of our not-being, the necessity and impossibility of its incorporabilty into the structure of care. In effect Heidegger is trying to resurrect an Eleatic, or radical, sense of not-being, *to mēdemos on*, not just *to mē on*. That is, he is trying to recover what he considers obscured by the "solution" to the problem proposed in Plato's *Sophist*. Since the sophist says what is not, it might look to an Eleatic that he violates the proscription on nonbeing, and so there cannot really be a sophist, or a distinction between sophist and philosopher, because nonbeing cannot be. But Plato's Eleatic stranger tries to show that *to mē on* cannot be some sort of radically empty being, just a *not*-being, but is instead "otherness," a kind of otherness "woven through" all the beings. To say what is not the case is not then to say what is not, but to say what is other than the truth at the time; that is, always to say *something else*, to say of something other than what is the case that it is the case. In Heidegger's 1924–25 Marburg course on Plato's *Sophist* this issue is brought to a head in §§ 78 and 79. See *Plato's Sophist*, trans.

Richard Rojcewicz and André Schuwer (Bloomington: Indiana University Press, 1997), pp. 386–401. But Heidegger is so self-restricted there in his role as a commentator that the issue is much easier to see elsewhere in his lectures, when he speaks more in his own voice.

46. Cf. also another such attempt, Hegel's—especially, in his introduction to the *Phenomenology of Spirit*, his remark that "in every case the result of an untrue mode of knowledge must not be allowed to run away into an empty nothing, but must necessarily be grasped as the nothing of that from which it results [*Nichts, desjenigen, dessen Resultat es ist*]." G. W. F. Hegel, *The Phenomenology of Spirit*, trans. A. V. Miller (Oxford: Oxford University Press, 1998), p. 56.

47. This is the passage from Heidegger's "What Is Metaphysics?" as quoted by Carnap, with ellipses, in "The Elimination of Metaphysics," p. 69.

48. *Being and Time*, p. 251/245. Hegel, *Phenomenology of Spirit*, p. 56; *Die Phänomenologie des Geistes*, in *Hauptwerke in sechs Bänden*, vol. 2 (Hamburg: Meiner, 1999), p. 61.

49. He wants to make the same point about the implications of the primordial situation of thrownness, about what happens to us, by coining such neologisms as "Die Angst ängstet sich um das Seinkönnen des so bestimmten Seiende [Anxiety is anxious *about* the potentiality-for-being of the entity so destined]" (*Being and Time*, p. 310/266).

50. Heidegger's example in *Introduction to Metaphysics* is from Knut Hamsun's *The Road Leads On*, where a poet sitting alone by the ocean, muses, "Here—nothing meets nothing and is not there, there is not even a hole. One can only shake one's head in resignation." *Introduction to Metaphysics*, p. 29.

51. *Being and Time*, p. 435/384. Cf. the remark in *Introduction to Metaphysics*: "The human being has no way out, in the face of death, not only when it is time to die, but constantly and essentially. Insofar as humans are, they stand in the no-exit of death. Thus being-there is the happening of the uncanniness itself" (p. 169). It would take several more chapters to try to show that this sort of account of meaning-failure is paradigmatic for what Heidegger wants to say in all contexts about the meaning of being. But I would want to argue that there are always parallels to this sort of account in those other contexts. Forms of life can also "fail" to mean, and there can be analogous anticipations of death in phenomena like "nihilism." The language of *Being and Time* is reconfigured as a kind of struggle between "Earth" (thrownness) and "World" (projection), in *On the Origin of the Work of Art*, and so forth.

52. It is certainly possible to characterize Heidegger's account as "transcendental" in a rather benign sense. One could say that Heidegger has shown that a necessary condition of Dasein's being making sense is the possibility of its not making sense; only such a condition can disclose this unavoidable "condition": the utter contingency of such care or mattering or significance when it happens. Or one could say, with Føllesdall, that Heidegger has shown that purposive action is a "necessary constituent" of the possibility of intentionality. But this is too benign to be very informative, and could be misleading. Heidegger's procedure is rather to establish a question, demonstrate both its supremely distinct and practically unavoidable character, and then argue that various possible candidate accounts (like Cartesian mentalism) fail to answer it. He does not, cannot, argue, say, that nonpractical inten-

tionality is "impossible." See Dagfinn Føllesdall, "Husserl and Heidegger on the Role of Actions in the Constitution of the World," in *Essays in Honor of Jaakko Hintikka*, ed. E. Saarinen, R. Hilpinen, I. Niiniluoto, and M. P. Hintikka (Dordrecht: Riedel, 1979).

53. Or: when Kafka's K cannot find the Court that has accused him, or even the charge against him, we are not to assume that if he tried harder or got lucky he *might have*. In a paradoxical way that exactly mirrors Heidegger's claim: this failure in no way lessens the bewildering guilt K begins to feel, the anxious sense that being alive itself is the situation of being guilty. In the parable of the law and the man from the country that closes the novel, there are three things true of the elements of the fable. The doorway to the law *is* for the man from the country; he may *not*, however, enter; and these two facts do not amount to a contradiction but instead "a necessity."

54. *Being and Time*, p. 374/326.

55. Ibid., p. 381/332.

56. Ibid., p. 427/375.

57. Preserving that connection also makes the relation between the so-called early and later Heidegger considerably easier to see for English readers, the Heidegger who will say very shortly after *Being and Time* (in a 1931–32 lecture course), "Being happens as a history of human beings, as the history of a Volk." *Vom Wesen der Wahrheit: Zu Platons Höhlengleichnis und Theätet*, ed. Hermann Mörchen, *Gesamtausgabe*, vol. 34 (Frankfurt am Main: Klostermann, 1988), p. 145. Stambaugh's word for *Geschehen* in her later translation of *Sein und Zeit*, "occurrence," is better, but it now conflicts with what has emerged as the preferred translations of *vorhanden* and *zuhanden*, John Haugeland's "occurent" and "available." *Being and Time*, trans. Joan Stambaugh (Albany: State University of New York Press, 1997).

58. *Being and Time*, p. 435/384.

59. *Phenomenology of Spirit*, p. 19; *Phänomenologie des Geistes*, p. 27.

60. *Phenomenology of Spirit*, p. 51; *Phänomenologie des Geistes*, p. 57.

61. See chapter 7, "Unending Modernity," in my *Modernism as a Philosophical Problem: On the Dissatisfactions of European High Culture*, 2nd ed. (Oxford: Blackwell, 1999), pp. 160ff.

CHAPTER 14: PROJECTION AND PURPOSIVENESS

I owe thanks to the participants in the 2003 conference Heidegger's Transcendentalism, held at Rice University in Houston, especially Steven Crowell, and to Joseph Rouse and Catherine Zuckert for comments on earlier drafts of this chapter.

1. Namely, Heidegger's Kant interpretation in *Kant and the Problem of Metaphysics* (trans. Richard Taft, 4th ed. [Bloomington: Indiana University Press, 1990]), and in the lecture course *Phenomenological Interpretation of Kant's "Critique of Pure Reason"* (trans. Parvis Emad and Kenneth Maly [Bloomington: Indiana University Press, 1997]), out of which *Kant und das Problem der Metaphysik* arose. Despite some differences in Heidegger's approach in these works, I shall treat them as complementary to one another. Heidegger's later discussions of Kant, in *What Is a Thing?* (*Die Frage nach dem Ding?*) and "Kant's Thesis About Being" ("Kants These über das Sein"), in

Pathmarks, ed. William McNeill (Cambridge: Cambridge University Press, 1998), pp. 337–63, are (as I shall suggest briefly below) not part of the same interpretive project, for in them Heidegger takes a more directly critical stance toward Kant. Citations to these works are to page numbers of the Indiana University Press translations. Citations to the *Critique of Pure Reason* (trans. Paul Guyer and Allen Wood [Cambridge: Cambridge University Press, 1997]) are to the A/B page numbers, and those to the *Critique of Judgment* (trans. Paul Guyer and Eric Matthews [Cambridge: Cambridge University Press, 2000]) and *Jäsche Logic* (*Lectures on Logic*, ed. J. Michael Young [Cambridge: Cambridge University Press, 1992]), are to the Academy volume and page numbers; translations quoted in the text are from the Cambridge translations.

2. See, e.g., *Phenomenological Interpretation*, pp. 14, 136, 196.

3. In *Kant und das Problem der Metaphysik*, §§ 1–2 (for example), Heidegger situates Kant's project in the context of the history of metaphysics, not epistemology, and takes Kant to be investigating the being of beings and the nature of human transcendence or finitude.

4. This (long-standing) approach to Kant is exemplified by Henry Allison (e.g., in his *Kant's Transcendental Idealism* [New Haven, CT: Yale University Press, 1983]). On this view, Kant's idealism comprises not a metaphysical claim about *what* objects *are*, but an epistemological claim concerning *how* they appear to us; correspondingly, any philosophical claims about the nature of being must appear "dogmatic": we may only consider what form things must take if they are to be recognized (by us) as "existing." Allison's interpretation of Kant seems, however, to inherit at least one aspect from Heidegger's, for he (like Heidegger, but not—textually speaking—like Kant) begins with the contrast between human, finite knowledge and God's knowledge or intuitive understanding.

5. This broader construal is not an unreasonable description of what it is to be engaged in transcendental philosophy in general: a recent writer characterizes transcendental arguments as those that argue "that one thing (X) is a necessary condition for the possibility of something else (Y). . . . In suggesting that X is a condition for Y in this way, the claim is supposed to be metaphysical and a priori, and not merely natural and a posteriori." Robert Stern, *Transcendental Arguments and Scepticism: Answering the Question of Justification* (Oxford: Oxford University Press, 2004), p. 3. And Kant's project in the *Critique of Pure Reason* may plausibly be said to begin with experience and/or knowledge and then to establish the legitimacy of certain claims (synthetic a priori judgments), because they are (or express) necessary conditions for the subject's knowledge or experience. (I cannot here enter into the disputes concerning possible differences between transcendental argument—Stern's concern—and transcendental philosophy—Kant's.)

6. Heidegger certainly takes his reading of Kant to concern the subjective conditions for the possibility of experience, and takes this philosophical approach to be his philosophical inheritance from Kant (e.g., *Phenomenological Interpretation of Kant's "Critique of Pure Reason,"* pp. 269, 289, 292–93).

7. In the Davos disputation. See *Kant and the Problem of Metaphysics*, pp. 195–96, 203–7. Cassirer argues, more specifically, that Heidegger ignores the nature of transcendental subjectivity as elaborated in the moral philosophy.

8. Ibid., §§ 4–6; as is most explicit in § 5, Heidegger is, then, engaging in "reconstructive" interpretation (supplying a basic, unstated premise).

9. I use *judgment* broadly here (to include synthesis), as Heidegger (and Kant) do: "Judgment," Kant writes, "is the representation of the unity of consciousness of various representations, or representation of their relation insofar as they constitute a concept" (*Jäsche*, para. 17, 9: 101). Or, on Heidegger's gloss, judgment is the representation of a unity which contains a commonness, with which (unity) many representations agree (*Phenomenological Interpretation of Kant's "Critique of Pure Reason,"* p. 163). I shall return to this broad meaning for "judgment" briefly below.

10. *Kant and the Problem of Metaphysics*, pp. 26–30.

11. See, e.g., *Critique of Judgment*, para. 76. Even Heidegger's rather less-Kantian-sounding claim that, for Kant, intuition is the primary mode of knowing, to which thinking is merely in "service," might be taken as "loyal" to Kant when understood within Heidegger's intellectual context, that is, the Marburg neo-Kantian interpretations of Kant, according to which (human) cognition comprises—exclusively—conceptual judgment. Heidegger's vindication, contra these neorationalists, of the role of intuition in cognition, as necessary to provide both "content" (or "matter") to be synthesized, and as the basic, "immediate" connection of thought to things other than the knower, seems to be in a (broadly) Kantian spirit.

12. Indeed Heidegger's interpretation might be understood as the "flip side" of the Anglo-American interpretive tradition, in which Kant's response to Humean skepticism has been emphasized to the exclusion of many of Kant's other concerns.

13. *Phenomenological Interpretation of Kant's "Critique of Pure Reason,"* p. 203; *Kant and the Problem of Metaphysics*, p. 60.

14. See § 7 of Heidegger's *History of the Concept of Time: Prolegomena* (trans. Theodore Kisiel [Bloomington: Indiana University Press, 1985]), in which he defends, more explicitly, this conception of the a priori as the "original" and properly understood conception (insofar as it explicitly recognizes the role of time as constitutive of the meaning of the a priori) than the epistemological conception. I owe Joseph Rouse for this reference.

15. This is an interpretive claim addressed against the neo-Kantians (and an issue still contested in Kant interpretation); see, e.g., *Phenomenological Interpretation of Kant's "Critique of Pure Reason,"* para. 2.

16. *Phenomenological Interpretation of Kant's "Critique of Pure Reason,"* pp. 26–27, 32; *Kant and the Problem of Metaphysics*, p. 158.

17. *Phenomenological Interpretation of Kant's "Critique of Pure Reason,"* p. 25.

18. Heidegger's claim is a bit more limited in scope: because Kant is engaged in ontology concerning beings only as "nature," Kant's project is a more specific "objectification," that is, it articulates the conceptual foundation for a specifically modern scientific point of view/comportment toward beings. *Phenomenological Interpretation of Kant's "Critique of Pure Reason,"* pp. 18–19.

19. *Kant and the Problem of Metaphysics*, e.g., p. 76.

20. Ibid., pp. 95–96. Heidegger's claim that Kant "shrank back" is, narrowly speaking, based on textual evidence: Kant identifies the imagination as the faculty of synthesis in the A edition, and then, in the revised B edition, claims instead that synthesis is a function of the *understanding*, or that the imagination is merely a subfaculty of the

understanding. *Kant and the Problem of Metaphysics*, pp. 112–15, *Phenomenological Interpretation of Kant's "Critique of Pure Reason,"* p. 191.

21. *Critique of Pure Reason*, A138–39/B177–78.

22. *Kant and the Problem of Metaphysics*, pp. 89–94; *Phenomenological Interpretation of Kant's "Critique of Pure Reason,"* p. 189.

23. *Kant and the Problem of Metaphysics*, p. 100.

24. *Kant and the Problem of Metaphysics*, pp. 121–23; *Phenomenological Interpretation of Kant's "Critique of Pure Reason,"* p. 192. This is, of course, a necessarily abbreviated overview of Heidegger's interpretation. In particular, in concert with Kant's full transcendental deduction arguments, according to which categorial synthesis is a necessary condition for the possibility of a unified experience for a single subject (for the possibility that the "I think" may be joined to any of the "I's" representations), Heidegger also describes this claim as the explanation how the "I think" may be joined to time (*Kant and the Problem of Metaphysics,* pp. 128–31, 135); for reasons of space, I cannot pursue this full argument (on either side) here.

25. *Kant and the Problem of Metaphysics*, pp. 58–59.

26. *Critique of Pure Reason*, A99–104.

27. *Kant and the Problem of Metaphysics*, p. 140.

28. Ibid., pp. 121–23.

29. Heidegger also argues that the projective imagination is the source of intuition, for we generate the "concepts" of (objective) space and time (pure intuitions) from the imagination as equivalent to primordial time. I leave these arguments aside because they are (broadly) consonant with Kant's considered view: Kant characterizes the Transcendental Aesthetic as a preliminary treatment of space and time as independent of the categories; ultimately (most explicitly at the end of the B-Deduction), however, Kant suggests that (objective) space and time are unified *by* the productive imagination synthesizing in accord with the categorial principles.

30. Heidegger's account need not preclude, however, orthodox Kantian claims concerning the illegitimacy of assertions about noumena. For (on Heidegger's reading) the categories apply meaningfully to objects (have "objective reality") only on the basis of imaginative synthesis, and thus may well apply only illicitly to objects that (as nonintuitable or atemporal) cannot be grasped in imaginative synthesis.

31. *Phenomenological Interpretation of Kant's "Critique of Pure Reason,"* p. 123.

32. *Kant and the Problem of Metaphysics*, pp. 168–71.

33. *Critique of Pure Reason*, A155/B194.

34. See, respectively, *Critique of Pure Reason*, A55/B79ff., B140–42; and *Kant and the Problem of Metaphysics*, pp. 20, 27, 42–45.

35. The oddity of Kant's transcendental conception of judging is less commented upon than it ought to be in much Kant scholarship (as in the common Kantian dictum, "all experience is judgmental"); for a good treatment of these issues, see Dieter Henrich, *The Unity of Reason* (ed. Richard L. Velkley, trans. Jeffrey Edwards [Cambridge, MA: Harvard University Press, 1994]).

36. As Heidegger suggests, e.g., in *Kant and the Problem of Metaphysics*, p. 121; see Michael Friedman, *A Parting of the Ways: Carnap, Cassirer, and Heidegger* (Chicago: Open Court, 2000); and Joseph Rouse, *How Scientific Practices Matter* (Chicago: University of Chicago Press, 2002), concerning Heidegger's deep-going concern with

just such questions in response to the neo-Kantian or logical positivist focus on the normativity of logic or scientific claims.

37. Or, in a Sellarsian vein, one might formulate this question as: how can "blind" or "the given" intuitions function as evidence or justification for conceptual, judgmental claims. The nature and severity of the schematism problem is, of course, a highly debated issue, a dispute I must pass over here.

38. *Kant and the Problem of Metaphysics*, p. 105; my emphasis.

39. Thus Heidegger's reading may be understood as a successor to the German Idealist complaint (as, for example, expressed by Schelling) against Kant that Kant overly restricts his "transcendental" investigation to "formal," conceptual, or epistemological considerations, refusing to recognize that these conditions themselves presuppose metaphysical conditions (or characteristics of the subject).

40. For instance, e.g., *Critique of Pure Reason*, B151–52.

41. *Phenomenological Interpretation of Kant's "Critique of Pure Reason,"* p. 203. Heidegger, like many others, also finds the table of judgments methodologically questionable, indeed question-begging: Kant introduces new types of judgments (Heidegger argues) in order to set up his table of categories (ibid., pp. 176–77). Béatrice Longuenesse, in the most sophisticated recent reconstruction of the Metaphysical Deduction, like Heidegger provides an alternative derivation of the categories from the activity of reflection. *Kant and the Capacity to Judge* (Princeton, NJ: Princeton University Press, 1998).

42. *Kant and the Problem of Metaphysics*, p. 38. In *Phenomenological Interpretation of Kant's "Critique of Pure Reason,"* pp. 186–87, Heidegger provides a somewhat different account (to the same purpose, however).

43. *Jäsche Logic*, 9: 94–95.

44. *Phenomenological Interpretation of Kant's "Critique of Pure Reason,"* pp. 158–59; see also *Kant and the Problem of Metaphysics*, p. 37.

45. *Kant and the Problem of Metaphysics*, pp. 38–39.

46. Kant discusses many different kinds of reflective judgment in the *Critique of Judgment*, but I shall discuss only two, empirical concept formation and (very briefly) aesthetic judgment.

47. *Critique of Judgment*, 5: 179.

48. Ibid., 5: 184.

49. This is a controversial reading of the *Critique of Judgment* that I defend more fully elsewhere; see, however, ibid., 5: 220 and 229.

50. Ibid., 5: 190, 354.

51. Ibid., 5: 183–86.

52. One might, correspondingly, gloss Dasein's authenticity (as characterized in *Being and Time*) as a state in which it recognizes itself as purposive without a purpose.

53. *Kant and the Problem of Metaphysics*, p. 112, n. a; app. 1, pp. 175–76. Heidegger discusses the *Critique of Judgment* very little and states that he consulted the *Critique of Judgment* only to make sure that it was not in conflict with his reading. See also Heidegger's comments on Kant's aesthetics in his Nietzsche lectures; for example, Heidegger there writes that aesthetic judging, on Kant's view, is "a basic state of human being in which man *for the first time* arrives at the well-grounded fullness of his essence" (Heidegger, *Nietzsche* [2 vols. bound as one], trans. David Farrell Krell

[New York: Harper Collins, 1991], p. 113; my emphasis), where we do not take up the object "with a view to something else," but "let what encounters us, purely as it is in itself, come before us in its own structure and worth" (*Nietzsche*, p. 109).

54. *Critique of Judgment*, 5: 353.

55. *Critique of Pure Reason*, A104.

56. Ibid., A106.

57. Ibid., A105.

58. Despite Heidegger's recognition of the A-Deduction passages (*Kant and the Problem of Metaphysics*, pp. 51–52, 58–59, 108–9); see ibid., p. 203, for Heidegger's celebration of the "accidentality" of Dasein.

59. In his later works on Kant, Heidegger is more cognizant of the importance of necessity in Kant's project (in *What Is a Thing?* as constitutive for Kant's [Cartesian] conception of knowledge as founded upon a priori *principles* necessarily known and legislative for nature, and in "Kant's Thesis on Being," as characterizing that which can be formally attributed to nature *because* of its connection to the judging subject). He is *therefore* (I suggest) less friendly to Kant, less willing to see Kant's project as anticipatory of his own. Such Cartesian, subjectivist, and necessitarian impulses, Heidegger argues, exemplify the very forgetfulness of being, the occlusion of the ground beyond the knowing subject, that Heidegger wishes to uncover and rectify.

60. *Kant and the Problem of Metaphysics*, pp. 165, 189.

61. On this, see Joseph Fell, "The Familiar and the Strange: On the Limits of Praxis in Early Heidegger," in *Heidegger: A Critical Reader*, ed. Hubert Dreyfus and Harrison Hall (Blackwell: Oxford, 1992).

62. For another view on this, see David Carr's chapter in this volume.

Bibliography

Allison, Henry. *Kant's Transcendental Idealism*. New Haven, CT: Yale University Press, 1983.

Apel, Karl-Otto. "Regulative Ideas or Truth-Happening? An Attempt to Answer the Question of the Conditions of the Possibility of Valid Understanding." In *The Philosophy of Hans-Georg Gadamer*, ed. Lewis Edwin Hahn, pp. 67–94. Library of Living Philosophers 24. Chicago: Open Court, 1996.

Aristotle. *Physics*. Trans. Daniel W. Graham. Oxford: Oxford University Press, 1999.

Bieri, Peter, Rolf-Peter Horstman, and Lorenz Krüger, eds. *Transcendental Arguments and Science*. Dordrecht: Reidel, 1979.

Blattner, William. "The Concept of Death in *Being and Time*." *Man and World* 27 (1994): 49–70.

———. *Heidegger's Temporal Idealism*. Cambridge: Cambridge University Press, 1999.

———. "Is Heidegger a Kantian Idealist?" *Inquiry* 37 (1994): 185–201.

———. "Is Heidegger a Representationalist?" *Philosophical Topics* 27 (1999): 179–204.

———. "Laying the Ground for Metaphysics: Heidegger's Appropriation of Kant." In *The Cambridge Companion to Heidegger*, 2nd ed., ed. Charles Guignon, pp. 149–76. Cambridge: Cambridge University Press, 2003.

———. "The Primacy of Practice and Assertoric Truth: Dewey and Heidegger." In *Heidegger, Authenticity and Modernity: Essays in Honor of Hubert L. Dreyfus*, ed. Mark Wrathall and Jeff Malpas, vol. 1, 231–49. Cambridge, MA: MIT Press, 2000.

Blumenberg, Hans. "Das Sein—Ein MacGuffin." *Frankfurter Allgemeine Zeitung*, May 27, 1987, p. 35.

Brandom, Robert. "Holism and Idealism in Hegel's *Phenomenology*." In *Tales of the Mighty Dead: Historical Essays in the Metaphysics of Intentionality*, by Robert Brandom. Cambridge, MA: Harvard University Press, 2002.

Breeur, Roland. "Randbemerkungen Husserls zu Heideggers *Sein und Zeit* und *Kant und das Problem der Metaphysik*." *Husserl Studies* 11 (1994): 3–63.

Brelage, Manfred. *Studien zur Transzendentalphilosophie*. Berlin: de Gruyter, 1965.

Brueckner, Anthony. "Transcendental Arguments I." *Nous* 17 (1983): 551–75.

Carmen, Taylor. *Heidegger's Analytic: Interpretation, Discourse and Authenticity in "Being and Time."* Cambridge: Cambridge University Press, 2003.

Carnap, Rudolf. "The Elimination of Metaphysics Through Logical Analysis of Language." In *Logical Positivism*, ed. A. J. Ayer, pp. 60–81. New York: Free Press, 1959.

———. "Empiricism, Semantics, and Ontology." In *Meaning and Necessity*, by Rudolf Carnap, 2nd ed., pp. 205–29. Chicago: University of Chicago Press, 1956.

———. *Der logische Aufbau der Welt.* Berlin: Weltkreis, 1928.

———. *Scheinprobleme in der Philosophie: Das Fremdpsychische und der Realismusstreit.* Berlin: Weltkreis, 1928.

Cerbone, David R. "World, World-Entry, and Realism in Early Heidegger." *Inquiry* 38 (1995): 401–21.

Crowell, Steven. "Heidegger's Phenomenological Decade." *Man and World* 28, no. 4 (1995): 435–48.

———. *Husserl, Heidegger, and the Space of Meaning: Paths Toward Transcendental Phenomenology.* Evanston, IL: Northwestern University Press, 2001.

———. "Lask, Heidegger, and the Homelessness of Logic." *Journal of the British Society for Phenomenology* 23, no. 3 (October 1991): 222–39.

———. "Metaphysics, Metontology, and the End of *Being and Time*." *Philosophy and Phenomenological Research* 60 (2000): 307–31.

———. "Subjectivity: Locating the First-Person in *Being and Time*." *Inquiry* 44 (2001): 433–54.

Dahlstrom, Daniel O. *Heidegger's Concept of Truth.* Cambridge: Cambridge University Press, 2001.

———. "Heidegger's Kantian Turn: Notes to His Commentary of the *Kritik der reinen Vernunft*." *Review of Metaphysics* 45, no. 2 (December 1991): 329–61.

Davidson, Donald. "Three Varieties of Knowledge." In *A. J. Ayer: Memorial Essays*, ed. A. Phillips Griffiths, pp. 153–66. Royal Institute of Philosophy Supplement 30. Cambridge: Cambridge University Press, 1991.

Depraz, Natalie. *Transcendance et incarnation: Le Statut de l'intersubjectivité comme altérité à soi chez Husserl.* Paris: Vrin, 1995.

Dreyfus, Hubert. *Being-in-the-World: A Commentary on Heidegger's "Being and Time," Division I.* Cambridge, MA: MIT Press, 1991.

———, and Charles Spinosa. "Coping with Things-in-Themselves: A Practice-Based Phenomenological Argument for Realism." *Inquiry* 42 (1999): 49–78.

Ebbs, Gary. "Putnam and the Contextually A Priori." In *The Philosophy of Hilary Putnam*, ed. Lewis E. Hahn and Randall E. Auxier. La Salle, IL: Open Court, forthcoming.

Fell, Joseph. "The Familiar and the Strange: On the Limits of Praxis in Early Heidegger." In *Heidegger: A Critical Reader*, ed. Hubert Dreyfus and Harrison Hall, pp. 65–80. Oxford: Blackwell, 1992.

Føllesdal, Dagfinn. "Husserl and Heidegger on the Role of Actions in the Constitution of the World." In *Essays in Honor of Jaakko Hintikka*, ed. E. Saarinen, R. Hilpinen, I. Niiniluoto, and M. P. Hintikka. Dordrecht: Riedel, 1979.

Frede, Dorothea. "Heidegger and the Scandal of Philosophy." In *Human Nature and Natural Knowledge*, ed. A. Donagan, A. N. Perovich, and M. V. Wedin. Dordecht: Reidel, 1986.

Frege, Gottlob. *Begriffschrift und andere Aufsätze.* 2nd ed. Ed. Ignacio Angelelli. Darmstadt: Wissenschaftliche Buchgesellschaft, 1971.

Fried, Gregory. *Heidegger's Polemos: From Being to Politics.* New Haven, CT: Yale University Press, 2000.

Friedman, Michael. *A Parting of the Ways: Carnap, Cassirer, and Heidegger*. Chicago: Open Court, 2000.

Gadamer, Hans-Georg. *Heidegger's Ways*. Trans. John W. Stanley. Albany: State University of New York, 1994.

———. "Reflections on my Philosophical Journey." In *The Philosophy of Hans-Georg Gadamer*, ed. Lewis Edwin Hahn, pp. 3–63. Library of Living Philosophers 24. Chicago: Open Court, 1996.

———. "Rhetorik, Hermeneutik, Ideologiekritik." In *Gesammelte Werke*, vol. 2, pp. 232–50. Tübingen: J. C. B. Mohr, 1993.

Gethmann, Carl-Friedrich. *Verstehen und Auslegung: Das Methodenproblem in der Philosophie Martin Heideggers*. Bonn: Bouvier, 1974.

Gram, Moltke S. "Transcendental Arguments." *Nous* 5 (1972): 15–26.

Hacker, P. M. S. *Appearance and Reality: A Philosophical Investigation into Perception and Perceptual Qualities*. Oxford: Blackwell, 1987.

Harries, Karsten. "Death and Utopia: Towards a Critique of the Ethics of Satisfaction." *Research in Phenomenology* 7 (1977): 138–52.

Hartmann, Eduard von. *Kritische Grundlegung des Transcendentalen Realismus*. Berlin: Carl Duncker, 1875.

———. *Grundriß der Erkenntlislehre*. Bad Sachsa im Harz: Hermann Haacke, 1907.

Haugeland, John. "Dasein's Disclosedness." In *Heidegger: A Critical Reader*, ed. Hubert Dreyfus and Harrison Hall, pp. 27–44. Oxford: Blackwell, 1992.

———. "Truth and Finitude: Heidegger's Transcendental Existentialism." In *Heidegger, Authenticity, and Modernity: Essays in Honor of Hubert L. Dreyfus*, ed. Mark Wrathall and Jeff Malpas, vol. 1, pp. 43–77. Cambridge, MA: MIT Press, 2000.

———. "Truth and Rule-Following." In *Having Thought: Essays in the Metaphysics of Mind*, by John Haugeland, pp. 305–61. Cambridge, MA: Harvard University Press, 1998.

Hegel, G. W. F. *Phänomenologie des Geistes*. In *Hauptwerke in sechs Bänden*, vol. 2. Hamburg: Meiner, 1999.

———. *The Phenomenology of Spirit*. Trans. A. V. Miller. Oxford: Oxford University Press, 1998.

Heidegger, Martin. *Aus der Erfahrung des Denkens, 1910–1976*. Ed. Hermann Heidegger. *Gesamtausgabe*, vol. 13. Frankfurt am Main: Klostermann, 2002.

———. *Basic Concepts*. Trans. Gary E. Aylesworth. Bloomington: Indiana University Press, 1993.

———. *The Basic Problems of Phenomenology*. Trans. Albert Hofstadter. Bloomington: Indiana University Press, 1982.

———. *Basic Questions of Philosophy*. Trans. Richard Rojcewicz and André Schuwer. Bloomington: Indiana University Press, 1994.

———. *Basic Writings*. Ed. David Farrell Krell. Rev. and exp. ed. New York: HarperCollins, 1993.

———. *Being and Time*. Trans. John Macquarrie and Edward Robinson. New York: Harper and Row, 1962.

———. *Being and Time*. Trans. Joan Stambaugh. Albany: State University of New York Press, 1997.

———. *Beiträge zur Philosophie (Vom Ereignis)*. Ed. Friedrich-Wilhelm von Herrmann. *Gesamtausgabe*, vol. 65. Frankfurt am Main: Klostermann, 1989.
———. *Besinnung*. Ed. Friedrich-Wilhelm von Herrmann. *Gesamtausgabe*, vol. 66. Frankfurt am Main: Klostermann, 1997.
———. *Zur Bestimmung der Philosophie*. Ed. Bernd Heimbüchel. *Gesamtausgabe*, vols. 56–57. 2nd ed. Frankfurt am Main: Klostermann, 1999.
———. "Building Dwelling Thinking." In *Poetry, Language, Thought*, trans. Albert Hofstadter, pp. 143–61. New York: Harper and Row, 1971.
———. *Contributions to Philosophy (from Enowning)*. Trans. Parvis Emad and Kenneth Maly. Bloomington: Indiana University Press, 1999.
———. " Conversation on a Country Path." In *Discourse on Thinking*, trans. John M. Anderson and E. Hans Freund. New York: Harper and Row, 1966.
———. "Davoser Disputation zwischen Ernst Cassirer und Martin Heidegger." In *Kant und das Problem der Metaphysik*, ed. Friedrich-Wilhelm von Herrmann, *Gesamtausgabe*, vol. 3, pp. 274–96. Frankfurt am Main: Klostermann, 1976.
———. *Towards the Definition of Philosophy*. Trans. Ted Sadler. London: Continuum, 2002.
———. ". . . dichterisch wohnet der Mensch . . . " In *Vorträge und Aufsätze*, ed. Friedrich-Wilhelm von Herrmann, *Gesamtausgabe*, vol. 7. Frankfurt am Main: Klostermann, 2000.
———. *Einführung in die Metaphysik*. Ed. Petra Jaeger. *Gesamtausgabe*, vol. 40. Frankfurt am Main: Klostermann, 1983.
———. *Einführung in die phänomenologische Forschung*. Ed. Friedrich-Wilhelm von Herrmann. *Gesamtausgabe*, vol. 17. Frankfurt am Main: Klostermann, 1994.
———. *Einleitung in die Philosophie*. Ed. Otto Saame and Ina Saame-Speidel. *Gesamtausgabe*, vol. 27. Frankfurt am Main: Klostermann, 2001.
———. *Elucidations of Hölderlin's Poetry*. Trans. Keith Hoeller. New York: Humanity Books, 2000.
———. "The End of Philosophy and the Task of Thinking." In *On Time and Being*, trans. Joan Stambaugh, pp. 55–73. New York: Harper and Row, 1972.
———. *Erläuterungen zu Hölderlins Dichtung*. Ed. Friedrich-Wilhelm von Herrmann. *Gesamtausgabe*, vol. 4. Frankfurt am Main: Klostermann, 1996.
———. *The Essence of Truth: On Plato's Cave Allegory and Theaetetus*. Trans. Ted Sadler. London: Continuum, 2005.
———. *Die Frage nach dem Ding*. Tübingen: Niemeyer, 1962.
———. *Frühe Schriften (1912–1916)*. Ed. Friedrich-Wilhelm von Herrmann. *Gesamtausgabe*, vol. 1. Frankfurt am Main: Klostermann, 1978.
———. *The Fundamental Concepts of Metaphysics: World, Finitude, Solitude*. Trans. William McNeill and Nicholas Walker. Bloomington: Indiana University Press, 1995.
———. *Die Grundbegriffe der Metaphysik: Welt, Endlichkeit, Einsamkeit*. Ed. Otto Saame and Ina Saame-Speidel. *Gesamtausgabe*, vols. 29–30. Frankfurt am Main: Klostermann, 1983.
———. *Die Grundprobleme der Phänomenologie*. Ed. Friedrich-Wilhelm von Herrmann. *Gesamtausgabe*, vol. 24. Frankfurt am Main: Klostermann, 1975.

———. *History of the Concept of Time: Prolegomena*. Trans. Theodore Kisiel. Bloomington: Indiana University Press, 1985.
———. *Holzwege*. Ed. Friedrich-Wilhelm von Herrmann. *Gesamtausgabe*, vol. 5. Frankfurt am Main: Klostermann, 2003.
———. *Identity and Difference*. Trans. Joan Stambaugh. Chicago: University of Chicago Press, 2001.
———. *Introduction to Metaphysics*. Trans. Gregory Fried and Richard Polt. New Haven, CT: Yale University Press, 2000.
———. *Kant and the Problem of Metaphysics*. Trans. Richard Taft. 4th ed. Bloomington: Indiana University Press, 1990. 5th ed., Bloomington: Indiana University Press, 1997.
———. *Kant und das Problem der Metaphysik*. 4th ed. Frankfurt am Main: Klostermann, 1951, 1973.
———. "Kant's Thesis About Being." In *Pathmarks*, ed. William McNeill, pp. 337–63. Cambridge: Cambridge University Press, 1998.
———. *Die Lehre vom Urteil im Psychologismus*. In *Frühe Schriften (1912–1916)*, ed. Friedrich-Wilhelm von Herrmann, *Gesamtausgabe*, vol. 1, pp. 59–188. Frankfurt am Main: Klostermann, 1978.
———. *Logik: Die Frage nach der Wahrheit*. Ed. Walter Biemel. *Gesamtausgabe*, vol. 21. Frankfurt am Main: Klostermann, 1995.
———. *Metaphysical Foundations of Logic*. Trans. Michael Heim. Bloomington: Indiana University Press, 1984.
———. "Per mortem ad vitam: Gedanken über Jörgensens 'Lebenslüge und Lebenswahrheit'" (1910). In *Reden und andere Zeugnisse eines Lebensweges*, by Martin Heidegger, ed. Hermann Heidegger, *Gesamtausgabe*, vol. 16. Frankfurt am Main: Klostermann, 2000.
———. "My Way to Phenomenology." In *On Time and Being*, trans. Joan Stambaugh. New York: Harper and Row, 1972.
———. "Neuere Forschungen über Logik." In *Frühe Schriften (1912–1916)*, ed. Friedrich-Wilhelm von Herrmann, *Gesamtausgabe*, vol. 1, pp. 17–43. Frankfurt am Main: Klostermann, 1978.
———. *Nietzsche*. 2 vols. Pfüllingen: Neske, 1961.
———. *Nietzsche*. Trans. David Farrell Krell. San Francisco: HarperSanFrancisco, 1991.
———. "Nur Noch ein Gott Kann Uns Retten." Interview. *Der Spiegel* 23 (1976): 193–219.
———. "'Only a God Can Save Us': The *Spiegel* Interview (1966)." Trans. William J. Richardson. In *Heidegger: The Man and the Thinker*, ed. Thomas Sheehan, pp. 45–67. Chicago: Precedent, n.d.
———. *Ontology: The Hermeneutics of Facticity*. Trans. John van Buren. Bloomington: Indiana University Press, 1999.
———. *Parmenides*. Trans. André Schuwer and Richard Rojcewicz. Bloomington: Indiana University Press, 1992.
———. *Pathmarks*. Ed. William McNeill. Cambridge: Cambridge University Press, 1998.

———. *Phänomenologie der Anschauung und des Ausdrucks*. Ed. Claudius Strube. *Gesamtausgabe*, vol. 59. Frankfurt am Main: Klostermann, 1993.
———. *Phänomenologische Interpretation von Kants "Kritik der reinen Vernunft."* Ed. Ingtraud Görland. *Gesamtausgabe*, vol. 25. Frankfurt am Main: Klostermann, 1977.
———. *Phenomenological Interpretation of Kant's "Critique of Pure Reason."* Trans. Parvis Emad and Kenneth Maly. Bloomington: Indiana University Press, 1997.
———. "Zur philosophischen Orientierung für Akademiker" (1911). In *Reden und andere Zeugnisse eines Lebensweges*, by Martin Heidegger, ed. Hermann Heidegger, *Gesamtausgabe*, vol. 16. Frankfurt am Main: Klostermann, 2000.
———. *Plato's Sophist*. Trans. Richard Rojcewicz and André Schuwer. Bloomington: Indiana University Press, 1997.
———. *Poetry, Language, Thought*. Trans. Albert Hofstadter. New York: Harper and Row, 1971.
———. *The Principle of Reason*. Trans. Reginald Lilly. Bloomington: Indiana University Press, 1996.
———. *Prolegomena zur Geschichte des Zeitbegriffs*. Ed. Petra Jaeger. *Gesamtausgabe*, vol. 20. Frankfurt am Main: Klostermann, 1994.
———. *The Question Concerning Technology and Other Essays*. Trans. William Lovitt. New York: Harper and Row, 1977.
———. "The Rectorial Address." Trans. Lisa Harries. In *Martin Heidegger and National Socialism*, ed. Günther Neske and Emil Kettering. New York: Paragon, 1990.
———. *Reden und andere Zeugnisse eines Lebensweges*. Ed. Hermann Heidegger. *Gesamtausgabe*, vol. 16. Frankfurt am Main: Klostermann, 2000.
———. Review of *Autorität und Freiheit: Betrachtungen zum Kulturproblem der Kirche* (1910), by Friedrich Wilhelm Förster. In *Reden und andere Zeugnisse eines Lebensweges*, by Martin Heidegger, ed. Hermann Heidegger, *Gesamtausgabe*, vol. 16. Frankfurt am Main: Klostermann, 2000.
———. *Zur Sache des Denkens*. 2nd ed. Tübingen: Niemeyer, 1976.
———. *Sein und Zeit*. 17th ed. Tübingen: Niemeyer, 1993.
———. *Sein und Zeit*. Ed. Friedrich-Wilhelm von Herrmann. *Gesamtausgabe*, vol. 2. Frankfurt am Main: Klostermann, 1977.
———. *Seminare*. Ed. Curd Ochwadt. *Gesamtausgabe*, vol. 15. Frankfurt am Main: Klostermann, 1986.
———. "Time and Being." In *On Time and Being*, by Martin Heidegger, trans. Joan Stambaugh, pp. 1–24. New York: Harper and Row, 1972.
———. *On Time and Being*. Trans. Joan Stambaugh. New York: Harper and Row, 1972.
———. *Unterwegs zur Sprache*. Pfüllingen: Neske, 1959.
———. *Unterwegs zur Sprache*. Ed. Friedrich-Wilhelm von Herrmann. *Gesamtausgabe*, vol. 12. Frankfurt am Main: Klostermann, 1985.
———. "Der Ursprung des Kunstwerkes." In *Holzwege*, by Martin Heidegger, pp. 7–68. Frankfurt am Main: Klostermann, 1972.
———. *Der Ursprung des Kunstwerkes*. Stuttgart: Reclam, 1960.
———. *Vorträge und Aufsätze*. Ed. Friedrich-Wilhelm von Herrmann. *Gesamtausgabe*, vol. 7. Frankfurt am Main: Klostermann, 2000.

———. *Was ist Metaphysik?* Frankfurt am Main: Klostermann, 1969.

———. *On the Way to Language.* Trans. Peter D. Hertz. New York: Harper and Row, 1982.

———. *Wegmarken.* 2nd exp. ed. Ed. Friedrich-Wilhelm von Herrmann. *Gesamtausgabe*, vol. 9. Frankfurt am Main: Klostermann, 1978.

———. *Vom Wesen der Wahrheit.* Frankfurt am Main: Klostermann, 1949.

———. *Vom Wesen der Wahrheit: Zu Platons Höhlengleichnis und Theätet.* Ed. Hermann Mörchen. *Gesamtausgabe*, vol. 34. Frankfurt am Main: Klostermann, 1988.

———. "What Is Metaphysics?" In *Basic Writings*, rev. and exp. ed., ed. David Farrell Krell, pp. 89–110. New York: HarperCollins, 1993.

———. *What Is a Thing?* Trans. W. B. Barton, Jr., and Vera Deutsch. Chicago: Regnery, 1967.

———. *Zollikon Seminars: Protocols, Conversations, Letters.* Trans. Franz Mayr and Richard Askay. Evanston, IL: Northwestern University Press, 2001.

Henrich, Dieter. *The Unity of Reason.* Ed. Richard L. Velkley. Trans. Jeffrey Edwards. Cambridge, MA: Harvard University Press, 1994.

Hölderlin, Friedrich. *Hymns and Fragments.* Trans. Richard Sieburth. Princeton, NJ: Princeton University Press, 1984.

Hume, David. *A Treatise of Human Nature.* Ed. L. A. Selby-Bigge. 2nd ed., Peter Nidditch. Oxford: Clarendon, 1978.

Husserl, Edmund. *Analysen zur passiven Synthesis: Aus Vorlesungs- und Forschungsmanuskripten (1918–1926).* Ed. M. Fleischer. *Husserliana*, vol. 11. Dordrecht: Kluwer, 1988.

———. *Analyses Concerning Passive and Active Synthesis: Lectures on Transcendental Logic.* Trans. Anthony J. Steinbock. Husserl Collected Works 9. Dordrecht: Kluwer, 2001.

———. *Aufsätze und Vorträge.* 1922–37. Ed. T. Nenon H. R. Sepp. *Husserliana*, vol. 27. The Hague: Kluwer, 1988.

———. "Bericht über deutsche Schriften zur Logik in den Jahren 1895–99, Erster Artikel." *Archiv für systematische Philosophie* 9 (1903): 113–32.

———. *Cartesian Meditations: An Introduction to Phenomenology.* Trans. Dorion Cairns. The Hague: Nijhoff, 1967.

———. *Cartesianische Meditationen und Pariser Vorträge.* Ed. Stephan Strasser. *Husserliana*, vol. 1. The Hague: Nijhoff, 1950.

———. *The Crisis of European Sciences and Transcendental Phenomenology: An Introduction to Phenomenological Philosophy.* Trans. David Carr. Evanston, IL: Northwestern University Press, 1970.

———. *Einleitung in die Logik und Erkenntnistheorie: Vorlesungen, 1906/07.* Ed. Ullrich Melle. *Husserliana*, vol. 24. Dordrecht: Kluwer, 1985.

———. *Erste Philosophie (1923–24). Erster Teil: Kritische Ideengeschichte.* Ed. R. Boehm. *Husserliana*, vol. 7. The Hague: Nijhoff, 1965.

———. *Erste Philosophie (1923–24). Zweiter Teil: Theorie der phänomenologischen Reduktion.* Ed. R. Boehm. *Husserliana*, vol. 8. The Hague: Nijhoff, 1965.

———. *Formal and Transcendental Logic.* Trans. Dorion Cairns. The Hague: Nijhoff, 1978.

———. *Formale und transzendentale Logik: Versuch einer Kritik der logischen Vernunft.* Ed. Paul Janssen. *Husserliana*, vol. 17. The Hague: Nijhoff, 1974.

———. *Ideas: General Introduction to Pure Phenomenology.* Trans. W. R. Boyce Gibson. New York: Collier Books, 1962.

———. *Ideas Pertaining to a Pure Phenomenology and to a Phenomenological Philosophy: First Book.* Trans. F. Kersten. The Hague: Nijhoff, 1983.

———. *Ideen zu einer reinen Phänomenologie und phänomenologischen Philosophie. Husserliana,* vol. 3. The Hague: Nijhoff, 1976.

———. "Kant and the Idea of Transcendental Philosophy." Trans. Ted E. Klein and William E. Pohl. *Southwestern Journal of Philosophy* 5 (Fall 1974): 9–56.

———. *Die Krisis der europäischen Wissenschaften und die transzendentale Phänomenologie: Eine Einleitung in die phänomenologische Philosophie.* Ed. Walter Biemel. *Husserliana,* vol. 6. The Hague: Nijhoff, 1962.

———. *Logical Investigations.* Trans. J. N. Findlay. 2 vols. Rev. ed., with a new introduction by Dermot Moran. London: Routledge, 2001.

———. *Logische Untersuchungen.* Halle a.S.: Niemeyer, 1900 and 1901 (= ed. A). Tübingen: Niemeyer, 1913 and 1921 (= ed. B).

———. *Logische Untersuchungen.* Vol. 1, *Prolegomena zur reinen Logik.* Text of the 1st and 2nd ed. Ed. E. Holenstein. *Husserliana,* vol. 18. The Hague: Nijhoff, 1975.

———. *Logische Untersuchungen.* Vol. 2, *Untersuchungen zur Phänomenologie und Theorie der Erkenntnis.* Ed. Ursula Panzer. *Husserliana,* vol. 19. Dordrecht: Kluwer, 1984.

———. *Phänomenologische Psychologie: Vorlesungen Sommersemester 1925.* Ed. Walter Biemel. *Husserliana,* vol. 9. The Hague: Nijhoff, 1968.

———. *Phenomenological Psychology: Lectures, Summer Semester 1925.* Trans. J. Scanlon. The Hague: Nijhoff, 1977.

———. *The Phenomenology of Internal Time-Consciousness.* Ed. Martin Heidegger. Trans. James S. Churchill. Bloomington: Indiana University Press, 1964.

———. "Philosophy as Rigorous Science." In *Phenomenology and the Crisis of Philosophy,* trans. Quentin Lauer, pp. 71–147. New York: Harper and Row, 1964.

———. *Psychological and Transcendental Phenomenology and the Confrontation with Heidegger (1927–31).* Trans. Thomas Sheehan and Richard E. Palmer. In Husserl Collected Works 6. Dordrecht: Kluwer, 1997.

Jacobi, Friedrich Heinrich. "Beylage über den transscendentalen Idealismus" (1815). In *David Hume über den Glauben oder Idealismus und Realismus: Ein Gespräch.* In *Friedrich Heinrich Jacobi's Werke,* ed. Friedrich Roth, vol. 2. Leipzig: Gerhard Fleischer d. Jüng, 1812–25.

Jaspers, Karl. *Notizen zu Martin Heidegger.* Ed. Hans Saner. Munich: Piper, 1978.

Kant, Immanuel. *Critique of Judgment.* Trans. Werner S. Pluhar. Indianapolis: Hackett, 1987.

———. *Critique of the Power of Judgment.* Trans. Paul Guyer and Eric Matthews. Cambridge: Cambridge University Press, 2000.

———. *Critique of Pure Reason.* Trans. Paul Guyer and Allen Wood. Cambridge: Cambridge University Press, 1997.

———. *Critique of Pure Reason.* Trans. Norman Kemp Smith. London: Macmillan, 1968.

———. *Kritik der reinen Vernunft.* In *Kants gesammelte Schriften,* ed. Royal Prussian [later German] Academy of Sciences, vol. 3. Berlin: Georg Reimer [later Walter de Gruyter], 1900–.

———. *Kritik der reinen Vernunft*. Hamburg: Meiner, 1976.

———. *Kritik der Urteilskraft*. In *Kants gesammelte Schriften*, ed. Royal Prussian [later German] Academy of Sciences, vol. 5, pp. 165–486. Berlin: Georg Reimer [later Walter de Gruyter], 1900–.

———. *Lectures on Logic*. Ed. J. Michael Young. Cambridge: Cambridge University Press, 1992.

Katz, Jerrold J. *Realistic Rationalism*. Cambridge, MA: MIT Press, 1997.

Kisiel, Theodore. *The Genesis of Heidegger's "Being and Time."* Berkeley and Los Angeles: University of California Press, 1993.

Körner, Stephan. "The Impossibility of Transcendental Arguments." *Monist* 51 (1967): 317–31.

Lafont, Cristina. *Heidegger, Language, and World-Disclosure*. Cambridge: Cambridge University Press, 2000.

Locke, John. *An Essay Concerning Human Understanding*. Chicago: Regnery, 1956.

Longuenesse, Béatrice. *Kant and the Capacity to Judge*. Princeton, NJ: Princeton University Press, 1998.

Löwith, Karl. "Wahrheit und Geschichtlichkeit." In *Truth and Historicity*, ed. Hans-Georg Gadamer. The Hague: Nijhoff, 1972.

Maimon, Salomon. *Versuch einer Transscendentalphilosophie* (1790). Darmstadt: Wissenschaftliche Buchgesellschaft, 1963.

Malpas, Jeff. "Locating Interpretation: The Topography of Understanding in Heidegger and Davidson." *Philosophical Topics* 27 (1999): 129–48.

———. *Place and Experience: A Philosophical Topography*. Cambridge: Cambridge University Press, 1999.

———. "The Transcendental Circle." *Australasian Journal of Philosophy* 75 (1997): 1–20.

———. "From the Transcendental to the Topological." In *From Kant to Davidson: Philosophy and the Idea of the Transcendental*, ed. Jeff Malpas, pp. 80–86. Routledge Studies in Twentieth-Century Philosophy. London: Routledge, 2003.

Moore, G. E. "A Defence of Common Sense" (1925). In *Philosophical Papers*, by G. E. Moore, pp. 32–59. London: George Allen and Unwin, 1959.

———. "Proof of an External World" (1939). In *Philosophical Papers*, by G. E. Moore, pp. 127–50. London: George Allen and Unwin, 1959.

Moran, Dermot. "Making Sense: Husserl's Phenomenology as Transcendental Idealism." In *From Kant to Davidson: Philosophy and the Idea of the Transcendental*, ed. Jeff Malpas, pp. 48–74. Routledge Studies in Twentieth-Century Philosophy. London: Routledge, 2003.

Mueller, Axel. *Referenz und Fallibilismus*. Berlin: de Gruyter, 2001.

Mulhall, Stephen. *Heidegger and "Being and Time."* London: Routledge, 1996.

Nietzsche, Friedrich. *Philosophy and Truth: Selections from Nietzsche's Notebooks of the Early 1870s*. Trans. and ed. Daniel Breazeale. Atlantic Highlands, NJ: Humanities Press, 1979.

———. "On Truth and Lies in a Nonmoral Sense." In *Philosophy and Truth: Selections from Nietzsche's Notebooks of the Early 1870s*, trans. and ed. Daniel Breazeale, pp. 79–97. Atlantic Highlands, NJ: Humanities Press, 1979.

———. "Über Wahrheit und Lüge im aussermoralischen Sinne." In *Kritische Studienausgabe*, ed. Giorgio Colli und Mazzino Montinari, vol. 1, pp. 875–90. Munich: Deutscher Taschenbuch, 1980.

Okrent, Mark. "Heidegger and Korsgaard on Human Reflection." *Philosophical Topics* 27, no. 2 (Fall 1999): 47–76.
———. *Heidegger's Pragmatism: Understanding, Being, and the Critique of Metaphysics.* Ithaca, NY: Cornell University Press, 1988.
———. "Intending the Intender; or, Why Heidegger Isn't Davidson." In *Heidegger, Authenticity, and Modernity: Papers Presented in Honor of Hubert Dreyfus*, ed. Jeff Malpas and Mark Wrathall, vol. 1, pp. 279–301. Cambridge, MA: MIT Press, 2000.
Olafson, Frederick. *Heidegger and the Philosophy of Mind.* New Haven, CT: Yale University Press, 1987.
Ott, Hugo. *Martin Heidegger: Unterwegs zu seiner Biographie.* Frankfurt am Main: Campus, 1988.
Philipse, Herman. *Heidegger's Philosophy of Being: A Critical Interpretation.* Princeton, NJ: Princeton University Press, 1998.
———. "Should We Be Kantians?" *Ratio: An International Journal of Analytic Philosophy* 13 (2000): 239–55; and 14 (2001): 33–55.
———. "Transcendental Idealism." In *The Cambridge Companion to Husserl*, ed. Barry Smith and David Woodruff Smith, pp. 239–322. Cambridge: Cambridge University Press, 1995.
Pippin, Robert B. "On Being Anti-Cartesian: Hegel, Heidegger, Subjectivity and Sociality." In *Idealism as Modernism: Hegelian Variations*, by Robert B. Pippin, pp. 375–94. Cambridge: Cambridge University Press, 1997.
———. "Fichte's Alleged One-Sided, Subjective, Psychological Idealism." In *The Reception of Kant's Critical Philosophy: Fichte, Schelling and Hegel*, ed. Sally Sedgwick. Cambridge: Cambridge University Press, 2000.
———. "Heideggerian Historicity and Metaphysical Politics." In *Idealism as Modernism: Hegelian Variations*, by Robert B. Pippin, pp. 395–414. Cambridge: Cambridge University Press, 1997.
———. *Modernism as a Philosophical Problem: On the Dissatisfactions of European High Culture.* 2nd ed. Oxford: Blackwell, 1999.
———. "Naturalness and Mindedness: Hegel's Compatibilism." *European Journal of Philosophy* 7, no. 2 (1999): 194–212.
Putnam, Hilary. "It Ain't Necessarily So." In *Mathematics, Matter, and Method: Philosophical Papers*, by Hilary Putnam, vol. 1, pp. 237–49. Cambridge, MA: Cambridge University Press, 1975.
———. "Replies." *Philosophical Topics* 20, no. 1 (Spring 1992): 347–408.
———. "Rethinking Mathematical Necessity." In *Words and Life*, by Hilary Putnam, ed. James Conant, pp. 245–63. Cambridge, MA: Harvard University Press, 1994.
———. "'Two Dogmas' Revisited." In *Realism and Reason: Philosophical Papers*, by Hilary Putnam, vol. 3, pp. 87–97. Cambridge: Cambridge University Press, 1983.
Quine, W. V. O. "Carnap and Logical Truth." In *The Ways of Paradox and Other Essays*, by W. V. O. Quine, pp. 100–125. New York: Random House, 1966.
———. "The Elusiveness of Reference." In *Sprache, Theorie und Wirklichkeit*, ed. Michael Sukale. Frankfurt: Lang, 1990.
———. *Theories and Things.* Cambridge, MA: Harvard University Press, 1981.
———. *The Ways of Paradox and Other Essays.* New York: Random House, 1966.

Richardson, William J. *Heidegger: Through Phenomenology to Thought*. The Hague: Nijhoff, 1963.
Rorty, Richard. "Strawson's Objectivity Argument." *Review of Metaphysics* 24 (1970): 207–44.
Rosen, Stanley. *The Question of Being: A Reversal of Heidegger*. New Haven, CT: Yale University Press, 1993.
Rouse, Joseph. *How Scientific Practices Matter*. Chicago: University of Chicago Press, 2002.
Ryle, Gilbert. *Dilemmas*. Cambridge: Cambridge University Press, 1964.
Schalow, Frank. *The Renewal of the Kant-Heidegger Dialogue*. New York: State University of New York Press, 1992.
Schatzki, Theodore R. "Early Heidegger on Being, the Clearing, and Realism." In *Heidegger: A Critical Reader*, ed. Hubert Dreyfus and Harrison Hall, pp. 81–98. Oxford: Blackwell, 1992.
Schulze, Gottlob Ernst. *Aenesidemus oder über die Fundamente der von dem Herrn Professor Reinhold in Jena gelieferten Elementar-Philosophie* (1792). Ed. Manfred Frank. Hamburg: Meiner, 1996.
———. *Kritik der theoretischen Philosophie*. Hamburg: Bohn, 1801.
Shaper, Eva, and Wilhelm Vossenkuhl, eds. *Bedingungen der Möglichkeit: "Transcendental Arguments" und transzendentales Denken*. Stuttgart: Klett-Cotta, 1984.
Sheehan, Thomas. "Husserl's Marginal Remarks in Martin Heidegger, Being and Time." In *Psychological and Transcendental Phenomenology and the Confrontation with Heidegger (1927–31)*, by Edmund Husserl, trans. Thomas Sheehan and Richard E. Palmer, pp. 258–422. Husserl Collected Works 6. Dordrecht: Kluwer, 1997.
———. "Kehre and Ereignis: A Prolegomenon to *Introduction to Metaphysics*." In *A Companion to Heidegger's "Introduction to Metaphysics,"* ed. Richard Polt and Gregory Fried, pp. 3–16. New Haven, CT: Yale University Press, 2001.
Sherover, Charles. *Heidegger, Kant, and Time*. Bloomington: Indiana University Press, 1971.
Smith, A. D. *Husserl and the Cartesian Meditations*. London: Routledge, 2003.
Stern, Robert. *Transcendental Arguments and Scepticism: Answering the Question of Justification*. Oxford: Oxford University Press, 2004.
———, ed. *Transcendental Arguments: Problems and Prospects*. Oxford: Oxford University Press, 1999.
Stroud, Barry. "Transcendental Arguments." *Journal of Philosophy* 65 (1968): 241–56.
Thomä, Dieter. *Die Zeit des Selbst und die Zeit danach: Zur Kritik der Textgeschichte Martin Heideggers*. Frankfurt am Main: Suhrkamp, 1990.
Truffaut, François. *Hitchcock*. New York: Simon and Schuster, 1985.
Tugendhat, Ernst. "Heideggers Idee der Wahrheit." In *Heidegger*, 2nd ed., ed. Otto Pöggeler. Cologne: Kiepenheuer and Witsch, 1970.
———. *Self-Consciousness and Self-Determination*. Trans. Paul Stern. Cambridge, MA: MIT Press, 1986.
———. *Der Wahrheitsbegriff bei Husserl und Heidegger*. Berlin: de Gruyter, 1967.
———. "Wir sind nicht fest gedrahtet: Heideggers 'Man' und die Tiefdimension der Gründe." In *Aufsätze, 1992–2000*, by Ernst Tugendhat, pp. 138–62. Frankfurt am Main: Suhrkamp, 2001.

Vallega-Neu, Daniela. "Poietic Saying." In *Companion to Heidegger's Contributions to Philosophy*, ed. Charles E. Scott, Susan M. Schoenbohm, Daniela Vallega-Neu, and Alejandro Vallega, pp. 66–80. Bloomington: Indiana University Press, 2001.

van Buren, John. *The Young Heidegger: Rumor of the Hidden King*. Bloomington: Indiana University Press, 1994.

Weatherstone, Martin. *Heidegger's Interpretation of Kant*. London: Palgrave, 2003.

Williams, Bernard. *Ethics and the Limits of Philosophy*. Cambridge, MA: Harvard University Press, 1985.

Zahavi, Dan. *Husserl and Transcendental Intersubjectivity*. Trans. Elizabeth A. Behnke. Athens: Ohio University Press, 2001.

———. *Husserl's Phenomenology*. Stanford, CA: Stanford University Press, 2003.

Index